THE
ANIME
ECOLOGY

THE ANIME ECOLOGY

A GENEALOGY OF TELEVISION, ANIMATION, AND GAME MEDIA

THOMAS LAMARRE

University of Minnesota Press
Minneapolis | London

Published by the University of Minnesota Press
111 Third Avenue South, Suite 290
Minneapolis, MN 55401–2520
http://www.upress.umn.edu

Printed in the United States of America on acid-free paper

The University of Minnesota is an equal-opportunity educator and employer.

24 23 22 21 20 19 18   10 9 8 7 6 5 4 3 2 1

Library of Congress Cataloging-in-Publication Data
Names: LaMarre, Thomas, author.
Title: The anime ecology : a genealogy of television, animation, and game media / Thomas Lamarre.
Description: Minneapolis : University of Minnesota Press, 2018. | Includes bibliographical references and index.
Identifiers: LCCN 2017042800 | ISBN 978-1-5179-0450-0 (pb) | ISBN 978-1-5179-0449-4 (hc)
Subjects: LCSH: Animated films—Japan—History and criticism. | Television programs—Social aspects. | Video games—Social aspects. | Cultural industries—Social aspects. | BISAC: PERFORMING ARTS / Animation. | SOCIAL SCIENCE / Popular Culture.
Classification: LCC NC1766.J3 L34 2018 | DDC 791.43/340952–dc23
LC record available at https://lccn.loc.gov/2017042800

CONTENTS

INTRODUCTION
TELEVISION ANIMATION AND INFRASTRUCTURE ECOLOGY

THIS BOOK EXPLORES THE RELATION BETWEEN TELEVISION AND ANIMATION. IT DEALS WITH HOW TELEVISION AFFECTS animation, and how animation allows for a different perspective on television media, one more in keeping with the contemporary situation in which what has traditionally been designated as television is now thoroughly mixed with a host of other media and media practices. Such an exploration is necessarily broad in reach and synthetic in impulse. It draws on research conducted in a number of disciplines, including cognitive science, neuroscience, economic and sociological studies of telecommunications, infrastructure studies, as well as in the vast middle ground of cultural studies, film and media studies, and critical theory and philosophy, not to mention the field of Japanese studies.

In this Introduction, I wish to provide an overview of and guidelines to my approach to the key concern of this study: how the relation between television and animation hinges on infrastructures, multimedia franchises, and media ecologies. The result is a far-reaching introduction to a capacious and synthetic study. Yet I feel such an introduction is both necessary and desirable in order to situate my approach and findings in the context of contemporary debates within television, film, and media studies. I thus provide here an overview of some of the current questions about what is happening with television today and what is happening with animation, infrastructures, and multimedia franchises. This Introduction addresses what is happening concretely and pragmatically with television out there, and what is happening conceptually or speculatively within our interpretations of television. The speculative "in here" follows from the pragmatic "out there": interpretation tracks, follows on, and hovers over concrete changes in practices, discourses, and technologies of the production, distribution, and consumption of television and animation. As such, I tend to situate myself more as a tracker and gatherer than as a keeper of fields or a builder of monuments. But television's appeal, despite its thoroughly sedentary tendencies and statist legacies, may not ultimately lie in its association with settled worlds or monumental histories but rather in its calling for other kinds of society.

Television

Something's happening with television. TV industries around the world are producing record numbers of new shows, and these programs are finding their way into new markets via streaming services, cable and satellite services, and downloads, both in regular and informal economies. What is more, although there are pronounced generational differences, surveys tell us that people of all ages are watching as much or more television than ever.[1] Still, it is equally plausible in response to such surveys to declare, as a young friend did, "How is that even possible? No one I know even has a television!"

The sense of what's happening to television depends on what your image of television is—media platform (the television set), mode of reception or cultural practice (domestic versus ambient viewing), content (specific patterns of serialization), communications infrastructure (broadcast, cable, streaming), globalized experience of synchronicity, a bid for national or global unification based on demographic segmentation of content, or some combination of these modalities.[2] Because any or all of these modalities may be called on to define television, it is equally plausible today to speak on the one hand of the marginalization or even the demise of television, specifically of broadcast television, as a result of its being subsumed within telecommunications networks and being received on tablets, phones, and computers. On the other hand, the conversion of broadcast television in Japan to digital terrestrial television, which is a digital update of the prior broadcast system, together with the completion of the Tokyo Sky Tree in 2012, at 634 meters the world's tallest broadcast tower, duly attest that broadcast television is far from over, as much in its symbolic dimension as in its financial dominance of media ownership.[3] In the North American and European contexts, the term "posttelevision" is increasingly used to split the difference between the two contemporary sides of television.[4]

The first wager of this book is that what's happening with television today is a continuation of what's been happening with it for a long time. Interestingly, accounts of posttelevision in the North Atlantic region usually make reference to the rise of transmedia storytelling. In the context of Japanese television, however, transmedia storytelling is nothing new. It meshes with all periods of television. Japanese scholars thus tend to speak in terms of periods and generations of transmedia storytelling, or media mix, and to address transformations in it rather than isolate it as posttelevision (see chapter 5).[5] Similarly, the buzz over posttelevision in the North Atlantic context stresses the recent "unbundling of TV from the medium that delivers it and the machine you watch it on."[6] There is buzz in Japan, too, about TV that is not TV as a result of its medium and platform. A Nippon Telegraph and Telephone Company (NTT) service launched in 2013 bears the provocative name NOTTV *(nottīvī)* yet delivers television programming such as news and sports to smartphones. This not-TV form does not break with broadcast television; in fact, it is promoted as Japan's first smartphone-oriented broadcaster. As such, NOTTV builds on a deeper history of the unbundling of TV from medium and platform that was hotly debated in 1980s Japan under the rubric of new media (see chapter 7). For these reasons, I do not adopt the rubric of posttelevision. Japanese television, which remains the world's second largest industry, affords a different historical perspective on transformations in television media, platforms, and infrastructures. The rubric of posttelevision runs the risk of erasing the sociohistorical and geopolitical dimensions of contemporary television formations by introducing a globally synchronized break.

Recent developments in information technologies and telecommunications infrastructures have profoundly affected television modalities. Yet they have not resulted in a definitive rupture with prior modalities. In fact, I would like to up the ante here: thinking of television history in terms of rupture merely tends to sensationalize certain kinds of practices in certain parts of the world at certain times, fragmenting and detotalizing television only to retotalize its world preemptively, even if unwittingly. Presenting Japan as always already posttelevision, or as entering into a postposttelevision era, simply posits North Atlantic history as a normative point of reference, with Japan alongside the master. This is why this study, in its historical dimension, takes the form of genealogy: both continuity and discontinuity are evident at the level of television platforms, content, and infrastructures, which is also to say modes of reception, transmission, production, and serialization. What is deemed television at any one moment is an assembling of these modes.

One might also take another step back, as Siegfried Zielinski does, and consider television as an entr'acte in a deeper history of audiovision, which is to say, as one assembling of modalities in an even larger history of audiovisual media.[7] Here too the problem is that the articulation of historical depth is also the articulation of a (European) center, without any account of how that center was produced. Again, adding Japanese television to this deeper history of audiovision would demand some reckoning with how Japan has come to be constructed as a center or in relation to a center. For these reasons, the focus of this study is on Japanese television rather than the larger history of audiovisual media—not to isolate Japan in advance but to understand its formation as an urbanized media center. In addition, instead of delineating periods of television, the focus is on genealogical transitions between one assembling of television and another. The overall emphasis falls on a particular lineage, in which domestic television practices centered on the family TV set were gradually expanded into the home media network in two registers: at the same time that game consoles and VHS, LD, VCD, DVD, and DVR devices were being plugged into the TV, new infrastructures of distribution (closed-circuit television, cable, satellite) were altering broadcast infrastructures.

This domestic lineage of television has profoundly affected geopolitical reflection on audiovisual media, encouraging a focus on national television, or more precisely nationalized television, which Yoshimi Shun'ya nicely captures with his rubric "national domestic television formation."[8] Television was both domesticated and nationalized. To take seriously the processes of domestication and nationalization without reinforcing or reinscribing them, I move back and forth across two levels: the macrohistorical level of television (the formation of nationwide networks and nation-orientated programming) and the microsociological level (the relations between audiences, platforms, and content). Looking at how these two levels interact serves to disclose the regional, international, transnational, and cosmopolitan registers of nationalized television. What's happening with television today in terms of contemporary trends toward transnational and regional TV presents important continuities with what was happening in prior eras. Arguably, television was only ever transmedial and transnational. Nationalized television introduces a kind of geopolitical segmentation that amplifies transnational flows instead of reinforcing territorial boundaries.

The second wager of this book is more original, and as such potentially more polemical and controversial. The wager is that animation will afford a better perspective on this genealogical lineage of television than the usual historical emphasis on the liveness and presentness of television.[9] Accounts of television have often lingered on the trend toward simultaneity of the capture of image and its transmission, which has generally encouraged a bias toward live broadcasting as the key to understanding the impact of television. Its reality or actuality effects are thought to derive from its telecommunicational drive toward immediacy, simultaneity, and synchronicity. Such an understanding is often extended to the electronic and the digital. As Vivian Sobchack describes it, "Unlike the cinema, the electronic is phenomenologically experienced not as a discrete, centered, *intentional projection* but rather as a simultaneous, dispersive, and *neural/'neutral'* *transmission*."[10] Other scholars, notably Jane Feuer, have noted how such a metadiscourse on television relies on the allusiveness of the term "live," resulting in a degree of imprecision that has hindered the analysis of television.[11]

Animation, precisely because it need not rely on live broadcast or on live action, provides a way to work past the ontological and phenomenological compartmentalizing of media types. The wager here is that animation affords a better understanding of how television has continuously mutated through a series of assemblings and yet has persisted, and how it has taken on computational modalities and telecommunications technologies by making way for them within its very operations. To grasp television from the angle of animation, however, demands some reconsideration of animation itself.

Animation

Something's been happening with animation. Generally speaking, until the 1990s, the wisdom was that animation was a genre, a kind of content whose form of expression relied on the sequential photography of paintings or drawings (hand-drawn cel animation), or of clay figures, puppets, or other objects (stop-motion animation). In the North American context, animation as a genre had become conflated with two formats: children's TV programming (Saturday morning cartoons) and theatrical animated films to which the family took children (Disney films). This was never all there was to animation, of course; among its diverse lineages, significant forays into experimental art animation persisted. Yet it was the increased usage of digital technologies in filmmaking in 1990s that would shatter this prior image of animation and introduce a new one: animation as a kind of technicity, that is, a set of technical operations that made for a distinctive mode of technical existence. Lev Manovich captured this new image of animation with a series of provocative claims, including this: "Manual construction and animation of images gave birth to cinema and slipped into the margins . . . only to reappear as the foundation of digital cinema. . . . Born from animation, cinema pushed animation to its periphery, only in the end to become one particular case of animation."[12]

In retrospect, it is easy enough to take issue with Manovich's exclusive reliance on cinema as a point of reference, and on his characterization of cinema in terms of photography and photography in terms of indexicality.[13] Nonetheless, he provocatively demonstrated how, with the rise of digital technologies, a notion had emerged that would utterly change the conceptualization of animation: live-action cinema. Suddenly everything that was not live action could be taken as animation. It thus became difficult to determine the actual limits of animation, the technical mode of existence of which was now deemed pervasive and ubiquitous.[14] This new image of animation, partly because of its very capaciousness, has spurred a boom in animation studies. The feeling that emerged in the 1990s—of something happening with animation—made it possible to approach animation once again from the abstract side, in a more philosophically speculative manner.[15] Such an image of animation is a far cry from the notion of animation as cartoons for kids or family films.

Still, if the perception of animation as children's cartoons has nonetheless proved surprisingly persistent alongside the notion of animation as a pervasive technical mode, it is because both ways of thinking about animation are necessary. While I don't endorse the idea that animation is best thought of as a film genre or a kind of television programming, I do think it crucial to maintain something of both perspectives on animation—abstract and concrete, speculative and pragmatic.

Not surprisingly, as with the feeling that something's happening with television, this new orientation in the 1990s toward the happening of animation has also made it possible to perceive that what was happening had been happening for some time.[16] The emergence of digital technologies may not have introduced the definitive rupture they were so often purported to introduce. Indeed, the central problem that emerged in the digital production of moving images—compositing—turned out to have precedents in the production of cel animation, that is, animation composed of celluloid layers. The key problem of cel animation was how to manage the relation between multiple layers of the image under conditions of movement, as movement tended to make the gap between layers perceptible. A variety of solutions to this problem arose through experimentation with concrete materials: animators might, for instance, use techniques to suppress the perception of the gap between layers; they might try to mobilize the movement of layers to heighten a sensation of movement; they might try to call attention away from the movement between layers by focusing attention on the movement of a character. There are yet other possibilities for drawing attention from the gap, such as the use of color or music to impart a sense of seamlessness of the experience of moving images.[17] The multilayered image thus implies the generation of a translayer force.

Digital animation and special effects present a transformation of this problem of compositing in that digital images frequently resort to different media sources: some elements of the image come from live-action photography. Others come from computer-generated imagery, including computer techniques for drawing and painting, motion capture, and digital photography of models or figures.[18] The term "plane" thus is probably preferable to "layer" in the digital context. In any event, one plane of the image may appear photographic or photoreal while another plane may appear to be drawn by hand; one plane may appear volumetric, and another rather flat.[19] Various strategies for compositing these media planes have been worked out, with different tonalities. The interval between the multiple layers in cel animation and the interval between "media textures" or "media planes" in digital production are not different in nature but rather are different in kind. The problem of managing the relation between components of the image under conditions of movement is the same. While the term "montage" is sometimes used to designate this problematic,[20] I prefer the term "compositing" because montage has historically been associated with structuring movement, and I wish to give priority to what happens in relation to movement and to consider process as well as structure. The problem of process runs deeper: the multiplanar image implies the generation of a transplanar force of movement, which appears to precede it.

The study of animation as moving images thus invites a genealogical approach, for the basic problematic of compositing remains without definitive solution. This is why it is impossible to define what animation is. It is only possible to track what animation is becoming. The genealogical approach thus proposes lineages of animation instead of genres. These lineages are technoaesthetic lineages based on tentative experimental solutions derived from working with the abstract machine implicit in the problem of compositing, which became concretized in history of cel animation in a series of variations on the base apparatus used to work with cel layers: the animation stand. Solutions are also made, abetted by, and prolonged through social and financial investments as well as received aesthetic conventions, even though they are not reducible to any of them. In sum, a lineage of animation hinges on the formation of a distinctive technosocial assembling that is at once concrete and abstract.

In a prior study, I delineated three lineages of Japanese animation with reference to three different ways of grappling with the problem posed by the abstract machine for animated movement, which I styled the anime machine in that context. The first two lineages were associated with major studios and famous animation directors—Studio Ghibli and Miyazaki Hayao, and Gainax Studio and Anno Hideaki—which offer polarized solutions to the problem of animation. They correspond to what historian of Japanese animation Tsugata Nobuyuki calls the two axes of Japanese animation.[21] Miyazaki situates his animated films in a lineage of classical full animation, which emerged in 1930s Japan and flourished in the theatrical animated films of Tōei Studios *(Tōei dōga)* of the 1950s and 1960s. Although Miyazaki explicitly differentiates his "cartoon films" *(manga eiga)* from television animation, he does utilize a range of techniques associated with limited animation. If his films impart sensations akin to full animation, it is because he deftly opens the movement of layers within the image while playing with the orientations of weightless characters to enhance the overall feeling of a "movementful" cinematic world. In contrast, Anno Hideaki and Gainax Studios embrace the lineage Miyazaki so adamantly rejects: the highly limited television animation that began with Tezuka Osamu's *Tetsuwan Atomu* (*Astro Boy* or *Mighty Atom*) in the early 1960s. Anno Hideaki's animations use various techniques that tend to flatten the sense of a gap between layers, which forces movement to the surface, encouraging a zigzagging, scanning sensation.

These polarized solutions are not purely technical solutions; they imply technosocial assembling. Put another way, they imply worlds that extend beyond the animation object to affect makers and users, producers and consumers. Miyazaki's animations, for instance, dream in general of a minimally technologized eco-logical relation to the world. For much of his studio's history, this dream was enmeshed with minimally technologized animation techniques that demanded specific kinds of work and labor relations; it also encouraged a minimally com-mercialized franchise to harmonize with the contemplative stance expected of its audiences. In contrast, Anno Hideaki's animations develop an alternative kind of technological capture, a structure of exploded projection that solicits a high de-gree of interaction on the part of audiences, encouraging fan production and par-ticipation as a key component of a commercialized franchise while strategically mobilizing social discourses on the allegedly antisocial behavior of otaku (that is, "fan cultures" or "subcultures") fandom. Such animations become interactive milieus, easy to repurpose and easy to outsource.

To discourage a reduction of the contrast between Miyazaki and Anno to a binary opposition between cinema and television, I introduced a third lineage of animation, one centered on the adaptation of manga series into animated television series, where the source manga and its creators matter as much as (and often more than) the animators. I used the example of *Chobits* where the animated series is calculated to harness the creative energies of the four-woman manga team known as CLAMP. While this lineage of animation shows a good deal of affinity with the Gainax lineage in its technical solutions of the problem of the anime machine, it differs in significant ways in its technosocial assem-bling. Specifically, its story hinged on the idea of reset, and the animation series intuitively expanded the notion of reset into a general logic for understanding the relation between the different media instances or instantiations of a multimedia series: manga, toys, television animation, films, light novels, console games, and visual novels, to mention a few.[22]

The genealogical approach to the creation of animation thus reaches the point where another problem is appearing: that of the relation between media instances in a multimedia series or franchise. Put another way, the problematic governing animation production (managing the relation between layers) has shifted into another register, toward a problem that is like that of the multiple planes of the animated image but is clearly not identical to it. The problem of production shifts into that of distribution. The distribution of anime is the focus of this book.

Distribution is also where questions about the role of television must be ad-dressed. After all, as mentioned previously, Japan has the world's second largest television industry (after the United States), and Japanese animation studios have been the largest producers of animation in the world since the 1970s. The bulk of that animation production has been for television or for television-related audio-visual formats such as the OVA (Original Video Animation), the OAD (Original Animation Disk), and the ONA (Original Net Animation), all of which may be screened today on mobile phones, televisions, or computers. What is more, at the box office, animated films based on manga and anime series outnumber the cinematic animations we associate with such directors as Miyazaki Hayao and Takahata Isao (Studio Ghibli) and Hosoda Mamoru (formerly Madhouse and now Studio Chizu). Prime examples of such franchise anime films are the annual cinema installments in the *Crayon Shin-chan* and *Doraemon* series, and anime films related to more recent franchises such as *Naruto* and *Fairy Tale*. While these anime films are exhibited in a cinematic fashion, they are equally, perhaps principally, of the world of television in both their aesthetics and their distribution. They move quickly onto DVD and into broadcasting or streaming markets, which is ultimately their commercial base. As such, the actual theater release of the anime film feels more like promotion for DVD sales, or like a public event acknowledging the broad-based public success of a multimedia franchise. Significantly, the two biggest films of 2016 were made by animation directors associated with otaku circuits: Shinkai Makoto's animated film *Kimi no na wa (Your Name)*, which broke box-office records for animated films, and Anno Hideaki's live-action special effects feature, *Shin Gojira (Godzilla Resurgence)*. Not surprisingly, interpretations of their success oscillated between two poles: either otaku-related television anime had been absorbed into mainstream and thus crushed by it, or cinema had finally been overtaken and crushed by television anime.

The distributive force of television is formidable beyond the Japanese markets too: it has played a crucial role in the movement of Japanese animation into regional and national markets across the world. The general pattern has been as follows: television anime travels first, with the manga and other related products in its wake; subsequently, as the franchise system becomes established, the sequence for the release of other media instances such as toys, soundtracks, and novels occurs, but in a more variable fashion.

Television is not merely a distributive force behind animations, however. It is not as if animated series are made, and then television picks them up like so many objects, distributing them in the sense of putting them into circulation. When animation is considered from the perspective of its creation, for instance, the impact of television on animation is already palpable. On the one hand, the basic parameters for television series—rapid production of weekly episodes—made techniques of limited animation the best option, the funnel for creative energies. On the other hand, television is already within and across animation series at the level of segmentation within program episodes (openings, endings, ads, story segments) and across episodes (series). Television is a transversal force: it works through and acts with animation.

It is here that my wager about animation begins to take shape. As television works its way through animation, animation becomes something other than a self-contained object or self-identical content existing apart from its distribution. It becomes a kind of nondiscrete object. As it folds the segmentations and flows of television into it, it takes on something of the distributive force of television. After its encounter with television, animation is not only a form of content but also (and, I will argue, principally) a force of distribution. This force of distribution is particularly evident in four registers of anime series: (1) the use of limited animation to solve the problem of the compositing within the image; (2) segmentation within each episode; (3) serialization of the anime, or the segmentation of the whole into serial components, and (4) serialization across media, or the formation of multimedia franchises, commonly called "media mix" in the Japanese marketplace. These four registers of segmentation and flow make the anime series difficult to localize and to treat as a discrete form or object. They may be considered as nondiscrete objects akin to what Timothy Morton calls hyperobjects, "things that are massively distributed in time and space relative to humans."[23] Indeed, I would push the notion further and would argue that in its encounter with television, animation ceases to be an object in the received sense of the term, instead turning into a mode of existence. This way of looking at animation returns me to Manovich's proclamation about animation subsuming cinema, but with a different spin: if animation seems to be everywhere and nowhere, it is because it is no longer a localizable discrete object but a technosocial mode of existence.

Still, rather than simply conclude that animation has always already been the ultimate multimedia or omnimediating entity, I would like to consider how this anime technosocial mode of existence has emerged as an internal limit on the distributive force of television, appearing where television folds back on itself in an assembling of polarized tendencies that at once affects and follows from specific kinds of content and audiences as well as platforms and infrastructures.

Infrastructures

Something's happening with infrastructures. As audiovisual experience is increasingly organized around ever smarter mobile devices with wireless service, everything appears to be structured like a network, with any point in the network potentially connected to any other point, and with so many connections being made that data proliferate to the point where they allow for innumerably diverse pathways through them. The impression is one of network logic being pushed toward its absolute limit, tending toward pure horizontal or lateral connectivity without an external boundary, which makes for an emergent system whose limits cannot be perceived or known—a frictionless cloud, akin to what Deleuze called in a different context "gaseous perception," echoing Marx's notion of sublimation, in which "all that is solid melts into thin air."[24] This situation seems diametrically opposed to the situation commonly attributed to broadcasting: the histories of radio and television broadcasting are frequently characterized in terms of a subsuming of point-to-point or networklike tendencies within the one-to-many paradigm in which a signal is transmitted from a central source to multiple locations. Contemporary discussions about broadcast vis-à-vis networks often make reference to an inversion of the prior situation: the ascendency of networks has not merely liberated point-to-point connections but has also over-turned their prior subsuming within the one to many: the network formation is now subsuming broadcast. Now that each point can connect to many other points, what was once the central point has lost its privilege. Broadcast is but one point among others.

Such a story about broadcasting recalls Manovich's story about animation and digital media: animation, previously subsumed by cinema (old media), is now subsuming cinema. The new has not emerged through a rupture with the old, however. Rather, something that had been subsumed within a prior formation has emerged to subsume that prior formation. Television historian Shiga Nobuo, writing on the emergence of new media in 1980s Japan, presented the relation between television and telecommunications in exactly that manner: where television had previously gained autonomy from telecommunications and established control over its networks, telecommunications had now begun to bring television back into their fold.[25]

Such stories invite a reconsideration of the notion of subsuming in the context of infrastructural transformations. The term "subsuming" has gradually come to imply a totalizing historical movement. Now that it has become possible to speak of an inversion of subsuming (what was subsumed is now subsuming) in the context of television, the received notions of subsuming might be effectively stretched and reconsidered as well. If the subsuming associated with broadcast television has been desubsumed and resubsumed, then it is probably time to introduce another concept alongside subsuming—in this case, assembling. To take into account the possibility of an historical movement in which one-to-many broadcasting effectively subsumes point-to-point networks only to be sub-sequently overturned and subsumed by them, I propose a genealogical approach to television media centered on assembling.

Assembling happens between, and strives to hold together, the two polarized tendencies (point to point, one to many), resulting in a continuous process of as-sembling, disassembling, and reassembling. The actual functioning of media infrastructures will tend toward one pole or the other—toward point-to-point net-working or toward one-to-many broadcasting. When an overall tendency toward one pole becomes pronounced as a result of a variety of social factors, it is possible to speak of subsuming. Yet subsuming is not totalizing—or at least, it is only total-izing in the last instance. There will always be a mixture of tendencies; each ten-dency will retain and work with features of the polarized tendency. As such, even if the one-to-many tendency appears historically to subsume the point-to-point tendency, this does not mean that the point-to-point tendency disappears. Even in the heyday of broadcast television, the point-to-point tendency subsists, insists.

Assembling occurs because there is a problem or problematic implicit in the formation of telecommunications and television infrastructures that cannot be resolved once and for all: some points take on greater weight than other points, contingently. So even if television flows today are no longer organized around a central point or central points (broadcast monopoly or oligopoly), and even if those points in the network are all deemed equivalent, they are not equal when it comes to the actual functioning of the network. Hence one of the salient socioeconomic tensions of contemporary media flows: in an era noted for horizontal, lateral, nonhierarchical connectivity and participation, media ownership is concentrated in fewer and fewer hands. Dealing with such problems is the goal; looking at processes of assembling allows for a more finely grained discussion of historical transformations than is available through global narratives of subsuming. Yet insofar as the perspective of assembling strives to understand something of the overall movement of television rather than atomize it, it is not in opposition to the notion of subsuming. It radically complicates it.

In his account of television, Raymond Williams dwells on the subsuming of point-to-point connections within the one-to-many structure of broadcast television, yet he shows an awareness of the insistent generative irritation posed by network tendencies. Subsuming, then, is not a once-and-for-all solution; it is just one concrete instance of the assembling of polarized tendencies; one with teleological ambitions. Nor does Williams's account preclude the possibility of other kinds of assembling. His account remains open to other possibilities because he strives to grasp the social technology of television from the angle of its distributive force. Indeed, Williams may be said to sometimes exaggerate this point: in contrast with cinema, where products are made and then distributed, Williams argues that with television (and telecommunications in general), distribution comes prior to, and takes priority over, the production of content.[26] Still, his point is sound. The problem or problematic of television lies in its harnessing of a genetic or generative force prior to either the point-to-point or one-to-many tendency. Broadcast television is one way of managing this distributive force and one manner of solving the basic problem posed through the development of infrastructure.

Williams's emphasis on distributive force opens a strand of thinking in Marx that has been largely ignored because of the insistence on a limited economic model in which the production of goods is taken to be the economic base or infrastructure, with all else being superstructural.[27] In one of his rare comments on the impact of communications in *Capital*, however, Marx remarks, "A relatively thinly populated country, with well-developed means of communication, has a denser population than a more numerously populated country, with badly-developed means of communication."[28] Means of communications serve to intensify something that initially appears to be entirely extensive and thus imminently measurable: population. Population, however, turns out to have two kinds of density, one related to extensive quantities (the number of inhabitants) and the other to intensive magnitudes (the connections between them). As a result of these intensive effects, the means of communication must be deemed productive; such means are not superstructural to an economic base or production proper. Elsewhere Marx notes, "The conclusion we reach is not that production, distribution, exchange and consumption are identical, but that they all form the members of a totality, distinctions within a unity. Production predominates not only over itself, in the antithetical definition of production, but over the other moments as well."[29] It is this line of inquiry in Marx that encouraged Gilles Deleuze and Félix Guattari to speak of the production of production, the production of distribution, and the production of consumption.[30] While tacking the term "production" onto all three modes feels awkward, the shift in perspective is essential to this study for three reasons.

First, the production of goods is not the sole or primary infrastructure. The notion of infrastructure can be extended to distribution and consumption without distorting Marx's insight.[31] This is in effect what Williams does in his account of television: he sees infrastructures of distribution as productive in themselves, and he gives priority to them. He thus makes it possible to consider infrastructures in terms of forces of distribution and relations of distribution.

Second, the focus then falls on what happens between or across these three (or four or more) infrastructures—production, distribution, consumption, and circulation, to name the obvious ones. The production of distribution, for instance, overlaps with or intersects the production of production, but the two infrastructures are not identical or reducible to one another. They are members of a totality, to use Marx's term. The resultant unity or totality may be conceptualized as a society effect (Althusser), a socius (Deleuze and Guattari), or the social (Foucault). Here my point of departure is the technological assembling that happens within the television infrastructure, but in agreement with Williams's emphasis on television as social technology, I understand technical assembling in terms of social implications and practices. The forces and relations of television distribution make for technosocial assembling.

Third, when Deleuze and Guattari tack the term "production" onto production, distribution, and consumption, it is their way of calling attention to the two sides of each infrastructural mode of production: forces of distribution and relations of distribution; what distribution produces, and what produces distribution. Take television distribution: on the one hand, something produces distribution (technical experimentation, financial, military, and government investments in platforms and infrastructures), and on the other hand, distribution produces something (affects and values).

These three points allow me to build on Williams's approach to take into account the productivity of both faces of infrastructure: extensive and intensive. The extensive side of television infrastructure is what is normally thought of as the actual infrastructure—for instance, platforms (television sets, computers, mobile phones) and all the rigging used to connect them (relay towers, satellites, power lines) that permit broadcast, cable, satellite, and wireless networks. When it comes to studying the extensive side of infrastructures, there exists a well-established academic tradition of research, commonly associated with the sociology or social sciences of communications. I draw a good deal on such studies, for they have laid the foundation for understanding the territorial distributions and populations of television—its actual coverage, as it were. The focus of this study is more on the intensive side, however, where recent trends in media studies and science and technology studies have invited a renewed consideration of technologies and infrastructures in terms of experience, affect, and values.[32] Already two distinct orientations have begun to emerge in the study of the intensive side of infrastructures.

First there are accounts, such as Brian Larkin's seminal discussion of infrastructures in Nigeria, which place greater emphasis on large-scale transformations, grand spectacles, and public display: "Just as the ritual surrounding the opening of the Kano Water and Electric Light Works was designed to represent the plant as a technical object, so that plant was itself involved in a representational project intended to signify the future and promise of an electric Nigeria, bright and modern." Thus Larkin focuses on the "provision of infrastructures as a work of state representation as well a technical process."[33]

The history of television in Japan abounds with analogous spectacles orchestrated on the part of the government, corporate broadcasters, or both in attempts to make the modernity of the Japanese nation or economy both perceptible and desirable to consumers. Examples from the earlier years of television continue to be cited: the placement of television sets in public places to encourage sales in the mid-1950s *(gaitō terebi)*, the use of the imperial wedding of 1959 to spur television sales, and the hype around satellite broadcast for the 1964 Olympics. Contemporary examples are equally striking. The Tokyo Sky Tree is a powerful recent example of the infrastructure-related entwinement of technical processes with state (and corporate) representation. A whirlpool of discourses swirls around it, including those attesting to the Japanese qualities of its design and those signaling a new era of prosperity for Japan's export economy.

Studying large-scale events orchestrated around infrastructures provides insight into the social and cultural values, or symbolic values, enmeshed with the actual technical processes. This sort of technosocial assembling turns the components of television infrastructure—broadcast towers, large television screens in public places, and even the humming array of transformers and power lines— into symbols of modernization, internationalization, and globalization, as well as into purveyors of social and cultural values. Such an approach runs parallel to and complements the study of the extensive side of infrastructures. While it evokes something of the intensive side of infrastructures, it sustains a focus on what is perceptible, primarily on a large scale and at a macro level. As such, this approach tends to subordinate the intensive side of infrastructure (what it produces—affects and values) to the extensive side of infrastructure (what produces it—governments, corporations, and engineers and technicians). As I will show in this study, it thus tends to focus primarily on the one-to-many tendency of infrastructures—on centralizing tendencies—in a symbolic register.

Second are accounts of infrastructures that strive to give more latitude to their intensive side by shifting attention away from the perceptible and focusing more on the imperceptible. Two general manners of thinking have emerged in this respect. The first may be characterized by its emphasis on the disruptive.

The emphasis on the disruptive finds its classic expression in Heidegger's account of the tool: when the tool fails to function, the excess of its being, suddenly revealed, is felt.[34] Similarly, when infrastructure does not function—if, for instance, water does not flow from the tap or if there is a blackout—one must suddenly confront the practices and technologies that sustain the functioning of the infrastructure, which normally fade into the background. Such an emphasis on the moment of disruption gravitates toward large-scale disruptions. In effect, it addresses the large symbolic or poetic functions of infrastructure that Larkin highlights but focuses on the site or moment of their breakdown.

Although Heidegger acknowledges that disruption serves to disclose something of the smaller practices and technological negotiations that ordinarily sustain the infrastructure, his interest lies elsewhere than in infrastructures and technologies. What stands revealed in disruption is being itself, which had been covered over by the metaphysical condition that makes humans absent to themselves: a promise of salvation from a technoscientific condition. His focus on the disruptive is part of a larger philosophical project interested in the play of the presence/absence of Being, which has often been adopted in psychoanalytic and deconstructive approaches to questions of technology. In the psychoanalytic version, however, humans are deemed absent to themselves in a different manner: humans are always already internally disrupted, that is, constituted through negation (constitutive lack). The disruption of infrastructures is thus read in terms of the disruption of the symbolic or symbolization—which, again, is useful in that it steers toward the intensive flip side of Larkin's poetics of infrastructure.

The problem is an emphasis on the disruptive lends itself to a tortured metaphysics because what you experience when tools, technologies, and infrastructures fail to function is the human condition writ large. Still, it is possible to overturn this orientation toward absence or lack by resituating the problematic within the history of telecommunications, as John Durham Peters does in his account of the telephone. He considers the anxious interpretations that arise when you are waiting for a phone call that does not arrive: "The exploding of dialogue into two remotely linked halves makes the validity of interpretation obscure. The inability to distinguish inner projections from outer messages flourishes in conditions where interpreters have to bear the weight of the entire communication circuit. This inability, psychologically conceived, is called paranoia; socially conceived, we should call it mass communications."[35]

Peters also tends to look at telecommunications from the angle of the breakdown or disruption of communication, and from an explicitly Heideggerian angle, which dwells on the interplay of presence and absence. Treating infrastructures and media as akin to Heidegger's ground of being, he focuses on how moments of failed communication or noncommunication (between humans and cetaceans, for instance) bring the ground to the fore, revealing or disclosing the medium (environment and vessel).[36] But in that context, as in the above quote, his account implies an important shift in emphasis as it teases out the nonrelation at the heart of relatedness: breaking down is essential to functioning; disclosing or revealing is productive, even operative. Discontinuities are built into continuous functioning. It is discontinuity that generates continuity, but now continuity is happening in two registers. One appears to be objective: the continuous functioning of the telecommunications infrastructure through physically engineered linkages. The other appears to be subjective (paranoia and mass communication): you feel all the possible connections impinging on the point where an interval opens between you and the caller, for the lack of a call feels like a call. The discontinuous or the interval, then, is not disruptive but rather disjunctive. It allows for a disjunctive synthesis of these two distinct faces of continuity, holding them together across an interval.

It is useful here to introduce Deleuze's terminology. In *Difference and Repetition*, Deleuze refers to the one side of continuity as passive determination or connective synthesis. The other side of continuity is conjunctive synthesis. Between them lies a second synthesis, disjunctive synthesis. Subsequently, in *Anti-Oedipus*, Guattari collaborated in the transformation of these concepts through their encounter with Marx's conceptualization of production, distribution, and consumption.[37] For the sake of clarity, let me present it schematically:

        connective synthesis   →   production of production
        disjunctive synthesis   →   production of distribution
        conjunctive synthesis   →   production of consumption

As noted previously, in contrast with Marxist accounts that take the production of production as the primary infrastructure, Guattari and Deleuze pave the way to consider each of these syntheses or productions as infrastructures. What is more, even if these infrastructures enjoy some degree of autonomy, they do not occur in isolation from one another: disjunctive synthesis (assembling) also happens across infrastructures (connective synthesis) and implies socius or society effect (conjunctive synthesis). What some Marxists call the primary mode of production in fact entails a threefold synthesis instead of the two-sided economic determination of base and superstructure.

When it comes to the study of television or telecommunications infrastructures, the point of departure is the production of distribution, which implies disjunctive synthesis. On this point Raymond Williams's account of television agrees with Deleuze and Guattari. In fact, Williams pushes the point: what characterizes television and telecommunication is the dominance of the production of distribution. The novelty of Williams's approach becomes clearer when contrasted with recent trends in infrastructure studies, which tend to look at media infrastructures primarily from the point of view of their production (connective synthesis), or to assume subjectivity all the way down (conjunctive synthesis). Still, these approaches are not incompatible with a focus on the disjunctive. The problem is that they are all too one-sided.

Susan Leigh Star and Karen Ruhleder sum up the Heideggerian impasse of infrastructure studies: "Common metaphors present infrastructure as a substrate: something upon which something else 'runs' or 'operates,' such as a system of railroad tracks upon which rail cars run. This image presents an infrastructure as something that is built and maintained, and which then sinks into an invisible background. It is something that is just there, ready-to-hand, completely transparent. But such a metaphor is neither useful nor accurate in understanding the relationship between work/practice and technology. It is the image of 'sinking into the background' that concerns us."[38] They then begin to delineate an approach complementary to Williams–Deleuze–Guattari's emphasis on production of distribution.

Star and Ruhleder do not recommend turning to moments of massive disruption of infrastructural services as a way to bring them to the fore. Indeed, they argue generally against the infrastructural inversion that favors an account of the impact of infrastructures on humans at the expense of what humans do with infrastructures. They note how the emphasis on the disruptive tends to give greater weight to infrastructures than to humans. To counter such a tendency, Star and Ruhleder strive to bring both infrastructure and human agency to the fore, exploring how infrastructures are produced and maintained through the agency of humans, acknowledging not only engineers and technicians but also users: "Within a given cultural context, the cook considers the water system a piece of working infrastructure integral to making dinner; for the city planner, it becomes a variable in a complex equation. Thus we ask, when—not what—is an infrastructure."[39] When they enumerate the principal dimensions of infrastructures, "becomes visible upon breakdown" is but one dimension alongside the following: embeddedness, reach or scope, learned familiarity, links with other conventional practices, embodiment of standards, and built on an installed base.[40]

Their focus is thus largely on production, on designing or making infrastructures. Star and Ruhleder attend to how discontinuities—that is, the various problems and challenges presented to design—allow for the construction of technical continuities, which involve a complex ongoing process of maintenance and fixes. This is precisely what Deleuze and Guattari call connective synthesis or the production of production: it is the discontinuity, the cutting or segmenting, that generates flow. Bruno Latour presents a similar understanding in his account of the discontinuities and heterogeneity implicit in the construction of networks, which he calls "paths of reference." From the angle of users of infrastructures, he notes that these discontinuities may not be perceived: "There are paths of reference that resemble gas pipelines or mobile phone networks: once they are in place, no one (except someone responsible for maintaining them) is interested in the other meaning of the word 'network' (the one involving heterogeneous associations that were necessary for putting the functioning networks in place)."[41]

This way of thinking about infrastructures is useful in that it brings to the fore the complex series of actors and actions that go into producing, sustaining, and altering infrastructures. Yet as Guattari and Deleuze point out, and as Latour too is well aware, although such a focus on connective syntheses demonstrates a keen sense of technical processes, its account of the human and the social remains thin. Star and Ruhleder's account, for instance, often speaks of human agency without considering any sort of constraints—internal or external—on it. The risk, then, is that human agency becomes conflated with human sovereignty, thus presupposing mastery over objects and the ascendency of the subject. It is for this reason that Latour introduces the agency of nonhuman actors and proposes to treat them symmetrically with human actors. To present his stance somewhat crudely, the TV set and its audience might both be considered agents or actors, meriting equal attention for their active contributions to the network or infrastructure—but so too might electrons, photons, cathode ray tubes, cable boxes, modems, antennas, and relay towers, to name a few possible nonhuman actors. The big question emerging from Latour's work is, once you acknowledge all these nonhuman actors, how are you to represent them? Latour moves directly to the matter of political—or rather cosmopolitical—representation of nonhumans.[42]

Latour's approach intersects with that of Deleuze and Guattari in its attention to distributed agency (distributed across human and nonhuman actors), yet the latter thinkers take a different tack. In keeping with Marx's insights—first, that circulation produces unevenness, and second, that circulation is produced via a social distribution that occurs through assembling across infrastructures of production, distribution, and consumption—Guattari and Deleuze are interested in how technical processes (connective synthesis) and psychosocial processes (conjunctive synthesis) are at once held together and held apart (disjunctive synthesis). Peters's example is relevant: the person waiting for a phone call does not know whether the problem lies in technical processes (is there a technical breakdown?) or in the one who should call (is the caller dead, has the caller forgotten to call, does the caller intend never to contact him again?). On the one hand, there are technical processes with their discontinuities and continuities, and on the other hand, there are psychosocial processes of paranoia, of feeling the burden of the entire system of communication. The two processes do not map neatly onto one another in a causal manner or through a system of correlation, yet they are undeniably entangled. This is a matter of technosocial assembling—or more precisely technopsychosocial assembling, in which technical processes and psychosocial processes enter into disjunctive synthesis.

Disjunctive synthesis implies a perspective similar to Latour's principle of symmetry in that it gives equal weight to technical and psychosocial processes. As such, it provides a way to situate and build on the approaches to infrastructure presented above. For instance, Larkin's attention to large-scale events tends to see technical processes subordinated to psychosocial processes, such as state-organized cultural events operated as representations that "subjectify" technical processes. In contrast, Star and Ruhleder tended to bracket questions of subjectivity, instead bringing technical processes to the fore and showing how engagement with them at different moments in the making of infrastructure creates a sort of community. A similar contrast plays out in the studies of Japanese television history. Yoshimi Shun'ya, for instance, offers a detailed analysis of the national subjectification of domestic television through mass-targeted events, synchronized scheduling, and other symbolic means. In contrast, Katō Hidetoshi lingers on the technologies of television, seeking sites and moments where they might be turned in other social directions. The perspective of disjunctive synthesis does not rule out these two levels of interpretation. It is always possible to subjectify technical processes, and conversely to technologize human agency. What is more, disruptions may serve to expose something of operations of infrastructures, revealing dysfunctions internal to functioning.

Ultimately, however, the perspective of disjunctive synthesis is broader in that it does not rule any of these possibilities. At the same time, however, it is narrower in that it is attentive to the relation prior to the two terms—technical and social—that is active as they emerge together, assembled. In this respect, disjunctive synthesis acknowledges both the symmetry and asymmetry between two registers of continuity implicit in infrastructures. To give a simple example, a human being and a television set are not normally thought to be symmetrical in terms of their agency. After all, humans construct and operate televisions. Still, humans and televisions may in fact act symmetrically in some instances. They may even begin to feel asymmetrical in the other direction: the charge of television feels more forceful than its listener. As these inversions and conversions become entangled and stabilized, the result is what Guattari calls an "infrastructure complex."[43]

Where Freudian lineages of psychology speak, for instance, of Oedipus and Electra complexes, Guattari evokes infrastructure complex in order to break with the Freudian penchant for confining psychology to the nuclear family and domestic space, and to consider how psychosocial and technical "machines" enter into entangled, socially operative complexes. In effect, this complex arises where the disjunctive synthesis is already fueling a conjunctive synthesis, and a form of subjectivity is beginning to condense or cohere. Because disjunctive synthesis is always happening together with the production of production and the production of consumption, it is often overlooked. Yet there is something at stake in focusing on it. Today it is generally acknowledged that the interval between production and consumption seems to be shrinking, compressing, or collapsing. Fan cultures are one prime example because the fan mode of consumption is so productive that it scarcely feels like consumption at all; it feels like a mode of production in itself. This observation, although valid, often encourages a simplistic account of technologies and infrastructures, in which digitalization is at once everything and nothing, ontologically. As such, the digital or the computational may appear to be all controlling or all liberating in social terms simply because it is productive. It is here that Star and Ruhleder's intervention is apt: the question is not what but when is the digital.

This is also where the Marxist insight into the intensive side of communications, which informs Raymond Williams's account of the distributive force of television, proves invaluable. The when of broadcast television infrastructures lies in the encounter between tendencies—the one to many and the point to point—that have become polarized through a set of relations catalyzed or precipitated around the historical event of television. In the context of experiences of television, that is, the kinds of experience implicated in using, watching, listening to television, which are the focus of this book—the when of television infrastructures happens in the moment when you feel the pressure of the encounter between the one to many and the point to point at once: you alone are experiencing television, you and innumerable others linked to you; those entities on the tube are small and intimate, at your disposal, and at the same time, you feel some powerful unilateral force beyond your control lies behind them; you are the one among many, you are but one among many, and you are many vis-à-vis the one. But this when is not simply your personal experience. The very pressure on "you" serves as a reminder that the when of television for you is also genealogical.

But what does animation have to do with any of this? How does Japanese television animation in particular contribute to an understanding of television infrastructures?

Approaching Electromagnetic Reality

This study began with a simple observation: alongside its generating and harnessing of transplanar forces through multiplanar images (connective synthesis), Japanese television animation has a penchant for transmitted light effects, and especially for various kinds of flash and flicker effects. Such effects populate the screen to different degrees, from the twin beams of automobile headlights to the elaborate luminosity of control panels. Transmitted light effects are widely applied: they represent electromagnetic events ranging from lightening bolts to extrasensory-power attacks and mind-control waves. They also run the gamut in intensity, from slow pulsing or blinking to eye-searing flashes. Flashing and flickering effects have often been evoked as a cliché of anime, especially after the Pokémon Incident of 1997, when thousands of children experienced photoepileptiform seizures watching an anime episode with particularly intense red–blue flashes. Needless to say, given that anime is audiovisual in nature, sound and music are frequently mobilized to intensify such effects, to the point where the audio and the visual often feel entirely fused within the flash.

I began to pay closer attention to such effects and to track them across numerous series because I was interested in exploring how anime dealt with television and computer screens. It occurred to me that if I were interested in the relation between television and animation, then I should not only consider the history of television and of broadcasting animation but also how anime series deal with television screens. Because animation relies fairly heavily on hand-drawn elements (even if they are drawn into a computer), the presentation of screens within anime introduces a wrinkle into the photographic model of realism associated with live-action cinema, in which screens would be captured by a movie camera. As it turns out, anime has its own distinctive manner of realism when it deals with television, computer, and other kinds of screens. The presentation of screens in anime generally oscillates between two possibilities: either screens pulse blankly with light, glowing and flickering, but do not show images, or screens show images, yet these images are usually drawn in the same style and with the degree of intensity as the nonscreen components of the image. In the latter case, the boundary between screen world and actual world is tenuous or nonexistent.

The oscillation between these two screen modalities in anime opens a truly novel and significant perspective on television. Much of the literature on television, including film studies, has tended to portray it in terms of a unified and simplified effect: immediacy. Discussions of the immediacy of television tend either to dwell on presentness and liveness (simultaneity) or on distraction, that is, inattentive attention (the boob tube). In the 1950s and 1960s in Japan, as Yuriko Furuhata has shown, an emphasis on the liveness and presentness of television was fueled by a fascination on the part of avant-garde artists with television news reports and live broadcast.[44] Filmmakers in particular described and championed such effects as a mode of actuality that promised to revolutionize cinema and to bring about an aesthetic revolution.

Such an emphasis on actuality in the theorization of television in 1950s and 1960s Japan strongly parallels the account of television that Dudley Andrew teases out of André Bazin's writings. Andrew explains that Bazin saw photography as a document of the past that addressed the present, which allowed photography-based cinema to preserve the ongoingness of phenomena but at a remove.[45] In contrast, Bazin associated television with presentness, for it strove to eliminate the temporal interval between photographic capture and its experience. In other words, television was characterized largely in terms of immediacy, which tended to eliminate the sort of spatial or temporal interval that was thought to allow for an ethical or political aesthetic engagement with reality—critical realism, as it were. Cinema, in contrast, afforded a spatial and temporal interval through which memory allowed for a thoughtful and ethical relation to documentation and thus history.[46]

Such a characterization of television was part of broader orientation toward contrasting cinema and television. In his books on cinema, for instance, Deleuze contrasts cinema and television by situating television within telecommunications, with unfavorable implications: television is closer to the production of clichés, the greatest obstacle to a genuinely thinking cinema.[47] Still, it should be noted that neither Bazin nor Deleuze aimed to separate cinema and television in a definitive manner. In fact, much like the interest in actuality among Japanese filmmakers in the 1960s, Bazin's and Deleuze's emphasis on the presentness of television was calculated as a challenge to the contemporary complacency of cinema, to force it into new kinds of ethical reflection and political action. As William Marotti has demonstrated, for instance, avant-garde artists in 1950s and 1960s Japan proposed to extend the contemporary revolution in aesthetic representation to the entire social and political field of representation.[48]

Clearly these earlier biases toward reality or actuality in television, grounded in strong assumptions about its presentness and liveness, do not seem to leave much room for animation, let alone television. Yet I will later draw on Andrew's recent presentation of Bazin's writings on television, for Bazin stresses one the aspects of television that is integral to this study and closely associated today with animation and media mix: its parasocial effects. What is more, in her account of actuality in Japan, Furuhata notes that as avant-garde filmmakers interested in actuality began to experiment with the remediation of one medium by another (say, comics by cinema), they entered a domain that might be called animation.[49] Such a take on animation recalls that of Manovich: animation is defined in terms of a technical mode enabling multimediation rather than as a genre. The interest in actuality thus shifted seamlessly into social experimentation with multimedia precisely because artists and filmmakers were focused on the ways in which cinema might be transformed through its remediation of television and other media. The result was, above all, cinema expanded in its use of media in order to enlarge its scale to the point of immersing audiences.[50]

Something different was happening in the domain of television animation, however, and what we loosely call anime arrives at a far different understanding of the social experience of television. The genealogy of that "something different" is the focus of Part II of this study. By way of introduction, suffice it to say that anime developed its own take on the television experience, an experience polarized between two possible modes of reception that hinge on two kinds of imperceptibility. On the one hand, when the screen flickers, the content becomes imperceptible. It is surely there, but it is acting below the threshold of perception and thus of consciousness. On the other hand, when the screen shows images, the distinction between screen world and real world becomes imperceptible. Again, the distinction may indeed be active, yet it remains beneath the threshold of perception and consciousness.

There are thus two modes of address, which in turn imply two kinds of attention in reception practices. The second mode of address is easier to characterize: it implies "worlding," or the production of a parasocial field. The boundary between screen world and real world disappears, allowing television entities to swarm into the real world, and conversely real persons to enter the television world. The result is a distinctive social field in which television entities and real-world entities mingle freely. It levels ontological and hierarchical distinctions in the encounter between humans and TV personalities and characters. Usually this sort of television effect is placed under the rubric of parasocial relations or parasociality to indicate that it is like sociality but not real sociality. While I take on the term "parasocial," I do not consider its like-social relations to be less real than real-world sociality. For better or worse, our media have definitively eroded a binary opposition between real sociality and media sociality. The parasocial has its own social reality. To adopt something of Simondon's perspective, this parasocial field is one on which nonhuman actors may be ontologically distinguished from humans in their mode of existence yet not are different from them essentially or substantially.

The first mode of reception is harder to characterize because the blank flickering or pulsing glow of the television screen is so different from the presentness and liveness of television often evoked in film studies. This flicker effect does not dwell on the tendency toward simultaneity of image capture and its transmission (presentness), which allows for increased synchronization of broadcasting in various locations around the world (liveness). It implies a play with frequencies or wavelengths, evoking frequency allocations and separations within the signal. Crudely put, it is about noise instead of signal. More precisely, it is about an experience in which signal is imperceptible from yet is somehow felt through noise. Such an experience opens a zone in which what is liked (or not liked) about television is its hum, glow, fuzziness, snow, flicker, scan lines, bands, or hiss, to name a few qualities; these are what audiences engage with first and foremost. It might be characterized as an analog experience, in that analog media are commonly defined in terms of the entanglement of noise and signal (whereas the digital strives to eliminate noise for the sake of compression). Such an experience, however, carries over into digital television and onto liquid crystal displays. It is akin to the experience of glitch, that is, an experience of discontinuity within the seemingly continuous process of scanning, transmitting, and receiving the image flow.

This sort of glitchy discontinuity may be characterized in terms of connective synthesis; it is the discontinuity that produces continuity, or the segmenting that generates flow. It concerns the production of the production of distribution—the productivity of electromagnetic wavelength and frequency whose weird space–time particle–wave existence are the stuff that go into making actual infrastructures work. Here I call it the stuff of blink. But when I do so, I am already treating it as it passes from connective synthesis into disjunctive synthesis, for I am also addressing how it feels. The discontinuity at the level of the production–transmission of the television image is prolonged into a discontinuity at the level of its transmission–reception, where the glitch implies a disjunctive synthesis.[51]

Here the contrast between cinema and television in the Bazinian line of film studies pays off, if reconfigured. The Bazinian line looks at cinema in terms of approaching reality.[52] It considers how the interval between reality and its mechanical capture is then prolonged across registers of cinematic experience.[53] Television may also be characterized in terms of approaching reality, but it adds another dimension of capture to the capture of moving images—an electromagnetic capture. Cinema has tended to grasp the capture of reality in terms of a particulate reality, treating light as particle, while television approaches light both as particle and as wave. Television might thus be described in terms of approaching electromagnetic reality, in which that reality is both particulate (discontinuity) and wavelike (continuity). Capture is thus diffuse and heterogeneous. For historical reasons, it is the wavelike continuum of television that has been emphasized, either to celebrate it (global village) or demonize it (boob tube). The productivity of its glitches has been largely ignored.

When addressing television in this way, one of the challenges comes of the basic intuition, so often hardened into dogmatic position, that television waves are somehow like brain waves. In Part I, I deal extensively with this sort of discursive hardening of the problematic of approaching electromagnetic reality, showing that it makes for a specific kind of apparatus: the screen–brain apparatus. The screen–brain apparatus is a major part of the story of television, allowing television to be conceptualized and harnessed as a force acting directly on brains, allegedly in a unilateral fashion. Significantly, in the context of the Pokémon Incident, which is arguably the most important incident to date for grappling with the electromagnetic effects of television, everything hinges on television animation. But now, I hope, it is more evident why animation, instead of live broadcast or live-action programming, may provide a better way of understanding the electromagnetic reality of television.

Animation production has always used, and continues to use, photography-inspired modes of image capture in the digital era, yet when rendering movement, it takes on a different problematic from cinema: the separation of the image into multiple layers and multiple planes. These planes may also imply distinct media textures or tones. With its techniques of compositing, animation pragmatically tended toward multiple capture and thus toward a multimedia image instead of a photographed profilmic reality.[54] This process entails connective synthesis; it concerns the production of production of animation, wherein a specific sort of discontinuity or interval generates a specific sort of continuity or flow, which makes for a distinctive kind of animated movement. Subsequently, as cinematic animation went onto broadcast television, its connective synthesis meshed with the televisual domain of distribution in a distinctive manner. With the rise of so-called limited animation, the interval within the multiplanar image became flattened, moving toward the surface of the image and becoming distributed across the image. At this juncture, these animated moving images started, as if spontaneously, to lend themselves to the production of distribution. Simply put, the interval at work in the domain of animation production meshed readily with the interval at work in television distribution.

Japanese television animation pushed this tendency toward the distributive image to a remarkable degree, which allowed its anime to take on an unusual and distinctive relation to television distribution. That relation comes to the fore in the way in which anime portrays television screens oscillating between two modes of reception. The screen approaches the flicker and hum of electromagnetic reality, only to flip, as if naturally, into a parasocial field, a world of social relations in which human and nonhuman actors mix and mingle. This ability of television animation to switch between (and effectively fuse) electromagnetic reality and parasociality allows it to generate what might be called the electromagnetic socius or electromagnetic society effects. This twofold nature of the television screen in anime recalls the two sides of television infrastructures: the entangling of psychosocial machines and technical machines. Time and again, at different levels, in different registers, the study of television encounters this yoking of the technical and social. Still, what is happening at the level of the screen in anime and what is happening at the level of infrastructures is not the same thing. Although they are like one another, they are neither structurally identical nor isomorphic. They are semblances, so to speak.

Studying television animation thus brings into play a distinctive register of technopsychosocial assembling: media ecologies. In terms of their scale and magnitude, television media ecologies may be said to be smaller than infrastructures and larger than screens. In the context of anime, for instance, the most important media ecology is the expanded home television network, that is, the expansion of the television through the addition of plug-ins or peripherals such as VCRs, DVD players, and video game consoles. In terms of scale, the expanded home television network is larger than the television screen (or computer screen) and smaller than broadcast television infrastructures (or Internet). It is situated between the two in terms of magnitude. But scale is just one way of looking at the situation. This sort of television media ecology has also its intensive side, particularly evident when the television screen becomes the site of switching between the (large) broadcast network and the (small) home network that comprises recorders, players, game consoles, and sometimes computers. The result is a zone of encounter between two tendencies of television infrastructure. The one-to-many tendency of broadcast television is shunted and transformed into point-to-point tendencies within the home television network. Here too television animation plays an integral role, which encourages one other shift in emphasis in this study: from media mix to media ecology.

Prior studies of multimedia franchise models, such as Japan's media mix and America's media convergence, have tended to treat them as simple combinatory systems, a gathering together or mobilizing of components. When seen from the angle of television, however, it becomes clear that something like media mix depends on a site of encounter between polarized infrastructural tendencies, which makes for a charge running through the components and provisionally ordering them. While "ecology" is a loaded term, thanks to its naturalistic connotations, it is not an entirely inapt term either. Just as the biome becomes organized around flows of energy that give rise to increasingly enmeshed life pathways, so the media ecology takes form through and with the distributive force, the coursing energies of which allow for cuts and segmentations that generate flows. Nevertheless, to avoid naturalizing multimedia formations, I frequently refer to media ecology by Guattari's quirkier term: infrastructure complex. Thus the case studies of different kinds of media mixes and media ecologies in Part III take on monikers such as "family broadcast complex," "home theater complex," "game play complex," and "interface complex."

Overview

To address the range of concerns evoked in this Introduction, this study consists of three parts, each of which deals with the relation between television and animation in a different register. Part I centers on the famous (or infamous) incident in which thousands of children across Japan simultaneously experienced photosensitive epileptiform seizures or symptoms during a broadcast of the *Pokémon* animated series in 1997. This incident forced a closer look at the physiological and neurological effects of animation. Also, because it gradually became clear that the effect resulted from both the animation and the television, the incident led to government regulations for both broadcasters and animators. Given the double origin of the incident (animation and television), it is perhaps not so surprising that, even though the facts of the matter are fairly clear, a strictly causal scientific explanation has eluded researchers because cofactors began to multiply. The Pokémon Incident thus served as a catalyst for the formation of a new set of relations vis-à-vis television and animation. I refer to this set of relations as the screen–brain apparatus and explore how it meshes with the contemporary surge in discourses on media addiction, where the Pokémon Incident is commonly a major point of reference.

What also interests me about the Pokémon Incident is the challenge it presents to received ways of thinking about discursive construction and apparatuses. It is frequently assumed that discourses and apparatuses are culturally, socially, or discursively constructed all the way down—that is, top to bottom—irrespective of physical reality. In the context of the Pokémon Incident, however, some sort of electromagnetic reality is evidently pushing back, precisely because it is entangled with social realities from the outset. To address this very real entangled stuff, I turn to William James's notion of pure experience, offering a characterization of the plane of immanence of television animation: the stuff of blink. It is the stuff of blink that is cut, stitched, and patched together to form the electromagnetic social reality of television. Put another way, Part I deals with two connective syntheses: the connective synthesis implied in the relation between television screens and the human eye, and the connective synthesis active in the relation between animation and television.

Part II takes up the disjunctive synthesis of television and animation, that is, the production of television distribution. Using Raymond Williams's account as a point of reference, this section follows the historical formation of a national television network in Japan but with a genealogical spin, that is, with attention paid to the ways in which the one-to-many tendency of broadcast infrastructures have remained in constant antagonism with the presumably subsumed point-to-point tendency. The aim of this genealogical spin is to move beyond a fundamental divide within historical studies of television, whereby television is construed either as totalizing or individualizing, either as social or technical, but rarely are both aspects taken seriously together. Point-to-point tendencies are all too often treated as synonymous with individualizing techniques and are placed in opposition to the totalizing procedures of the one-to-many broadcast system. When television is examined genealogically from the angle of distribution, however, the assembling of tendencies comes to the fore: television is simultaneously totalizing and individualizing, social and technical.

Here a focus on the national dimensions of television threatens to become a liability. The risk is that of resting content with an account of the assembling of the Japanese nation-state (totality) and the Japanese subject (individual) within the domestic household. To counter such a naturalizing of Japanese domestic nationness, I work through histories of Japanese television that are critical of its national dimension, especially those of Yoshimi Shun'ya, taking up the alternatives arising in that context. As I shift my focus toward the assembling that occurred within domestic space, I track the ways in which the platform devoted to reception of national broadcast was gradually networked through the addition of various plug-ins and peripherals, from the dream of interactive TV in 1960s, through the emergence of VCRs and game consoles in 1970s and 1980s, to arrive at the era hailed as "new media" in Japan of the 1980s and early 1990s. Such an approach allows me to consider how the social technology of television media stretches across the sovereign power of the family, the disciplinary spaces of school and work, and biopolitical sites of crisis, disaster, and emergency. If the social technology of television remains a considerable force in the era of new media (and through new media), it is because it contributes to a regime of what Brian Massumi calls ontopower that helps to stabilize the relations between these power formations, promising modes of social existence able to work across and through the family, work, and emergency.

In Part III, I explore the relation between disjunctive synthesis and conjunctive synthesis to consider television ontopower from the angle of practices of self. Across the four chapters comprising Part III, I work through four media ecologies or infrastructure complexes, each implying a distinctive subjectivity, or an affective ecology: the *Crayon Shin-chan* series, the *Detective Conan* series, the *.hack* series, and the *Persona* series. In each case, I begin by considering the series' media mix configuration, that is, its serialization across media. Yet to counter the received tendency to treat media mix as a combinatory system, I draw on the prior discussion of television infrastructures to consider how the underlying media ecology channels the distributive force of television through the media mix. In this context, I explore how the television-animation ecology bifurcates beyond one-to-many and point-to-point tendencies into hierarchical and heterarchical tendencies as well as unidirectional and environmental tendencies. A media ecology, then, is not a simple combination of elements but rather a complex assembling of infrastructural tendencies relative to a distributive force.

I selected these four case series from a truly daunting array of multimedia franchises because I thought they provided the best spread of possibilities, both in terms of their television media ecology and in terms of how they move toward a metamodel of their infrastructure complex.[55] I had initially assumed that more cyborgesque and technophilic fare, such as the *Cyborg 009* series and *The Ghost in the Shell (Kōkaku kidōtai)* series, would furnish the most challenging material for thinking through technosocial assembling. Of course, I address robot and cyborg anime as well as other series such as *Pokémon* and *Doraemon*. Surprisingly enough, the *Shin-chan* and *Detective Conan* series ultimately permitted keener insight into television media ecology.

Such a surprise may well be the point of this study: expansile and scopious multimedia series are now familiar features on our local and global mediascapes. Yet because we are heirs of modernist legacies of interpretation that favor discrete art objects, we have yet to develop concepts and terms adequate to them. Even though our experience of them feels increasingly intimate as well as integral to our social experience of the world, these nondiscrete objects still feel cumbersome and unwieldy in conceptual terms. In media and cultural studies, the preference is still highly modernist in that discrete art objects are critically leveraged against large social forces and power formations. We are at a loss when it comes to nondiscrete objects. Thus it always feels like something's happening with them, but you never really know for sure when or how it is happening with you. One of the principal aims and potential contributions of this study, then, is to begin to address their complexity, to generate concepts and terms for dealing with what makes them significant, happening, and eventful. It all begins by putting pressure on that site and moment when television and animation are happening together.

Part I

THE SCREEN—BRAIN APPARATUS

1 POPULATION SEIZURE

IN THE FIRST FEW SECONDS OF EACH EPISODE OF ANIMATED SERIES SHOWN ON TELEVISION IN JAPAN, A MESSAGE TO this effect usually appears: "Please watch television animation in a well-lit room, and do not sit too close" (Figure 1.1). The warning comes in response to the so-called Pokémon Shock of December 16, 1997, when an episode of the animated *Pokémon* series provoked photosensitive epileptic seizures in about 700 children across Japan as well as photosensitive epileptiform responses in a far larger population, perhaps as large as 100,000.[1] The broadcaster (TV Tokyo) suspended the series, and together with the National Association of Commercial Broadcasters and the NHK (Nippon Hōsō Kyōkai, or Japan Broadcasting Corporation), it worked with government ministries to study the event and formulate guidelines for animation production.[2] These study teams also made recommendations for animation broadcasters and producers to include an advisory message for children viewing television—hence the commonly seen warning at the opening of television animations, enjoining viewers to refrain from watching television in the dark or sitting close to the screen.

Similar incidents had already occurred. A British TV commercial provoked seizures in three individuals in 1993. This incident "prompted the Independent Television Commission (ITC)—the statutory regulatory body for all commercial TV in the United Kingdom—to request the drafting of guidelines to prevent a recurrence," which led to the adoption of a similar code by the British Broadcasting Corporation (BBC).[3] There were a series of incidents, in Japan and other countries, in which Nintendo video games induced seizures. What is more, something like the Pokémon Incident had already occurred earlier the same year (1997) in Japan: NHK's broadcast of an episode of *YAT Anshin! ūchū ryokō* (Yamato Anshin

テレビアニメをみるときは、部屋をあかるくして、
近づきすぎないようにしてみてくださいね。

FIGURE 1.1. *Marvel Disk Wars: The Avengers* (2014) includes the television animation advisory over its opening battles sequence: "When you watch TV anime, please try not to approach the screen, and keep the room well illuminated."

Travel: galactic travel, no worries!) apparently induced epileptiform seizures in some viewers, but on a lesser scale.[4]

The very scale of Pokémon Shock, as the incident also came to be known in Japan, in conjunction with extensive news coverage, both domestically and internationally, made it impossible to ignore. Indeed the anxiety and uproar around it led to a second rubric, Pokémon Panic. Nonetheless, because there was a body of scientific research as well as precedents for broadcasting guidelines in the United Kingdom, even while animators and broadcasters in Japan continued to claim in all sincerity that they were not sure what exactly triggered such widespread epileptiform phenomena, guidelines and advisories went into effect fairly quickly.

In this chapter, by way of introduction, I propose to explore the implications of these advisories and regulations in order to begin to delineate the contours of the power formation that the Pokémon Panic served to catalyze. I also aim to show how Foucault's notions of positive unconscious, apparatus *(dispositif)*, and productive power provide the best points of departure for understanding the implications of the Pokémon Incident. These notions will pave the way for a more general understanding of a new form of media-related power, the screen–brain apparatus. In addition, I will contrast this understanding of power with some of the received paradigms and hypotheses for understanding media apparatuses.

Circling the Anomaly

The animated *Pokémon* series recommenced broadcast some four months after the Pokémon Incident, on April 16, 1998, with an hour-long special episode called "Pikachū no mori" (known as "Pikachu's Good-bye" in English). Not surprisingly, this episode deliberately presents a sharp contrast with the previous combat-heavy, flash-laden, cyberadventure episode responsible for the epileptiform phenomena, which will be discussed more fully in chapter 2. In the follow-up episode, the young male protagonist Satoshi's best-loved "pocket monster," Pikachu, discovers an entire forest full of wild pikachus. The central question, then, is, will Pikachu leave Satoshi and return to his kind in the wild? Ultimately Pikachu decides to stay with his Satoshi, even though Satoshi is prepared to let him go. In the meantime, the possibility that Pikachu might leave Satoshi allows the episode to include a heartwarming review of all of their best moments together.

Before the episode, a sequence entitled "to all of you in the front of the television" was aired, with the title superimposed onto a collection of Pokémon toys as if they were addressing the audience (Figure 1.2).[5] Host Yadama Miyuki appears on screen in the middle of a huge collection of Pokémon toys and proposes, with the utmost courtesy and gentleness, to discuss the Pokémon Incident with children, to treat them as adults. Naturally, she softens the impact of incident, mentioning that many children felt ill, and some went to hospitals. Upon offering an apology, she then explains, with the use of visual aids, how the show was suspended while a research team was formed to look into the causes (Figure 1.3). The visual portrayal, cartoonish as it is, deserves closer attention because it starkly presents a new constellation of forces precipitated by the Pokémon Incident: medical professionals (men in white coats at a table), television broadcasters (a dish atop a building sending forth a signal like a lightning bolt), and government officials (a government building with "country" written on it). Yadama also illustrates the cause of the incident—rapid alternation of red and blue—with cardboard squares, clarifying that the effect was not (as initial reports assumed) the result of light flashing directly from the screen. In the future, she concludes, they will be more careful with the use of alternating red and blue as well as spiraling patterns. The preshow ends with a reading of various letters from all over Japan asking that the station not to put an end to *Pokémon*.

Significantly, while the research team had more or less identified the trigger for seizures, extensive in-depth scientific research only commenced after the incident had in effect been handled administratively and commercially. Such rapid

テレビの前のみなさんへ

4月16日/1998
PM 7:00

FIGURE 1.2. When *Pokémon* resumed
broadcasting on April 16, 1998, a
brief explanation of the Pokémon
Incident preceded to the episode,
in which Pokémon toys seem
to directly address the audience
with the words "To all of you
sitting in front of the TV."

management of the crisis was possible because information gathered from prior incidents, in conjunction with clinical observations, created a sense of confidence that developing guidelines for animators, broadcasters, and viewers could indeed prevent such incidents. As a result of the wealth of prior incidents, initial assessments of the Pokémon Incident were not far from the mark.

The day after the Pokémon Incident, the Asahi newspaper printed a fairly substantial article covering various aspects of the event. In the opening paragraph, the article attributed the incident to the use in "anime and SF" of powerfully flashing lights. Then the article presented the analysis of a specialist in otaku culture, Okada Toshio. Okada calls attention to two common effects: flicker and "transmitted light" *(tōkakō)*. Flicker is a matter of rapid alternation of contrasting saturated colors, such as red and blue, white and black. Transmitted light is a technique of double exposure. Footage is first shot normally; then it is filmed

FIGURE 1.3. Preshow host Yadama Miyuki explains the research team mobilized to determine the cause of Pokémon Shock, with a drawing to illustrate the coming together of doctors, broadcasters, and government officials.

a second time with strong light projected through it from behind. Some areas are masked so that light does not pass through, while the areas that are not masked are brilliantly, even aggressively, illuminated. The flashing eyes of giant robots are a classic instance of transmitted light, and indeed Okada traces the technique back to war scenes in two famous television series of 1970s, *Majingā Z* (*Mazinger Z*, 1972–74) and *Ūchū senkan Yamato* (*Space Battleship Yamato*, 1974–75). But he adds that from the early 1990s, when anime styles became faster, it became so common as to be ubiquitous today. This technique is so pervasive in Japanese animation that it has both a proper name, *tōkakō,* and a nickname, *paka-paka.*

Even if the Asahi article does not actually mention the specific effect that eventually emerged as the cause of the incident—12 Hz red–blue flicker—what is striking is that by exploring prior less-publicized incidents and looking into accounts of television seizures, the Asahi article not only comes close to that explanation but also succeeds in formulating the basic advisory: keep the room well illuminated, stay as far away from the screen as possible, and avoid watching TV for extended periods.[6] The question thus arises: if it was relatively easy to figure out what happened, and what should be done, why were animators so surprised? The temptation is to conclude that animators should have known that their attention-grabbing techniques might produce such responses, or that they did know but chose to ignore the fact. As it turns out, however, the 12 Hz flicker was not produced by animators. Animation at the time was still shot on film, with a frame rate of 24 frames per second. But because television is broadcast at 60 frames per second, the transfer of the film to television produced a new frame rate and frequency. As Takashi Takeo and Tsukahara Yasuo report, "Changing the film's two frames into the TV scene results in three red fields and two blue fields. The resultant alternating red/blue light frequency is therefore 12 Hz."[7]

In other words, all of the elements that went into the guidelines and advisories were largely in place and available for use before the incident, but Pokémon Shock nevertheless served as the catalyst for the formation of a new set of relations vis-à-vis television and animation. With the Pokémon Incident, an operative set of relations precipitated out of the mix, as it were, generating what I will initially call the television-animation apparatus. In the next chapter, I will look at the role of brain sciences and neuroscientific research on the effects of television, and I will resituate this particular television-animation apparatus in the context of a more general screen–brain apparatus comprising other media and platforms. In this chapter, however, to set the stage for that discussion, I wish to consider the implications of regulations, guidelines, and advisories generated by the Pokémon Incident. I also wish to avoid imposing an order onto the events that is ultimately misleading: beginning with scientific accounts of photosensitive response might make it seem that scientific knowledge was driving the formation of the apparatus, when in fact analysis of Pokémon Shock brings a whole series of elements into relation, with neuroscience but one element among them.

In sum, governmental, clinical, and commercial groups worked together to find a scenario to reduce anxiety about the effects of television animation on children. Yet even as they labored to situate the incident as an anomaly, they could not explain it away; they could not guarantee its complete eradication. This ineradicable anomaly triggered the precipitation of an apparatus, a set of relations across these various groups and concerns, as they began orbiting around the nonanomalous anomaly that had suddenly appeared in television animation.

What Is a Media Apparatus?

As my choice of terminology thus far makes evident, I am using the term "apparatus" in the Foucauldian sense of *dispositif*: "a thoroughly heterogeneous ensemble consisting of discourses, institutions, architectural forms, regulatory decisions, laws, administrative measures, scientific statements, philosophical, moral and philanthropic propositions—in short, the said as much as the unsaid. Such are the elements of the apparatus. The apparatus itself is the system of relations that can be established between these elements."[8] In the instance of Pokémon Shock, we are dealing with a system of relations coursing through a heterogeneous ensemble that comprises media practices (animators), discourses on media (media scholars were included in the study teams), institutions (research laboratories, hospitals), architectural forms (household layouts for television viewing), regulatory decisions (advisory messages and other measures to inform the general populace), administrative measures (guidelines for animation production), scientific statements (by doctors, engineers, neurologists, and psychiatrists), and of course philosophical, moral, and economic propositions concerning relations between scientists and children (one brave teacher warned that the rush to collect data about Pokémon Shock might constitute a violation of their rights and expose them to discrimination),[9] parents and children (does television viewing require supervision, and what are parents' responsibilities?), and awareness of the global reach of Japanese animation, made keener by the Asian financial crisis in July of the same year (anime was now seen as an important export and relatively stable business proposition).

At the same time, I place greater emphasis on technological and what might be termed medial elements (television sets, in-camera effects, broadcast networks, and other infrastructures) than Foucault might.[10] Such an emphasis is keeping with the television-animation apparatus itself, which invariably refers us to the operations of actual technological devices (televisions, screens, cameras) and to various media-related techniques. Such an emphasis on technologies and media runs the risk of falling into a deterministic argument, of assuming that a technological apparatus fully determines or unilaterally causes the *dispositif*. Indeed, discourses surrounding Pokémon Shock often tend toward such determinism, for the entire incident seems to hinge on a simple fact, which is frequently taken as a straightforward unilateral determination. Takahashi Takeo et al., in their research on the Pokémon Incident, neatly state this fact: "TV images with 12 Hz red/blue flicker provoked photosensitive seizures in a number of children distributed over a wide area of Japan."[11]

While I do not contest these scientific statements or deny that specific frequencies of screen and flicker directly provoke photosensitive epileptiform seizures, I begin with the governmental advisory because my focus is on the television-animation *dispositif* or apparatus that Pokémon Shock served to precipitate out of the general media economy of Japan. I see the television-animation–induced seizures more as catalyst than a cause for the television-animation *dispositif*. To stick with variations on Foucauldian language for the moment, I would propose that we think in terms of different kinds of spacing, abruptly forced into relation:

(1) the interval between television and viewers, (2) the interval between animation and viewers, (3) the interval between television broadcasting and animation production, and (4) the interval or intervals within television, within animation, and within audiences. Bringing these spacings or intervals into relation serves catalytically to increase the rate of articulation of relations between sciences, media, homes, schools, and government while these sites and institutions struggled to grapple with what was happening with television, animation, and children.

From the Cinema Apparatus to the Television Apparatus

If we return to the warning message with such qualifications in mind, then what is initially striking is how the proposed ideal for viewing television appears diametrically opposed to cinema. After all, cinema viewing is associated with watching images in the dark, and if you do not need to sit close to the screen in a movie theater to have a cinematic experience, it is surely because the screen is so large that it sufficiently fills your view. You are already close to it, and you are not supposed to look away or close your eye—at least, such is the cinematic experience as it came to be formulated in film discourses, exhibition practices, and institutions, particularly from the 1910s. Siegfried Zielinski, in his account of the cinema *dispositif*, emphasizes the relation between the discourses on cinematic motion and illusion, in conjunction with technological developments and the construction of a sort of culture and sphere for viewing: "The cinema, where the filmic discourse of perfect illusionisation of motion in space and time in the intimate–public sphere became concretized and where the culture–industrial element came to dominate."[12] Raymond Bellour focuses more on the specific combination of parameters that make for a particular kind of aesthetic experience: a relation of the force of the image to its temporal consequences. Such an experience is related, but not reducible to, viewing films in movie theaters on fairly large screens in the dark, and so forth. He notes, "As soon as the lights go off, and the spectator begins to forget the room and the other spectators whose presence he nonetheless vaguely feels, and images appear, shot after shot, take after take, to which he entrusts his body and soul, forgetting himself but also finding endless opportunities, diverse as the diversity of film, for coming back to himself, for thinking the film as if it were thinking within him—as soon as all this comes together, the spectator, thus embodied in this singular time knows he is at the movies."[13] Naturally, as Bellour is aware, such a combination of parameters need not be obeyed in all instances.[14] It is more like a field of possible engagements arising across audiences, movies, theaters, critics, owners, distributors, and police.

In contrast, recommendations for television viewing in the wake of Pokémon Shock advise a well-lit room and a good distance from the screen. In the governmental and scientific literature, there are additional recommendations, which do not appear in the warning message but follow naturally from it: the image should not fill your view (thus the larger the screen the farther away you should sit), and if you feel yourself becoming too absorbed in the image, you should look away or close an eye before it causes discomfort. Narrative and diegesis may also come into play: the seizure-inducing 12 Hz red–blue flicker happened at the moment of greatest narrative absorption, when the beloved Pikachu finally launched his famous thunderbolt attack against incoming missiles. Arguably, the narrative pattern contributed to keeping children's eyes glued to the TV set when they should have looked away. In sum, the ideal situation for television viewing (bright room, distance, diminished image size, avoiding absorption) stands in sharp contrast to received ideals for cinema viewing (dark room, sense of proximity to screen, large image, diegetic absorption).

This opposition to something like cinematic experience in the context of the television-animation apparatus merits closer attention because it delineates the apparatus while bringing us closer to the internal limit of that apparatus—and thus its potentiality. The initial temptation may be to blur distinction between cinema and television, between live-action movies and animations, and to think in terms of a general (and maybe quintessentially modern) paradigm of "haunted media" or "cursed technologies." After all, the idea that you may become ill, go crazy, or lose consciousness while watching movies is one that goes back to the early days of moving images. Tanizaki Jun'ichirō's 1917 story, "The Tumor with a Human Face," comes to mind, in which there is a silent black-and-white film that terrifies and eventually kills those who watch it alone in the dark: "To watch a film all alone in a dark room without sound or dialogue somehow causes ghostly and quite uncanny sensations. This is true of course with quiet, desolate images, yet even with scenes of banquets and skirmishes, as the images of so many people in action flicker, you feel not so much that they are lifeless but rather you have the sensation that you who watch, you yourself are about to vanish."[15]

Other, more recent popular examples of haunted media also come to mind, such as Suzuki Kōji's novel *Ringu* (*Ring*, 1991) and its film adaptation (dir. Nakata Hideo, 1998), in which a videotape kills those who watch it within seven days;[16] or Kawamata Chiaki's 1984 novel *Genshigari (Death Sentences),* in which a surrealist poem kills those who read it by spurring an addiction to the sensation of being transported into other dimensions; readers eventually leave their body behind to perish. There are numerous other examples of spirit media in Japan, including the divination games called *kokkuri* popular in the Meiji period and phenomena like spirit photography.

Such examples may encourage the formulation of a generalized mechanism whereby, to use Brian Rotman's phrase, "ghosts cling to communicational media."[17] Rotman's project, which centers specifically on the remediation of speech by writing, nonetheless strives to formulate a general paradigm: "To illuminate the way communicational media can facilitate new psychic entities and objects of belief. Such facilitation occurs when a new media confronts and absorbs its predecessor."[18]

Read in Rotman's terms, the injunction against something like cinematic experience in the television-animation warning appears to be an instance in which a newer medium (television or animation) confronts and absorbs its predecessor (cinema or movies), which facilitates new psychic entities (flicker-sensitive children's brains) and objects of belief (dark shadows of media influence can be dispelled by illuminating rooms and adopting a respectful distance vis-à-vis dangerous entities such as the television set). Rotman's paradigm helps to draw attention to the occult sensibilities that frequently spring up around technologies related to the commercial distribution and personalized consumption of media: the home movie projector, cranked by hand, in Tanizaki's story; the circulation of videotapes in *Ring*; technologies of mass reproduction and circulation (print and audio formats) in *Death Sentences*. Similarly, the warning about television animation, while grounded in an actual event and scientific research, serves to generate new dispositions toward television viewing and children. More precisely, it serves to make a set of existing dispositions more salient and dominant.

Some caution is needed, however, in mobilizing these high modernist paradigms of cursed media and haunted technologies. I do not wish to fall into a deterministic stance by placing too much weight on technological devices and media forms. Yet if we blur distinctions between, say, the haunted videotape of *Ring* and the investment of television-animation with new powers in the wake of Pokémon Shock, we risk falling back on dubious cultural generalities and become unable to address the positivity at work at the scientific research and governmental practices. Simply put, we risk ending up with a thoroughly idealist account in which everything is culture, ideas, or ideology all the way down, and natures appear only the form of ghosts, specters, and curses, that is, materiality under erasure.

To avoid such idealism, and to deal effectively with the positive effects of sciences and screens, I propose that we turn the mechanism of remediation on its head. We need to avoid positing two self-identical media, followed by a struggle in which one tries to assimilate and preserve (that is, sublate) the other, which results in a historically newer, higher, or more omnivorous medium (say, the digital) in a caricature of Hegelian epochal history. Instead, we need to attend to how Pokémon Shock, for instance, served to produce and enact medium specificity. Government reports and scientific experimentation went to great lengths to identify and define animation techniques, and to hone in on the ones that potentially produce seizures. Something like medium specificity begins to emerge through discourses and practices that orbit around a potentiality, the ever-present, not entirely localizable potential for animation to produce a specific effect, which makes for an animation field.

Oddly enough, while the specificity of animation became a hot topic in the context of Pokémon Shock, television only later emerged as a site of medium specificity: government ministries and sciences tended to highlight animation effects and downplay those of television. Gradually, however, other practices, statements, and institutions drew television into the *dispositif*. In this way, efforts to locate the cause of seizures generated a sense of medium specificity. Of course, entities like animation, television, and even cinema cannot be defined categorically, once and for all. But this does not mean they are haunted by what they are not. On the contrary, they begin to act as fields in relation to the television-animation apparatus.

Limit-Experiences and Potentiality

The warning message may give the impression that it is intent on stripping all traces of cinema experience from television viewing. Television-animation appears, then, to take on consistency through a simple negation of cinematic experience. Yet it is clear that cinematic experience verges on becoming a quasi-orgiastic, horror-filled, death-ridden limit within television viewing: as you darken the room and approach the TV screen, you may experience headaches, nausea, or convulsions; you may even black out. For some viewers, the possibility may prove tantalizing: how close can you come to such an experience without completely losing yourself? What would it feel like to lose consciousness?

Affirming the power of flickering televisual images to overwhelm and harm the TV spectator may serve to reenchant television watching, which usually is seen as such a daily and ubiquitous viewing practice that it scarcely deserves special attention. In any event, it is clear that the warning message takes on an expressive function as it strives to articulate the specific parameters for television viewing. On the one hand, it forms a field of potential stances and experiences vis-à-vis the TV screen. On the other hand, it sets up a specific arrangement within domestic space or personalized space. This is not to say that television viewing is limited to domestic or personalized spaces.[19] Television screens are ubiquitous in public places in Japan, but the viewing parameters associated with ambient television do not generally allow viewers to come close to the screen in the dark. In effect, the warning assumes a viewer enclosed in a space that can be made dark and a screen that can be physically approached.

A field of variation also arises around displaying the message. The Japanese government recommends including the message in the first few seconds of an animation broadcast, but the recommendation is not legally binding, and many broadcasters, especially smaller local stations, do not include it. Sometimes it is broadcasters that add the message using "telop" (*teroppu*, an abbreviation for "television opaque projecting device"), that is, superimposing the message directly during broadcast. Sometimes producers add the message, "hard sub-bing" it into the show, where it extends beyond the context of its initial broadcast to appear on the video or DVD releases. As such, the display of the message does not correspond case by case with the actual situation addressed by the message. For instance, when the animated film *Road to Ninja: Naruto the Movie* showed on big screens across Japan in summer 2012, the television-animation warning incongruously appeared. Such incongruity arises because animation producers are more intent on DVD release than on theatrical release. They thus included the message on the master copy before its screening. For movie viewers, for better or worse, it is as if the cinema experience had been absorbed into or coded by television. Indeed, the yearly increase in animated films associated with manga, television anime, and video game franchises are sometimes taken as evidence of ongoing destruction or invasion of cinema by television; although such animated films are feature-length theatrical releases, their aesthetics are not deemed particularly cinematic.

In the case of the warning appearing in movie theaters, the crossover from television animation to other screens and media might be deemed a side effect. But the warning may also extend to animated films (that is, animations not intended for television) when they are shown on television, and to video and DVD releases of nonanimated children's movies destined for home viewing, presumably on a television screen. Such instances show concern specifically about the television screen rather than targeting animation per se. Thus the television-animation apparatus is readily extended to other small screens and other media. A similar safety warning about seizures appears in pamphlets accompanying Nintendo handheld consoles and games played on them, and more recently for the Wii. A number of incidents have occurred in which gamers have experienced epileptic seizures while playing arcade games, console games, and Game Boys. Before the Pokémon Incident, the association of seizures with Nintendo games became so pronounced that such seizures became styled as "Nintendo seizures" in the press in 1994, in the context of John Ledford's lawsuit against Nintendo. Ledford allegedly experienced his first seizure at the age of twenty-seven while playing one of their games at a video arcade. In 2004, the BBC aired a documentary, *Outrageous Fortune,* which exposed evidence showing that Nintendo had deliberately suppressed knowledge of game-induced seizures.[20] In sum, although responses to Pokémon Shock initially emphasized the specificity of animation, there were previous game-related instances of seizures that had focused attention on screens, interfaces, and hardware.

Significantly, despite the seriousness of the actual seizures, the warning becomes caught up in forms of expression, especially in the context of television animation. This is not because producers and broadcasters do not take the message seriously but rather because the message has become part of the experience

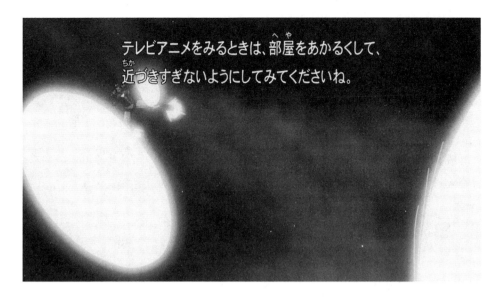

テレビアニメをみるときは、部屋をあかるくして、
近づきすぎないようにしてみてくださいね。

FIGURE 1.4. The use of intense transmitted light effects in conjunction with the television-animation advisory over the opening battle in *Marvel Disk Wars: The Avengers* (2014) seems to enact the very effects it warns against.

of watching animation. The Japanese broadcast of recent Disney–Tōei–Marvel coproduction, *Marvel Disk Wars: The Avengers* (*Disuku uōzu: Abenjāzu*, 2014) deploys the message in its conventional form with telop. Yet the seemingly child-friendly message plays over a fast-paced, light-riddled aerial battle that seems to belie the expressed concern for young viewers (Figure 1.4). Or maybe it serves to remind and possibly tantalize young viewers with the possibility that animation is always on the verge of inducing a shock to the brain? In the animated *Fairy Tale* series, one of the characters, Natsu, appears and cheerily enjoins viewers to keep the room nicely lit and not to get too close to the television (Figure 1.5). Such a presentation may be read as a clever way to channel both the shock of animation and emotive concern into the character form. In contrast, Anno Hideaki's 1998–99 anime adaptation of the manga *Kareshi kanajo no jijō* (His and her circumstances) presents the warning with highly stylized, honorific expressions hardly suited for an audience of children, which may impart a sense of haughty impudence and a slyly mocking tone (Figure 1.6). Again, such expressive variations do not necessarily mean that animators wish to undermine the warning. Rather, the warning cannot stand outside television animation and effectively provide a perspective

FIGURE 1.5. *Fairy Tale* plays with the television-animation advisory with one of its heroes, Natsu, directly reading the message to the audience in his own style: "Hey kids, when you watch *Fairy Tale,* keep away from the TV and keep the lights on!"

on it because the warning and the television animation now function as elements within a set of relations, the television-animation *dispositif.*

As an enunciation, the television-animation warning unfurls variations across media (animation, game software), exhibition and interaction sites (homes, theaters, arcades), technologies (game hardware, television screens), broadcast situations, production sites, and creative practices. What at once empowers and consolidates the enunciation across such variations is the articulation of a limit-experience—convulsions, headaches, seizure, and loss of consciousness. If something like cinematic experience comes into play at the limit, conjuring up older paradigms about the dangers of letting yourself become absorbed into the screen in the dark, such an experience is not evoked as an external limit. It does not mark a line between the desired television viewing practice and the undesirable cinema-like relation to the screen. It does not make for a bounded territory called television animation. Rather it implies an internal nonlocalizable limit, which generates a field with shifting fringes.

A nonlocalizable limit serves to potentialize a field. While it works through the field, it remains somehow outside it. Yet this nonlocalizable limit is not a for-

FIGURE 1.6. *Kareshi kanajo no jijō* (*His and Her Circumstances,* 1998–99) adopts an arch tone when conveying the advisory: "On those occasions when you view television animation, please take care so as not to approach the screen, and keep the room illuminated."

eign medium or invading entity that become lodged inside territory; it is not an inassimilable foreign entity that must be continually repressed or held under erasure (like a negative unconscious). Nor does it entail generalized mechanism of remediation in which television or animation confronts and absorbs its cinematic predecessor. Put another way, if something like cinematic experience appears as the nonlocalizable limit of the television-animation apparatus, it is not because cinema has invaded the sovereign realm of television and set up shop, alienating the television-animation apparatus from itself. Although negation and regression come into play, they do so in a second instance in the same way that government injunctions follow the scientists testing the children who tend to scatter and mutate under pressure, while the company buries evidence of seizures. Likewise, even if it is possible to speak of an "expanded television" in which television is entering into or overcoding cinematic experiences, aesthetics, and spaces (the appearance of the television-animation advisory in movie theaters is the tip of the iceberg), the warning itself implies that there is something positive in television animation that is already in communication with cinema, as it is with manga, video games, and other media forms.

Positive Unconscious and Productive Power

In speaking about how seizures catalyze the formation of a television-animation apparatus in the context of Pokémon Shock, I am using terms such as "positive" and "productive," which may trouble some readers. Shouldn't I be directing attention to all the negative effects, to the suffering of victims and their families, to the criminal irresponsibility of corporate profiteering, and to the indifference of a government that remains content to place responsibility on consumers rather than slow down the generation of profits from lucrative TV shows? Isn't it wrong for seizures to be associated, however tangentially or provisionally, with positivity and productivity? Any response to such questions will necessarily be a complicated one because Pokémon Shock has incited an outpouring of concern for children and fears about media in conjunction with the need for consumers to shoulder increased responsibility. In this respect, Pokémon Shock has already proved productive in reinforcing a general trend toward replacing governmental and corporate responsibility with forms of media care. Referring to power as productive does signal an affirmation of it, however. If I adopt something of Foucault's emphasis on positivity, productive power, and the positive unconscious, it is for specific reasons.

First, while I would be happy to join in direct action against government ministries and media corporations, I tend to agree with Foucault that merely denouncing power is an ineffective tactic, particularly in this context. What would it mean to denounce television or television animation in general? As Said put it in the context of Orientalism, "One ought never to assume that the structure of Orientalism is nothing more than a structure of lies or myths which, were the truth about them to be told, would simply blow away."[21] The television-animation apparatus is configured to deflect such denunciations through its production of a system of relations between discourses, institutions, media, architectures, and laws. Not only do government officials and research scientists show genuine concern about media effects but also individuals and social groups are enjoined to care for themselves in their use of media and to care about how media affects them. In other words, this apparatus consolidates and reinforces media practices of self, which deflect and diffract indictment and incrimination of media producers and broadcasters by evoking media care. Suddenly politics takes the form of pointing fingers at someone or something who does not appear to care—not really.

Second, as scholars like Vicki Kirby, Elizabeth Grosz, Judith Butler, Karen Barad, and Pheng Cheah have persuasively argued for some time, Foucault's focus on productivity and positivity is calculated to avoid treating everything as culture or ideas, as culturally or ideationally constructed, all the way down. A new challenge arises. Addressing the question of materiality or mattering has moved in a number of directions in recent years, among them the object-oriented ontology of speculative realism; the natures, actors, and modes of existence associated with Bruno Latour; and the ecology of practices of Isabelle Stengers. If I begin with an emphasis on Foucault's notions of positivity and productive power, it is because I feel that the questions about power have not been as thoroughly or forcibly addressed in these other approaches as in Foucault. At the same time, as I have already indicated, and as Friedrich A. Kittler signaled some years ago, Foucault's approach tends to avoid directly addressing the positivity of media and technologies.[22] Foucault also generally avoids any account of what Thomas Kuhn, one of his sources, calls "normal sciences."[23] Consequently, while my account of television begins with Foucauldian paradigms, I do so in hopes of drawing more effectively on approaches that speak to modes of existence, objects, ecologies, technologies, and mediality.

To give a more concrete sense of what such an approach means, let me turn to an interpretation of Pokémon Shock that calls attention to the production of objects, beings, and modes of existence. This brief account touches on a number of the same concerns as my account, and so I wish to work through it in some detail.

Beyond the Metaphysical Hypothesis

Spyros Papapetros writes, "The Pokemon incident acts as a painful reminder that humans instinctively attribute agency to inanimate images and things when something *bad* is happening to them."[24] Drawing on some of the horrifying personal accounts ("Her eyes rolled back and she went into convulsions . . . she didn't come round for more than ten minutes," reported a mother),[25] Papapetros refers us to a general response mechanism in which humans attribute malevolent agency to what harms them. Yet he also wishes to complicate such a response to the terrifying effects of episode 38 of the animated *Pokémon* series. His account thus highlights two points about animation made evident by the seizures: first, "we can never *know* much about animation," because as soon as we begin to produce knowledge, we have left behind the immediate experience; and second, animation produces "complementarity" between subject and object, as evidenced in the "white blasts and flashing lights on the television screen were replicated by the 'whitening out' and 'hot and cold flashes' on the spectators' faces."[26]

In other words, the experience of animation is one in which subject and object are not readily separable but are mirroring each other. Then knowledge steps in, and subject and object are held apart. Although he does not make the point explicitly, his insistence on the apparently inevitable phobia toward the harmful object implies that the emergence (or return) of human agency in the wake of the immediate experience of subject–object complementarity is a formation in which the subject not only stands apart from the object but also strives to stand over and above it, striking back at it, expressing anger, and treating it as a source of malign intentions. "Things are not considered for the good they may produce, but rather for the harm they are capable of inflicting,"[27] Papapetros notes. What is at stake in Papapetros's account is not merely challenging the separation of subject and object but also the ascendency of subject over object, that is, subjectification of the object.

What attracts me to his approach to Pokémon Shock comes of its evocation of what William James called pure or immediate experience. Papapetros signals an experience of animation that is nonconscious (not experienced consciously) and nonsensuous (not localized perceptually or sensuously). In a similar vein, Tohkura Yoh'ichi uses the phrase "unexperienced information" to describe Pokémon Shock in order to indicate that the effects were not experienced consciously, perceptually, or sensuously.[28] Insofar as immediate experience is nonconscious and nonsensuous, it might well be described as nonexperienced experience, or nonexperience. But I will stick with the terms "pure experience" and "immediate experience" used by James and other philosophers. In any event, Tohkura's point is that information does something: "Information acts on humans just as medicine does."[29] Similarly, Papapetros proposes that animation does something and implies that what it does is not consciously or perceptually experienced. It is not an object but a process. In this respect, I am entirely in agreement with Papapetros and Tohkura.

It is the next move in Papapetros's account that troubles me. He suggests that knowledge steps in and transforms the nonconscious nonsensuous something into an object. Two problems arise. First there is a problem of temporality: Pokémon Shock encourages us to think in terms of a traumatic event followed by perceptual and conscious responses, that is, in terms of an immediate experience that is subsequently unpacked or covered over, through perception and consciousness. The temptation is to think of the event in terms of loss and recovery (of perception, of conscious). In fact, however, perception and consciousness are not lost and then found, any more than immediate experience is lost. Consciousness, perception, and the nonconscious nonsensuous something are always there, even if relative intensities fluctuate. Likewise, the actual experience of animation is always a combination of conscious experience, perceptual experience, and immediate experience.

Second, when Papapetros considers the formation of animation as an object of perceptual and conscious knowledge, he presents us with a general mechanism of phobia, of fear and hatred toward the object. The title of his essay implies that this is a "cultural response," yet he turns primarily to Western art theory and to Warburg's assertion that humans and animals invariably perceive everything that looks alive or merely moving as hostile.[30] In other words, in this approach, knowledge is not formed culturally in the usual sense of culture (national culture, global culture, or subculture). It is instead formed metaphysically, as formulated in the metaphysics of Western art theory. As such, rather than address practices per se, the account verges on a psychologistic and anthopologistic primitivism. Thus, in a final twist, Papapetros proposes to invert Warburg's values: where Warburg claims that art pacifies humans by endowing objects with a liveliness that counters our inherent phobic response, Papapetros wishes to hang onto the possibility of the animation object as an encounter with "a being that is radically different from our own."[31] He proposes, somewhat obliquely, for us not to "obliterate the enigmatic power of an object," for us not to "strip the *thing* of all of its deathly connotations."[32]

The strength of such an approach lies in its reminder that experiences of and responses to animation are not primarily rational and thus may not be explicable in cognitive terms. Papapetros forces us to acknowledge a magical or nonrational mode of relation arising between viewers and animations, between subjects and objects, which runs counter to received ideas about the subjection of objects, about the subject's mastery over them. Indeed, through Pokémon Shock, a new series of things emerge as objects of concern: television sets, animation techniques, architectural layouts and lighting, parental absence, advertising and the attention economy, the transformation of children into research data, and the global economy, not to mention cinematic experience, broadcast infrastructures, and networks. Modes of magical thinking and behavior vis-à-vis objects may play a role, and even a significant one, within this field of knowledge and power. Nevertheless, a purely metaphysical account of knowledge formation (the failed drive for mastery over moving objects and our consequent fear of them) does not help us to understand the formation of a knowledge/power field or to assess its implications.

Again, this is why I have begun with a more Foucauldian approach, exploring the warning message in order to begin a tentative delineation of a television-animation apparatus that generates a knowledge/power field that produces media techniques of self. I would argue that although animation and other objects appearing in this field undoubtedly have an existence outside this field (they are not culture or idea all the way down), they take on a specific mode of existence through this field. As Alfred North Whitehead remarks, "The molecules within an animal body exhibit certain peculiarities of behavior not to be detected outside an animal body."[33] Likewise, we interact with animation through this *dispositif* in a particular manner, and it is the power of an apparatus that it makes a certain range of interactions feel possible. The apparatus does not need to make an interaction feel thoroughly natural or ineluctable. It need only assure that it feels possible, at once constrained and potentialized, promising a possibility that is not airy fantasy or ideological illusion. Indeed, as we will see, the television-animation apparatus catalyzed by Pokémon Shock both constrains and potentializes specific practices of self—at the moment when, in a darkened room, the viewer approaches the flickering screen.

An ethical concern nonetheless lingers when potentiality is evoked in the context of Pokémon Shock. Because there were victims who experienced epileptic seizures as well as those who underwent the ordeal of witnessing their loved ones experience headaches, convulsions, and blackouts, commentators tend to convey their concern for victims by casting a pall of horror over every aspect of the event. The problem is, victimhood may thus become generalized to the point where we speak of how images harm "us." Foucault encourages us to resist this sort of hysterization of power. It is crucial to dehystericize our account of power because its effects are not evenly distributed among "us." It is possible (and desirable) to introduce gradations among those affected—victims, witnesses, bystanders, and perpetrators—and gradations within these gradations. It is also possible (and necessary) to establish degrees of responsibility. Are animators to blame, or broadcasters, or parents?

By the same token, however, it is precisely because responsibility cannot be definitively localized and assigned that Pokémon Shock can serve to catalyze the formation of an apparatus. For as we step back and try to account for the set of relations that makes up this apparatus, we find that it all hinges on what is commonly called the attention economy. Everything circles around experimentation with ways of capturing and holding attention, which inevitably places the nonconscious and nonsensuous something at the center of a vortex—let's call it a brainstorm. We may of course denounce the attention economy, yet no one takes seriously proposals to abandon televisions, computers, or cell phones, along with all advertising and image making. We opt instead for regulation, which tends to rehystericize the understanding of power, attributing quasi-magical agency to images, television sets, animation techniques, lamps, and darkened rooms while producing an understanding of the human body as inherently passive, frail, precarious, and under siege, and hence in need of regulatory governance based on studies of neurological development. All this productive activity circles like a storm system around a nonconscious nonsensuous something that potentializes the field of knowledge and power.

Brainstorm

Is it possible to be more specific about this nonconscious nonsensuous something? Max Tegmark's definition of two nonconscious states provides some insight: "Although our neurons remain alive and well during sedation and deep sleep, their interactions are weakened in a way that reduces integration and hence consciousness. During a seizure, the interactions instead get so strong that vast numbers of neurons start imitating one another, losing their ability to contribute independent information, which is another key requirement for consciousness according to IIT [integrated information theory]."[34]

I will resort again, at the risk of overdoing it, to the running contrast between cinema and television-animation. Cinema has often been likened to a waking collective dream in a dark theater, with a dreamlike loss of self that is spurred by an uncanny doubling with the screen, a loose integration at the level of unconscious investment. With the television-animation apparatus, seizures become the major issue, and Tegmark's descriptions point to a far different kind of nonconscious state, one in which individuals start to do exactly the same thing at the same time, losing autonomy as their interactions become stronger. Is this not precisely what happened during Pokémon Shock, with individual children across a wide area of Japan starting to experience exactly the same thing at the same time, interacting with one another so strongly that they lost their ability to contribute independent information? This is the possibility that Pokémon Shock brings to the fore, and here is the potentiality around which a set of relations circles like a storm around a vortex: a nonconscious nonsensuous something that overintegrates individuals through the television infrastructure.

What is striking about the relation between individuals is that it is unconscious—or more precisely nonconscious—and so the group it draws together is not imaginable in the usual sense of an imagined community. I am thinking of imagined community of the sort hypothesized by Benedict Anderson, in which participants in media networks (readers of newspapers, for instance) imagine other participants participating at the same time as a result of effects of synchrony (everyone reads the same headline on the same day), which are largely confined to the borders of a nation.[35] Newspaper readers thus feel a sense of belonging to a national community as a result of this imagining of proximity over distance. Media such as newspapers may be said to mediate the flattening effects of capitalism to create an imagined community.

The population seized by Pokémon Shock, in contrast, is not experienced as mediation to generate a bounded territory. Pokémon Shock happened only in Japan as a result of broadcast zoning, and it can be said to be more statistically likely to affect children between the ages of six and twelve. Yet it is not inclined toward producing an imagined community of, say, Japanese children—at least not in the first instance. National discourses and institutions do not fail to swarm onto the gathering storm, but they are riding its wind, trying to determine the shape of a coming community. The Pokémon Incident suggests that at the heart of mediation there is immediation, and at the heart of imagined community there is an image economy wherein it is impossible to separate neurons and television infrastructures. This economy may be called an attention economy, with the caveat that it is precisely because attention to specific features or objects can never be assured that an economy actually emerges, gathering, vortexlike, around something prior to attention. Likewise, governmental, medical, parental, and media concerns begin to circle around the anomaly they cannot dispense with. This is the brainstorm that the first part of this study aims to explore. To track it, we may have to come closer to the screen, closer to both television and animation, than is perceptually or consciously comfortable.

2

NEUROSCIENCES AND TELEVISION

A GROWING NUMBER OF ESSAYS WITH STRONG SCIENTIFIC BACKING TELL US THAT TELEVISION IS BAD FOR US. THERE IS nothing new about talking about the ills of TV and deploying cognitive sciences, psychological research, and physiological studies to do so, but there has been a gradual yet pronounced shift in emphasis. In "Television Addiction Is No Metaphor," published in *Scientific American,* Robert Kubey and Mihaly Csikszentmihaly put it this way: "Scientists have been studying the effects of television for decades, generally focusing on whether watching violence on TV correlates with being violent in real life. . . . Less attention has been paid to the basic allure of the small screen—the medium, as opposed to the message."[1]

Anyone familiar with Marshall McLuhan will probably not find such a statement particularly novel. Within communication, media, and film studies, a resolute distinction between medium and message feels as tired and overworked as nature versus nature in popularized biology. But there is something other than a dubious distinction between medium and message at stake. As Kubey and Csikszentmihaly's essay suggests, prior studies tended to highlight the impact of television on social behavior and to link physical issues to mental health (for instance, violence, obesity, sociality, or school performance), whereas newer studies place greater emphasis on the physiological, primarily neurological, effects of media. The shift is from psychology to neurology. As such, even though the echoes of media determinism in these new discussions of why television is bad for us often lack nuance and novelty in accounting for the effects of media, what demands attention is the shift toward neurosciences, which brings something new into the mix.

Intoxication and Brain Health

The shift from psychology to neurology brings with it a shift in social concern. Studies of the effects of television on violence, antisociality, obesity, numbing of emotion, and reduced ability to learn, for instance, displayed concern for deviant behavior, as if television—or more precisely an excess of it—interfered with the processes of healthy development in accordance with received social norms. Such studies have not disappeared, of course, and will not soon disappear.[2] But as neurosciences gain in explanatory range and scientific authority, they are displacing them. A different concern is appearing. No longer is television primarily a matter of social norms and deviancy but of brain health and controlled intake. Kubey and Csikszentmihaly's conclusion clearly articulates such a shift in concern: "Maintaining control over one's media habits is more of a challenge today than it has ever been. TV sets and computers are everywhere. But the small screen and the Internet need not interfere with the quality of the rest of one's life. In its easy provision of relaxation and escape, television can be beneficial in limited doses."[3]

Simply put, media are increasingly treated as intoxicants, comparable in effect to other everyday yet potentially harmful substances such as alcohol and cigarettes. Research on media addiction thus faces problems similar to those faced by addiction research more generally. An article in *Nature,* for instance, compares the difficulties faced by those who wish to conduct research on television with the difficulties faced by those who conducted research on the effects of smoking: objections to such research arise because it is seen as ethically intrusive, and effects are exceedingly difficult to track.[4] Difficulties arise because culture gets in the way: not only do families resist studies because they feel their practices are acceptable but there is also always the possibility of hidden factors not directly related to media exposure that interfere with solid results based on isolable effects.[5] In any case, even if no one is proposing that television screens are like cigarettes in terms of degree of toxicity, it is clear that television and other media, especially video games and the Internet, are being treated in light of how they affect and alter the brain in the manner of intoxicants or toxic substances. Troubling questions arise. What does it mean to rely on neurosciences and cognitive science to define doses and limits of media based on brain health?

References to the Pokémon Incident frequently appear in the literature on why television is bad for your (brain) health. This is not surprising: in terms of sheer numbers and news coverage, the incident remains the most spectacular instance of television-induced neurological effects. Consequently, the Pokémon Incident is almost invariably cited in the neurological literature as proof of the direct effect of television on audiences. Discussions of television effects commonly move rapidly from Pokémon Shock to video games. The evocation of video games is not surprising for a number of reasons. First, the *Pokémon* anime series derived from the globally popular handheld Nintendo game. Second, incidents in which both Nintendo handheld games and arcade games had apparently induced seizures had been widely reported in Japan and North America. Finally, although quickly discredited, Mori Akio's account of "game brain" was highly popular in Japan and widely cited in the international press and online reviews, and its very popularity has given it a good deal of currency.[6] Noting a decline in beta brain wave activity in gamers, Mori claimed they "were hardly using the frontal regions of their brains, which are important for emotional processing, planning and self-control."[7]

It is not surprising, then, that the effects of television, animation, and video games should be folded into a general discourse on the neuronal impact of screens. Indeed, discussions of media addiction move readily from television screens to "electronic game screens" (as they are frequently styled), conflating them. In the *Scientific American* article, for instance, the Pokémon animation is actually described as a "video game broadcast":

> In 1997, in the most extreme medium-effects case on record, 700 Japanese children were rushed to the hospital, many suffering from "optically stimulated epileptic seizures" caused by viewing bright flashing lights in a Pokémon video game broadcast on Japanese TV. Seizures and other untoward effects of video games are significant enough that software companies and platform manufacturers now routinely include warnings in their instruction booklets. Parents have reported to us that rapid movement on the screen has caused motion sickness in their young children after just 15 minutes of play.[8]

Even as the article proposes to call attention to the effects of the medium (television), the scope rapidly expands from television to other media, such as video games, mobile phones, the Internet, and screens in general. Similarly, broadcast and cable, the wireless and wired, merge into general paradigm of screen exposure. In contrast, in the actual research on photosensitive epilepsy (PSE), scientists introduce basic distinctions between media, distinguishing between animations and video games when considering, for instance, the effects of light, color, and flicker, and when distinguishing between different kinds of screen technology such as cathode ray tube (CRT), liquid crystal display (LCD), plasma screens, and combinations thereof. The scientific accounts generally agree that CRT screens and low-wavelength deep red flicker present the worst-case scenario for evoking seizures. But ultimately, despite the distinctions drawn between media platforms and mediums in their research, they nevertheless conclude that newer screen technologies and moving image techniques present similar risks. Scientific research on epilepsy thus winds up endorsing the idea of screen ecology, which is to say that although screens may be empirically different in their technological parameters, they may induce similar effects. As Charles Acland writes, "The concept of the 'screen' stitches together an identifiable and mean-ingful array of artifacts" but "technical specifications—screen size, aspect ratio, resolution, frame and refresh rate, brightness, color scale—only [get] us so far in our job of actually understanding the related senses, sensibilities, and prac-tices that form as a consequence of media use."[9] A sort of "virtual unity" arises through and across distinctive kinds of screens, these "surfaces for animation."[10]

A variety of new research projects propose to identify how media affect brains, not merely for the sake of gathering information but in the name of prevent-ing harm to children's development and brain health, which is posed in terms of neuroplasticity. Because of the scale of the incident and the extensive media coverage, the Pokémon Incident is equally often evoked to justify such research. Take, for instance, the research initiative launched in Japan in the first decade of the new century under the rubric "Brain Science and Education."[11] A review of international trends on brain science and neuroethics, published in *Neuroscience*, conveys the concerns of the Japanese initiative:

> One of the greatest societal demands in Japan is for accurate information
> about critical periods in brain development. When is the best time to begin
> teaching English? Or sports? What is the influence of video games, cell
> phones and "anime" (Japanese animations) on children? Many of the modern
> ills emerging among Japanese youth are attributed to excessive technology.
> Staggering increases in violent crimes, vagrancy and suicide among this sector
> of the population raise many questions about what can be done for children
> who burn out (known as "kireru"). In response, large cohort studies that will
> follow 10,000 Japanese children during the first several years of life have
> been launched under the rubric of "Brain Science and Education." This links
> pediatricians, educators, parents and scientists on a scale that has not previ-
> ously been attempted.[12]

A number of assumptions about Japanese society are at work in this brief pas-sage. Note that the passage does not make an appeal for accurate information about crime, vagrancy, and suicide, and the facts are mistaken: crime has not shown "staggering increases" in Japan, and insistence on such increases is argu-ably an ideological position adopted by an aging media elite of journalists and intellectuals; vagrancy is more readily linked to socioeconomic inequality than to youth brain burnout.[13] Instead, there is an appeal to understand how children's brains develop. Similarly, rather than call for an in-depth account of social prac-tices related to media, there is a call for accurate information about brain develop-ment. Needless to say, even if there is a "societal demand" for such information about children's brains, such a demand may not necessarily be socially progres-sive or even socially acceptable. The warning of a teacher in Kanagawa, Japan, published the day after the Pokémon Incident makes the point clearly: the push to collect scientific data on children might permit an abuse of power by violating basic human rights. Likewise, the collection of data on children cannot be presented as a neutral process, even if it is in the name of protecting neuroplasticity. Claims for a societal demand in Japan for such research need not be accepted at face value. Indeed, as if in compensation for the shakiness of arguments linking social ills to childhood brain development, the essay turns to Pokémon Shock as if to provide incontrovertible evidence: "One need only consider the synchronized, photic seizures that were induced in almost 1,000 Japanese children by an episode of Pokemon to see the relevance of the basic biology of neural plasticity to humans."[14]

In signaling some of the misguided assumptions about society and Japan within this call for neuroscientific research, I do not aim to dismiss neurosciences. The basic biology of neural plasticity poses a profound challenge to received ways of doing cultural studies, area studies, and media studies, and that challenge should be taken up. As William Connelly presents the challenge beautifully, "Although cultural theorists do have things to teach neuroscientists, some research by the latter can teach us a thing or two about the layered character of culture. It can show us how the inwardization of culture, replete with resistances and ambivalences, is installed at several different levels of being, with each level interacting with the others and marked by different speeds, capacities, and degrees of linguistic sophistication."[15] In fact, it is impossible to understand television and animation in Japan without taking the Pokémon Incident seriously, which also means taking brain sciences seriously. Caution is needed, however. To meet that challenge and to build bridges between neurosciences and what might loosely be called culture and technology studies, I wish to address the problems that arise if neurosciences are not understood to operate in two ways at once.

The Two Neurosciences: Apparatus and Diagram

On the one hand, as is evident in the continual evocation of Pokémon Shock as incontrovertible proof of the effects of television screens and/or moving images on brains, neurosciences have come to function as key elements within a set of relations, forming a screen–brain apparatus. This apparatus is for all practical purposes synonymous with the television-animation apparatus presented in chapter 1, but now television may be expanded to comprise a broader range of screens; instead of an exclusive focus on animation, a broader range of techniques used in moving images may be considered. The screen–brain apparatus gravitates toward and revolves around brain mechanisms of attention (orienting response, flicker fusion, for instance) and their dark precursor (seizures) in relation to screen experience. It should be noted that although eyes and vision are often the point of departure, multisensory experience is ultimately at stake as a result of the focus on general processes entailed in brain, mind, and consciousness. As Antonio Damasio reminds us, "The brain maps the world around it and maps its own doings. Those maps are experienced as *images* in our minds, and the term *image* refers not just to the visual kind of images but to images of any sense origin such as auditory, visceral, tactile, and so forth."[16]

Neuroscientific experiments and statements are not the source or cause of this screen–brain apparatus or *dispositif.* They constitute key elements brought into relation through the apparatus. As examples cited thus far suggest, the screen–brain apparatus tends to confer responsibility on viewers, to recommend self-control and personal management, and to naturalize rather than dismantle the attention economy, all under the aegis of media-orientated protectiveness, that is, media care. As such, the orientation of the screen–brain apparatus around media care resonates with key features of neoliberal ideology. For instance, the screen–brain apparatus meshes smoothly with what Maurizio Lazzarato dubs the "work on self" characteristic of the incessant generation of indebtedness within neoliberalism: "Debt is an economic relation which, in order to exist, implies the molding and control of subjectivity such that 'labor' becomes indistinguishable from 'work on the self.'"[17]

It is important, however, not to collapse these different registers, and so I will repeat: neurosciences are not the apparatus or its cause but rather are key elements contributing to the set of relations that is the apparatus; likewise, the apparatus is not in and of itself neoliberalism. The apparatus must be linked to techniques of work on self if it is to be yoked to the production of debt to drive profits. Nonetheless, the screen–brain apparatus contributes to a distinctive power formation, in which knowledge and power are intertwined and mutually constitutive—what I have called media care.

On the other hand, Deleuze's widely cited aphorism "the brain is the screen" has become the major point of reference for bringing neurosciences into film and media studies, philosophy, and political theory.[18] Deleuze situated neuroscientific insights in a highly specific way, however. He stressed how contemporary neurosciences had dismantled both the Cartesian legacy (in which the mind implied subjective mastery) and the Freudian legacy (of neurosis and psychic health): "Psychology has a good deal to say about a lived relationship with the brain, of a lived body, but it has less to say about a lived brain. Our relationship with the brain becomes increasingly fragile . . . The brain becomes our problem or our illness, our passion, rather than our mastery, our solution or decision."[19]

When Deleuze calls on neurosciences against Cartesianism and Freudianism, his stance resonates with Foucault's work (he was writing a book on Foucault at the time). Foucault's work had painstakingly recast Cartesianism and Freudianism as distinct knowledge/power formations. Psychoanalysis, for instance, was presented as an apparatus of power in *The Birth of the Clinic* wherein the

Freudian superego turned out to be a production of the panopticon. Foucault's work generally associated Cartesianism with early modern forms of sovereignty and grids of universal knowledge. In his later works, however, Foucault began to delineate practices of self *(techniques de soi)* in the wake of an extended critique of neoliberalism. Deleuze's evocation of neurosciences seems consonant with this aspect of Foucault's critique of the subject as formulated both within Cartesianism and Freudianism, and with Foucault's subsequent turn to practices of self.

Behind Deleuze's aphorism "the brain is the screen," then, there lies an effort to address a political shift away from the apparatuses of Cartesianism (sovereignty) and Freudianism (disciplinization) to "societies of control." When Deleuze refers to the brain as our problem or our illness, he is evoking something akin to Foucault's "practices of self" and "care for self" against forms of politics based on mastery, or critical reason, or psychological norms. Deleuze's use of neurosciences should not be taken as a straightforward endorsement of neurosciences. Oddly, however, despite the cautious precedents set by scholars such as Brian Massumi,[20] accounts of the neurosciences within film and media studies often seem to assume that neurosciences are automatically Deleuzean, which has skewed analyses toward presuming that neuroscientific paradigms invariably afford new possibilities for social or political resistance.

Because Foucault and Deleuze were more intent on challenging Cartesian and Freudian paradigms, neither thinker directed much attention specifically toward the neurosciences in terms of their social relations and political implications. Awareness of the basic problem posed by neurosciences is nonetheless evident within Foucault's discussion of neoliberalism and affect-based economy. His remarks there provide some insight into how we might begin to understand what neurosciences contribute to an apparatus of power: "Action is brought to bear on the rules of the game rather than on the players . . . and there is an environment of intervention instead of the internal subjugation of individuals."[21]

In sum, understanding how the neurosciences contribute to the screen–brain apparatus calls for a twofold approach. For instance, the paradigm of media care may be seen to oscillate between two kinds of self-practice, work on self and care for self, which entail a tension between self-enclosure and self-activation, between self-instrumentalization and self-potentialization. Deleuze's aphorism—the brain is the screen—may also be construed in terms of a pivot between apparatus and "diagram" in the Deleuzian sense. Diagrams, he writes, "mark out possibilities of fact, but do not yet constitute a fact."[22] The diagrammatic, then, is a specific marking, mapping, or distributing of potentiality. While it has specificity, it is not about something else; it is not a model, illustration, or blueprint for something.[23] Whereas the apparatus is the set of relations that constitutes facts and depends on constituted facts, the diagram marks, maps, or distributes possibilities of fact.

In the context of the Pokémon Incident, for example, photosensitive epileptic seizures are widely cited as proof of the effects of the television ecology. Seizures become facts. At the same time, as I will discuss below, the Pokémon seizures have tended to elude received forms of measurement. Some neurological effects were not in fact recognizable as seizures. Something is happening before recognition, something that also extends beyond recognition and beyond the constitution of the fact of TV-anime-induced seizures. Because something was happening before and beyond the demonstrable seizures, it became possible for subsequent discussions to characterize the entire incident as a kind of overdose, a tipping point where intoxicating doses of television reach a saturation point, becoming fully toxic for the viewer and doing genuine damage.[24] The transition from possibility (possible seizures) to facts (measurable seizures) is thus articulated in terms of a transition from harmless intoxication to harmful toxicity. Permeating the facts in advance, then, is a distribution of attention-grabbing effects, which may suddenly coalesce into the fact of toxicity, causing headaches, nausea, vomiting, and blackouts. Yet the same distribution may be experienced below the threshold as pleasant, mildly intoxicating, possibly relaxing and benevolent doses of television. The distribution of toxicity, then, is at once inside and outside TV screens. This is how an apparatus, a set of relations, is able to arise across the facts of neurosciences, layouts of living rooms, parent–child relations, techniques of animation, screen parameters, and governmental institutions. This apparatus harnesses the potentiality of the distribution of toxicity and gives structure to it. Toxicity is at the tipping point between possibility and fact, potentiality and factuality, the diagrammatic and the apparatus.

Let me turn now to neuroscientific accounts of the Pokémon Incident with these concerns in mind, and with the caveat that brain sciences alone do not make for an apparatus.

Pokémon Shock

When "Dennō senshi Porigon" (Computer warrior polygon) went on air on December 16, 1997, it was via TV Tokyo, which broadcast the show to twenty-seven prefectures in Japan, predicting that of the approximately ten million people who would watch it, over seven million would be schoolchildren.[25] The estimate was based on the show's ratings, which, at over 15 percent, were the highest in the 6:30 to 7:00 PM slot. The *Pokémon* franchise enjoyed phenomenal popularity from the launch of its handheld console Nintendo game in 1996, and the debut of the animated series (April 1, 1997) had spurred the franchise to new heights of popularity. By the time the first season's episode 38, "Dennō senshi Porigon," went on the air, the animated series had hit its stride, with a fairly distinctive look and feel, a recognizable set of characters, and a growing collection of brand products, such as card games, foodstuffs, figures, and other toys.

At about 6:50 PM, however, roughly two-thirds into the episode, a large number of viewers, especially children between the ages of six and twelve (the age group most prone to PSE), experienced headaches, nausea, blurring of vision, convulsions, and other symptoms characteristic of photosensitivity. By 7:30 PM, 618 children had been taken to hospitals, and as word spread, several television stations replayed the flash sequence, which may have triggered additional cases. Ultimately, the Fire and Disaster Management Agency reported that 685 children (310 boys and 375 girls) were rushed to hospitals and were seen by physicians.[26] This figure has become the official count for Pokémon Shock, generally cited in subsequent news reports as "about 700 children." Of these children, however, hospitals only admitted about 150 to 200 children because symptoms cleared up in the other children either on the way to the hospital or at the hospital.[27] In addition to this core group of children whose cases were actually reported at the time, subsequent surveys by doctors indicate that larger numbers of children experienced symptoms of neurological distress, running the gamut from headaches, blurred vision, loss of vision, nausea, vomiting, and abdominal pains.[28] The affected population was probably much larger than actually reported through hospital cases. Some reports calculate that because statistical analysis showed that about 5 percent of children viewers experienced neurological distress, even a conservative estimate would put the number of affected children closer to 100,000 among the over seven million school-age viewers.[29]

On the basis of how different populations were affected, some commentators use the term "Pokémon phenomenon" to refer to these broader effects in which children clearly showed symptoms in keeping with epileptic phenomena, but their symptoms were not immediately recognizable as such because the affected children did not require hospitalization or medical treatment and recovered fairly quickly. Indeed, it may be useful to think of the Pokémon Incident as comprising three overlapping yet distinct sets of responses: Pokémon Shock (the induction of recognizable PSE), the Pokémon Phenomenon (photosensitive epileptic phenomena of a less recognizable sort), and Pokémon Panic (widespread anxiety and contagion-like propagation of social panic vis-à-vis *Pokémon* in particular and television animation in general).

What, then, produced such effects according to subsequent scientific studies? Although occasional reports point out that the episode as a whole may have contributed to the induction of seizures, scientific studies tend to ignore nonisolable elements such as story, as they are not well equipped to reproduce the effects of content or narrative. Yet the events in the episode seem to prefigure the incident. "Dennō senshi Porigon" opens with the main characters—the boy Satoshi (Ash in English) and his "pocket monster" or pokémon, Pikachu—agreeing to go to the Pokémon Center in a nearby town because Pikachu is feeling tired after all his prior battles and competitions. Apparently his charge of energy can be renewed there. With his close friends Kasumi and Takeshi (Misty and Brock) and

FIGURE 2.1. In episode 38 of *Pokémon*, Professor Akihabara and Nurse Joy consult the computer to determine why the pocket monsters, zapped into the computer with lightning flashes, are not arriving at their destinations.

their pokémons, Satoshi arrives at the Pokémon Center, only to find that the center's nurse (all Pokémon Center nurses are identical women called Joy) is having trouble with their pokéball transfer apparatus *(tensō sōchi)*. When they try to transfer a pokémon via the computer (which entails intense flashes of jagged light to send the pokémon's ball into cyberspace), the pokémon disappears. Something is seizing up within the system. The inventor of the system, Professor Akihabara, shouts that it cannot be the system itself malfunctioning because his invention simply cannot break down in this manner (Figure 2.1). The professor abruptly runs to his laboratory. The children pursue him, but instead of the professor in the flesh, a glowing computer-generated image of the professor projected from a mobile unit greets them and takes them into the facility.

The professor then traps the children inside a device designed to transport humans into the computer, explaining that the three members of nefarious Team Rocket have stolen his prototype for a pocket monster who can live in cyberspace, Porigon or Polygon. (Presumably the polygonal surfaces of this pokémon convey an enhanced sense of dimensionality, hence its ability to go into other dimensions.) Team Rocket has entered the computer with Polygon and has made a blockade to prevent the transfer of Pokémon, apparently in hopes of seizing all of them en route. Gotta seize 'em all! The professor transports the children, against their express wishes, into cyberspace to stop Team Rocket. The episode lingers on the body of the girl Kasumi as it is erased while she screams in terror (Figure 2.2). The spiral whorls on the professor's glasses begin to occupy more and more of the screen (Figure 2.3). Brilliantly glowing concentric circles fill the screen as the children fall, still screaming, into computer space, and brilliant flashes of white mark a series of electronic transitions (Figure 2.4).

FIGURE 2.2. Kasumi screams as Professor Akihabara sends her body into the computer against her will.

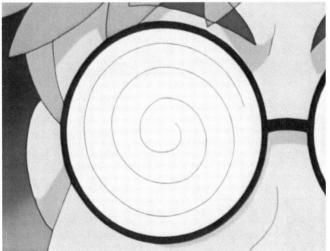

FIGURE 2.3. Professor Akihabara's glasses with their whirling spirals, a common accessory for mad scientists in anime, begin to fill more and more of the screen as episode 38 progresses, contributing to the overall effect of vertigo.

FIGURE 2.4. Screaming in terror, the three kids and Pikachu are transmitted into cyberspace by Professor Akihabara.

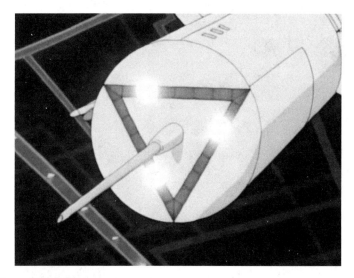

FIGURE 2.5. Unaware that the children are in the computer, to combat the computer virus, Nurse Joy and a computer technician send in "vaccine missiles," which look like injection needles as manifested in cyberspace.

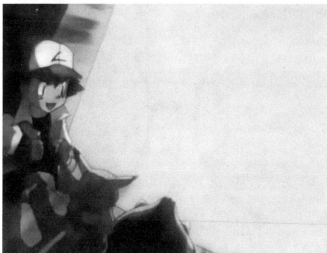

FIGURE 2.6. When Pikachu launches his thunderbolt attack against the incoming vaccine missiles, a large portion of the screen flashes rapidly between red and blue for some seconds.

When the children finally find the blockade and Team Rocket, a new problem arises. Nurse Joy has called in a computer technician, who launches an antivirus program designed to erase everything in the system, including the children. The episode plays with images of viral contamination: the antivirus program shoots giant hospital needles at the children in the form of "vaccine missiles" (Figure 2.5). Anyone afraid of injections should not watch this episode! Although Satoshi and friends have sufficient time to escape, they linger, as vaccine missiles explode around them, to save the members of Team Rocket. At about the twenty-minute mark, at approximately 6:50 PM, as a final massive grouping of vaccine missiles bears down on the children, Pikachu uses his famous thunderbolt attack to destroy the missiles. A rapid series of deep red and bright blue flashes cover most of the screen for some seconds (Figure 2.6).

It is this 12 Hz red–blue flash that was taken as the principal cause for the seizures because it was right at 6:50 PM that children began to experience epileptic phenomena, leading to the approximately 700 children being rushed to hospitals. News reports immediately identified this flash sequence as the culprit, and they quickly mobilized media experts, animators, broadcasters, and producers to comment. Initially news reports targeted the effect of flicker and transmitted light, while neuroscientists quickly detected the effects of color inducing seizures.[30]

But what are we to make of all those children who were not rushed to hospitals but who (it was later claimed) had experienced symptoms? Should the Pokémon Phenomenon be considered as part of Pokémon Shock or as part of Pokémon Panic?

Pokémon Panic

Among the few commentators on Pokémon Shock who read the Pokémon Phenomenon in terms of social panic are Benjamin Radford and Robert Bartholomew. In a coauthored essay, "Pokemon Contagion," they call attention to the fact that only a small fraction of children demonstrably exhibited PSE. They provocatively characterize the response of children who exhibited signs of Pokémon Phenomenon as "mass hysteria" or "conversion disorder" (as it is now commonly called), that is, "converting emotional conflicts and anxiety into physical symptoms."[31] The essay denies any organic basis to the widespread symptoms among the Pokémon Phenomenon children: "The outbreak of illness symptoms coinciding with the broadcast of the *Pokemon* television program fit the profile of the mass anxiety hysteria triggered from either observing someone having a genuine seizure or learning of the illness from mass media reports or word of mouth."[32]

To highlight processes of epidemic hysteria and contagion, Radford and Bartholomew have to downplay the physiological trigger for the actual seizures while offering an exceedingly reductive vision of Japanese society: they ground their argument for an irruption of mass anxiety in Japan at that moment by calling attention, albeit tentatively, to a "strong compulsion to conform" in conjunction with high school entrance exams in December.[33] They later reworked this account of the Pokémon Incident in their book on media-driven panics and hoaxes, casting additional doubt on the scientific explanation and amplifying the diagnosis of epidemic hysteria: "The researchers *believe* that the children's sensitivity to color—in particular, rapid changes between red and blue—*may have* played a role in triggering the seizures. As for the vast majority of other children who fell ill, mass hysteria was the culprit."[34]

It is not surprising that in response to Radford and Bartholomew's essay two renowned neuroscientists, Benjamin Zifkin and Dorothée Kasteleijn-Nolst Trenité, point out that the symptoms—"headache, nausea, vomiting, visual changes, and nonspecific abdominal symptoms"—associated with the wider Pokémon Phenomenon are "highly suggestive of migraine or of photically-induced occipital seizures, a recently recognized and less common epileptic phenomenon that is difficult to discriminate from migraine."[35]

Zifkin and Kasteleijn-Nolst Trenité also worry about belief. They express concern that Radford and Bartholomew's diagnosis of mass hysteria does not make clear whether they believe that the initial outbreak really entailed photosensitive seizures.[36] As such, to prove that the seizures were real, Zifkin and Kasteleijn-Nolst Trenité indicate that the effects are reproducible in the laboratory: "The unusual potency of that particular Pocket Monsters sequence in causing photosensitive epileptiform EEG activity has been confirmed in other settings. One of us (D.K.N.T.) found that 25 or 35 known photosensitive patients (71%) were even sensitive to that specific 12 Hz colored flashing sequence segment when it was shown on a 100 Hz television, which generally reduces the chance of seizures triggered by the screen."[37]

Although I concur with Zifkin and Kasteleijn-Nolst Trenité's diagnosis and do not endorse Radford and Bartholomew's bid to eliminate the physiological and to homogenize the social, Radford and Bartholomew are nevertheless correct to point out that something strange is happening with the population of children (Pokémon Phenomenon) whose experience lies somewhere between the children who demonstrably experienced PSE (Pokémon Shock) and all those people who were anxious, frightened, or shocked in different ways (Pokémon Panic). And what are we to make of subsequent reports that adults experienced seizures upon watching recordings of the episode? For instance, the Asahi evening paper reports on the evening of December 18, 1997: "According to contacts made on the night of the 17th with the Fire and Disaster Unit in Ibaraki Prefecture, at about 6:30 in evening of the same day, a man (age forty-two) from Nagareyama in Chiba Prefecture lost consciousness and collapsed while watching a recording of TV Tokyo's popular anime, *Pocket Monster,* at a friend's house in Tsukuba in Ibaraki Prefecture."[38]

The Asahi article also reports on governmental measures for stopping sales and rentals of *Pokémon* videos, expressing concern that offers are already appearing on the Internet to buy copies of the episode. In this instance, physiological and social factors appear inextricably intertwined. While the man's seizures were presumably genuine (or could be disproven scientifically), his experience moves the Pokémon Phenomenon well beyond the expected age distribution— children aged six to twelve are the most sensitive population. Moreover, in a manner recalling popular science fiction stories and films like *Ring* and *Death*

Sentences, distribution networks are now subject to suspicion and therefore subject to control.

The new article does not specifically cite episode 38 yet mentions that government officials were taking measures to stop sales and rentals of videocassettes and DVDs of the second volume of the *Pokémon* anime. The article thus tends to enlarge the scale of Pokémon Phenomenon to include other *Pokémon* episodes on the same disc. This example shows that there is a diagrammatic distribution at work. This diagrammatic distribution comes prior to the establishment of the facts of epileptic seizures, tends to extend beyond them, and spurs regulatory efforts in a number of ways. It incites additional fact-finding studies to curb the not fully perceptible and not fully known distribution by producing reproducible evidence; it tracks measures that develop a series of correspondences between a not-yet-known distribution (who exactly will prove photosensitive?) and actually existing distribution networks (rental stores, convenience stores, and media retail stores, as well as online modes of distribution); and it encourages speculation, which comprises gains in symbolic capital or hard cash for possessing copies of the episode (a kind of economic speculation), affective contamination (physiological effects without demonstrable causes), and a speculative movement of thought (pursuing the implications of the nonsensuous nonsconscious diagrammatic distribution, as I am here). In sum, there is a diagrammatic distribution from which facts are carved and from which points of correspondence with existing networks of distribution are established, both of which will allow the elements of the apparatus to hold together. Setting aside for now the question of the effects produced by distribution networks, let me continue to explore what happens as scientific facts are carved out of the Pokémon Phenomenon.

Epileptiform Phenomena and Singularity

For over a century, flickering sunlight has been known to induce epileptic seizures in susceptible individuals, and similar effects have been observed with artificial light and striped patterns. Yet it is only in recent decades that PSE seizures have become associated with television and video games in particular.[39] PSE has come to be measured in terms of an abnormal response, called photoparoxysmal response (PPR), provoked by intermittent photic stimulation during an EEG.[40] What proved unusual about the Pokémon Phenomenon is that many children who experienced actual seizures, which is indicative of PPR, did not test for PPR on the EEG. For instance, one research team found that of 685 children studied, 560 had actual seizures.[41] Among those who experienced seizures, at least 70 percent had no history of epilepsy,[42] and 81 percent of these children showed no recurrence of epileptic seizures in a five-year follow-up study.[43]

There are various ways to interpret such results. A team headed by Yamasaki

Takao concludes that even healthy individuals may experience image-induced seizures, proposing "chromatic sensitive epilepsy" as a variant of PSE and recommending study of "the neural basis of latent color-luminance sensitivity in healthy people to prevent epileptic seizures occurring when watching TV."[44] Takada Hiroyuki and colleagues, who conducted an extensive questionnaire survey in Aichi, also call for a shift of thinking about PSE: the previous belief in generalized seizures must be supplemented with attention to partial seizures. Their study concludes, "Photosensitivity may not be an all-or-none phenomenon as has been believed. It may be possessed by any individual in whom a maximal visual stimulus can eventually produce abnormal paroxysmal discharges, as chemical convulsants or electric shock will do. The TV program may have been so highly epileptogenic as to induce epileptic seizures even in 'subphotosensitive' persons."[45] Likewise, Zifkin and Kasteleijn-Nolst Trenité's interpretation of the Pokémon Incident calls attention to more unusual and recently discovered forms of epileptic phenomenon. In sum, even as neuroscience research strives to determine the underlying physiological causes of the seizures observed during the Pokémon Incident, the incident is altering the definitions of seizures, effectively broadening them as they are more fully described, precisely because the experienced seizures did not fit the received forms of measurement. In the absence of a strictly measurable, isolable, and reproducible effect, it is not possible to localize the effect definitively in specific bodies. Even healthy teenagers, for instance, might be subphotosensitive and thus prone to partial seizures, which may involve a previously unrecognized form of epileptic phenomenon, akin to but mistaken for migraines.

This difficulty in localizing the cause for the effect is a sign that neurosciences are confronting a singularity.[46] In physics, a singularity is understood as a breakdown in the geometrical structure of space-time. Black holes, for instance, are often said to contain a space-time singularity at their center, but a singularity is not a thing that resides at some location. The singularity, sometimes described as a tear in space-time, brings with it notions of incomplete paths and missing points: when structures of location are torn, it is not possible to assign origins to movements. Put another way, particles function as intensities, not extensities. Consequently, in one interpretation of singularity, the relation between measurement (extensive) and intensity goes haywire: "For example, some measure of the intensity of the curvature ('the strength of the gravitational field') may increase without bound as one traverses the incomplete path."[47] This is one way to explain the phenomenon of a black hole.

Because singularity is associated with a boundless increase in the measure of intensity, Vernor Vinge used the term to explain Irving J. Good's prediction about a possible "intelligence explosion" due to an "ultraintelligent machine [that] could design even better machines; there would then unquestionably be an 'intelligence explosion,' and the intelligence of man would be left far behind."[48] Vinge used the term "singularity" to underscore that a point would arrive where we could no longer make accurate predictions about the development of intelligent machines. While the jury is still out on whether such a singularity will soon happen (and what the impact on humans will be),[49] philosophers have noted other implications, showing how the notion of singularity takes us beyond the philosophy of mind.[50] The singularity arising in the context of Pokémon Shock points to something similar, but in reverse, as it were. The singularity is already there, already operating before and beyond the philosophy of mind.

In any event, scientific studies of epileptic phenomena in the context of the Pokémon Incident, while seeking to pin down the cause of the seizures, confront a singularity: the cause evades received forms of measurements (subphotosensitive), eludes definitive localization (even if seizures can be located in the occipital lobe, the phenomenon may entail partial seizures), and threatens to spread rapidly to populations not previously recognized as photosensitive. There is an underlying nonisolable "brain singularity" on the brink of exploding into a nova or collapsing into a black hole, so to speak. Again, my aim in raising this problem is not to cast doubt on the facts of neurosciences or on the reality of image-induced seizures (as Radford and Bartholomew do). On the contrary, there is nothing like the sciences for producing empirical encounters with singularities. The question, then, is, what do we make of this (brain) singularity?

What to Make of Singularity?

Sciences, as the prior discussion indicate, tend to make singularities into recognizable, demonstrable, and reproducible facts, which makes for usefulness. Massumi puts it this way: "The processings of science run usefully from recognizability to reproducibility."[51] Sometimes this reproducibility is taken for universality. For instance, a specific kind of 12 Hz flicker will induce photosensitive epileptic seizures or other epileptic phenomenon, primarily in children aged six to twelve, anywhere and everywhere. Because this demonstrable and reproducible fact is not dependent on cultural determinations or symbolization, it might be taken as a universal truth. It is nonetheless important to point out that this allegedly universal truth depends on a process of universalization, which is grounded in the production and maintenance of highly specific material networks: for instance, laboratories with specialized equipment are needed to produce the exact frequency of flash so they can measure children's responses, with procedures to rule out the influence of other factors—not to mention the need for obtaining permission from parents as well as long-term clinical data on patients and families.

Bruno Latour makes a similar point when he provocatively declares that scientific facts do not exist outside their networks and that scientific truth expands its networks to expand the scope of their effectiveness in the world.[52] This point may seem scandalous if taken to mean that facts and realities do not exist. But that is not the point. Latour, for instance, writes, "When I discuss the invention-discovery of brain peptides, I am really talking about the peptides themselves, not simply their representation in Professor Guillemin's laboratory."[53] My point is likewise simple and reasonable: it does not make sense to speak of the universality of certain kinds of television-induced epileptic phenomena in the absence of the prior universalization of television and its infrastructures as well as neurosciences and their infrastructures. In sum, it does not make sense to speak of universals without taking into account actual processes of universalization. When actual processes of universalization are ignored in favor of the universality of facts, the result is what I will call enclosure.

Enclosure builds on the neurosciences' act of processing singularities into reproducible facts, but it transforms those facts into universals while obfuscating the process of universalization. Enclosure makes for selves that appear to be personalized, particularized instances of universal brain. As I will discuss in later chapters, enclosure also tends to collapse the distinction between person and nation, or more precisely between personal sovereignty and national sovereignty, seeing them as identical processes of self-formation. Enclosure thus depoliticizes what the brain can do and what the self can make of its self. It lends itself wholeheartedly to the screen–brain apparatus. This is why Massumi proposes a reconsideration of processes in relation to singularities. He sees philosophy and art "concerned with eventful expression of singularity," and as such functioning as bookends to science, "working from opposite scientific termini."[54] He continues, "The processing of philosophy runs uselessly from accompaniment (actual qualitative expression) to relationality (virtual connection to singularities). Those of art cleave to actual qualitative expression, running from quality to quality in a way that envelops actual movements (in a composition that can be either seamless or disjunctive, contagious or off-putting)."[55] What would such distinctions mean in the context of the Pokémon Incident?

Philosophy might run this sort of process: while admitting that the epileptic phenomena observed in the incident are scientifically isolable and reproducible, the incident as a whole cannot be isolated or reproduced. In additional to ethical constraints on reproducing it (researchers can't ethically or seriously propose to recreate an event that proved harmful to so many people), there are too many accompaniments to take into account: the content of the episode, the degree of absorption into the narrative and into the franchise, time of day, time of year, illumination, relation to parents, advertising, prior exposure to the attention economy, history of attention economy, and a variety of socioeconomic factors that might have affected the child's sense of exposure to or absorption in *Pokémon*, and the parents' response as well. As such, philosophy might call attention to the virtual unity arising in relation to these diverse accompaniments—what I have called a diagrammatic distribution prior to the apparatus.

For its part, art might take all the elements of the Pokémon Incident—loss of self, absorption into the television, emission of harmful effects, parental concern, quasi-criminal activities of corporations vis-à-vis the attention economy, school-yard discussions of television effects, and so forth—and across these different qualities of the incident compose an animation that would envelop the actual movements that took place around the incident. In chapter 13, I will talk about the animated series *Persona 4* in precisely such terms, as producing a new composition of the elements and relations of Pokémon Incident. At this juncture, a fan fiction entitled "The Mysterious Original Pokemon Red and Green Incident," circulated as an anonymous message, provides a good example. The anonymously circulated message describes horrible effects on children spurred by the *Pokémon Red and Green* Nintendo game, as if the game were a mysterious precursor to the incident with Pokémon animation. It begins:

> During the first few days of the release of Pokemon Red and Green in Japan, back in February 27, 1996, a peak of deaths appeared in the age group of 10–15.
>
> The children were usually found dead through suicide, usually by hanging or jumping from heights. However, some were more odd. A few cases recorded children who had began sawing off their limbs, others sticking their faces inside the oven, and choked themselves on their own fist, shoving their own arms down their throat.[56]

The rest of the story can be found online. I will let readers decide if this sort of composition is compelling or off-putting.

Other examples of compositions with the elements associated with the Pokémon Incident may be found in tales of extrasensory perception, telekinesis, and a range of other psychic powers or supernatural abilities *(chōnōryoku),* which are typically located in the brain, the mind, or the brain–body interface. How often the recipient or bearer of a special brainpower or additional sensory organ suffers from it, and in the process of adopting and using it undergoes seizurelike contortions, writhing and convulsing, and usually emitting bursts and flashes of light, accompanied with zapping noises and other electronic sound effects. Such enhanced powers of brain, mind, and perception appear as if uncanny intensifications of the singularities related to photosensitive seizures, as if the human being had really become both the screen and its audience, taking on and also expending those electrifying powers. Such fictions are not merely allegories of the effects of television on brains and perception, in the sense of representing and commenting on them. Rather, they are actual qualitative expressions of them, compositions of sensations, affording an experience of them.

This example brings me to the fourth line of processing, which Massumi describes as "from relationality to expressed quality," which "would distinguish itself from both art and philosophy by taking their political middle as its eventual terminus."[57] It is precisely this fourth line of processing that I would like to follow, with help from philosophy and art, in the context of the Pokémon Incident. The actual problem can be stated simply enough at this juncture. What are the potential politics of flash and blackout? How can they amplify effective resistance or empower a new collective within the screen–brain apparatus? What effect do compositions offering an experience of qualities such as special brainpowers, journeys in cyberspace, or killer media have on the screen–brain apparatus?

Expression of Singularity in Media Networks

To summarize, I began with an exploration of how neurosciences address the effects of television, which helped me to delineate a specific set of relations. But this set of relations is two-sided, entailing on one side a screen–brain apparatus and on the other an underlying–overarching diagrammatic distribution. The apparatus moves from relationality—that is, relations between terms prior to their constitution as terms (screen neurality)—toward relationships between constituted terms (screen and brain). The diagrammatic distribution, in contrast, moves from relationships toward relationality. As such, distribution is where the political middle ground is happening, as it moves us closer to the expressed qualities and the intensity building up around singularities. Now that I can delineate, with some confidence, four lines of processing within the expanded empirical field afforded by neurosciences and television, I wish also to address some of the difficulties arising in the context of pursuing the fourth line of processing.

Massumi draws attention to these difficulties when he writes, "This [fourth] process line could well be cultural studies. But it isn't. . . . As it is widely practiced, cultural studies falls short of singularity at both limits because it clings to the notion of *expression of a particularity*. It realizes that expression is collective. But it takes the collectivity as already constituted, as a determinate set of actually existing persons (in common parlance, a constituency)."[58] Needless to say, nation-based or region-based area studies, such as Japan studies or China studies, reach a similar impasse, taking the nation or the region as an already constituted set of persons rather than considering how this constituency is actually being constituted, enacted, and processed. The flip side of such a presumption of (Japanese) particularity is, as Naoki Sakai has so insistently shown, (Western) universality.[59] Likewise, Jyotsna Kapur warns us of the "inadequacy in assuming *children* to be a natural category, an audience that is simply found rather than constructed."[60] Indeed, the challenge of the Pokémon Incident comes precisely of how it defies reduction to the expression of a particularity, of a preconstituted set of actors, either Japanese people or Japanese children.

On the one hand, what appear to be familiar constituencies, such as children, parents, and nation, are brought into relation with other familiar constituencies, such as television screens, flash effects, animators, broadcasts, and networks, but in entirely unfamiliar ways. Although such actors—parents, scientists, or government officials, for instance—may act on precedent, how they act and the meaning of their actions do not necessarily follow precedent. There is a transformation underway. On the other hand, actors that seem to be already solidly constituted come into relation with new actors in unprecedented ways: children across Japan experience analogous symptoms at the same time. In both instances, we encounter another actor that all accounts thus far presume yet largely ignore: television infrastructures.

Radford and Bartholomew, for instance, insist on social contagion rather than physiological effects, yet when they try to ground their discussion, they conclude with McLuhan's notion of the global village, highlighting that contemporary media networks aid and abet social contagion.[61] Accounts of television addiction, such as that of Kubey and Csikszentmihaly, often characterize their approach in terms of a focus on medium rather than message. Likewise, neuroscientific studies tacitly assume the agency of media: television networks allow for both synchrony and instantaneity, which assures scientists that the events of the Pokémon Incident "occurred with no warning or societal exposure as individual acute events in private homes,"[62] inadvertently providing the ideal parameters for large-scale randomized clinical trial on the effects of television. In other words, accounts that are polarized at the level of nature (physiology) versus culture (society) nonetheless share assumptions about television networks. Even as the functioning of television networks is ignored, they are presumed to be integral to the incident. This is precisely where attention needs to be directed: to this middle ground that is neither nature nor culture but surely both, and that allows for the expression of a singularity.

In conclusion, the Pokémon Incident does not allow for a purely cultural interpretation, that is, an analysis based on reading the event as an expression of received cultural positions. Rather, it forces us to reckon with neuroscientific data, making clear that fields such as cultural studies or culture and technology studies will have to move beyond their reliance on expression of a particularity and grapple seriously with singularity. This shift in emphasis might be underscored by heralding a new field, which perhaps might be termed sensory ethnography or media ethnography. But it may be too soon for that. In any case, we can no longer maintain the reigning separation between the cultural studies question "what do audiences do with media or technologies?" and the sciences' question "what do media or technologies do to audiences?" The political middle ground is already appearing in the screen–brain apparatus, with its incitement for work on self and care for self through media. With and through this apparatus, a brainstorm gathers, vortexlike, around a singularity, spinning elements into new trajectories.

3

THIS STUFF
CALLED BLINK

A CHILD IS WATCHING AN EPISODE OF *POKÉMON* AND BARELY BLINKING. CONCENTRIC CIRCLES, GLOWING WHITE, RADIATE outward from one of the pocket monsters, filling the screen (Figure 3.1).[1] The child's father, noting her tendency not to blink as well as her fits when the flow of images ceases, begins to wonder: what is the tube doing to us?

This scene appears near the start of a documentary film, *The Tube* (*Le Tube*, 2001), directed by Peter Entell. The film follows Luc Mariot, who plays himself (father and journalist) as he delves into the effects of television. Mariot remarks at a number of points how his daughter scarcely blinks while watching TV, and unblinking eyes become a refrain in the film, a sign of passivity toward, and exposure to, what is happening on the screen (Figure 3.2). The screen, on the other hand, appears active, with light flickering, pulsing, and radiating (Figure 3.3). *The Tube* gradually builds up and dramatizes this contrast between

FIGURE 3.1. In the documentary *The Tube*, a young girl is raptly watching this scene from *Pokémon*, apparently from episode 24 of the first season, featuring the pocket monster Gengar.

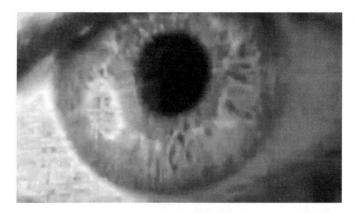

FIGURE 3.2. Scarcely blinking eyes become a motif in *The Tube*, signaling both the exposure and the passivity of television audiences.

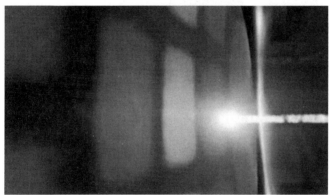

FIGURE 3.3. *The Tube* continually underscores the activity of the television screen vis-à-vis its viewers, as in this image of a CRT firing at the television screen.

the unblinking eye, passive and vulnerable, and the flickering television screen, active and even coercive.

Don't Blink

When I watch this scene of the child not blinking while watching *Pokémon,* another actor catches my attention, precisely because it too rarely blinks: the pocket monster Gengar. Indeed, if you pay attention to the eyes of the characters in the "Dennō senshi Porigon" episode of *Pokémon,* no one blinks much—not the friendly little monsters, not the kids, not any of the other characters. (One possible exception is Takeshi's eyes, drawn as slashes, yet they presumably are open even if they look closed.) The large round eyeglasses of the mad scientist, Dr. Akihabara, with their psychedelic spiral whorls, feel more like an amplification of than an exception to the generally oversized, wide-open, almost never blinking eyes of the characters. For the first three and a half minutes of the "Dennō" episode, for instance, no one blinks. Nearly three more minutes pass before a character blinks again. If you carefully follow their eyes for signs of blinking, you will probably feel your own eyes begin to strain: when you focus intently on such large, open eyes, you tend to keep your eyes open longer and wider than usual. This makes it difficult to see anything, yet you don't want to blink because you might miss the character blinking.

Eyes remain wide open throughout the introductory sequence of the "Dennō" episode, throughout the montage of the opening song (although Satoshi once seems to be looking down), and well into the action of the first segment. When blinking does occur, it tends to convey emotion of some kind, often anticipating a smile or some manner of interaction with another character, sometimes in response to a pleasant surprise. Thus, at about three and a half minutes, Satoshi blinks as he turns his head in surprise, and then Kasumi blinks at him as if in acknowledgement. Later Pikachu closes his eyes in pleasure. This limited use of blinking primarily to express emotion runs counter to human physiology, for we are constantly blinking. If our perception feels continuous despite our constant blinking, it is because the brain and sense organs are continually filling in the scene during our moments our eyes are shut.

Years ago, researchers conducted studies of the nonblinking eyes common in cartoons for kids. Nonblinking is especially common in limited animation, where minutes of dialogue may occur with only mouths moving (in a loop) without a single blink or any other kind of movement. The studies suggested that unblinking eyes were disturbing to children. In compensation, animated characters in Saturday morning cartoons in North America started blinking all the time. But because the eyes of such characters tend to be proportionally larger than those of actual humans, constant blinking can also be quite distracting, even disconcerting. The largeness of the eyes makes us perceive the blinking as excessive. Indeed, sometimes sound effects are added to underscore the blinking of the eyes. It was a common procedure in classic cartoons, but the effect crops up in the strangest places, such as the cat heroine of *Tamala 2012*, with weird effects.

It is difficult to determine exactly what effect characters' blinking or not blinking has, and whether different frequencies of blinking have different effects on different viewers. In any event, largely nonblinking characters are fairly typical of the styles and conventions used in limited animation for television in Japan. Of course, a fuller study of blinking (or nonblinking) across historically, generically, and stylistically different kinds of animation would surely help us better understand the range of its functions. My aim is at once smaller and larger, however. On the one hand, I am rather narrowly interested in the effect of characters' generally not blinking in *Pokémon* and similar animations. On the other hand, as my evocation of the problem in the context of Entell's film *The Tube* implies, I wish to focus on a larger set of relations that comes into play when screens appear to be blinking all the time while audiences and characters are not. I am deliberately introducing three points of reference—audience eyes, character eyes, and screen—in order to avoid a binary model that presupposes a closed or linear model of interaction. To make clear what is at stake, let me contrast the account of not blinking while watching TV that appears in *The Tube* with David Bordwell's meditations on the effects of the reduced blinking of actors in movies.

The Art of Not Blinking

Bordwell observes:

> In ordinary life blinks lubricate our eyes, and when relaxing or conversing, we blink between 10 and 25 times per minute. A blink lasts about one third of a second. Interestingly, in conversation, playing the role of speaker tends to raise the blink rate, whereas playing the role of listener lowers it. Once more, in film, aspects of the listener's role are transferred to the speaker, and the speaker becomes less of a blinker, just as his or her gaze wanders much less.[2]

In other words, the reduction of blinking, in conjunction with the tendency of movie characters rarely to look away from one another, and to make mutual eye contact frequently, signals for Bordwell the characters' mutual attentiveness to the situation.[3] While he initially focuses attention primarily on actors in movies, he gradually widens the scope to include the viewer-listener. Bordwell notes that the listener's role is mapped onto the speaker within the film, and he underscores how not blinking is an indicator of attentiveness (listening or watching attentively) on the part of the audience as well: "When do we not blink? It seems that absorption in a visual task creates longer intervals between blinks. Several Japanese researchers have found that blink rates slow down when people are engrossed in television watching."[4]

Bordwell is interested in how the effect of such eye behaviors in movies comes to serve the ends of filmmakers, to assure the audience's deep engagement with story information. His emphasis thus falls on the artful use of blinking: "An occasional blink humanizes, but the trick is to make it significant." He concludes, "Cinematic style often streamlines ordinary human activity, smoothing the rough edges, and reweighting its features in order to create representations that are densely informative and emotionally arousing."[5] Ultimately, then, Bordwell evaluates the artful use of blinking or not blinking in movies, both on the part of filmmakers and actors (at one point described in terms of an intuitive sense of audiences), which transforms everyday activities into art. Blinking, then, is subordinated to cinematic form in his account. Blinking is a means to achieving an end, a densely informative and emotionally arousing representation.

While Bordwell's mode of formal analysis is useful in opening new sites of analysis (such as eye behavior in films), formal analysis tends to deactivate the very sites it opens by making them into forms to be guided and ultimately constrained or managed by artful intentions. The result is a classicist model with rather normative implications. What happens, for instance, if blinking or not blinking is not used as a means to an end? What if blinking becomes an end in itself? Is the result not an art, or is it a different art? Who decides?

Bordwell himself relies on a distinction between daily life and the art of film: "Japanese etiquette discourages people from looking fixedly at their conversational partner, but in films they do so frequently, and they seldom blink. Ozu Yasujiro's films are remarkable repositories of staring, nonblinking conversations."[6] His account suggests that the heightening of daily behaviors through film art may stand in contrast to everyday activities. By extension, film art may even be construed as affording a site of critical reflection on daily behaviors. But again, questions arise: who determines which degree of nonblinkingness is neutral, critical, or excessive? To what extent should a film hold attention, arouse strong physiological responses such as feelings and emotions, or densely pack in information? While Bordwell's account of blinking doesn't actually provide guidelines for using increased attention, arousal, and information to make better art, his choice of materials places artful—that is, formal—limits on the experience of not blinking. Formal analysis relies on a hylomorphic model in which form is imposed on matter, and so form constrains matter in advance.

Pokémon Shock reveals one impasse of formal analysis: if we place "population seizure" (attention, arousal, information density) outside television or cinema in a psychologistic manner, as an external limit (an exceptional event), as Bordwell does, then we are effectively siding with the screen–brain apparatus, setting forth normative parameters for art and experience, or positing them in advance. My point is not that inducing seizures should be validated as art. My point is that the evidence of seizures demonstrates that blinking (or not) constitutes the ground (or more precisely the plane or fabric) for the experience of animation (and cinema), not an external limit or a passive material. Of course, blinking or not may indeed be deployed in an artful fashion by animators, filmmakers, or actors, but the intensity of certain performances of blinking or not blinking only happens because some sort of blinkingness serves as the ground for experience.

The point can be better understood by contrasting Bordwell's account of the formal use of not blinking with Entell's account of the media effects of not blinking in The Tube.

The Pressure of Flickering Screens

Profoundly affected by his daughter's tendency not to blink while watching Pokémon, father and journalist Luc Mariot heads for Japan, where he interviews one of the doctors, Funatsuka Makoto, who treated many of the children affected by Pokémon Shock at Tokyo Women's Medical College Hospital.[7] Funatsuka carefully explains that one in 4,000 children will show signs of photosensitivity. Then, in response to a question from Mariot as to whether the television screen alone can induce such effects, Funatsuka suggests that the cause lies in how the screen blinks *(tenmetsu suru)*, underscoring that such effects occur regardless of the actual program content *(dono bangumi de mo)*.

As in the neuroscientific studies of television discussed in the last chapter, the focus of *The Tube* falls on how "the medium is the message." In fact, Mariot later films one of Eric McLuhan's experiments, the Fordham experiment, which shows the effects of light-through media (transmitted light, like television) versus light-on media (reflected light, like cinema). Ultimately, however, the emphasis in *The Tube* is not primarily on "light through," that is, light radiating from the TV screen. Gradually the film comes to place greater stress on the flickering or blinking of the screen, which comes of the interlacing of television image due to CRTs firing half the image at a time but at a frequency that cannot be perceived or recognized. In effect, the television is actively emitting light and thus is blinking, while the audience apparently is passive, receiving light without blinking. It is as if the screen were blinking its audiences—controlling their actions, as it were.

The Tube imparts a sense that there is something nonsensuous and nonconscious that is always operative, always there, but not perceptible or recognizable. In this respect, Entell's bias toward the blinking screen comes closer than Bordwell's account to calling attention to the "blinkiness" through which screens, audiences, and animations happen together. This blinkiness is, to use Karen Barad's term, intra-active: the screen, the viewer, and the animation entail the "mutual constitution of entangled agencies."[8] They do not so much interact as preconstituted unchanging elements as they intra-act as intensive elements. This level of blinkiness may also be characterized as infraindividual, to use Massumi's term, because "what resonates on that level are not separable elements in interaction."[9]

The Tube backs away from such an insight. *The Tube* situates blinkiness as an agency arising in the interval between the two interlaced images. On CRT screens, half the image flashes, then the other, and between them arises a blink or flicker, which blinking is deemed responsible for the nonblinking of the viewer. Yet a number of empirical problems arise with this interpretation of the effects of television screens: (1) localizing the nonlocalizable effect entirely within the screen, that is, in a medium, technology, or media platform; (2) ignoring the message or subordinating it to the medium (indeed, the untenable dichotomy between message and medium produces such a dilemma); and as a result (3) interpreting television as a totalizing force by eliminating evidence of personalizing or individualizing forces. Each of these problems demands closer attention.

Entell made *The Tube* in 2001, a time when CRT screens were common. Today they have all but disappeared; the production of CRTs ceased in 2013, imparting the sense of a definitive end to the CRT TV. Yet as mentioned in the previous chapter, scientific studies on the effects of television have generalized those effects beyond CRT screens, and even beyond television, to include a variety of other screens associated with social and mobile media, such as those of cell phones and computers. CRTs may disappear, but the screen effects associated with them have not vanished, at least not from the scientific literature.

Scientific studies have gradually had to expand their scope beyond their initial focus on CRTs. Pioneering research on PSE by Graham Harding, for example, gravitated toward television, which had emerged as the most common stimulus in provoking seizures, triggering first seizures in about 60 percent of patients subsequently diagnosed with PSE.[10] Harding's studies stressed the flicker effects related to the frequency of image interlacing on CRT screens. Much of the subsequent research on PSE thus stressed the impact of different frequencies of image interlacing (25, 50, and 100 Hz), demonstrating that inducement diminished with increasing frequency: 100 Hz screens are less likely to induce seizures than 50 Hz screens. Screen flicker thus appeared to be the primary mechanism of inducement, and *The Tube* builds on that bias. Pokémon Shock, however, was something of a game changer.

Studies of seizures induced by video games had already broadened the scope of questions because they drew more attention to nonphotosensitive seizures, that is, seizures related to geometric patterns and movement.[11] Yet perhaps as a result of their more isolated occurrence, seizures related to pattern stimulation generally attracted less attention than those related to photic stimulation. Frequently, in fact, discussions of video game seizures still imply some potential for a photic dimension to the event, referring to electronic game screens. In any event, the scale of the Pokémon Incident generated a surge of interest in PPR while shifting the field of inquiry. Attention turned to animation effects.

As mentioned previously, in the news media, reports initially focused on flicker and transmitted light effects in animation. Transmitted light photography or *tōkakō*, colloquially styled *paka-paka*, is a technique common in Japanese animation in which animators take an already photographed sequence and flash light through it from below; portions of the image that are not supposed to flash are masked.[12] This effect makes for the brilliant headlights and streetlights, the flashing cherries of police cars, the flashing eyes of mecha, eye-searing explosions, and glowing, flickering screens, to name a few instances. Subsequent research, however, showed *paka-paka* was not the cause—at least, not in itself. Scientific attention gradually settled on the rapid alternation of red and blue (12 Hz red–blue flicker). An article by the doctor who appears in *The Tube*, Funatsuka Makoto, sums it up thus: "Continuous alternately flickering red and blue lights that occupied almost the entire screen (60–100 percent) and lasted for approximately 4.5 seconds, was responsible for the incident. As the red and blue colors were alternated at intervals of 1/20 and 1/30 of a second, respectively, the reversal frequency of 'red–blue' was approximately equivalent to a 12-Hz flickering light."[13] Subsequent studies succeeded in further localizing the effect, demonstrating the importance of long-wavelength red, that is, deep red.

In other words, around Pokémon Shock, effects came to be localized not in the screen (CRT) but in animation. In one of the first major studies of the incident, Takashi Takeo and colleagues note: "Harding and his colleagues have demonstrated that 50 & 25 Hz flicker produced by PAL-TV and 60 & 30 flicker produced by NTSC-TV, particularly the former, can provoke photosensitive seizures. The TV seizure is thus due to 'hardware dependent stimulus.' On the other hand, the Pokemon seizures were due to a 'software dependent stimulus' or 'programme-content dependent stimulus.'"[14]

What do such studies tell us about Entell's emphasis on CRTs in *The Tube*? Is it simply a matter of Entell getting the facts wrong, of focusing on the effect of CRTs when he should have focused instead on the flicker, flash, or strobe effects within moving images?

The problem with Entell's tendency to focus exclusively on CRTs is analogous to the one discussed in the prior chapter: trying to locate a cause when the cause is, in fact, not entirely localizable. There is instead a singularity. In fact, even as studies of Pokémon Shock gradually started to localize the cause of seizures in deep red flicker within animation, other studies appeared that emphasized the role of the accompaniments to deep red flicker. One study connected the emission of long-wavelength red light to CRTs.[15] Takahashi and Tsukahara suggest that blue may well have had a facilitating effect. They stress that researchers, broadcasters, and producers should not forget the effects of flickering geometric pattern stimuli.[16] Indeed, a later study found that alternating red and blue flicker has a greater effect than simple red flicker.[17] Another series of studies focused on effects of different kinds of screens, on the use of various filters with different screens, and other variables. In experiments with filters to reduce or eliminate Pokémon seizures, the 50 Hz NTSC television used in Japan and North America is distinguished from the 60 Hz PAL television used in Europe.[18] As filters and other modifiers are tested with different screens, studies find that increased frequency is always safer (100 Hz is better than 50 Hz),[19] and plasma screens and LCDs are safer still. Yet scientists nonetheless underscore the importance of maintaining the basic guidelines regulating a flicker, flashes, and high-contrast patterns.[20] This is why the general guidelines address not only flicker and flash but also the smoothness of movement and the percentage of screen used:

a. Flicker. Repetitive flashes of ≥3/s are not allowed.

b. High-contrast patterns that alternate, reverse, or oscillate are not allowed if more than five repetitions are present on the screen. High-contrast stationary patterns are similarly controlled but are allowed to occupy a larger screen area. However, patterns that move smoothly across, into or out of the screen, are allowed.

c. Flashes of long-wavelength red at ≥3/s are not to be used. In addition, clauses specify the amount of the screen that may be occupied by the flashes or patterns exceeding the guideline limits (typically ≤25% of screen area).[21]

As the above examples attest, even as one cause was experimentally isolated with a fairly high degree of certainty (such as deep red flicker), it turned out to have a number of facilitators, and yet other co-causes or accompaniments also appeared. Likewise, even when the cause of Pokémon Shock was attributed to 12 Hz red–blue flicker, a number of other animation effects were shown to have similar effects. In fact, upon closer inspection, the "Dennō senshi Porigon" episode turned out to be riddled with such effects, as did other animations. As a consequence, the definition of what qualifies as an epileptiform phenomenon had to be at once refined and expanded. In sum, as effects are localized into facts, they are simultaneously enlarged in scope, and this twofold process of localization and expansion happens in all three registers: animations, screens, and audiences (epileptiform phenomena). Simply put, blinkiness turns out to be intra-active and infraindividual.

Bordwell's emphasis on the artful use of not blinking (formal analysis) and Entell's use of the medium–message dichotomy reach an impasse for the same reason: because they only deal with two points of reference for data, their accounts remain focused on causal interaction between individuals, ignoring the intra-active reality of blinkiness. Bordwell deals with how movies affect audiences but he does not address screens, and Entell focuses on how screens affect audience but largely ignores moving images. Both studies, then, focus exclusively on causal interaction between individuals: between formal elements and viewers in Bordwell, and between CRTs and viewers in Entell.

Entell's approach readily transforms into a highly deterministic argument about television. Such an outcome is to some extent inherent in Marshall McLuhan's framework: even as the famous phrase "the medium is the message" promises to overcome the dichotomy, it may actually serve to reinforce it.[22] This is because the temptation is now to think in terms of overcoming the dichotomy or blurring the distinction between terms, rather than developing a method that does not rely on such dubious dichotomies at the outset. These dubious dichotomies have larger ramifications: in *The Tube,* the insistence on linear interaction between individuals borrowed from McLuhan becomes amplified into a geopolitical effect.

FIGURE 3.4. With the remark that the television experience could be totalitarian, *The Tube* cuts a CGI animation of digital men dancing in perfect synchrony to techno dance music that was playing on screens in Shibuya earlier in the film.

Techno-Orientalism and Global Pokémon Panic

In *The Tube,* journalist Mariot discovers that alpha waves increase when you're watching television; alpha waves signal that your brain is less active, that you're not paying attention. The film playfully assumes an aura of conspiracy theory by providing clips from *Invaders from Mars* (1953), in which aliens implant mind-control devices in humans. Gradually, however, the aura of a mass conspiracy and mass control loses its tone of levity. In a discussion with Eric McLuhan, Mariot postulates that the society inherent in the television experience (group orientation, right brain, loss of objectivity) "could be very totalitarian—if every-body's immersed in the same dream, it's one definition of totalitarianism." The film suddenly cuts back to Japan, to a CGI animation playing on a large screen in Shibuya, with largely identical digital men dancing in perfect synchrony to techno dance music with vaguely Japanese overtones (Figure 3.4).

Thus, in high techno-Orientalist fashion, *The Tube* projects its anxieties about televisual control over the masses (which is also described in the film in terms of the fall of Western culture into group culture) onto an alien invader: Japanese animation.[23] It's no longer just a matter of television inducing unblinking passiv-ity and generating controllable masses; it's also a matter of Japanese animation invading France, capturing the attention of French children, and thus under-mining Western values. Entell's form of Orientalist panic contrasts sharply with Marshall McLuhan's brand of Orientalist fantasizing. McLuhan opines, "Since the point of focus for a TV set is the viewer, television is Orientalizing us by causing us all to begin to look within ourselves."[24] While McLuhan's comments may feel more positive, Said's work constantly reminds us that the problem with Orientalism is not simply one of making negative statements about the Orient; positive statements about the Orient also serve to transform a vast, heteroge-neous area of the world into a unitary object, whose function is to feed identity and reality into myths about the West and to deny the genuine sociohistorical complexity of the non-West. Nonetheless, the difference in Orientalist tone in Entell and McLuhan deserves some attention.

The global success of *Pokémon* in the late 1990s generally inspired a sense of shock and panic around the impact of things Japanese on European and North American markets and on children. Gilles Brougère writes, "Pokémon has been a big commercial success in France, as elsewhere. At the end of its first year in France (2000), over 2.5 million Pokémon game cartridges had been sold and the Pokémon license had generated over $300 million in revenue. Episodes of the TV series were broadcast three times a week on TFI (on of the four major French broadcast channels) with a very high audience rating."[25] Similarly, in the United States, Elaine Gerber writes,

> The "Pokemon" fever began in September 1998 when "Pokemon" first debuted on TV in America. The 2.5 billion dollar profits harvested in seven months' time by Nintendo in marketing the "Pokemon" Game Boy cartridges made it the fastest selling product in company history. Warner Brothers further fueled the "Pokemon" frenzy by distributing *Pokemon* to 1,500 to 2,000 theaters in November 1999, the largest U.S. release of any Japanese film ever.[26]

In her analysis of the ensuing moral panic vis-à-vis Pokémon, Christine Yano remarks, "What these critiques express is Euro-American and other ambivalences toward global (late) capitalism—here fanatic consumerism—even as we adults live, create, and sometimes glorify a world of consumption. Pokemon is nothing more than capitalism running at its smoothest."[27] Put another way, panicked responses to Pokémon projected localized anxieties over capitalism onto this global Japanese franchise, thus disavowing their own capitalist excesses, while "depicting Japan and the Japanese as variously monstrous, mystical, and unscrupulous."[28] In contrast, Yano finds, criticism in Japan was muted at best, where the general tendency was to construe the success of Pokémon as a Japanese economic triumph. Indeed, government reports on Pokémon Shock express concern about how such an incident might affect the global Pokémon market: "In terms of market share, Japanese animation accounts for 65 percent of the entire world market. It is thus extremely important to take responsibility to ensure the safety of visual imaging display in order for the world's audience to watch it safely."[29]

The Asian financial crisis of July 1997, about four months before the Pokémon Incident, surely exacerbated such anxieties about Japanese economic success, making all too clear to Japanese citizens the extent to which their national economy lay exposed to regional and global flows of currency, and raising fears in North America and Europe of the Asian crisis spreading to their nations in a domino effect. A series of overlapping concerns appeared at once: fear that consumption was outstripping production, fear that financial capital was outstripping industrial capital, and fear that national boundaries were not proving effective in softening the blow.

Given such a context, it may not be surprising that Entell's film links the noxious effects of TV screens to the destruction of Western values by Japanese audiovisual culture, that is, Japan's highly advanced attention economy, in a thoroughly techno-Orientalist way. Yet this tendency to pick up and amplify Orientalist anxieties is not a bias that comes to the documentary from without. Its Orientalism cannot be neatly separated from its account of television. Part of the reason why Entell's film so readily takes on an Orientalist bias comes of its reliance on a binary media model, tracing movement unilaterally between two individual points. The film draws a line from television to audience, which it then exploits to draw a line from Japan to the West.

While the normative implications of Bordwell's account are less salient, it shows a similar tendency to assume a unidirectional movement from form to receiver, a projection of art forms from the screen toward audiences, which may easily turn into a defense of modernist art and a dismissal of other arts. In sum, the tendency toward cultural and geopolitical normativity, however unwitting, follows directly from the model that posits interaction between individuals, drawing a line between two points. This is why three points are needed. Three points make for a plane, and on a plane, points become complex, allowing for intra-actions as well as interactions.

The Plane of Radical Empiricism

Using a plane as a point of departure is precisely what William James invites in his philosophy of radical empiricism. Realizing that prior forms of empiricism had tended to draw lines and retrace them (from sensory data to subjectivity, from objects to subjects, and back again), James went back to the roots of empiricism, that is, the blank slate or tabula rasa. James radicalized this blank slate, however, by stripping it of epistemological dualisms, that is, binary categories such as subject and object, spirit and matter, and form and matter, to which we might also add medium and message. Simply put, the blank slate for James did not belong to anyone or anything—neither to a subject nor to sensory data. He thus established "a plane where nothing is pre-established, where no form of knowledge, no certainty—even virtual—has yet appeared, such that everything has the right to be constructed."[30] Such a plane he called pure experience or immediate experience.

The term "experience" may be a source of confusion, for it conventionally implies someone who experiences. James uses pure experience in a nonsubjective way, however, explaining that there is "one primal stuff or material in the world, of which everything is composed, and . . . we call that stuff 'pure experience.'"[31]

As such, everything is made of pure experience—not only perceiving and knowing subjects, but also perceived or known objects. Pure experience doesn't belong to someone or something, and there is nothing behind it. James underscores the primordial nature of the stuff of pure experience by describing it as a mosaic without bedding: "In actual mosaics the pieces are held together by their bedding, for which bedding the Substances, transcendental Egos, or Absolutes of other philosophies may be taken to stand. In radical empiricism there is no bedding; it is as if the pieces clung together by their edges."[32]

Drawing on David Lapoujade's reading of James, I would like to introduce the term "plane" to refer to the mosaic without bedding that is pure experience.[33] The term "plane" has the advantage of avoiding the potential misunderstanding of pure experience as subjective experience. It also recalls Deleuze's plane of immanence, suggesting some commonalities between radical empiricism and "transcendental empiricism" (as Deleuze once described his approach).[34] More importantly, the term "plane" will allow me to tease out the methodological dimension of radical empiricism in the specific context of the effects of television. We have seen how other approaches (form centered or medium centered) tend to select two points of reference, to posit them as indivisible individuals, to impose a dichotomy on them, and then to draw a line between two individual points. In contrast, the three pieces of our mosaic—animation, screen, brain—may be said to hold together by their edges, constituting a plane. Previously I referred to this plane as a ground, but the term "ground" is a misnomer if it is taken to be a substance or essence underlying the three terms. Rather, as with James's mosaic, the three terms cling together, and the plane is the clinging. This is why James also uses the terms "fabric" or "stuff" for this plane.

Another observation follows from the above. Both Bordwell and Entell begin and end their discussion with a linear relation between dichotomous terms—subject and object, form and matter. For Bordwell, it is the subjectivity of film-makers and actors that counts: they fashion forms that heighten everyday experiences. For Entell, a mechanical form (CRT flicker) imposes itself on minds, which threatens to reverse the ascendency of subject over object, making the active and objective subject into a passive influenced object. In contrast, scientific studies remain open to the operation of a singularity. Even though the search for causes in scientific studies implies a linear, deterministic relationship between object and subject—namely, this cause (deep red flicker) induces this effect (PPR, PSE)—such studies nevertheless remain open to a series of cofactors or accompaniments, which are changing interactions into intra-actions. Even as scientific studies aim to produce facts, their experimental procedures bring them closer to a plane where forms of knowledge and facts are not established in advance. Thus experimentation continues to make discoveries, which at once narrows and widens, constricts and dilates the domain of investigation, making the plane of pure experience into a field of inquiry.

My goal is not to champion the sciences over the humanities but rather to indicate a genuine challenge afforded by the sciences to humanistic assumptions about subjects and objects, forms and matter. The reason that William James is so often cited appreciatively within the sciences, especially brain sciences, lies in his move beyond psychology into radical empiricism,[35] avoiding Cartesian dualisms while stripping empiricist philosophy of its residual tendency to rely the interactive ascendency of subject over object in advance—or to watch in horror when the dichotomy is reversed, and the object seems to gain the upper hand.

Because I have taken issue with the normative implications of Bordwell's and Entell's accounts, I should signal my bias: in James's emphasis on "things in the making," I see an alliance with currents in Marxist thinking that stress the productivity of production, which currents will in later chapters allow me to reconsider Marx's account of infrastructure in the context of television networks. Infrastructure is not for Marx an underlying substance or ground but rather implies, like James's plane, a mosaic without bedding, at once subjective and objective, agency and structure, culture and nature. For Marx, infrastructure is infraindividual. In addition, James's planar approach affords a critique of linear geopolitical models that focus on movement from Japan to the West or the West to Japan, or from center to periphery or periphery to center. The goal is not to say that such linear movement does not happen but rather to consider the plane (or conditions, if you will) on which it is possible to restrict movement to a linear relationship between nations or regions or between centers and peripheries.[36] But that discussion will have to wait for later chapters. At this juncture, I wish to continue to explore the methodological implications of radical empiricism for transforming analyses of the effects of television on brains.

The Stuff of Blink

James's radical empiricism conceptualizes pure experience in general in a philosophical vein, but I am dealing with a concrete pure experience—a specific plane, as it were, related to the clinging together of animations, screens, and brains. It is a matter of *this* stuff or *this* material. Previously I used terms such as "nonblinking" and "blinkiness" to describe this plane. I could equally well have called it "flashiness" or "flickeriness" because this stuff might be likened to a fabric of light and dark, interlaced spatially and temporally, rhythmically. For the sake of convenience, let me call this specified tissue of pure experience "blink."

Although "flicker" may be an equally apt term, I prefer "blink" because, for me at least, it has connotations of tactility. Experiments on the effects of blinking on eye flicker (or saccadic movement), for instance, use a puff of air to the eyeball.

The eye is touched. The term "blink" may thus serve as a reminder that although the major point of reference for neuroscience work on screens and animations is the relation between eyes and brains (there is some research on ears and the effects of sounds in moving image media on brains, and even on seizures, but far less of it), the discussions are not ocularcentric in the sense of isolating the modality of vision from other perceptual modalities. On the contrary, blink implies an amodal mixture of the visual and the tactile, what is sometimes called the haptic.

The haptic is neither visual nor tactile; it is touch in sight, or sighted touch. It is a matter of eyes touching and being touched, of eyeballs jumping and being jumped, which is consonant with James's descriptions of pure experience as stuff, fabric, and tissue. Simply put, the plane does not belong to a single perceptual modality any more than it does to a subject. It is multisensory, or rather its expression is multisensory. The plane itself entails what Richard Cytowic in his studies of synesthesia refers to as the union of the senses prior to their separation into distinction modalities.[37] This union is nonsensuous and nonconscious, which explains for Cytowic why the experience of synesthesia tends toward singularity (synesthetes rarely make the same cross-modal associations).

Brains, animations, and screens are holding together by their edges, and such a clinging together or interweaving of elements makes for the fabriclike stuff I now call blink. Naming the stuff, however, is not the end of the exploration but the beginning, for now it is possible to speak not in terms of interactions between individuals but in terms of intra-active infraindividual actions that arise between screens and brains, between animations and screens, and between animations and brains. Dispensing with the form–matter distinction, James invites us to think of intra-actions in terms of the cutting and sewing of fabric stuff. Different functions or operations, then, cut up the stuff of blink and then piece it together.

I previously explored one function of blink that allows animations and brains to be at once held apart and held together: blinking eyes on the screen. Bordwell drew our attention to this function in his discussion of movie actors not blinking but then misconstrued this function as a form. Entell explored a different yet related function of blink: viewers not blinking while the screen was flickering. But he mistook this alpha wave sort of clinging together for a lack of brain activity rather than a distinct brain–screen function. Finally, scientific studies provided reminders that screens and animations may also cling to one another, with CRT facilitating deep red, for instance, or interlacing frequency affecting strobe patterns.[38]

It is possible, then, to begin to delineate several functions that are like one another but do not resemble one another. In reference to animation, we have been introduced to transmitted light photography or *paka-paka,* flicker effects, flash effects, reversing patterns and other geometric forms, and the nonblinking eyes of characters. In reference to screens, we have attended to transmitted light, interlacing (in CRT screens), proximity to screen, and surrounding illumination. In reference to brains, accounts have referred us to patterns of neuron firing, brain waves, dreamlike states, and seizures.

When matters are thus tabulated, animation seems to entail the greatest diversity of elements and potential functions, but this is surely because it is the easiest to analyze, that is, to treat in terms of isolable elements, which are construed as so many forms. With screens, the technological parameters are easy enough to enumerate, but their functions receive less attention, for they are more difficult to treat in isolation and thus to make into forms. Finally, brains are notoriously difficult to divide into discrete functions, that is, to treat at the levels of part and whole simultaneously, whether the approach be psychoanalysis, schizoanalysis, or neuroanalysis. This is surely why brains in contemporary neurosciences are construed primarily in terms of functions, not forms, and why form is treated as secondary to function, as a specific expressive contraction of it.

One way to understand how animations, brains, and screens hold together by their edges, making for the plane of blinky stuff, is to highlight the semblance between the phenomena associated with each of them. Blinking eyes, red–blue flicker, image interlacing, ambient lighting, neurons firing, for instance—such functions are like each other. But they do not resemble each other. They do not entail representation. A neuron firing, for instance, is not a representation of something in the world. Nor does it resemble red–blue flicker in its construction. These various functions are produced in quite different ways: electrochemistry of the brain, CRTs, transmitted light photography, and so forth. Their likeness is what Walter Benjamin calls semblance, or nonsensuous similarity, to distinguish it from resemblance, when he talks about the mimetic faculty.[39] Put another way, where resemblance (and representation) address interactions between individuals taken to be indivisible, semblance is a matter of infraindividual intra-actions.

In the instance of PSE, the relation between eyes blinking, 12 Hz red–blue flicker, and neurons firing is like Benjamin's mimetic faculty. Funatsuka, for instance, uses an analogous term to describe the affected children's eyes (*tsuka tsuka*, eyes stinging as when affected by smoke, and thus stinging and blinking rapidly) and the flickering of red and blue (*tenmetsu suru*), terms that are often used together in a common phrase (*tsuka tsuka tenmetsu suru*). Similarly, the scientific description of seizures (a neuronal overintegration in which neurons start imitating one another) entails semblance with the overintegration of children across Japan during the incident, with all of them doing the same thing at the same time.

This sort of semblance is not merely an effect of word choice or a linguistic effect. Semblance happens as if prior to language. Again, synesthesia comes to mind, as Cytowic explains it: "What I am saying is that cross-modal associations are the foundation of language."[40] Yet semblance is not really a ground or foundation. It is transindividual in that it appears to come both before language (ontologically) and after it (epistemologically); it happens with and through language.

Semblance is not reducible to an effect of technology on brains. Take the example of the recent hype about how social media can change brain circuitry. Neuroscientist Susan Greenfield has been widely cited to validate the threat posed by social networks.[41] The basic claim is that our brains were not evolved to deal with such media. In contrast, Stanislas Dehaene offers a theory of recycling: "The brain did not evolve for culture, but culture evolved to be learnable by the brain. Through its cultural inventions, humanity constantly searched for specific niches in the brain, wherever there is a space of plasticity that can be exploited to 'recycle' a brain area and put it to a novel use. Reading, mathematics, tool use, music, religious systems—all might be viewed as instances of cortical recycling."[42] Both Greenfield and Dehaene resort to rather mechanistic models that recall classical empiricism in being narrowly axed on enumerating correspondences. In contrast to both, I would point out that neuroplasticity entails singularities—and thus a plane, not a line (or point-by-point binary correspondences). The relation between a cultural function and a brain area entails semblance in that it is not preestablished in the cultural function or in the brain; nor is it closed to transformation. As Jason Read so beautifully phrases it, "A culture is nothing other than transindividuality, but transindividuality exceeds any delimited culture."[43]

Now that I have presented my basic approach (radical empiricism) to what is happening between screens, brains, and animations through the stuff of blink, I propose to take a closer look at claims made about television addiction (which segue readily into arguments about Internet addiction and social media addiction) rather than dismiss them out of hand.[44] In doing so, I hope to accomplish three things, albeit not necessarily in this order: (1) to show how the use of brain sciences in arguments about the neurological basis for media addiction culminates in a more reductive account of self than neurosciences actually offer; (2) to explore how the stuff of blink, which does not imply a simple on–off model of brain activity but a fabric of functions, provides a way to build a more complex understanding of the self; and (3) to show how the functioning of television screens within animated films and TV series affords an understanding of their effects that may lead us more directly to the heart of the problem—the relations of self to self through media.

The goal is thus to follow the fourth line of processing of singularity discussed in the prior chapter, locating the political middle between art and philosophy (the diagrammatic distribution prior to seizures) without taking it in advance to be the expression of a particularity (for instance, Japanese children) in the manner of cultural studies or area studies. This doesn't mean that cultural studies and area studies have nothing to contribute to this discussion. They have a great deal to contribute, provided we do not assume particularity but consider how (and how much) particularity is produced. But this is the topic for the next chapter, in which I propose to proceed toward questions about media addiction via the stuff of blink. Because there are large gaps in the current generalizations that strive to relate neurology to everyday practices, I will work across scientific data and speculative approaches, coming up with a sort of science fiction between art and philosophy as they run parallel to science.

4

A THOUSAND TINY BLACKOUTS

BLINKING IS RATHER STRANGE. INITIALLY YOU MIGHT THINK OF BLINKING, THE EYELID COMING DOWN OVER THE EYE, AS a momentary punctuation in a continuous flow of seeing. Blinking seems to disrupt the continuous act of perceiving. Oddly enough, however, blinking does not interrupt the act of seeing. It produces it.

Three Syntheses

Seeing doesn't just happen when the eyes are open but also when they are shut. Seeing is happening across the opening and closing of the eyes. This is why neurosciences sometimes claim that seeing really happens in the brain, or more precisely through the eyes and brain. Seeing, then, entails a connective synthesis: the flow of data when the eyes are open does not make for seeing. It is on the segmenting of the flow, when the brain fills in, that seeing occurs. A better example of connective synthesis, however, is the saccadic movement of the eyes. A passage from Mark Haddon's novel *The Curious Incident of the Dog in the Night-Time* provides a compelling description that is worth citing at length:

> And when we look at things we think we're just looking out of our eyes like we're looking out of little windows and there's a person inside our head, but we're not. We're looking at a screen inside our heads, like a computer screen.
>
> And you can tell this because of an experiment [. . .] You put your head in a clamp and you look at a page of writing on a screen. [. . .] After a while, as your eye moves around the page, you realize that something is very strange because when you try to read a bit of the page you've read before it's different.

And this is because when your eye flickers from one point to another you don't see anything at all and you're blind. And the flicks are called *saccades*. . . .

But you don't notice that you're blind during saccades because your brain fills in the screen in your head to make it seem like you're looking out of two little windows in your head.[1]

Part of the attraction of the narrator's description in Haddon's novel lies in its articulation of a doubling that takes place around the act of reading. On the one hand, there is a screen. The screen entails a relation between brain and data: the brain fills in the gaps to make a picture on the screen despite the discontinuity in data due to saccadic movement of the eyes. The separation in the flow of data amounts to a segmentation of a continuous flow that raises the flow to another level, what may be called a connective synthesis. Connective synthesis makes for a screen in the brain, or more precisely a brain screen. On the other hand, there is a window. The window affords a sense of a separation between someone seeing and the world seen, but the separation is supposed to be transparent, impalpable. The windows appear because the infilling of connective synthesis runs in parallel with a second moment, a disjunction, through which segmentation seems to have been raised to another level: that of an interval between self and world.

Raising segmentation to another level makes for disjunctive synthesis. Disjunctive synthesis arises from connective synthesis in various intra-active ways, as connections are prolonged affectively. Haddon's narrator enacts disjunction rather than describes it. A feeling of connectedness or disconnectedness, of attraction or repulsion, occurs across the interval between self and world, not despite the separation (two little windows) but with and through it. The world is not only *that* world but also *your* world, for better or worse, somehow *you*. This disjunctive synthesis may also be articulated in terms of semblance: you and the world are like each other; although you do not resemble one another. It is also the realm of affect: you two are mutually constituted in entangled feelings. Indeed, Haddon's narrator highlights how it feels: "To make it seem like you're looking out of two little windows."

Disjunctive synthesis makes for something perceptible (with feeling attached), while the relation between eye data and brain screen, the process of infilling, remains imperceptible and nonconscious. The picture on the brain screen is not yet anybody's picture. It is nobody's picture. The infilling may be intuited, perhaps, but you don't perceive it. Also, you do not perceive it belonging to you, unless it somehow becomes broken, and the alleged dysfunction is then attributed to you.

Connective synthesis, then, is close to immediate experience, the stuff I'm calling blink. With disjunctive synthesis, there is another moment of relation vis-à-vis immediate experience, something temporally different, maybe affinity or maybe uncertainty, maybe attraction or maybe repulsion, but something hovering between this sensation of a world (like the ground beneath your feet) and a perception of this world (like the sky overhead). Temporally, it jibes with what James calls the specious present.

A third synthesis also occurs, what may be called conjunctive synthesis.[2] It happens, for instance, when you begin to feel that the world out there is so radically different from you that it isn't really your world at all, at least not entirely, a world where deities, demons, objects, things, and other forces appear, requiring propitiation, negotiation, manipulation, codes, acts, and so forth. At the same time, it is by placing yourself within a story, by knowing yourself, that you relate to this world. Thus the feeling self, which holds together feelings and perceptions, tips toward another kind of self, a knowing self. The knowing self strives to connect or conjoin with external forces (or conversely to withdraw from or to master them), succeeding in various degrees in different contexts and cultures, hovering between perception and cognition, perceiving and knowing.

In some philosophies, especially those of a Cartesian bent, the conjunctive synthesis is called the subject and is taken for the full reality and for the ground of feeling, perceiving, and thinking or knowing.[3] Neurosciences, however, tend to highlight the simultaneous functioning of all three syntheses. In fact, the three syntheses might be mapped, tentatively and cautiously, onto what Antonio Damasio refers to as brain, mind, and consciousness, in *Self Comes to Mind*. I will later complicate this map considerably, but first, before the screen drops out of the picture, I wish to turn to a related problematic that has affected how film and media studies think about screens, the notion of persistence of vision versus flicker fusion and apparent motion in explaining how we perceive moving images.

Moving Images Moving Brains

Joseph Anderson and Barbara (Fisher) Anderson have made the strongest statements about the mythical status of the idea of persistence of vision within film studies, publishing an initial essay debunking the persistence of vision in 1978 and revisiting it in 1993:

> Dudley Andrew has observed that "persistence of vision . . . might be associated with a psychoanalytic view of mind, since the passive eye retains the effects of stimuli like a mystic writing pad, a palimpsest, that is like the unconscious."[4] Indeed in the past 15 years, psychoanalytic-Marxist film scholars have retained the model implied by persistence of vision: theirs is a passive viewer, a spectator who is "positioned," unwittingly "sutured" into the text, and victimized by the "dominant" ideology.[5]

The Andersons and other writers have amply demonstrated that the persistence of vision does not explain how we perceive motion in a series of consecutively photographed still images that are projected in quick succession, that is, motion pictures.[6] Demonstrations of why persistence of vision is wrong are readily available online, as are more accurate accounts of our perception of moving images that are based on flicker fusion and apparent motion.[7]

Flicker fusion concerns the frequency at which we no longer perceive the interval of an intermittent light stimulus, for instance, a flickering, flashing, or strobelike light. But fusion is a matter of a threshold rather than a fixed quantity. It varies with brightness and how light strikes the retina; peripheral vision detects flicker at higher frequencies than foveal vision. In the case of movies or digital video files, if the frame rate falls below the flicker fusion threshold, you see flickering, and the movement of objects may appear jerky or jumpy. The flicker fusion threshold for humans is conventionally taken to be 16 Hz, and the frame rate for projection of cinema, television, and computer displays must be considerably higher. Although film footage is generally shot at 24 frames per second, it is today generally projected at 48 frames per second (with double shutter projection). This is because flicker is still detectable when movies are projected at 24 frames per second, as was done in the earlier days of cinema (with projection rates at 24 frames per second or lower, or even variable), which is how movies came to be called "flicks." Television displays, as we have seen, use image interlacing at 50 or 60 Hz, which is sometimes detectable, because, as it turns out, humans often detect flicker even at frequencies of 70 to 75 Hz. Even these figures are not absolute, however. Other studies show that "although retinal neurons respond to flicker at rates as high as 120 Hz, perceptual studies show that flicker cannot be detected at frequencies nearly this high."[8] Flicker entails both imperceptible and perceptible experience.

The low frequencies of movie projectors and CRTs are a thing of the past, and flat-panel LCD is becoming the preferred format for television and computer displays. LCD panels do not seem to flicker at all because the light through the screen happens at a very high frequency, nearly 200 Hz, and unlike the CRT display, in which each pixel is fired individually (flashing on and off), LCD changes pixels through a scan. Nonetheless, light through the LCD screen can induce flicker: because it is difficult to dim the LEDs used for lighting, LCDs use pulse-width modulation to produce an effect of dimming. Some viewers may perceive the frequency of such modulation as flicker. In sum, even with contemporary screen displays, flicker persists, hovering on the threshold of perception.

But how is it that flicker fusion affects our perception of motion, of apparent motion, in moving images?

Accounts of apparent motion add spatial intermittency to the mix. The Andersons, for instance, cite work in which two dots of light, spatially separated, are flashed simultaneously or sequentially. When the two dots are close together, flashing them simultaneously results in an experience of a single dot. When they are flashed sequentially, however, you perceive smooth motion. This perception of smooth motion, also called close-range or short-range apparent motion, occurs with multielement or closely spaced displays, such as movie and television screens. When the dots are spaced farther apart, however, you reach a point where you still see motion, but it is not smooth.

The Andersons call on studies indicating that these two types of motion perception are neurologically different. Significantly, the close-range apparent motion may "share a common base with the perception of real motion."[9] Apparently patients who "are 'blind' to still images in the real world can nevertheless see the succession of still images presented on the TV screen."[10] Thus the Andersons conclude: "Motion in the motion picture is, as we have said, an illusion, but since it falls within the short-range or 'fine-grain' category, it is transformed by the rules of that system, that is, the rules for transforming real continuous movement. The human visual system can (and does) distinguish between long-range and close-range apparent motion, but it seemingly cannot distinguish between short-range apparent motion and real motion. To the visual system, the motion in a motion picture *is* real motion."[11] The Andersons' conclusion is significant, potentially with far-reaching implications, and so it is worthwhile to rephrase it directly: while the movement in moving images may be abstract and constructed, it is nonetheless concrete and real—as concrete and real as real motion in the world. But what are the implications of such an insight?

The Andersons wish to leverage the fact of apparent motion against the legacy of Freud and Marx in film theory. They argue that psychoanalytic-Marxist film scholars have stubbornly clung to the notion of the persistence of vision and have ignored the actual facts about moving images because the persistence of vision model suits their theory. This is why the Andersons refer to it as myth. Persistence of vision is not merely an error but a willfully sustained ignorance. Here the oft-cited phrase of Slavoj Žižek seems ironically to convey the Andersons' point: "They know very well, but all the same . . ."

Subsequent accounts of the dominance of the persistence of vision model in film studies adopt and extend the Andersons' judgment. Bill Nichols and Susan J. Lederman write, "The very persistence with which this 'explanation' [persistence of vision] has been recited says more about the hermetic and impressionistic world of some film scholarship than it does about the actual mechanism involved."[12] Rod Munday's account is more recent and more judicious, signaling how an emphasis on apparent motion (the phi phenomenon) "privileges a more constructivist approach to the cinema (David Bordwell, Noël Carroll, Kirsten Thompson), where the persistence of vision privileges a realist approach (André Bazin, Christian Metz, Jean-Louis Baudry)."[13]

There is indeed today a sharp divide between two approaches to the experience of moving images. I think that a somewhat different set of questions may emerge from this split within film studies, so I propose working through it.

Between Psychoanalytic-Realistic and Ecological-Constructivist Theories

On the one hand, there are film theories that place emphasis on the subject, tending to begin and end with it. The currently dominant approach to psycho-analytic film criticism, consolidated in Žižek's film analyses, for instance, is reso-lutely indifferent to any materiality other than what it dubs the weird substance of human enjoyment. It posits a cryptic or enigmatic relation to objects or material conditions, which consequently drop out of the discussion, or reappear in the schematic structural form of grand epochal regimes of subjectivity in a loosely Hegelian manner. In any event, what comes of the fore is a dreamlike yet oddly militant relation to Otherness.

Similarly, even as its realism acknowledges a kind of energizing charge be-tween the screen image and the movie audience, the Bazinian legacy has tended to press that charge into the production of a reality for the subject. It favors a linear movement from indexical capture through modes of realism to the sub-ject. This is what David Rodowick refers to as the photographic ontology of cin-ema.[14] What the Bazinian legacy finds in cinema are the ideal parameters for the production of a temporally transformed reality for the subject—memory—as a dreamlike relation to reality.

The psychoanalytic and realist models have tended to rule out the study of animation and television, or at the very least to make it exceedingly difficult. This is because television and animation entail the wrong kind of temporal mediation: animation is considered too removed from an indexical relation to reality, while television is too much in the present.

On the other hand, as the Andersons' account attests, there is nothing dream-like in the actual mechanism of apparent motion for the ecological model. Mo-tion in moving images may be styled as an illusion, but such an illusion is not in opposition to reality. It does not entail wish fulfillment or memory. It is an eye–brain function. How are moving images able to mobilize this existing eye–brain function? It might be surmised, if we extrapolate from Dehaene's studies of reading, that moving images have evolved to suit the human brain. We might even speak of a mutual adaptation or coevolution. In any event, to dramatize the contrast, let me say that the psychoanalytic and realist approaches linger on a shock to the psychological subject (thwarting its desires or intensifying its memo-ries), whereas the constructivist model envisions shock to the organism, to its neurological system or cognitive system, in measurably physical or bodily ways.

The constructivist approach may quickly come to an impasse. When the screen image is taken to be real, the temptation is to use this insight to anchor a limited empiricism based on subject–object correlation, which is to say that what is on the screen is assumed to correspond to something in the brain and thus in the individual human. In his account of reality programming, for instance, William Evans writes, "Viewers frequently come to feel as if they have a personal relationship of sorts with television actors and television personalities. Parasocial interaction is neither pathological nor rare. It is especially likely to be manifested by viewers who follow a show over several years. Parasocial interaction seems to be cultivated by people on television who make eye contact with the camera or who offer self-disclosure regarding their personal life."[15]

While there is nothing particularly objectionable about such observations, there is a marked tendency to eliminate the screen from discussion, beyond formal techniques such as eye contact and self-disclosure. The screen is replaced by a series of terms conveying likeness or verisimilitude: "The people on television and in film *seem real*, and their activities *seem real*."[16] The function of the screen is consistently relegated to a series of terms conveying likeness: para-, as if, seeming, like. Here I am still in agreement with the constructivist approach. Evans's emphasis on likeness meshes nicely with my emphasis on semblance. And I will subsequently use the notion of parasociality too.

The problem, then, lies not in the elimination of the screen per se. The problem is that when the screen (its techniques) is eliminated, there is a tendency to leap from immediate or direct experience (the experience of the television is a real experience) to affective response (people feeling as if they have a relation), and to rule out what happens between them. The affective response, for instance, is not immediate in temporal terms. It takes time. It entails hesitations and enthusiasms, attraction and repulsion. This also makes it inherently social. Maybe parasocial interaction with TV characters builds on infectious fads, or requires feedback from friends, or entails a desire for connections with people at work. In any event, affect is not immediacy. Between affective experience and immediate experience, disjunctive synthesis happens. Something happens to the "brain" (connective synthesis with its screen–brain filling in) that makes for "mind" (feelings and perceptions at once held apart and together), to which interval a "self" may be added—what James refers to as a process of appropriating or possessing immediate experience.

In other words, what is called the ecological or constructivist approach to film studies risks collapsing the difference between connective synthesis and disjunctive synthesis. It always looks at disjunctive synthesis from the angle of connective synthesis. The risk is precisely the dead-end forms of empiricism that James struggled to reform with radical empiricism: both classical and rational empiricism tend to construct a series of correlations, proclaiming them rational and objective. Nothing appears pathological, excessive, or irrational, but only because there is an assumption that a scientific explanation will eventually be found for everything. There are many critiques of correlative thought, among them the new polemic stance within speculative realism and object-oriented ontology,[17] but in this context, I wish simply to note that while the ecoconstructivist approach does not begin with the subject, it certainly ends with it: the neutrality and objectivity of the observer is guaranteed by the promised arrival of total objectivity in the future. We are enjoined to take part in the construction of a scientific utopia in which all thought will be understood and thereby neutralized.

In contrast, the psychoanalytic and realist approaches tend to look at disjunctive synthesis from the angle of conjunctive synthesis: everything points to the emergence of the subject. Oddly, however, as the constructive critique of the persistence of vision points out, these approaches begin with passivity, and then passivity is, in effect, powered up. There is a sort of activation of passivity.[18] Yet passivity continues to dominate the treatment of the subject. This is why the Andersons protest that in psychoanalytic approaches, "theirs is a passive viewer, a spectator who is 'positioned,' unwittingly 'sutured' into the text, and victimized by the 'dominant' ideology."

When the constructivist approach replaces this passive viewer with the active viewer, however, activity is located at the level of neurological and cognitive activity. The result is the ecological approach: organisms do not passively receive data and respond to it, but rather they actively pursue data, experiment with it, and shape their niches or worlds. When this approach grapples with the potential passivity of viewers, modes such as empathy and parasocial interaction come to the fore. The risk, then, is the inverse of the psychoanalytic approach: instead of powering up passivity, the ecoconstructivist approach tends to favor pacified activities, which take on the feel of laboratory situations.

I have dwelled on the schism between these two ways of dealing with the perception of movement in moving images in hopes of making some basic points clearer. First, the schism occurs because both sides tend to pass quickly over disjunctive synthesis. On the one hand, the ecological and constructive approaches always turn back toward connective synthesis, which runs the risk of it having nothing to look forward to but a future utopia of pacified, neutralized brain activity. On the other hand, the psychoanalytic and realist approaches rely on a sort of originary passivity, seeking a future in which passivity is intensified to the point where it finally transcends its origins.

Second, there is a middle ground. Not surprisingly, the schism between approaches opens in the register of disjunctive synthesis, for this is where passivity becomes intensified and starts to feel active, and activity begins to lose its buzz and bloom and to settle into tamer modes. This is the domain of affect and of semblance. My goal is not, however, to settle the differences between the two sides, to produce a synthesis in the classic sense. Rather, in keeping with disjunctive synthesis, my aim is to seize and to hold the schism.

Third, radical empiricism provides a way to talk about disjunctive synthesis, concretely and methodologically: (1) calling attention to singularity at work within scientific facts, which (2) allows for the construction of a plane with functions instead of falling back on simple linear relationships with forms and correlations, and thereby (3) calling attention to a diagrammatic distribution by which a set of relations holds together, which is also where the *dispositif* or apparatus arises. From the angle of disjunctive synthesis, I would say that radical empiricism segues into, and indeed cannot go on without, what Foucault calls radical historicism. In effect, the schism between ecoconstructivist and psychoanalytic approaches repeats a false schism between individualizing procedures and totalizing formations. Such a schism produces a false view of power. Power is at once individualizing and totalizing, as Foucault insists.

Fourth, Marx's critique of classical political economy takes on new relevance in this context, for it calls attention to how circulation and distribution—flows of capital—produce and sustain unevenness. This is why Deleuze and Guattari were able to retool disjunctive synthesis in Marxist terms as the production of distribution. Indeed, that is the central question of this study of brains, screens, and animations: what produces distribution, and what does distribution produce? In the specific ecology of television and animation, tentative schematic answers have already appeared: a nonsensuous, nonconscious population seizure produces distribution, while distribution in turn produces expanded television addiction to be managed by an apparatus of media care targeting the brain screen.

Fifth, while I do not wish rule out psychoanalytic and realistic approaches to moving images, I do not intend to dwell on them either. I have, however, lingered over neurosciences, extending that discussion into ecoconstructivist and cognitive approaches. This is because a shift is already underway, which the previous chapter characterized in terms of a shift from the psychological paradigm geared toward mental health and deviant psychological behavior to a neurological paradigm gravitating toward brain health and self-management. Under such conditions, to return to psychoanalytic and realistic approaches at the expense of addressing ecoconstructivist approaches would be a reactionary or at least backward-looking gesture, conceptually and institutionally. For better or worse, in film and media studies today, we need to understand thinkers like William James, J. J. Gibson, Julian Hochberg, Antonio Damasio, and Giulio Tononi. This is not because they are more accurate or scientific. This is because their work is historically and conceptually caught up in the screen–brain apparatus in ways the work of Freud, Lacan, or Bazin is not. These latter thinkers will take on renewed significance in the extent to which they are called upon engage with neurological, ecoconstructive, or cognitive approaches, not to confirm or reject them but to enter into the current terrain of conflict.

Tube Addiction

The sharp divide between psychoanalytic-realist approaches and ecoconstructivist approaches helps to explain how the question of media addiction has become discursively salient, supplanting concerns about ideological and psychological effects of media.

The paradigm of addiction introduces a wrinkle into the emphasis on the buzzing activity of our brains, flirting with a kind of passivity (addiction) without giving up on the primacy of active forces. The paradigm of media addiction centers on passive brain activity only to enjoin a more active brain care through media—take care of yourself, work on yourself. Addiction, then, occupies the middle ground, arising in the register of disjunctive synthesis where subject and object are only virtually distinguished, where activity and passivity, subjectivity and objectivity, are crossing paths in affective states of mind. As such, the details of television addiction are worth closer attention despite their wild leaps in logic.

Kubey and Csikszentmihaly's study confirms what prior studies and discussions have suggested: "People who were watching TV when we beeped them reported feeling relaxed and passive. The EEG studies similarly show less mental stimulation, as measured by alpha brain-wave production, during viewing than during reading."[19] Research associating alpha brain wave activity with television viewing goes back to the 1960s and 1970s. In his 1978 book *Four Arguments for the Elimination of Television*, Jerry Mander built on such studies of alpha wave activity to make one of his key arguments for getting rid of TV altogether: "Television produces neurophysiological effects which are probably unhealthy and which condition people to accept autocratic control."[20]

This is precisely the argument that came to the fore in *The Tube*: alpha wave activity presents a decrease in alertness (which is associated with beta wave activity), which makes television audiences willing to accept whatever the tube tells them. Unfortunately, no one can say exactly what the TV is telling people, and so arguments about the effects of alpha brain waves have gradually shifted: from mass mind control (the influencing machine) to more personalized problems with addiction. At the same time, the emphasis has shifted from alpha wave activity itself to the ways in which such activity is cut off. Kubey and Csikszentmihaly discovered, for instance, that "what is more surprising is that the sense of relaxation ends when the set is turned off, but the feelings of passivity and lowered alertness continue. Survey participants commonly reflect that television has somehow absorbed or sucked out their energy, leaving them depleted. They say they have more difficulty concentrating after viewing than before."[21] On a similar trajectory, Mori Akio's discredited notion of game brain stressed the reduction of beta brain wave activity in gamers, conflating this apparent cutting off of beta wave activity with a self that would feel cut off, ready to snap, or ready to explode into violence *(kireru)*.

Such observations bring us back to the stuff of blink. As you would expect of a fabric-like blink, addiction is not just a matter of turning the set off and then wanting to turn it back on. What matters are the different speeds of on and off for different kinds of brain activity, the weave of speeds and intensities. Accounts of the effects of television underscore that alpha wave activity returns quickly, unlike the gamma brain waves that are associated with the "orienting response" and involuntary attention—something catching your eye or ear, a sudden unexpected stimulus. Turning the tube back on may restore alpha wave activity relatively quickly, yet the very fabric of television is also crosscutting and undermining that relaxation. Annie Lang, for instance, has developed a limited capacity model for understanding how viewers responded to television, stressing that the "passage from environmental stimulus to mental representation is . . . complex, idiosyncratic, and inexact."[22] Her research team explored the effects of edits (transitions from one camera angle to another within a scene) and cuts (transitions from one scene to another) on memory recognition. Frequency of edits and cuts increased memory recognition, apparently by mobilizing the viewers' attention via an orienting response, but only up to a certain point. When the frequency of cuts, for instance, exceeded ten in two minutes, memory recognition dropped sharply. Such results invited the limited capacity model. Simply put, the brain becomes overloaded.

Television addiction thus cannot simply be a matter of alpha wave relaxation because the orienting response is constantly triggered by edits, cuts, and other movements. This is the basis of what is called the attention economy: capturing your attention and presumably evoking memory recognition. Yet the gamma wave activity runs counter to alpha brain waves: while the alpha wave activity recovers quickly, orienting response becomes overloaded and cannot recover quickly.[23] What is more, it is said that you never become habituated to the television triggers for orienting response, which is in keeping with the lack of distinction between apparent motion and real motion in terms of how it is processed. Similar observations appear in the context of Pokémon Shock: the use of flash effects and other attention grabbers, which eventually results in brain overload, does not allow for adaptation and thus undermines the capacity for learning.[24]

It is easy to understand how such research encourages tales of mass indoctrination and mind control. Yet if general assessments of the data on the effects of television lean toward addiction, it is because the upshot of studies of brain waves is that the experience of television is full of interferences: it entails a state of mind combining high attention and distraction, alertness and lack of focus. No wonder commentators seem divided over whether to consider such an experience to be pleasure or pain. It is as if pleasure and pain were fired into every pixel and neuron to weave a fabric of pure affect, with a thousand tiny blackouts and startups. What is to done with such a fabric, this blinking stuff?

Tales of television addiction make some interesting suggestions. First, what is called attention economy might better be described as addiction ecology. Rather than simply grabbing our attention and blazing signs in our memories, the blinking stuff of screen ecologies is a matter of interferences and resonances between different kinds of activity, neuronal and cultural, with intoxicating effects not attributable to a single source yet gravitating toward certain forms. Second, although "addiction" is an awkward term, full of unstated presumptions, it may nonetheless suggest a productive take on television effects: the emphasis no longer falls on an erasure or distortion of the subject, with connotations of mass control and conspiracy, but on a relation of self to self, what Foucault described as an opening within your self, making for two selves, present to yet distant from each other.[25] This is the political middle ground, which is one of the key concerns of this book: not the subject but subjectivity and selfhood, oscillating between work on self and care for self; not the expression of a particularity but the expression of an interval, or rather, a relation; the expression of a singularity, which is inherently social and implicitly political.

A fairly conventional and surely familiar trope in Japanese television animation makes the point in another manner.

Eyes in Need of a Fix

Animation tends to produce an effect akin to the cinematic close-up by pulling closer to the unblinking eyes, often magnifying one unblinking eye. This is because, unlike faces in cinema, faces in animation show neither spatial distortion upon magnification or close-up nor an encounter with the grain of the screen. They grow larger, but the contours and proportions are not altered. As such, they do not generate a shift from perception to affect, from something seen to something felt, as in the cinematic close-up. Instead, in animation, in its search for fine-grained feely encounters, magnification tends toward the characters' eye: as the unblinking eye grows larger, it becomes populated with sparking, gleaming, jiggling flecks, specks, circles, and bubbles (Figure 4.1). It is an eye populated with saccadic entities, flashing things. You feel them and you feel that the character is feeling, yet without additional cues, you don't know what that feeling is. In fact, if you stick with the jittery stuff within the nonblinking eye, you feel it could be any feeling whatsoever, pure affect, intensity where light and movement, flash and jitter, spark and jump are indistinguishable. This jitter light and glow jump is the grain—or rather the weave—of animation; it is the stuff of blink extending between animation, brain, and screen. If the notion of addiction better captures the lure of the stuff of blink than attention, then it is because feeling this stuff entails something more complex than catching the eye or recognizing a name. It is like the experiment evoked by the narrator in Haddon's novel: if you read with your head clamped in a vice, with only your eyes moving, the words of the text start to move around, swim and swirl. But with the jiggling eye gems of television animation, orienting response and relaxation are happening together, folding attention into lack of focus and vice versa. This overlapping of affective states is what makes for an interval opening within the self, a relation of self to

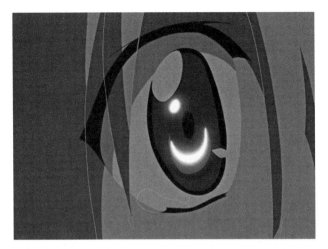

FIGURE 4.1. Magnification of eyes in anime functions like the cinematic close-up on faces, allowing for spatial distortion and discovering glowing lights and sparkling forms that tremble, jitter, and swim within the eye, as in these four examples (from top): episode 5 of *Iriya no sora, UFO no natsu* (*Iriya's Sky, UFO Summer*, 2005); *Gekijōban Shutainzu-gēto: fuka ryōiki no dejavu* (*Steins;Gate: The Movie— Load Domain of Déjà Vu,* 2013); episode 1 of *Nagi no asu kara* (*Nagi-Asu: A Lull in the Sea*, 2013); and episode 1 of *Nobunaga za fūru* (*Nobunaga the Fool,* 2013).

self. But the self no longer coincides with itself; nor does it unequivocally own itself. The self becomes a user of self, with only an intermittent self-possession. You may find that you're using your self more than you intend to, thinking about using your self less, making repeated unsuccessful gestures to quit, yet feeling symptoms of withdrawal when you do. You're addicted to blink.

Part II

A LITTLE SOCIAL MEDIA HISTORY OF TELEVISION

5

MEDIA GENEALOGY AND TRANSMEDIA ECOLOGY

A SERIES OF NEW RUBRICS HAS EMERGED IN RESPONSE TO TECHNOLOGICAL TRANSFORMATIONS AFFECTING HOW YOU receive television (broadcasting versus streaming) and how you watch television (TV set versus computer or mobile phone). Bold claims about the "end of television" and "not television" have been gradually extended and finessed into discussions of "television after television," "posttelevision," and "the postbroadcast era."[1] An emphasis on rupture persists, however.

Television and New Media

Naturally, for every claim for rupture, a countervailing account arises in the popular literature on contemporary television, insisting on continuity. In the context of French television, for instance, Gérald-Brice Viret contests much of the current wisdom about the future of television, reminding us, for instance, that a lot of people in France still own TV sets, corporate broadcasting is still powerful and profitable, and television still enjoys success with its use of standardizing modes of address.[2] In the context of Japan, news director Okumura Kenta argues that television is not dead; he stresses the ongoing importance of news reportage (in response to the terrorist attacks of September 11, 2011, in the United States and the March 11, 2011, Tōhoku, Japan, earthquake, tsunami, and nuclear meltdown, for instance), which he grounds in received wisdom about the liveness of television, its reality, immediacy, and simultaneity. He writes, "Why is it that television continues to exert so much influence? It is undoubtedly due to a certain zest for life only possessed by television. Its strength: 'events happening in far-off places are seen simultaneously in your household, in their reality.'"[3] With reference to the Pokémon Incident, I might add a twist: brains are really seized simultaneously in widely separated locations.

If I insist on a genealogical approach to contemporary transformations in television, it is to address both discontinuity and continuity. Something really is changing, but that transformation is happening because there was something unresolved or indeterminate at the heart of the old media formation called broadcast television, with its TV sets. Current transformations in television, in its delivery medium and platform, continue to revolve around that irresolvable problematic, which generates a new relation to television that is at the same time continuous with prior formations. As such, the new relation to television is continuous and discontinuous in both sociohistorical and technological terms.

In the chapters in this section, I will look at transformations in both platform and delivery medium. In both instances, I will consider continuity and discontinuity. Instead of focusing exclusively on a resolute break between the TV and the mobile phone or smartphone, for instance, I will consider how peripheral devices plugged into the TV set pave the way for more recent platform usages, and indeed might even be said to produce them. Likewise, instead of highlighting only the differences between broadcasting and streaming, I will frame the questions in terms of continuous and entangled transformations in television infrastructures that comprise broadcast, cable and closed-circuit television, satellite, and streaming.

Precedents for such an approach are abundant in studies of television. As Barbara Selznick notes in her account of global television when she considers the consolidation of media ownership in fewer and fewer hands, the "privatization and deregulation of the television industry in the 1980s and 1990s . . . paved the way for transnational television ownership."[4] Such processes of privatization and deregulation were underway at roughly the same time in Japan and are closely related to the global transformations discussed by Selznick. In this study, for practical reasons, I have to omit a full account of transnational and global dimensions of Japanese television and focus more on its transmedial dimensions.[5] Suffice it to say in this context, then, that the privatization and deregulation arising in the 1980s occurred alongside and relied on an unbundling of the delivery medium for television—not only as a result of new forms of broadcasting such as cable and satellite, but also as a result of new platforms such as the VCR and the game console, which made the TV set into site for the integration of nonbroadcast media, thus forming a site of transmedial encounter between television and computers. Not surprisingly, then, 1980s Japan saw a boom in discussions of new media in which the notion of new media was closely associated with transmedial transformations in television.

There is an eerie resonance between Japan's television-centered new media theories of the 1980s and English-language studies of television and new media in the 2000s. Indeed, in the North American context, it feels as if television studies were just now beginning to confront questions previously posed by new media studies in the 1980s and 1990s. The point of such observations is neither to claim that Japan was ahead of America when it comes to new media nor to suggest that English-language television studies have lagged in their discovery of new media. In fact, popular accounts of the transformation of television by new media had begun to circulate in North America by the early 1990s as well.[6] Instead, I wish to indicate something of the temporal and geopolitical complexity that the genealogical approach brings to the fore. It is impossible to order these three moments of new media in a purely chronological fashion. Indeed, my "discovery" of Japanese discourses on television and new media of the 1980s grew out of an interest in the relation between new media and animation in the 1990s, and these sites of inquiry in turn shape my perspective on contemporary accounts of television and new media. These three historical moments of new media demonstrate that television and new media have been interacting and intra-acting for some time, genealogically. They have been assembling with each other interindividually (as separable mediums and platforms) and infraindividually (what resonates are not separable elements in interaction).

From Transmedia Storytelling to Transmedia Ecology

Significantly, the current encounter with new media within television studies has gravitated toward a specific site of interaction: transmedia storytelling. This site has the advantage of allowing for an account of creative transformations across media. It also opens a site of encounter between producers and consumers or users of media where those roles become entangled. Although the overall emphasis in studies of transmedia storytelling still falls on the creative travails of producers within large media industries, such studies nonetheless avoid the pitfalls of an exclusively producer-centered account of creativity because they undermine a unilateral communications model by attending to the ways in which producers respond to and directly build on fan culture, and because they focus on the negotiations of smaller groups within media industries, undercutting the image of a huge monolithic industrial imposition of meaning. Denise Mann's account of television and new media is a prime example: while she highlights the persistence of broadcast-era production paradigms (partly as a result of the slowness of such industries to change), she shows how smaller groups within these apparent behemoths are the sites of innovation, often working at odds with larger agenda and other concerns.[7] As such, her account of transmedia storytelling, while producer centered, works to complicate their creative agency.

For similar reasons, this study focuses a good deal of attention on transmedia storytelling, or rather, something like it. In keeping with the genealogical approach, however, I do not situate transmedia storytelling as something radically new in the history of television. In fact, I will gradually introduce a shift from the paradigm of transmedia storytelling (and media convergence) toward that of media ecology (and infrastructure complex). There are two reasons for this shift in emphasis. First, as mentioned in the Introduction, in the context of Japanese television, transmedia storytelling is nothing new. For the Japanese forms of transmedia storytelling that are today grouped loosely under the general rubric of the media mix, the constitutive moment is the early 1960s.[8] The television genealogy of transmedia storytelling in Japan thus harkens back to the first forays of animation onto the small screen. Likewise, there are good reasons for avoiding terms like "posttelevision" in this context.

As Sheila C. Murphy remarks, "This dynamic, pitting old versus new in a narrative of progress, loss, innovation, or competition, unnecessarily creates an oppositional logic between industries, objects, and experiences that actually draw upon each other productively."[9] In addition, the term "posttelevision" tends to posit developments in the North Atlantic region as a normative frame of reference (the metaphysical construction also known as the West), endorsing a modernization paradigm that not only ignores how developments in different parts of the world have drawn on each other productively but also situates everything else in the world in a state of exception. Yet Japanese transmedia formations (among others) have long had an impact on American transmedia storytelling. They have in turn drawn on a wide range of media forms and formations, including Disney animations, Hong Kong action films, and Taiwanese and Korean television dramas. My point is not that everyone needs to be studying multiple locations. If multiple locations are treated as self-evident geopolitical individuals, then analysis remains limited to interaction among individuals (the international) instead of addressing the transnational (intra-action). My point is this: just as we need to avoid methodologically imposing the individual at the level of media forms and formats, so do we need to avoid treating the nation (or a region) as an unquestioned individual.

The second reason for shifting away from the paradigms of transmedia storytelling and media convergence has to do with the tendency of such accounts to focus exclusively on interaction and individual interactivity, downplaying or ignoring questions about intra-action and infraindividual resonance (semblance and affect) across media. Both levels merit closer attention. It is true on the one hand that the production of transmedia series depends on drawing on distinctions between individual mediums or media forms. Such distinctions may be as broad as print vis-à-vis electronic media, and analog vis-à-vis digital media, or they may be narrower: comics vis-à-vis movies vis-à-vis novels vis-à-vis television series vis-à-vis toys. In any event, it is impossible to ignore the existence of media individuals, for they are continually being constructed, performed, and enacted in our media worlds.[10] Yet this story about media convergence or media mix is only a half the story. This half-story is also partial in that its emphasis on interactions between media individuals also encourages recourse to normative liberal paradigms in which autonomously self-producing individuals appear to be a matter of fact, both at the personal level (users) and the political level (nations). Such individuals must be produced, however. They do not arise spontaneously.

The flip side of the transmedia story is infraindividual intra-actions: media ecology (which is always a transmedia ecology). Typically, accounts of media ecology linger on the idea that contemporary media have become so pervasive that they become an environment, which operates largely below the threshold of perception and cognition. Media are the ocean in which we swim, unaware of the water.[11] This environmental formulation of media ecology shows an interest in infraindividual intra-actions. Yet the environmental media model tends to remain highly binary, even dualist, focusing on relations between organisms and surroundings. The problem is, as is common with binary thinking, that the two-way mutually constitutive relation between organism and environment is frequently dropped in favor of a more unilateral focus, either on the impact of the media environment on its organisms (human animals) or of humans on the environment. In addition, even in studies in which the two-way relation is highlighted, both environments and organisms are generally treated as normative individuals.

Ecology, however, is not merely an environment surrounding an organism or group of organisms. Nor it is primarily a bilateral exchange between surroundings and individualized organisms. Ecology implies a set of relations between organisms and surroundings that is held together through common relation to what might be called an energy cascade. The energy cascade consists of smaller cascades and relations between them, but it is the overall effect of the cascade that is of interest. Therein lies the difference between the environmental media model and the ecological media model: where the environmental model dwells on individual interactions at the level of organisms and surroundings, the ecological approach explores the infraindividual intra-actions that are brought into relation (composed) via the energy cascade. Thus, if the goal is to look at media ecologically, attention must bear on forces of production, that is, the forces traversing the ecology, as well as relations of production, that is, the relations between surroundings and organisms arising at an infraindividual level, which make something transindividual out of what initially appears infraindividual. In the context of television studies, Raymond Williams's account provides one the best points for departure for thinking about television media ecology.

Williams actively resists a technology-driven history of television (hence his critique of McLuhan), stressing instead how established social hierarchies conferred authority on specific groups, permitting them to shape the development of television to their needs and interests, which were above all commercial interests. Television could have turned out quite differently. Williams does not ignore questions of technology, and yet because he always looks at them in relation to social, political, and economic structures, he is able to identify larger sociotechnological tendencies. These tendencies come to the fore when he draws attention to a decisive phase shift in television. In the first phase of television, an established and expanding commercial and military system tended to place the emphasis on person-to-person communications, from one operator (or operative) to another operator (or operative), as defined within specific structures.[12] In its second phase, however, broadcasting moved toward centralized transmission and privatized reception. In this respect, television repeats the history of radio, which was similarly transformed from a one-to-one network into a one-to-many system (broadcast).

Two social developments in particular affected this transformation of radio, and then television, into broadcasting: increased centralization and privatized homes. Williams argues that greater distances between homes, together with greater distance between homes and other centers (commercial centers, workplaces, centers of political power), contributed to the formation of a modern urban way of life that was consequently characterized by "two apparently paradoxical yet deeply connected tendencies": mobility and privatization. Williams refers to this mobile and home-centered way of life as a form of "mobile privatization."[13] Put another way, mobile privatization presents a specific manner of assembling of polarized tendencies, of composing with paradoxically yet profoundly connected tendencies: the point-to-point or one-to-one tendency, and the one-to-many tendency.

Williams stresses how broadcast television has historically subordinated or subsumed the point-to-point tendency within the one-to-many tendency. His is a history of centripetal forces, of centralizing and privatizing. Again, television follows from radio in this respect. In his account of radio, for instance, Edward D. Miller addresses the same sort of phase shift: "This feature of interactivity and reciprocity was part of radio's prebroadcasting appeal with radio adventurers—and indeed, with military users—but when the medium became administered by corporations with governmental cooperation, this aspect—one of the medium's 'selling points'—decreased. Radio became, on the manifest level, virtually a unidirectional, one-to-many broadcast medium."[14]

Although they are considering the history of broadcast from different historical perspectives and with different concerns, both Williams and Miller draw attention to the assembling of polarized tendencies within broadcast. Both show a keen awareness that although broadcast appears to subsume or subordinate the point to point within the one to many, the point-to-point tendency does not simply vanish. Insofar as Miller writes from the vantage of contemporary networks, it is easier for him to show how this other nonbroadcasting point-to-point "military" tendency of broadcast returns to the fore in the formation of cyberspace and the Internet. His account thus draws out the genealogical relation between radio and the Internet. Nonetheless, even though Williams focuses on the heyday of broadcast television, his notion of mobile privatization is likewise calculated to keep open the assembling of paradoxical tendencies, and his use of such terms as "flow" and "mobility" serve as a reminder that centrifugal forces persist, even if such forces now derive from inertia within the assembling rather than constituting an autonomous exterior force.

Technosocial Assembling

Williams's account of television provides a good point of departure for thinking about the media ecology of television because he shows how broadcast television formation is an assembling of polarized technosocial tendencies.[15] One tendency is toward one-to-many linkages, which is how we commonly characterize broadcast transmission: an emission from a (central) source to be received at multiple (private) points. The other tendency is toward point-to-point linkages without a centralized source, which might be called networks, and which we tend to associate more with new media and social media such as the Internet, smartphones, and streaming. Although Williams does not spell out how the paradoxical tendencies are deeply connected, his account of television is clearly concerned with both forces of production and relations of production. It is at the level of forces that these paradoxical tendencies are connected.

It is especially Williams's interest in forces of production that makes his account amenable to media ecology. Just as organisms and surroundings are related to one another ecologically through their relation in common to an energy cascade, so are relations of production set (or reset) in motion through forces of production. In the context of television, those forces might tentatively be glossed with Williams's term: flow. That flow will inevitably bifurcate, again and again, thus multiplying and dissipating. A great deal of social investment of energies (financial, psychological, technological) is needed to stabilize this bifurcation, to compose it into a standing bifurcation that appears to be a single-minded tendency but is in fact an assembling of tendencies. Relations of production thus come to temper and tamper with forces of production, harnessing while redirecting them, creating an assembling that may be characterized as ecological as well as environmental.

It is precisely this internal bifurcation that the current hype over posttelevision commonly ignores, intent on establishing its novelty by positing a break or rupture between broadcast television and new media. Broadcast is characterized in terms that place it in opposition to new media, and thus it appears that in the era of new media, or digital technologies, or streaming, the point-to-point tendency comes to broadcast television from without, striving to subsume it. Such a stance is understandable. Because it is common practice today to watch TV on computers and mobile phones, via streaming or downloads, it may indeed feel as if broadcast television has been subsumed, or is being subsumed, within new media. The title of a recent book nicely captures this feeling: *Netto ga terebi o nomikomu hi = Sinking of TV*. While the book furnishes its own gloss in English, "Sinking of TV," the title might be more literally rendered "The Day the Net Swallows TV." The sense of rupture between media formations easily translates into a paradigm of total remediation, in which the newer media appear to engulf, gulp down, and subsume the older. Theorists of the information revolution also often adopt such a stance, in which new information and telecommunications technologies not only break with prior formations but also seem to totally subsume them.[16] In such discourses of rupture and remediation, the current situation appears the exact inverse of the heyday of broadcast television: where Williams in 1975 stressed how the one-to-many tendency had effectively subsumed the point-to-point tendency, today it may seem that the inverse is true: the point-to-point tendency appears to be overcoming or subsuming the broadcast system.

In fact, however, as Williams demonstrated, the network tendency persists actively and operatively within broadcast television even as it is effectively subsumed. The history of television and new media thus presents us with an apparent paradox: new media come both before and after broadcast television. Also, because the point-to-point tendency of broadcast television is never fully subsumed, new media come to broadcast television from within and from without, at the same time.

In sum, I have opened Part II with a challenge to accounts of posttelevision and their tendency to insist on the novelty of transmedia storytelling, not because I claim to overcome or surpass them. On the contrary, in keeping with my call for a genealogical and ecological approach, I hope to complicate the external perspective they adopt, to fold it into the history of broadcast television. If we adopt a genealogical perspective on the history of broadcast television, it turns out that new media operate paradoxically as an "outside on the inside" of television.

It is because Williams is interested in both forces and relations of production that his account of television expands to include modes of political and social centralization, privatization, the formation of domestic space, and the commercial segmentation of programming. Thus, alongside the axis of relations of production, his account implicitly introduces a second pair of paradoxical yet deeply connected tendencies: individualizing techniques and totalizing procedures. Because he is primarily concerned with how the national broadcast system came to dominate television, his discussion tends to focus on totalizing procedures, especially centralization and privatization. Nonetheless, he does not place individualizing techniques in opposition to totalizing procedures, much as he avoids an opposition between point-to-point and one-to-many tendencies. Instead, he shows how totalizing procedures and individualizing techniques proceed apace. Individual and society are not placed in opposition. A certain kind of individual emerges with conjunction with a certain kind of society. The society of national broadcast (the nation-state) turns out to be a highly totalizing social and political formation that relies on a high degree of individualization (privatization). Thus, even as Williams focuses on totalizing procedures of television, his account also stresses how they rely on increasingly refined processes of segmentation.

In the chapters in Part II, I begin with a focus on the totalizing procedures associated with Japanese national broadcast and then shift my focus toward individualizing techniques. Such a shift follows from my interest in the genealogical relation between television and new media, which demands a careful account of individualizing practices. The current bias is to characterize broadcast formations almost exclusively in terms of totalizing procedures, reserving an account of individualizing procedures for new media such as social media, iOS games, and television streaming. Clearly, individualizing techniques are today reaching higher degrees of elaboration and refinement. They merit careful attention as such. Yet they never occur without totalizing procedures. With a nod to Williams's concept of mobile privatization, the current media juncture might tentatively be characterized in terms of private mobilization. How else to explain the apparently paradoxical concentration of media ownership in fewer and fewer hands at the very moment when media usage feels increasingly individualized, ever more selfie?

Precedents for such an inquiry abound, including Sherry Turkle's studies of a second self and of Internet identities, and Wendy Chun's account of tensions between freedom and control built into information networks.[17] Chun shows how the Internet, as a network of networks, does indeed allow users to make decisions autonomously, and yet the underlying processes are not visible, accessible, or controllable by users. Alex Galloway also addresses the totalizing procedures implicit in protocol, arguing that ideological control of subjects is built into, and is now inseparable from, the standardizing and homogenizing tendencies materially determined by protocol.[18] Both Chun and Galloway succeed in disrupting our contemporary fascination with the individualizing techniques of media users, which has favored a bias toward imagining that new media liberate individuals from the totalizing procedures associated with prior media formations, especially broadcasting. They thus pave the way for a thorough reconsideration of the relation between individualizing and totalizing tendencies in the context of contemporary networks.

Like such studies, the genealogical approach to the relation between television and new media is intended to challenge the ongoing conflation of new media with individualizing techniques while taking totalizing procedures seriously. The genealogical approach pursued in this study aims to introduce greater complexity into our local understanding of the social technology of television media. The general trend in media and cultural studies is to bypass or downplay the nation-state in order to address power globally. As such, when media and cultural studies speak of biopower and ontopower, they speak as if of the entire world. While I do not propose to reintroduce the nation or the nation-state in a normative fashion, to posit it as the key site of mediation in all geopolitical relations, the nation has played such an integral role in history of television that it cannot be bypassed or ignored. I begin, then, with accounts of national television. Working carefully through forces and relations of production in the history of television (the production of distribution or distributive capacity) paves the way for an account of its social technology. What ultimately come to the fore in the genealogy of television media are the complex relations arising across four power formations: the sovereign power invested in the family; disciplinary power and sites of disciplinary enclosure; biopolitical states of emergency comprising crises in sovereignty and environmental disasters; and finally ontopower or the ontopolitical, that is, power exercised over of modes of existence and their distribution.

6

A LITTLE HISTORY OF
JAPANESE TELEVISION

IN THIS CHAPTER, BEFORE DIRECTLY ADDRESSING THE RELATION BETWEEN BROADCAST TELEVISION AND NEW MEDIA, I wish to provide a little history of television in Japan, not only to provide some general background and specific points of historical reference but also to call attention to some of its central tensions and contradictions. Histories of Japanese television sometimes avoid these tensions and contradictions by introducing a divide between political history and the history of technology, either favoring one over the other or collapsing one into the other. As discussed in the prior chapter, it is the strength of Raymond Williams's approach to have shown how broadcast television works through an assembling of what he calls paradoxical yet connected tendencies—point to point versus one to many. I intend to build on and to extend his approach in two ways. First, while it surely made sense in the 1970s to think in terms of an effective subsuming the point-to-point tendency within the one to many, today such a gesture is not possible. Thus I propose to return to and reopen the paradox announced in Williams's approach. Second, reopening this paradox offers a way to revise and extend some of received social histories of Japanese television. Particularly important for me in this context is the work of Yoshimi Shun'ya. The historical focus in this chapter will largely be on the formation of Japanese television in the 1950s and 1960s, to pave the way for a discussion in the following chapter about the impact of new media during the heyday of Japan's broadcast television formation, roughly 1960 to 1990.

Paradoxical Yet Deeply Connected Tendencies

Histories of television in Japan, like histories of television in general, tend in one of two directions. First, there are histories emphasizing technological innovation and progress. In such histories, attention commonly falls, for instance, on Takayanagi Kenjirō, considered the father of Japanese television for his successful transmission of the katakana syllable *i* in 1926 through the development of a television receiver using the Braun tube.[1] Takayanagi's innovation lay in moving toward entirely electronic means of transmitting images, thus successfully addressing the key technical problem of transmission, that is, the synchronization of receiver and transmitter. Because technology-centered histories are generally keen to signal Japanese contributions to the international progress of television, they usually highlight another major Japanese contribution as well: Yagi Hidetsugu's 1925 invention of the prototype for what came to be the standard television antenna used throughout the world, one capable of receiving both VHF (very high frequency) and UHF (ultra high frequency) signals.[2]

In such histories of technological progress, attention also falls on appraising the degree of development of television in Japan. We thus learn that the predecessor of today's NHK (Nippon Hōsō Kyōkai), already under that name, transmitted the first television signals in Tokyo in 1937, and two electronics firms—Toshiba and Nippon Electric Company (Nippon Denki Gaisha or NEC)—began commercial production of television receivers. NHK aired Japan's first drama television broadcast in 1940. In retrospect, even if Japanese contributions were not quite as significant as those made elsewhere, and even if there remains some of the usual fretting about Japan lagging behind the Western powers, the history of television in Japan readily becomes a source of technological pride, for, generally speaking, the development of broadcast television in Japan roughly paralleled its development in Western Europe and North America.

Equally common in histories of technological progress is a tendency to present political problems as an obstacle to progressive movement. We might read in passing, for instance, and without any explanation, that plans were made to host and broadcast the 1945 Tokyo Olympics but were never realized. We understand implicitly that if such plans were not realized, it was because the advance of television was disrupted by the catastrophic culmination of Japan's fifteen-year Asia-Pacific war. Thus, speaking generally, technology and infrastructure histories tend to distance the development of broadcast television from its social and political context and to strip television of ideological connotations, or at least of those connotations that are deemed negative. Technological innovation thus appears to enjoy a high degree of autonomy from political and ideological problems.

Second are the histories emphasizing political centralization and state control over media. There are good reasons to highlight state control in the history of media in Japan. In the late nineteenth century, to extricate Japan from the unequal treaties forced on it by Western powers, the ruling elite put in place a modern political system including a constitutional system with political parties, parliamentary procedures, elections, and certain guarantees for freedom of political expression. Yet fearing a loss of their political control, the same elite felt obliged to crack down violently on political expression. The result was the Publication Law of 1893, which was harshly enforced. Subsequently, as Gregory Kasza writes, "Having jailed many opposition leaders and banished others from Tokyo, the government relaxed its newspaper ordinances in December 1887, as the constitutional project neared completion."[3] Ultimately, however, this was a temporary lull: concentration of political power increased, resulting in the censorship of newspapers, magazines, and books under the Press Law of 1909, and the enactment of the Peace Preservation Act in March 1925, which year also marked the start of radio broadcasting.

Censorship and state control became such salient features of broadcasting in Japan that even in its official histories today, NHK presents it as the first defining characteristic of Japanese broadcasting, albeit with some hemming and hawing:

> Pre-war broadcasting was subject to strict state control in accordance with the Wireless Telegraphy Law. Broadcasting had been conducted entirely by the NHK, which, though it was a private, public-service entity, had been especially entrusted to carry out a service regarded as the responsibility of the state. Accordingly, the communication ministry had long supervised the broadcasting business, and from September 1940 the Cabinet Information Bureau had also become involved as the official censor of broadcasting content. Under this regime, neither freedom of expression nor autonomy of programming was allowed.[4]

This process reached its culmination in the preparations made for the emperor's radio broadcast on August 15, 1945, in which Hirohito not only proclaimed Japan's surrender but also renounced his divinity. The broadcast was duly announced in advance, enjoining subjects to listen to the emperor's speech, and was subsequently presented as if such a use of radio were the most natural thing in the world, even though the emperor's voice had never previously been aired. Although accounts also exist to the effect that the message was in fact incomprehensible as a result of its highly formal language, everything conspired to make it seem that transparent communication to and centralized control of the Japanese masses were possible. Similarly, during the Allied occupation of Japan (1945–52), the American forces imagined that they could mold Japanese minds to American ends through the control of media. The justifications for retaining the emperor as the symbolic head of state in Japan meshed with this political imaginary based on centralized control and implementation, on addressing and shaping the masses unilaterally.

The strength of Raymond Williams's account of television lies in its strategy for dealing with both tendencies, respecting their polarization without collapsing their differences. This is evident in his identification of two apparently paradoxical yet deeply connected tendencies. Throughout his book *Television,* he works through paradoxical tendencies in different registers: flow, for instance, is matched by segmentation (programming), and mobility is coupled with privatization. While Williams does not provide a paired term for his other key term, centralization, it is clear that his overall strategy is to address a paradoxical mixture of centripetal and centrifugal forces, of pulling inward and pushing outward, of convergence and divergence. Divergent or centrifugal forces, then, may be paired with centralization. Indeed, Williams calls attention to the emergence of multiple centers.[5] In sum, assembling may be considered in three registers: mobile privatization, flowing segmentation, and multiplying centralization. I will return to these registers. But at this juncture, it is crucial to ask: What are the implications of his approach for working through technology-centered versus politically orientated histories of television?

When it comes to histories of technological innovation, Williams does not want to adopt the perspective of progressive development, which presents the current configuration of broadcast television as a natural and felicitous outcome, and as the only possible outcome. Nor does he wish us to conclude that the basic problem of television lies in its logistical or operative capacity as developed and mobilized within military operations. Williams would surely not accept Virilio's almost exclusive emphasis on logistics, for instance. Indeed, he situates the logistical tendency as a first phase, the implication being that it is to some degree subsumed by the tendency toward segmentation, privatization, and centralization. Williams's approach also differs from what is called media archaeology, where a technical device is seen as a kind of empty center or floating signifier, around which social trends and cultural behaviors revolve, as if attracted by its gravitational pull.[6] Yet Williams's notion of social technology actually seems to give greater weight to technology than media archaeology does, despite the latter's focus on technologies and devices. This is because, for Williams, even if the point-to-point tendency is to a high degree subsumed, the platforms and infrastructures for television nevertheless display a vague material tendency toward logistical point-to-point operations—toward network operativity, as it were. Technologies for him are neither place markers nor floating signifiers.

Conversely, when it comes to histories of state control, Williams does not want us to rest content with the idea that the problem of television lies in its use for propaganda by political elites. Thus he writes, "A fascist regime might quickly see the use of broadcasting for direct political and social control. But that, in any case, was when the technology had already been developed elsewhere. In capitalist democracies, the thrust for conversion from scattered techniques to a technology was not political but economic."[7] In other words, even if the technological or logistical is to some degree effectively subsumed by the political in his account, it is never totally subsumed. The paradoxical relation between polarized tendencies persists. This makes it possible to consider what holds these tendencies together and pulls them apart—relations of production and forces of production.

Production of Distribution

Williams's account of television is keeping with Marx's critique of political economy, the fundamental point of which, in contrast to liberal notions of economic freedom and the leveling power of free markets, is that circulation does not make for evenness or equality. Rather, circulation produces unevenness, and increased circulation will generate greater unevenness. What is more, unevenness is considered to be at once technological, political, and economic, which is to say, social. Thus one line of Williams's argument consists in showing how "a set of scattered technical devices became an applied technology and then a social technology."[8]

It is with this strategy that Williams avoids the economic determinism wherein the economic infrastructure (or base) comes first, and thus economic production determines the superstructure (society or culture). In Williams's account of television, capital exerts its effects first and foremost at the level of distribution instead of production. Indeed, he distinguishes television from cinema in this respect: "In the history of motion pictures, capitalist development was primarily in production; large-scale distribution came much later. . . . In broadcasting, both in sound radio and later in television, the major investment was in the means of distribution."[9] Elsewhere, he restates his point with added emphasis: *"It is not only that the supply of broadcasting facilities preceded the demand; it is that the means of communication preceded their content."*[10]

Thus, in 1930s and 1940s Japan, electronic companies launched into the production of commercial models of television receivers, and telecommunications companies began to build broadcast and relay stations, before the production of television content; media platforms (TV sets) and infrastructures preceded their content. This rush to put infrastructures in place continued into the postwar era. Before NTT took over responsibility for the telecommunications network in 1954, NHK was hastening to build television infrastructures, establishing experimental stations in Tokyo (1950), Osaka (1952), and Nagoya (1952) together with rebroadcasting stations with microwave relay trunks between them.[11] One of the key problematics of Japanese television, and indeed of television and new media in general, comes of the priority of investment in, and thus the excess capacity of, distribution and the means of communications over and above the production of content: will there ever be enough content to fill all those new channels during all the hours in a day? Who will make the content? Will it be sufficient to repurpose other media, such as showing movies on television? And who can take in all that content anyway?

Williams's attention to the generative force of the gap between distribution and production of content remains pertinent in the contemporary context, for historically, each time the production of content seems about to fill the gap, new investments in communications open the gap once again, and more widely. Today, even as the drive to increase the speed and efficiency of processing at the level of microchips seems to be reaching a material limit, the impulse to increase distribution capacity has not lessened. Everyone becomes drawn into the production of content (fans and netizens) and everything is turning into content (big data), but it will never be enough precisely because the productive power of distribution continues to take precedence over the production of content.

Another implication of Williams's account is worth emphasizing: when the production of distribution takes priority over the production of content, media platforms and infrastructures may become like content in their own right. The television receiver, for instance, may seem to be contentlike, even in the absence of actual transmission of content. Already in the history of early Japanese cinema audiences allegedly showed greater interest in the projector than what was being projected. Television redoubles and prolongs such an effect: apocryphal stories of early television are about audiences who are content to watch the set long after the actual programming had ceased; families would sit in front of a television receiver after broadcast hours, watching the effects of ambient radiation play across the screen. McLuhan's stance—the medium is the message—feels especially in tune with the broadcast era, for under conditions where distribution continuously exceeds content, technologies and media of distribution take on the feel of content. Distribution feels contentlike, and content in turn becomes increasingly nondiscrete, distributive in advance, medium-like.

Williams's prime example of such distributive content is programming, that is, the flowing segmentation of television content, across channels, by hour of the day, and within programs. Media mix, that is, multimedia franchising strategies characteristic of Japanese popular culture, provide another prime example, to which I will turn in the subsequent chapters.

As mentioned in the previous chapter, it makes sense that Williams, writing about television in 1975, would adopt the perspective of the one to many subsuming the point to point (not totally but effectively). Today, however, the scholarly trend is to reverse this priority, to see the point to point subsuming the one to many—and not simply effectively but totally. Such an emphasis tends to collapse the distinction between the technological and political while positing a total rupture between information media and broadcast media. This gesture makes it difficult to understand how new media may entail increased centralization, privatization, and segmentation alongside enhanced networking. Two explanations step in, almost by default, to address whatever appears as the exception to networking. One line of explanation evokes a powerful external force that intervenes to muck with, overcode, or expropriate point-to-point-generated networks; external forces intervene to undermine net democracy, for instance.[12] The other, conversely, finds centralization, privatization, and segmentation to be built into the very structure of networks at the level of protocol, software, or architectures. Such explanations are to some extent persuasive, yet without a conceptualization of disjunctive synthesis or the production of distribution, they make it all too easy to introduce a divide between the political and the technological, thus apotheosizing sovereignty or endorsing technological determinism.

It is with such concerns in mind that I now turn to the ways in which histories of Japanese television have come to stress centralization, privatization, and segmentation, to the point where they begin to posit the total subsuming of the point to point by the one to many.

Nationalizing Television

Histories of Japanese television dramatize its rapid spread and its connection to Japan's postwar economic recovery, the so-called economic miracle. Mass production of television sets lowered costs, while increases in salaries made purchase even easier. At the same time, relay systems improved, bringing television to remote areas of Japan, and the number of stations expanded, boosting the number of broadcast hours. By all accounts, villages in rural areas embraced television, even building the local infrastructure for reception if necessary. The overall image of the rapid spread of television in Japan, then, evokes a tendency toward complete coverage of the national territory, which advanced along two fronts, infrastructure (key stations, relay stations, and antennas) and receivers (television sets and antennas), and which was fueled by popular desire for the new medium alongside heavy commercial investment.

This image explains why television seems, at least at first, to fit nicely with Benedict Anderson's model of nationness: it apparently expands to the limit of the national territory, spreading sovereignty evenly across it. Television appears to advance in extensity to fill national territory, striving to deliver a signal to every town and provide a television in every home. The image is one of television spreading to the distant corners and isolated pockets of the territory called Japan, gradually expanding to fill it, smoothly and evenly. Such an ideal recalls Anderson's characterization of nationness in terms of flat, even sovereignty, a reworking of Walter Benjamin's characterization of modernity in terms of the production of empty, homogeneous time.[13] Ideally television would produce Japaneseness, at a formal or structural level, by bringing people throughout Japan into the same homogeneous temporality—television citizens, television nation.

It should be noted that for postwar Japan, which had only recently experienced defeat and relinquished its empire, this thoroughly Wilsonian ideal for national form—one language, one culture, one people, that is, an ethnically and linguistically homogeneous and rigidly circumscribed territory—constituted a dramatic and highly selective transformation of the imperial imaginary. Consequently, even as the postwar spread of television in Japan built on prior forms of media coverage, such as newspapers, magazines, novels, cinema, and radio, Japanese television differed from such prior media in being almost exclusively imagined within the territorial confines of the Japanese nation as defined immediately after World War II. Indeed, during the predominantly American-led Allied occupation of Japan, the occupying forces actively promoted such a vision of Japan, even in its media policy. The occupation saw to the enactment of the Broadcast Law of 1950, which provided for the existence of the NHK as a public service broadcaster drawing its funds from reception fees; every household was to sign a contract with NHK upon the installation of its television set. The formation of a public-service national television monopoly dovetails with the ideal of flat, even sovereignty and homogeneous national temporality. Yet a second vision arose to trouble this Wilsonian ideal. At about the same time, Shōriki Matsutarō fought against the establishment of a television monopoly in Japan in order to found Japan's first private television network. His intervention merits a brief digression.

In the 1920s, after his dismissal from his position as chief of staff of the Tokyo metropolitan police (and thus as head of the notorious secret police), Shōriki acquired the newspaper *Yomiura*, which he transformed into one of the world's largest selling newspapers through a combination of sensationalism, showmanship, and right-wing warmongering. One of the keys to the success of *Yomiura* lay in Shōriki's astute promotion of American baseball. Subsequently charged with and imprisoned for class A war crimes after the war, Shōriki was released in 1947, at the very moment when United States politicians, increasingly obsessed with the spread of communism, began to express concern that the Allied occupation was encouraging left-wing movements in Japan. Shōriki shrewdly exploited such concerns about communism to contest the NHK television monopoly and to form his private station. The *Economist* sums it up nicely:

> Shibata [Hidetoshi], a news reporter, heard of a plan put forward in America to use television to spread anticommunist propaganda around the world, with the former enemies West Germany and Japan as the bases. He brought the idea to Shoriki, who offered to help finance a new station—if the Americans helped persuade the Supreme Commander for the Allied Powers to lift his blacklisting. Using Shibata's American contacts, Shoriki browbeat the government to end the monopoly of NHK, the state broadcaster. His purge duly lifted, he raised more than ¥800m to establish Japan's first private network, Nippon Television, in 1952. Today it is the most popular TV station in Japan.[14]

Thus, about a year after the end of the Allied Occupation of Japan, two stations began regular broadcasts: the public service station NHK went on the air on February 1, 1953, and the commercial station Nippon Television (NTV) on August 28. Unlike NHK, which relies on subscribers' fees, commercial stations draw revenues from advertising. After the formation of NTV, four other Tokyo-based key broadcasters quickly emerged as the leaders in commercial broadcasting: TV Asashi, TBS, TV Tokyo, and Fuji TV. These five commercials broadcasters have tie-ins with Japan's five major newspapers, and regional private broadcasters are generally affiliated with one of these big five.[15] This is one prime instance of what Williams calls multiple centers: under conditions of flow due to the production of distribution, centralization tends to continuously multiply.

The point of this digression into Shōriki's NTV versus NHK is to signal a bifurcation inherent in the very formation of national sovereignty as realized in the postwar era: the Wilsonian ideal of nationness can only be enacted within a certain kind of world, or more precisely within a world order, which it helps to produce and sustain. That world order was Pax Americana, as established through the League of Nations (or U.N.) and the U.S. military-base empire. This situation—in which Japanese national reterritorialization and American global deterritorialization go hand in hand—can nonetheless be readily dramatized in terms of antagonism or conflict, as Shōriki was quick to realize. To attract audiences to watch television and to purchase TV sets, NTV aired sensational professional wrestling matches featuring Rikidōzan (a former sumo wrestler of Korean descent who presented himself as Japanese) enjoying victory over villainous American wrestlers such as the Sharpe Brothers (who were actually Canadian).[16] In other words, there is now a polarization within sovereignty producing two tendencies: on the one hand is a Japanese nation whose sovereignty (reterritorializing) takes place within an American world order (deterritorializing), and on the other hand is a Japanese sovereignty or Japaneseness that enters into conflict with American sovereignty, as if to emerge victorious or die trying.

This polarization is also linked to the historical movement of television that Williams glosses in terms of paradoxical yet connected tendencies, but the paradox is enacted in a register Williams largely ignores: national sovereignty. The one-to-many tendency entails centralization: Tokyo emerges as the television broadcast center for the national territory of Japan. Yet the point-to-point tendency is evident in the emergence of Japanese sovereignty within the American world order, which was itself being organized around its Cold War battle against communism. Oddly enough, this latter tendency has rarely been noticed or discussed in histories of the emergence of Japanese television. There is one important exception: in his study of Japanese television and the American CIA, Arima Tetsuo makes the situation abundantly clear: the American vision for Japanese television in the early 1950s consisted of a system of regional networks. In particular, above and beyond the capacity for one-to-many national broadcast, the CIA envisioned situating Japanese television within logistical point-to-point communication network amenable to military operations.[17]

As Arima shows, when Shōriki allied himself with the cause of using television for anticommunist propaganda, he also entered into this other vision of television networks. Shōriki was situating Japan not only within an ideological matrix but also within this logistical military telecommunications network. Significantly, in keeping with the American initiative to take over and sustain the southern arc of Japanese empire, which American strategists redubbed the Grand Crescent, Japan was situated at one end of the Southeast Asia network.

Ultimately the construction of this network met with resistance and was scrapped, and yet the ongoing bid to situate Japanese television within a neo-imperial Grand Crescent serves of a reminder of Japan's position in the postwar world order, one that continues to this day to shape Japan's media regionalism (flow of Japanese media in greater East Asia area) and soft power initiatives.[18] A full discussion of these regional and geopolitical dimensions of Japanese television media is beyond the scope of this study, however. Suffice it to say, I wish to underscore how histories of Japanese television have largely ignored or omitted any account of point-to-point tendencies, precisely because such tendencies undermine the ideal of national sovereignty, in which flat, homogeneous nationness appears to come first and only subsequently becomes internally fissured and ruptured by various forms of social segmentation such as gender, class, or ethnicity. Thus a pure form of the nation appears to take precedence over actual political struggles and social realities. Needless to say, such a bias may result in a desire for pure, untainted national community prior to social division and as such may rule out dissent and protest as a basis for society and for communal distribution.[19]

To summarize, because histories of television have omitted point-to-point tendencies from their accounts of national television or have treated them as totally subsumed, we have to be careful about how we introduce questions about the formation of national sovereignty to avoid dehistoricizing and naturalizing the ideal of flat, even sovereignty. While nationalization was and is a powerful current in the formation of Japanese television, nationalizing television is not a matter of representing a preexisting Japanese territory, or sovereignty, or Japaneseness; it produces Japaneseness, usually as a by-product (or epiphenomenon) of procedures of centralization, privatization, and segmentation.

Histories of Japanese television that draw critical attention to the production of nationness and nationalism thus provide a useful point of departure for historicizing formations of national sovereignty. Nonetheless, if we wish to challenge the logic and history of national sovereignty itself, we will need to return to the paradox of polarized tendencies, where a more complex material distribution occurs.

Segmentation

Understanding Japanese television primarily in terms of centralization makes sense in light of the national developmental imperatives of the late 1950s and 1960s. It seemed only a matter of time before broadcast coverage would cover the entire nation and every household in Japan would own a television set, or two. From the developmental perspective, statistics on ownership of a television receiver (and other electronic appliances) came to function as an index of national progress. Recourse to such an index tends, however, to obscure the multiplication of centers and thus to impart a sense of unified centralization, or more precisely a sense of unity through centralization, as if centralization and unification were the same thing. For instance, everyone knows that the Tokyo-based broadcasters, NHK and the big five, constituted different, competing centers from the outset, yet when we use TV ownership as a measure of progress, such competition becomes subordinated to the larger unity of Japanese television, imparting a greater sense of unity to the center than it may actually have.

It was above all the use of nationally orchestrated events to spur the acquisition of TV sets that reinforced the sense of Japanese unity. For instance, the royal wedding of 1959, between Shōda Michiko and Prince Akihito (the reigning emperor today), is a commonly evoked point of inflection in the increase of private ownership of receivers. As Yoshimi Shun'ya duly notes, "The numbers of TVs registered in Japan had already exceeded 1 million by April 1958, but the number increased even further later that year when the engagement was announced. It exceeded 2 million in April 1959 and 3 million by October the same year."[20] Similarly, the 1964 Tokyo Olympics spurred sales of color television sets. By 1973, 88 percent of households owned TV sets. In sum, statistics on national development of television, in conjunction with national spectacles, create the impression of a television unification of Japan. Consequently, television appears to represent its (national) audiences, and audiences may begin to seek their (national) representation via television.

This impulse to see centralization as producing unification has also had a profound impact on the formation of peripheries within the nation. In his social history of Japanese television, Jayson Makoto Chun recounts how, as television platforms and networks extended across Japan, attention quickly fell on the ways in which television might serve to lessen the distance, culturally and linguistically, between the rural periphery and urban center, which latter became largely synonymous with Tokyo and its key stations.[21] Moreover, at the time that television was spreading to the countryside, people were leaving rural areas to work in the city. In this postwar process of centralization, housing projects or *danchi*, with block upon block of 2LDK apartments, became characterized not only for their density of population but also for their density of television reception and hours of use.[22] Television thus went hand in hand with the homogenization and standardization of everyday life in urban areas, above all in Tokyo, which affected center–periphery relations within Japan. Chun calls attention to a process of standardized differentiation: "Ironically, the urban stations strengthened rural identities and economies by broadcasting scenes from rural areas on national television."[23] As such, what might be called for the sake of convenience "internal difference" (that is, rural, regional, and other differences within the national territory) was reterritorialized with reference to a Tokyo-television-centered Japan: "TV had become an important means to standardize regional differences."[24]

In sum, there were really totalizing strategies that constructed television in Japan through a combination of urban centralization, territorial homogenization, symbolic unity, and standardized difference. Later I will highlight the importance of other procedures (segmentation), but at this juncture, suffice it to say that the existence and apparent dominance of such totalizing strategies in the formation of Japanese television is what encourages us today to organize our histories around the one-to-many tendency. Yet when we organize our histories in such a manner, we tend to dwell on two kinds of facts about television.

First, because the center is not in reality unified, not one but multiple, when we focus on the emergence of the one-to-many tendency, we will tend to discover that the center is an empty or absent center, a symbolic center, a vanishing-into-the-clouds center. Consequently, even if Japanese television consists of multiple competitive centers, often in conflict with other centers (such as governmental and commercial centers), the emperor or some other sort of symbolic overexistence steps in to impart a sense of center, albeit an absent one. Actual historical developments, such as the connection between television purchases and imperial spectacles or sports events, lend support to such a vision.

Second, at the same time that the emphasis on the one-to-many tendency apotheosizes the center, it also subordinates the multitude to the one, either in the form of a mass (the national masses) or in the form of a mediating center (regional "centers" function as relays for the center, or connect to one another via the center, which becomes construed as a national center). It is through these two emphatic strategies that television across Japan was turned into Japanese television. Thus, when we track only these facts about television and focus exclusively on the emergence of the one-to-many tendency, it is all too easy to unthinkingly repeat the nationalizing gesture.

Yoshimi Shun'ya's work on television and nationalism is particularly important in this context because he carefully tracks the nationalist implications of television across different symbolic registers bearing on personal and social experience. For Yoshimi, television defined and stabilized nationalism or national consciousness from the early 1960s through the 1980s, making for what he calls the "national domestic television formation."[25] The constitutive moment of this formation was the movement of televisions into the household: "The intimate sphere of the Japanese household in its postwar form was itself created on a national scale through the medium of TV."[26] Yoshimi's account then turns to three different totalizing strategies for subordinating the domestic to the national as a result of the movement of television into private homes.

First, when the television set in Japan became one of three must-have electric appliances, it also provided "a symbol linked to the domestic subjectivity of the housewife and the productive national subjectivity of the engineer."[27] This was because, in advertisements in particular, the television set came to play a dual symbolic role: it produced an image of women as stay-at-home housewife consumers (although women soon had to work to purchase new luxury items), and it reinforced the image of men as commuting workers. In keeping with the new characterization of Japan as a high-tech producer, these commuter men ideally were to be engineers.

In effect, Yoshimi's first point addresses what Williams calls mobile privatization. The formation of broadcast television, by placing TV receivers in every household, meshed with a new organization of everyday life in which the private household became the anchor for new modes of social mobilization: workers began to commute to the workplace, students to school, shoppers to burgeoning new commercial centers, and then back home. Mobile privatization is thus reminiscent what Foucault calls disciplinary power: "Individuals are always going from one closed site to another, each with its own laws: first of all the family, then school (you're not at home anymore), then the barracks (you're not at school, you know), then the factory, hospital from time to time, maybe prison, the model site of confinement."[28] In sum, like Foucault and Williams, Yoshimi's account of television shows how such a formation operates through social segmentation.

Differences in emphasis appear across Williams, Foucault, and Yoshimi, yet these help to develop a fuller image of social segmentation. Williams's emphasis reminds us that segmentation does not happen only across the individual's life cycle but also within the regimens of everyday life: commuting. Yoshimi's account reminds us that such segmentation also implies different degrees and qualities of mobility: women are enjoined to move differently than men across segments. Foucault emphasizes the process of enclosure. Still, across their differences in emphasis, the three share a focus and paradigm—how social space is segmented to make for movement from closed site to closed site, from enclosure to enclosure. As such, movement (flow and mobility) is organized in accordance with social segmentation.

Second, Yoshimi sees television as "a flow of information structuring horizons of people's bodily sensations and experience through its broadcasts."[29] Above all, it is the broadcast timetable that structures everyday experience: "Until the 1980s, Japanese TV broadcasting was structured around these three contrasting time zones of morning, midday, and evening. Broadcasting at other times of day was relatively unstructured and formed a margin around these core time zones."[30]

Third, Yoshimi calls attention to how procedures of segmentation serve to connect domestic space-time to national space-time. The daily life of everybody in the nation is segmented in accordance with the daily timetable of programs, and at the same time there are symbolic codes within those program segments that introduce another kind of social segmentation: gender. Yoshimi looks at how these two kinds of segmentation work together to produce a symbolic center, a structure of national consciousness akin to Anderson's notion of the imagined community.

While I agree with Yoshimi that these procedures tend to work together, I would also add that they do not automatically work together, and so it is worthwhile taking a closer look at procedures of segmentation to consider how they might not always align and how new ways of assembling them are possible. There are three procedures of segmentation that merit attention in the context of broadcast television.

The first procedure of segmentation occurs in the process of allocating specific frequencies within the electromagnetic spectrum to different radio or television stations, making for a range of television channels, for instance. Significantly, something that is not fundamentally spatial (waves or frequencies) is transformed into something that feels spatial, like a definable and thus potentially enclosed space. This kind of segmentation is prolonged in the establishment of time slots for programs on a particular channel. Put another way, the stuff of blink has been cut into strips.

The second procedure of segmentation occurs within television programs, of which advertisement becomes the salient instance. With the establishment of NTV, for instance, revenues come from commercials, which appear during the program at regular intervals. A conflict arises between different ways of capturing attention: a sensational audience-grabbing show may draw lots of viewers to specific advertisements, but if the show is more compelling and eye-catching than the commercials, will they prove less effective? In other words, strips and patches of the stuff of blink are being folded and stitched together in various ways. Various planes of consistency are possible.

The third procedure concerns how, with the gradual establishment of twenty-hour broadcasting, different times of day are devoted to different kinds of programming that are based on who may be at home at that time to listen. Thus programming is targeted to niches comprising children, mother, father, or the whole family. In effect, the basic question is, who may fashion a garment from the stuff of blink, and who will wear it? Is it one size fits all? Or rather, how will you wear it? Do people even need to wear it in the intended way? Maybe a scarf becomes a turban or a *hachimaki* (helmet scarf), a halter top, a sash or a bellyband *(haramaki)* . . .

Focusing primarily on this third procedure (or third degree) of segmentation, Yoshimi calls attention to how television programming comes to articulate hierarchies: certain times of day (golden time) are more important than others because certain people (fathers) have more authority than others (wives, children). Consequently, Yoshimi sees segmentation producing—or more precisely reproducing—a structure of authority and hierarchy. Thus, moving away from an exploration of the production of multiple enclosures and movement between them, Yoshimi ultimately sees, in the segmenting procedures of television, the production of national ideology, a national structure of consciousness.

Yoshimi also contends that TV's procedures of segmentation turn into symbolic nationalism, an experience of national community. His account of "audience interpretation and meaning production through the various genres of texts and their customary codes" focuses on popular television series that link "the time of domestic memory with the time of national history."[31] Such a choice of programming adds weight to his general emphasis on the ways in which the domestic is yoked to the national.

Yoshimi is not mistaken to see the social technology of television producing a structure of national consciousness. What I wish to challenge is the implicit reduction of every procedure, tactic, and strategy to the formation of national consciousness. Yoshimi's account subordinates procedures of segmentation to the production of national sovereignty, either by introducing a causal relation between them (as if segmentation caused nationalism) or by positing nationalism as more powerful and fundamental than segmentation (as if the nation always already had the capacity to contain all procedures of segmentation and to press them into the reproduction of nationness).

Such an approach ultimately gives greater weight to symbolization than to material procedures, conditions, and struggles. It risks reimposing a symbolic center onto the actual practices, procedures, and polarities of broadcast television. It risks reinforcing a symbolic center in a form that inevitably turns out to be an empty, absent center, working across an immeasurable distance as if omnisciently, and in every crack and fissure of society as if omnipotent. This is why the center always retreats in Yoshimi's account of Japanese television, and as it retreats, it becomes larger, more distant, and yet more powerful. Thus, during the occupation, Yoshimi often calls attention to the United States as the hidden or overlooked social authority: "During the American military occupation following the Second World War, GHQ adopted the policy of conferring on media managers absolute and wide-ranging power over editorial matters."[32] And beyond the television as symbol lies the American imaginary: "This collective image of home electric appliances was introduced into postwar Japan particularly from the United States. However, this image was domesticated and 'orientalized' as an 'essential' element of Japanese culture."[33] Yoshimi's analysis implies that American managerial authority has consistently operated as a present absence or an absent presence. Beyond the corporations, behind emperorship, and behind the various symbols of Japaneseness, the United States is at once present and absent in the formation of Japanese television subjectivity.

To repeat, I do not think such a stance is entirely unwarranted. The problem lies in the reduction of the exercise of power to its symbolic dimension while adopting a narrow vision of sovereign power. The symbolic is only one dimension of how television operates, and it may not be the most significant. Indeed, the facts of television continually draw our attention back to procedures of segmentation, which are not necessarily subordinated in advance to the reproduction of national sovereignty. This is where Williams's emphasis on the multiplication of centers proves valuable, for it pulls us away from the monolithic paradigm of the absent center of national sovereignty. The multiplication of centers (or closed sites) brings us back to procedures of segmentation.

If we take a closer look at the third procedure of segmentation (who will wear this TV raiment, and how?), we do not see only unification and hierarchization of viewers. Part of the scandal of television was from the outset its ability to establish multiple sovereign centers and enclosures within the family. As soon as one TV set per household makes the family appear to be a seemingly solid and stable ground for television, the family threatens to break up and disperse. Debates arise about the television and the household. Is television holding families together or tearing them apart? Chun provides a judicious review of this debate in his account of Japanese television.[34] Naturally there is good evidence for both sides, because television is segmenting audiences.

On the one hand, there are reports of fathers spending more time at home with the family, even hastening home to watch television. And there are reports of members of the family talking more to one another—talking about television programs. On the other hand, with the advent of multiple channels and all-day programming, the television began to seek out and to produce different taste communities within the family.

Golden time, for instance, began at 7 PM with the news, followed by cartoons and family quiz shows, while drama and variety shows started after 8 PM. Professional ball games generally aired during golden time. Although golden time was intended to hold the family's attention, with an emphasis on the father's preference, differences of opinion arose within the family about what channel or show to watch at what time. Ratings wars started to play out within the family. At the same time, because household members followed different schedules (work, housework, school), non–golden time slots and niche markets (segments) increasingly took on importance.

Because segmentation works through the production of enclosures and the generation of movement between them, the enclosures cannot be consistently hierarchized. Children emerge as a recognizable segment that runs across and connects programming segments, such as children's hour, children's programs, and children's ads, which do not need to coincide perfectly to form a segment. Because the resulting children's segment enjoys a certain degree of autonomy, it cannot be assigned a lesser rank—below housewives and fathers, for instance.

In 1957, NHK surveys found children to be the heaviest viewers of TV, and discussions raged about whether television adversely affected children's physical, educational, psychological, and moral development, playing into and feeding off the new discourses on and anxieties about delinquency.[35] Because such a niche (children) cannot be readily assigned a place within a received hierarchy, it invites techniques of governance to set norms and regulate limits.

Raymond Williams's characterization of segmentation in terms of privatization makes sense in light of this production of closed sites. In effect, Williams looks at who wears the TV garment from the standpoint of commercial interests, where the question "who profits?" is closely related to the question "who owns?" But if we look at this question from the angle of the audience, television offers another paradox: you own the TV set, but you don't own the programs. Nonetheless, the programs are yours in another way: your path across them produces your niche, and your niche or segment generates a you, a TV self. This process might be called possession, but then we must carefully distinguish possession from ownership.[36]

Possession is related to a material continuum or plane of consistency underlying the who and the how of the TV garment. At its extremes, this plane of possession is for everyone and for no one. This is why it is possible to take up programs in different ways, just as a scarf may be worn as a turban. The act of "turbaning the scarf" is one of affective possession, not legal ownership. From the point of view of ownership, affective possession appears consonant with privatization, with taking something out of circulation and holding onto it. The self appears individualized, personalized, privatized—working on itself in a process of self-segmenting, so to speak. Yet from the point of view of flow and mobility, it seems that another "selfing" is possible via a self-animating process of care for self.

Outside Television

I will return to individualizing tactics of the self in subsequent chapters. For now, by way of conclusion, I wish to summarize the key points that have thus far appeared in this social history of television. Histories of broadcast television have tended to separate the social and political history of television from its technological and media history. The principal question is thus how to bring these two kinds of history together.

Building on Raymond Williams, I stressed that broadcast television is in fact an assembling of two tendencies, which are in turn related to these two kinds of histories. Histories centered on television technologies usually linger on the point-to-point tendency—progressive technoscientific development toward a network. Political and social histories focus primarily on the one-to-many tendency.

Williams himself tends in this latter direction. Although he calls attention to the two tendencies, his account of television as social technology situates the point-to-point tendency as a first phrase, effectively subsumed. Other social histories of television do not even acknowledge the first tendency, ignoring or omitting it to focus exclusively on the one-to-many tendency. This is generally the case in social histories of Japanese television.

My aim is not to renounce or reject social histories that focus on the one-to-many tendency but to complicate them. Thus I turned to social histories of Japanese television, especially Yoshimi Shun'ya's work, with two goals. First, I wished to show how an emphasis on the one-to-many tendency goes hand in hand with an assumption that power operates symbolically, and that's all there is to it. Yoshimi's account, for instance, gravitates toward symbolic operations, concluding with a totalizing structure of national consciousness, seemingly indifferent to material procedures. Second, I wished to show that even in social histories that ultimately stress the one-to-many tendency, procedures of segmentation come to the fore, however much they are subsequently muted. Procedures of segmentation allow for a more complex account of the social implications of television.

Yoshimi looks at segmentation from the point of view of complete centralization and nationalization. He thus subordinates segmentation to symbolic power. In contrast, Williams insists on the emergence of multiple centers and movement between them—mobile privatization. As such, although Williams, like Yoshimi, gives primacy to the one-to-many tendency, his account of segmentation hints at something else operating within it: material flows and movements that are never totally subsumed within what Yoshimi aptly calls the domestic national television formation.

To get a handle on this something else operating in procedures of segmentation, I sketched out three kinds of procedures: (1) the segmentation of programs into channels or stations that are based on frequency allocation, which transforms a wavelength into a protospace; (2) the segmentation within programs, most evident in the inclusion of commercials within shows, with the division of shows into modular units; and (3) segmentation by time of day, which, in conjunction with segmentation within programs, contributes to the formation of segments across segments, giving rise to niches to be personalized, which in turn are associated with the homes to which commuters return (mobile privatization).

When we look closer at these procedures of segmentation, we begin to detect another level of polarization, which expresses the polarization between point-to-point tendencies and one-to-many tendencies in a social register. Procedures of segmentation appear stretched between individualizing techniques and totalizing procedures. Segmentation simultaneously gives rise to specific kinds of individual and specific kinds of totality. Foucault's view of power comes to mind: "The state's power (and that's one of the reasons for its strength) is both an individualizing and totalizing form of power. Never, I think, in the history of human societies—even in the old Chinese society—has there been such a tricky combination in the same political structures of individualization techniques and of totalization procedures."[37]

Seen in this light, in their accounts of segmentation, Yoshimi and Williams appear more intent on accounting for the totalizing procedures of broadcast television. The fate of individualizing techniques in their accounts is to be always already totalized, whether via symbolization or privatization. Such a perspective on power is indispensable in the context of television and new media. Only by passing through such a perspective on power can we embark on a genealogy of television, to consider the assembling of the point to point with the one to many. Only by passing through such a perspective on power can we avoid the temptation to focus on point-to-point tendencies and imagine that we are somehow liberating the individual from the shackles of totalizing power, whether symbolizing or privatizing. Nor will we leap to the conclusion that totalization has always already occurred within point-to-point protocols. In the context of television and new media, point-to-point tendencies do not exist in a pure form, stripped of any relation to one-to-many tendencies, beyond totalizing procedures of power. Conversely, totalizing procedures do not exist in a pure form either.

Even this brief consideration of procedures of segmentation suggests that polarization arises within individualizing techniques—ownerlike personalization versus nonpersonal possession, which evokes the previous distinction between work on self versus care for self, and which might now be also styled in terms of self-segmenting practices versus self-animating ones. It is this polarization within individualizing techniques that I will gradually bring to the fore in subsequent chapters. Yet it is worth noting that polarization occurs within totalizing procedures as well. To evaluate these totalizing procedures, however, we would need to turn to transnational flows, regional effects, and imperial strategies, for television has never respected national borders. Such an account goes beyond the bounds of this study, but suffice it to say that when individualizing techniques and totalizing procedures enter into tricky combinations, national sovereignty may constrain the assembling but cannot contain it. Global–local assemblages arise.

One common objection to Foucault's focus on how power is exercised comes of its corollary: we are never outside power relations. Resistance, for instance, engages us on a field of power rather than liberating us from it. For some, the idea of resistance without a politics of emancipation of some sort feels vacuous. Yet in the context of television at least, it is the idea of liberatory politics that proves vacuous. To be sure, the revolution will not be televised—not on *their* television. But there are other possible televisions. Williams himself gravitates toward a politics of another possible configuration of television—community-access TV—not such a surprising choice in 1975.

Writing at the start of the new century, however, Yoshimi spins a bleaker yarn. Yoshimi not only tracks the birth of the national domestic television formation but also announces its death: "The stability of TV as national medium was threatened in all its dimensions from the end of the 1980s."[38] The death threat to television is not idle, in his opinion, and he speculates about the imminent disintegration and death of national television: "As the national medium, TV may be on its way toward a quiet demise."[39] What are sources of this possibly mortal threat to television? Yoshimi detects a shift from the home or household to new kinds of personalized communications media. He suggests, "Instead of 'home' technologies, 'personal' and 'body-conscious' technologies such as the Walkman, cellular phone, portable computer, pager (known in Japan as the 'pocket-bell') and *tamagocchi* came to play the leading role in the image of technology in everyday life."[40] Tentatively, then, Yoshimi posits the end of the era of the national television formation and the emergence of a new era: that of new mobile and personal communications media.

Japanese television, however, refuses to die: "In a society such as Japan, which during the Cold War developed into an extremely pure form of the nation state, acceptance of TV's demise may not come so easily, precisely because TV was the central medium in the creation of this postwar nation state. We are likely to witness many more counterattacks from the national backlash through the medium of TV."[41] To provide a contemporary instance of what concerns Yoshimi, in January 2014, the "new chairman of NHK [Momii Katsuto] said Saturday that its programming for foreign audiences should 'state Japan's positions in no uncertain terms' on territorial disputes with China and South Korea, while defending the nation's use of wartime 'comfort women' and dismissing press freedom concerns about the new state secrets law."[42] When the chairman of the nation's public service station openly advocates such blatantly revisionist and ultranationalist positions, it is indeed as if sovereign power were laid bare.

As the ideology and program scheduling that once used to stabilize national television vanishes, Yoshimi sees a morbid, zombielike living on of television as a nationalist mouthpiece, proclaiming and enacting more and more violent and virulent forms of nationalism. What now unite people in front of the television are disasters and emergencies. In this respect, Yoshimi agrees with news director Okumura Kenta's pronouncement that "even so television is not dead."[43] But Yoshimi sees its dystopian dimension. Across such takes on the living on of television (as it feeds, vampirelike, on natural disasters and political emergencies), it is possible to see a transformation in the way in which the nation-state draws together distinctive procedures of power. For instance, the demise of procedures of segmentation might also be considered to spell the end of disciplinary society.

After disciplinary society, another kind of power emerges, which in Yoshimi's and Okumura's accounts of Japanese television bears an uncanny resemblance to Agamben's reconsideration of Schmitt's theory of the state of exception.[44] It is as if television, in its death throes, has exposed the ontological drive of nationalism: pure sovereignty reducing its subjects to bare life, the absolute subordination of the many to the one that vanishes by burrowing into life itself. Yoshimi's account here reaches the point where it is no longer about television at all but about (national) sovereignty, pure and simple.

Consequently, if we look for traces of other possible televisions in Yoshimi's work, we will not find them in the era of national television (roughly 1960–90) or in the era of new media (1990–present). We will have to return instead to the moment of the birth of national television, in the 1950s, when another possibility briefly flickered: *gaitō terebi,* or "street TV."

Before people could afford to purchase their own receivers, television sets were placed in public places to attract audiences to the new medium and to encourage the purchase of televisions. In keeping with its public service profile, NHK placed sets in hospitals and community centers. In contrast, the head of the commercial station, NTV, Shōriki, opted to create a sensation, situating television sets at locations calculated to attract the largest number of viewers. Shōriki also had a flair for developing sensational programming, like the pro wrestling matches featuring Rikidōzan, which drew crowds to gather in the streets to watch or—because the large number of viewers often obscured the screen—to hear the match.

Gaitō terebi has taken on an almost mythical status within histories of Japanese television and popular culture for a couple reasons. First, the phenomenon evokes an almost naive fascination with television, which renews a sense of the extraordinary in a medium that today feels all too ordinary. Second, because televisions placed in the streets of Tokyo drew such huge crowds, *gaitō terebi* feels somehow communal, and spontaneously so, like the remnant of an urban community that would be lost when television moved into households and everyday life became increasingly privatized. *Gaitō terebi* feels like a lost possibility—not just another possible television, but another possible Tokyo, another possible Japan.

For Yoshimi, whose research generally focuses on mass events such as fairs, exhibitions, and other dramatic happenings in the city streets, the importance of *gaitō terebi* lies in its relationship to such mass events.[45] Thus he takes care to separate street television from Shōriki's sensational implementation of it, arguing on the one hand that Shōriki built on a tradition of technology exhibitions and fairs, and on the other hand calling attention to the importance of other forms of street television, which were not initiated by NHK or NTV, such as TV sets in the windows of shops selling electronics.[46] What attracts Yoshimi to this way of interacting with television lies in how it spurs face-to-face communication among people in the streets, with people commenting to one another about

TV events, asking each other about them, and picking up the conversation in other parts of the city, as if people were collectively piecing together a version of events, possessing what they could not own, as it were. Through the phenomenon of *gaitō terebi,* Yoshimi imagines a television unconstrained by walls, which is to say a television that is neither contained within households nor privatized. He liberates television from the prison house of the privatized household. Put another way, by imagining what happens with television outside the house, he liberates the first two procedures of segmentation (frequency allocation and code switching) from the third procedure (personalized, privatized niches). Yoshimi's gesture thus invites us to explore possibilities that arise within the first two procedures of segmentation.

Because the television set generates a nebulous semicircular zone for the audience, if it is not enclosed within walls, a strict distinction between inside and outside does not occur. People move into and out of the zone, may listen at a distance, may come close to the screen to watch, and so forth. The TV set does not of itself produce solid boundaries. Even within the household, the zone is variable over the course of the day in accordance with what the viewer is doing (preparing supper, watching intently, reading the newspaper, or doing homework while listening, for instance) and in accordance with such variables as the intensity of the signal, the quality of the sound, the resolution of the image, and the ambient sound and light, not to mention the kind of TV set, its hookup, its age, and so forth. Television experience, then, does not automatically entail form or structure. It is a matter of an encounter between the television and the human that opens a process of mutual experimentation. This is why Yoshimi associates street television with technology fairs. This sort of television formation calls for interaction based on curiosity and an experimental spirit, the intensity of which may be prolonged across the zone, thus extending it. Such a configuration of television, in which the TV set affords a zone of intensity, constitutes an amplification of the strange spatial effects inherent in frequency allocation.

Allocating a frequency to a particular station or channel involves a transformation of a wavelength into something spacelike, enclosure-like. When the television set is confined to the household, the enclosure-like tendency is reinforced. When the set is placed in the streets, the underlying intensity of wavelengths may be amplified, making for frequency-like effects rippling through the city. By the same token, switching codes within a program (that is, codes for program opening, commercial, credits, commercial, first story module, and commercial) may be seized from the angle of enclosure-like effects in terms of compartmentalizing both codes and programs. Yet the very same switching may be amplified into a cross-cultural nonpersonal chatter, echoing through the city. Such is the challenge Yoshimi discovers in *gaitō terebi*: if the third procedure of segmentation is removed, then the underlying intensity of the other two procedures may be amplified.

Once we understand Yoshimi's account of street television in this way, it is possible to look at television within the household in a different way. I agree with Yoshimi and Williams that the overall tendency of broadcast television as a social technology is toward pressing procedures of segmentation into the production of enclosed sites that are readily subordinated to the one-to-many tendency, which results in totalizing social structures. We cannot remove point-to-point tendencies from this historical process. Yoshimi's gesture of liberating television from the household—where procedures of segmentation appear to be completely enmeshed with privatization—opens a new line of thinking, however, because once we have imagined how television might operate without enclosures, we begin to notice similar zones within the household, zones of intensity where "outside television" is happening inside. This is where the genealogy of television and new media comes into play. If we take a closer look at the ways in which broadcast television has historically been configured with so-called new media, we confront the intensity arising where polarized tendencies are being assembled within domestic television. Thus, in the next chapter, I propose to reconsider the heyday of broadcast television, roughly 1960 to 1990, in terms of the ongoing assembling of new media and television.

7

TELEVISION AND NEW MEDIA

HISTORIES OF BROADCAST TELEVISION, INTENT ON CALLING ATTENTION TO THE HISTORICAL ASCENDENCY OF THE ONE-TO-many tendency, have generally downplayed or eliminated the point-to-point tendency. Williams treats the point-to-point tendency as effectively subsumed, and Yoshimi treats it totally subsumed, symbolically. As such, procedures of segmentation, such as frequency allocation, programming grids, and privatized households, have been looked at primarily from the angle of their capture by, or complicity with, the one-to-many tendency. Above all, it is the private household or domestic space that seems to seal the deal by aligning domestic space with private commercial interests (Williams) or with a structure of national consciousness (Yoshimi). While Williams finds some potential for breaking the privatized domestic–commercial alignment in community access TV, for Yoshimi the demise of the national domestic television formation in the late 1980s gives rise to a more virulent form of national sovereignty, one effectively liberated from its obligation to persuade and domesticate its citizens. To imagine what television might be outside its period of national domestication, Yoshimi turns to street television of the 1950s.

In this chapter, while continuing to build on those two accounts, I will to look at what is happening with television within domestic space or households during the heyday of the national domestic television formation, roughly 1960 to 1990, but I propose to look at household television from the angle of transformations in media platforms (plugging VCR and game consoles into the television) and media infrastructures (satellite and cable). What interests me is how the point-to-point tendency, almost as soon as it appears effectively subsumed within the one-to-many tendency, resurges from within the television formation, both within platforms and infrastructures. Consequently, rather than thinking about the history of television media only in terms of subsuming, we need also to think in terms of an assembling of the polarized tendencies that have to date been set in opposition and then narrowly attributed to broadcast (one to many) versus new media (point to point). Thus we arrive at a genealogy of television media, which affords a better understanding of both the continuity and discontinuity between broadcast television and various waves of new media—video games, personal media, mobile media, social media.

Polarized tendencies are never equal partners, of course. Assembling is thus not merely a matter of combining two tendencies bearing equal weight. This is why I have lingered on Williams's and Yoshimi's accounts of television, to make abundantly clear how the one-to-many tendency historically came to take priority over the point-to-point tendency, for both material and symbolic reasons. As a consequence, when the point-to-point tendency surges or resurges in the context of broadcast television, it appears as an intensification, as an outside of the inside, that is, as something that seems to come from without (the console is plugged into the television) even as it activates or reactivates the potential already implicit inside the domesticated television set (the television receiver has also the capacity to serve as monitor or computer).[1]

The discourses on new media that proliferated in 1980s Japan, around the time of the alleged demise of the national domestic television formation, lend additional support to the genealogical approach to television and new media. Those accounts of new media focused on transformations in television platforms and infrastructures as the site of a widespread social media transformation. In fact, in the Japanese context, the very idea of new media emerged through the "outside on the inside" of television.

Interactive TV (1960s)

Japanese television in the 1960s, which was television's second commercial decade and the first decade of Yoshimi's stabilized domestic television formation, has been characterized in terms of the territorial coverage of broadcasting infrastructures, the widespread movement of television sets in households, and the ability of domestic TV production to meet the challenge of providing shows all day, every day. Domestic reception of broadcast television became the dominant national cultural formation. Of course, nondomestic forms of television persisted, and television sets still beckoned from the windows of electronic shops and remained a familiar feature in shops and restaurants. Many of these ambient venues were also closely connected with privatizing reception of transmission from centralized sources—from the one to the many. At the same time, even in the 1960s, even as the dominant set of usages contributed to establishing the television set above all as a receiver, the television set was also being consistently

FIGURE 7.1. In a 1969 special feature written for *Shōnen Magajin* and illustrated by Minamimura Takashi, Ōtomo Shōji presents the futuristic possibilities of interactive television for educational purposes, with children typing on keyboards, writing directly onto screens, and accessing information.

articulated in a radically different manner: as an interactive computational device, like a computer or monitor.

The vision of the television set as a computer or monitor, as a site of interaction with a computational network, generally entailed a futuristic point of view in the 1960s. In 1969, for instance, in one of his special features written for *Shōnen Magajin* and illustrated by Minamimura Takashi, Ōtomo Shōji imagines the future possibilities of interactive television, with children typing on keyboards, writing directly onto screens, and accessing information within a computational network (Figure 7.1). Even while depicting a futurist scenario deploying fully computational TV, Minamimura and Ōtomo's vision also shows signs of an assembling of polarized tendencies.

On the one hand, their vision of children interacting with screens and participating in a network runs counter the dominant notion of the television set as a largely passive receiver of information transmitted from a centralized source, which in turn positions the television audience as a passive receiver. Their vision thus contrasts with the broadcast system, whose emphasis on the one to many makes for a formation that is at once directional (from the one to the many) and hierarchical (the one stands over and above the many). Minamimura and Ōtomo's vision of television brings environmental and heterarchical tendencies to the fore. Television appears environmental to the extent that its source is now an extensive archive that is activated at its point of access, through the computer or monitor, in response to the needs of and input from the student. Television is happening at the point of access rather than in the broadcast studio. Television also appears heterarchical in that it allows for nonhierarchical connections between nodes in the network: because elements are unranked, there is potential for the emergence of diverse ways of relating or ranking them.[2]

On the other hand, although Minamimura and Ōtomo's vision lessens the hold of the directional and hierarchical forces associated with broadcast television, it nonetheless situates these new computational activities with reference to a powerful center, an educational information center, with an apparently privatized and centralized archive. As such, it conjures up the strategies of social segmentation that Williams included under the aegis of mobile privatization: instead of eliminating the center, there is a multiplication of centers, and presumably students will be commuting from one center (the household) to another (the educational information center). The environmental experience of television thus depends on the construction of an environment, a specific location for access to data, with some form of centralization of data. Such an environment may then become another enclosed site, one amenable to social segmentation. Similarly, the heterarchical tendency implied in the student's interaction with the screen is nonetheless assembled with the hierarchical tendencies of education: even though the teacher has vanished into thin air, removing the frictions usually associated with the classroom experience, educational authority remains firmly in place.

In sum, despite its evocation of the environmental and heterarchical possibilities implicit in point-to-point network tendencies, Minamimura and Ōtomo's vision ultimately entails an assembling of polarized tendencies in a manner that may be characterized in terms of an experience of self-segmenting on the part of the young student. The experience of the student goes hand in glove with the vision of a self-segmenting society, that is, a society that appears to be developing spontaneously toward social movement among multiple centers as it implements ongoing advances in technology. Such a vision is entirely consonant with the discourses on information society emerging in the 1960s in Japan, which, for all their emphasis on the flattening or equalizing potential of the informationalization of industrial production, education, and communication, ultimately tended to shore up and even exacerbate received modes of social segmentation, as Tessa Morris-Suzuki has shown.[3]

It is worthwhile comparing such a vision to Yoshimi's emphasis on *gaitō terebi* as an extension of science and technology fairs. After all, fairs, exhibitions, and expos were among the major sites for envisioning and implementing the point-to-point network tendencies of the television screen, usually by configuring television screens into networked series, often with futurist connotations. Furuhata's discussion of media art installations using multiple screens to "expand" cinema at Expo 70 provides a useful example.

Furuhata describes filmmaker Matsumoto Toshio's "expanded cinema piece *Space Projection Ako,* which featured ten film projectors, eight slide projectors, and fifty-seven speakers," and which received praise for "the immersive effects of the circular screens and the sonic environment."[4] While the use of multiple screens and projectors implies a transformation of cinema into something networked to enhance point-to-point relations, the installation arranges its open series of screens to produce immersion, thus creating an enclosed site that is potentially an expansion of cinema that aligns it with the disciplinary modes of segmentation associated with television networks.

The example of Matsumoto's expanded cinema, like that of Minamimura and Ōtomo's computational TV, serves as a reminder that futurist visions of information networks often imply some sort of recourse to centers. Even when those centers are temporary, tentative, experimental sites that invite participation and interaction, they may also imply an enclosed site—an experiential immersion, privatization, or both. As such, instead of constituting a radical break with the one-to-many tendency, the very situation of fairs and exhibitions may instead invite participation in the multiplication of centers even as they experiment with network tendencies. Again, the result is an assembling of polarized tendencies instead of the radical futurist break that is so often proclaimed.

In the context of expositions, what comes into question is the status of avant-gardism. Sometimes media avant-gardism is discredited as a result of its reliance on corporate funding or government subsidies. This is one way of calling attention to how the multiplication of centers forecloses a genuinely nonhierarchical movement. But my aim is somewhat different. In calling attention to the occurrence of assembling in avant-garde media art, I am not trying to discredit such artwork or denounce its complicity. Instead, I am situating it within a genealogical transformation of the television formation. Nonetheless, such a gesture deliberately undermines the claims of media avant-gardism, even if it does not dismiss the interest of such experiments as art.

In this respect, Masuyama Hiroshi makes an interesting point in his account of Japanese television games or *terebi gēmu,* that is, video games played on a television screen via a plug-in console. In keeping with his stated goal of treating

FIGURE 7.2. Nam June Paik (1932–2006). *Magnet TV* (1965). Modified black-and-white television set and magnet. Overall: 38-3/4 × 19-1/4 × 24-1/2 inches (98.4 × 48.9 × 62.2 cm). Whitney Museum of American Art, New York; purchase, with funds from Dieter Rosenkranz 86.60a-b. Copyright Nam June Paik Estate.

television video games as media, in a section aptly entitled "An Other Television," Masuyama situates the origin of TV games in Nam June Paik's 1965 installation *Magnet TV*.[5] The setup for *Magnet TV* is simple: a large horseshoe magnet is placed atop a television set, and the TV set's reception of its magnetic field shows on the CRT screen (Figure 7.2). The implications of this simple setup are nevertheless profound. It is easy to understand why Masuyama calls on this work to establish the media origins of TV games: when you move the magnet, the pattern on the screen changes. The paradigm of televisual receptivity is fundamentally changed. Instead of patiently or faithfully conveying a transmission from a distant, absent source, the TV is receiving input from its would-be audience. The audience now is transmitting information and receiving it. The audience is playing the TV, rather as if they were playing a musical instrument. People play the TV in order to affect what appears on the screen. They receive feedback from their play too.

This play with the TV conjures up the charged field underlying the experience of television reception. In the 1960s, and even into the 1990s, this television field became especially tangible when people fiddled with antennas or jockeyed with the position of the TV in the room in order to improve the quality of reception, sometimes repositioning antennas and even the sets when they changed channels. The example of *Magnet TV* beautifully reveals how the television generates spaces of play—we might also say sociotechnological fields of interaction—in a medial fashion, prior to transmitting or displaying any particular content. In this respect, the example suits Masuyama's purposes well, for he proposes to look at television games first and foremost in terms of media rather than contents. The apocryphal scenario of TV audiences watching the fizz and snow on dead channels again comes to mind. For it is also an experience of the television field. Like any field or set of forces, the television field may not seem to be there, to be real, and yet it really is there, and is real—just as a magnetic field becomes visible and tangible when you sprinkle iron filings on a sheet of paper and apply a magnet. Television too generates a charged field. Needless to say, it is precisely this charged field that was targeted by regulatory measures in the wake of the Pokémon Incident.

The production of a TV field of play through *Magnet TV* also provides insight into the effects of frequency allocation, in which a frequency, which is not an enclosed space, starts to operate like an enclosed space. In frequency allocation, a charged field is being transformed into a zone, which then functions as a channel for a specific station. Likewise, *Magnet TV* transforms a magnetic field into a charged television field. Significantly, Masuyama describes it as a space. A charged field may indeed turn into a space or zone, for you can move into and out of the television zone, interacting with it with differing degrees and registers of attention. It does not contain or enclose you. In fact, with frequencies, fields, and zones, there is a built-in resistance to enclosure, so to speak. Where frequency allocation strives to transform the charged field and perceptual zone into an enclosed site, *Magnet TV* reopens the potential for field and zone effects around the television set.

In this respect, the example of *Magnet TV* seems closer to Yoshimi's account of *gaitō terebi* than to the large frictionless immersive spaces of multiscreen cinema installations at Expo 70 in Furuhata's account. It also stands in sharp contrast to the futuristic educational information center in Ōtomo and Minamimura's vision. Note, however, that the success of *Magnet TV* depends on avoiding networks. Its focus on the media platform brackets both broadcast and computer infrastructures. It thus differs profoundly from the educational information center and multiscreen installations that strive to bring network infrastructures to the fore. Oddly, however, when networks are brought to the fore in these futurist visions, the overall effect is toward a multiplication of centers (sites of enclosure) rather than a truly environmental and heterarchical media field. In contrast, by bracketing networks, *Magnet TV* provides a tool for repurposing your television set, for generating a charged field, outside the network. It thus enjoys greater success in generating an environmental and heterarchical media field of television play.

In sum, *Magnet TV* reconfirms that networks or point-to-point tendencies are not a guaranteed solution to or advance over the procedures of segmentation

a

b

associated with broadcast television, precisely because there is always an assembling. But what happens when the field of television play becomes configured with networks and broadcast infrastructures? Is it possible to envision something other than a multiplication of enclosed sites?

Surprisingly, television animation in the 1960s was already ahead of the game, precisely because it did not (indeed, could not) place itself beyond broadcast television. Consequently, its futurist visions of the computational dimensions of television directly address their assembling with the one-to-many tendencies of broadcast. Take, for instance, the series *Big X* (*Biggu ekkusu,* 1964–65).

After the tremendous success in 1963 of Tezuka Osamu's television-animation adaptation of his manga *Tetsuwan Atomu,* known as *Astro Boy* or *Mighty Atom,*

c

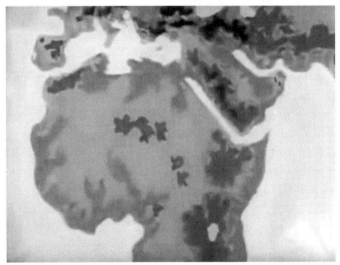

d

FIGURE 7.3. The first episode of the series *Big X* (*Biggu ekkusu*, 1964–65) begins with a scene of destruction unfolding (a). Then, as the viewing position pulls away from the scene, it appears on a large screen, with a professor standing in front of it to explain the perilous situation (b). As the professor speaks to the audience, the screen shifts to a map (c), and the viewing position pans across the map to seek the locations of the villains (d).

other TV stations and studios rushed to produce animated series for the small screen. *Big X* was an animated adaptation of another Tezuka manga title, produced at a time when demand for television animation was high yet experienced animators were hard to come by. Tokyo Broadcasting Station (TBS) thus financed its production with an emerging television studio, Tokyo Movie (Tōkyō Mūbī), intent on making animation under the direction of Fujioka Yutaka. The first episode of 1964 begins with a scene of destruction unfolding (Figure 7.3a), and then, as the viewing position pulls away from the scene, it appears on a large screen, with a professor standing in front of it to explain the perilous situation (Figure 7.3b). As the professor speaks to the audience, the screen shifts to a map (Figure 7.3c), and the viewing position pans across the map to seek the locations of the villains (Figure 7.3d). The same map later shows marks, as if someone had written on it to indicate positions. In other words, the scene uses the screen to move from location to location, with the viewing position moving out of the screen and back into it.

The conceit is so commonplace today that it may escape notice. Yet what happens is unusual: in the blink of an eye, the television screen has shifted from operating as a transmitter–receiver to operating as a computer–monitor. The scenario builds on techniques used in TV news: showing footage of an event, then turning to a map showing its location. In terms of image type, then, the sequence presents a quick shift from something like documentary or reportage to an operational or instrumental image—a shift not so uncommon in television news. In the sequence from *Big X*, however, the manner of panning over and focusing in makes the map appear interactive. In terms of media, the shift implies an ability to switch between receiver and computer within the television formation, which goes beyond what is normally associated with broadcast TV news—evoking what today is associated with interactive media technologies and applications, with computers and the Internet.

The effect may be attributed in part to the use of highly limited animation. There was little time or budget to produce smooth transitions or relationships between different types of images. In fact, you can sometimes detect inconsistencies in the rendering of the same character. Interestingly, however, the media effects attributable to limited animation prove consonant with contemporary media networks, in which media platforms switch readily between computer networks and broadcast networks. What is more, these effects display, albeit in the blink of an eye, an assembling of polarized tendencies. It all happens so easily that you might think it is being erased or eliminated. Yet the same effect of assembling becomes slowed down and prolonged in the series's dramatization of flash effects to depict frequencies and transmission, which are commonly rendered as brilliantly white lightning bolts.

The lightning bolt is an iconic figure for indicating electromagnetic or electric discharges of all kinds. In *Big X,* this iconic figure is used to signal acts of transmission. For instance, the young boy carries an amulet, a handheld device that emits lightning bolt flashes to transform him into the giant hero Big X (Figure 7.4). Similarly, the villain deploys some sort of electromagnetic discharge weapon to destroy the heroes' station, and this "electricity" is rendered with lightning bolts (Figure 7.5). The effect extends to radio transmissions, which are represented as jagged white bolts from a transmitter (Figure 7.6). Such electric or electromagnetic effects situate the action within a world of military operations that involve locating, monitoring, and tracking. This world of point-to-point logistical operations is contrasted with broadcast techniques, which are also rendered in an iconic manner, with wavelike circles radiating from the tip of a broadcast tower (Figure 7.7).

FIGURE 7.4. The young boy carries an amulet, a handheld device that emits lightning bolt flashes to transform him into the giant hero Big X.

FIGURE 7.5. The villain deploys some sort of electromagnetic discharge weapon to destroy the heroes' station. This "electricity" is rendered as lightning bolts that flash across the screen.

FIGURE 7.6. The flash of lightning effect extends to radio transmissions, which are shown as jagged white bolts from a transmitter.

In sum, in the 1960s, at the time when the one-to-many tendency of broadcast television had established its dominance through an effective subsuming of point-to-point tendencies, limited animation was discovering and experimenting with the point-to-point tendencies residing within broadcast television itself as a sort of intra-active and infraindividual potential. Consequently, unlike initiatives that sought a rupture with or overcoming of broadcast television by embracing network tendencies (Matsumoto's expanded cinema or Minamimura and Ōtomo's computational TV), television animation found itself internally constrained by broadcast tendencies, which encouraged experimentation with the assembling of polarized tendencies. Its experimentation was at once practical and imaginative, pragmatic and speculative. As the example of *Big X* indicates, the result might be described as "*gaitō terebi* in the house" or "magnet TV games in the street," implying a continuous assembling of militarized logistics and privatized centers (households and companies). Developments in the 1970s and 1980s, to which I now turn, would lend greater consistency to this limited

FIGURE 7.7. In contrast with the lightning effects that signal point-to-point logistical operations, broadcast is rendered with wavelike circles radiating from the tip of a broadcast tower.

television animation mode of assembling that was arising within the national domestic television formation.

Videocassette Recorders (1970s)

The 1960s saw various experiments speculating about the transformation of the television set from a broadcast-centered transmission-receiver to a network-based information-computer, which implied quite different kinds of media practices and experiences. Where broadcast television tended to impose directional and hierarchical patterns onto the audiovisual flow, the interactive computer or monitor promised to allow environmental and heterarchical flows. In the 1960s, situations were already arising in which television screens were being used as something other than receivers of transmissions, for instance, the broadcast booth and closed-circuit television. The broadcast booth offered a bank of screens that showed image feeds from various sources, which eventually enabled new techniques of live editing, especially for sports events. In effect, closed-circuit television followed directly from the broadcast booth: a bank of screens displayed the image feeds from cameras strategically situated to allow for surveillance of a building or complex—techniques of live monitoring. These new sets of techniques—live editing and live monitoring—are similar in that they involve ways of establishing and entering into a flow of images to produce a circuit or a closed system.

While such techniques remained in the background compared to speculation about and experimentation with computational television, they were already enabling a practical assembling of polarized tendencies. At the same time, even though they both use multiple screens in order to channel information instead of receiving transmissions, the broadcast booth and the surveillance booth reinforce the one-to-many tendency even as they transform it: there are now editing centers and monitoring centers. Such techniques would eventually come into play within the household assembling of television and new media, transforming everyone into editors and monitors of image flows. First, however, the household television set had to realize something of its potential as an information and computational device. This realization began with the introduction of two peripheral devices that came to be plugged into or hooked up to the television in the 1970s: television console games, and VCRs or videotape recorders (VTR). Remote controls also entered the mix, amplifying and delimiting the charged field of television play.

The history of this medial expansion of television within the household is exceedingly complex, with economic, governmental, social, cultural, and other implications. For my purposes, I wish to focus on how this expansion of television involved a suspending of the dominant one-to-many paradigm of broadcast television, which activated other possible formations for television through an intensification of the television screen.

Commentators in the early 1970s were quick to speculate about transformations of television due to the advent of VTR or VCR. In an overview of communication trends in Japan between 1970 and 1975 (written around 1977), for instance, Katō Hidetoshi speaks of an information explosion in conjunction with increased diversification of media, situating the VTR among "technological devices . . . made to 'tailor' information to the particular individual needs."[6] Katō shows enthusiasm for smaller media systems. In a medium such as cable radio, for instance, he sees "the basis for grass-roots democracy." His account of the VTR, however, remains descriptive and noncommittal: "Market researchers forecast that these simple video-cassette tape recorders will be among the most promising commodities of the 1980s, and the market is already rapidly expanding. With this new equipment, the nature of television viewing may gradually change. Viewers, after recording their favourite programmes, either for education or entertainment, may prefer to repeat these programmes rather than to watch broadcasting."[7]

The market for the VTR or VCR did expand rapidly, and Japanese companies were key players in the market, making the VCR one of the great success stories in Japan's bid to dominate the global electronics industry. In their marketing history of the VCR, Higuchi and Troutt note, "At the beginning of the VCR industry, nearly all manufacturing facilities were located in Japan. Even though a substantial global demand existed from the beginning, Japanese companies exclusively manufactured them in Japan and exported products to the rest of the world."[8] Indeed, for Higuchi and Troutt, the VCR offers the most complete paradigm for a successful product life cycle, shifting from local manufacture to the use of supply chains.[9]

Because sales of VCRs swelled throughout the 1980s, reaching a peak in the 1990s, we tend to think of the 1980s and even the 1990s as the heyday of the VCR. Yet already in the 1970s, speculation about their impact on broadcast television was common. As Katō predicts, people would begin to record programs to watch them when and as they pleased instead of adhering to broadcast schedules. People would also begin to rent, collect, and lend videos, not only developing circuits of exchange that often redefined the boundaries of what was considered legal but also watching and listening to materials in ways not anticipated by producers and distributors. Katō anticipates such developments when he emphasizes how the VCR allows for tailoring information to the particular individual's needs. In his gloss on the VCR in the late 1970s, Katō has, in effect, encountered the same problem as Yoshimi in the early 2000s. Recall how Yoshimi found, in the breakdown of audiences' adherence to stable programming schedules as a result of personalized media usage, evidence for the demise of television, that is, the national domestic television formation. Katō likewise imagines how the VCR undermines the formation of broadcast television because of the rise of an individualizing form of information usage.

This way of thinking about the implications of the VCR for broadcast television tends to introduce an opposition between on the one hand personalization and privatization, and on the other hand the public or public sphere. In this way of thinking, even if broadcast television is considered a flawed or degraded public sphere, it is nonetheless placed on the side of the public, and even community or citizenship. The VCR, however, is almost exclusively associated with the privatized household, which is now threatening not only to abandon its synchrony with the nation-state but also to lose all sense of community or collectivity. It is as if the "many" of the one-to-many tendency had dropped out of the picture, leaving only a lonely, isolated, privatized "one"—one whose connections to the many would bypass mediation via a communal formation, that is, some sort of community recognized or recognizable as such. Such concerns about excessively privatized individualization commonly arise in contexts in which personalization is associated with consumerism. The inverse interpretation—that individual consumers are forming new kinds of community—is equally common. The new kinds of community may then be (and often are) evaluated for the degree to which they make for a genuine public.[10] Thus it becomes possible to ask: is there such a thing as a VCR-based or VCR-mediated public sphere?

While such questions are important, they bring into play powerful and often normative assumptions about what constitutes a public or a community, which implies in turn certain assumptions about households and about media usage within households. Another level of abstraction, with less investment in these norms, thus merits careful consideration in this context: the diagrammatic forces of distribution brought into play by the VCR.

The VCR entails a complicated set of relations with broadcast television.[11] On the one hand, as a player or playback device, the VCR extends the basic orientation of television toward the production of distribution over and above the production of content. Just as broadcast television in Japan initially relied on importing content from other markets (particularly American TV shows) and from prior media formations (notably cinema) in order to make a dent in its distribution capacity, so did the VCR appear in advance of any original content specifically produced for it. The VCR thus spurred a process of repurposing and remediating television shows and movies, and of importing and subtitling foreign content, especially movies. The impulse was to put everything on videocassette, to make it a vehicle for transnational flows of content. Regulations were concurrently introduced to assure that videocassettes remained specific to regions, to avoid challenges to the established circuits of distribution.

On the other hand, as a recording device, the VCR allowed home audiences to do their own repurposing of content rather than wait for producers and distributors to provide original or remediated content. Indeed, the experience of the video copy, even if degraded, becomes an experience in its own right—for example, the delight of low-grade pirated circulation.[12] In this respect, the VCR appeared to ready to fill the gap introduced by the priority of the production of distribution over the production of content within television. It strives to fill the gap, however, by redistributing content, thus giving priority to processes of remediating or reformatting media forms. It is in this respect that it anticipates the computational: the priority of distribution over content production encourages a situation in which format begins to take priority over content, and ways of possessing content (personalizing) enter into conflict with laws about owning content (copyright).[13]

Williams, it may be recalled, stressed how television differed from cinema in this respect: the film industry made movies and then sought ways to distribute them; the television industry made distribution capacity and then sought ways to fill it. It is not surprising, then, that when the ascendency of digital media pushed film scholars to reevaluate the status of their medium, the historical transition of film to video also came to the fore. David Rodowick describes the situation poignantly: "I mark my personal experience of the end of cinema around 1989. . . . I saw that Pasolini's entire *oeuvre* was available on videocassette. . . . For film scholars, only a few short years marked the transition from scarcity to an embarrassment of riches, though at a price: *film had become video*."[14] It is interesting that Rodowick's account situates the end of cinema in the late 1980s, which is also the moment Yoshimi establishes for the demise of the domestic broadcast formation as well as the time when historians of Japanese television speak urgently of the transformation of broadcast television into new media. Evidently, then, the transformations wrought by the VCR, both to broadcast television and to cinema, had become abundantly clear by the late 1980s and early 1990s, marking the transition into an era of new media.

If we step back and consider the relation between video recorders and broadcast television, we may then move away from an epochal imaginary based on radical breaks in which there are successive era of media, with each new medium striving to totally subsume the previous one: cinema, television, video, digital media, computational cloud, and so forth. Instead of total subsuming, assembling comes to the fore. In the early 1970s, as Katō suggests, the VCR had already began to operate with and through broadcast television: suspending the reception of broadcasts, it suspends the effective subsuming of point-to-point tendencies within one-to-many tendencies. Point-to-point tendencies appear anew, but now they appear above all to be wired, jacked into the television set, in contrast with the wireless nature of broadcast. This is how the VCR would come to feel consonant with a wired world, with domestic networking and home computing. From the perspective of the 1970s, we see that the wired world, which will become dominant in the 1980s and 1990s, comes from an intensification of polarized tendencies born of the gap between distribution and production that broadcast television had allegedly, but not actually, overcome. By jacking into TV sets, video recorders produced a jacked-up TV—an intensified wired world television.

Home Video Game Consoles (1970s–1980s)

The home video game console is the other key component of this wired world of intensified television emerging in the 1970s. Like the VTR or VCR, the home video game console gives constitutive precedence to the production of distribution over the production of content, making for a generative interval that commercial and other interests strive to resolve or at least stabilize, to their profit. The production of devices for playing games on the TV screen outpaced the actual production of games at the outset. Although Magnavox released the first home video game console, the Odyssey, in the 1972, it is Atari's *Home Pong,* released in 1975, that is usually regarded as the first successful console.[15] The success of *Home Pong* came of adapting the wildly popular *Pong* arcade game for the television screen. The Odyssey did not catch on for a number of reasons, among them the lack of attractive content, while Atari's console had apparently solved the gap between distribution capacity and production of content by making the console and its content one and the same thing. The gap ran deeper than that, however: there was more money to be made by selling consoles than by selling games, yet without a range of interesting games, who would buy the console? This emerged as (and remains) the generative interval for home video games: without a gap between platform and content, the market stagnates, yet if the gap becomes too wide, the market collapses.[16] The entrance of Nintendo in the late 1970s and early 1980s provides an instructive, almost paradigmatic example.

The popularity of *Home Pong* encouraged Japanese toy manufacturers to leap into the business of exporting video games to the American market.[17] Thus, although historically known as a game and toy company, Nintendo entered the games console market at an historical moment when the bid to dominate the electronics market was spurring companies like Mitsubishi to consider licensing and manufacturing consoles. Indeed, Nintendo picked up the license for the Magnavox Odyssey, which Mitsubishi had dropped, and updated the Odyssey to meet the standards set by newer consoles from Magnavox and Atari. Thus Nintendo launched its Color TV Game 6 in 1977. In the meantime, drawing on the boom in popularity of Japanese arcade games licensed for distribution in North America, Atari had started to license and adapt these games for its home consoles. In 1980, Atari released a home console version of Taitō's 1978 arcade game *Space Invaders,* and in 1981 Namco's 1980s arcade game *Pac-Man.*

It seemed that a successful game could assure sales of a console, which inspired a reconsideration of the relation between platform and content, which were called, respectively, game hardware and game software *(gēmu sofuto).* It now seemed as if content might actually drive the market, which encouraged both increased production of game software and new strategies for controlling the relationship between platform and content.[18] As new brands of consoles emerged, regulatory measures gradually became focused on licensing and adapting content across platforms, including home computers. Thus, Parker Brothers received a license to produce cartridges of Konami's 1981 arcade game *Frogger* from Sega, which held distribution rights in North America—and the cartridges were compatible with various consoles as well as with home computers. In other words, licensed distribution of content promised to spur the sales and use of more kinds of platforms for playing games, yet the actual capacity of these platforms continued to outpace content.

In her study of television and new media, Sheila C. Murphy calls attention to the ways in which "companies like Atari, Commodore, and Magnavox maximized the connections between televisions and computers that were made in the 1970s and early 1980s, during the first wave of popularity for home video game systems and personal computers."[19] Put another way, in the context of home video games, a functional analogy was created between the television screen and the computer screen by way of the game console. As with the VCR, the game console suspended the transmission-receiver operations of the TV, transforming it into an information-computer. Using the terms "hardware" and "software" to refer to game consoles and cassettes reinforces such an analogy.

At the same time, at another level, the game console, like the VCR, expanded the constituent interval of broadcast television, for it once again relied on the production of distribution capacity over and above the production of content. What these platforms bring to the fore, albeit in a new register, is the basic television problematic of how to go about assembling polarized tendencies. By shifting the scope and sites of assembling, the process of plugging devices into the TV set brings new intensity to that constituent interval. Consequently, the history of video games cannot be treated in isolation from the history of broadcast television. In his philosophy of video games, Mathieu Triclot signals some of the consequences of functional and medial entanglement of video games and television:

> But the television set is not simply a vehicle for the diffusion of contents. The television is not some virgin space that the video game may force into compliance with its own logical ends, without consequences. First, because programs already exist, with contents, visual conventions, and an entire discourse in images, the video game must compose with them. If we envision the form that sports games will take on the console, it is not so much a matter of simulating the actual practice of a sport as it is of imitating how matches are represented on the screen.[20]

Video games, then, bring questions about transmedia to the fore, and Triclot's account invites a consideration of two levels. On the one hand, it is possible to speak concretely of an interaction between two media individuals, which would largely be a matter of resemblance, whether it arises in the register of character, genre, or stylistics. Looking at Japanese video games of the 1980s, for instance, it is difficult not to note certain kinds of resemblance with manga and anime in terms of character design, genre conventions, use of sound and music, and manners of movement that are linked to the distinctive flattening and compositing of foreground and background layers of the image that makes for a multiplanar image. On the other hand, something is also happening at an infraindividual level, where games, manga, and anime are intra-acting. You feel their semblance, but when you look at each of the media forms more analytically, you then start to perceive their distinctiveness; you begin to separate them in such a way that you only detect a play of resemblance and unlikeness. The media mix thus operates at both levels: a perceiving of resemblance and difference that can readily be made conscious and schematized, and a feeling of semblance that happens on the fringes and in the interstices of media individuals.

This is precisely where Nintendo transformed the video game scene. As sales of its consoles became significant as a result of the popularity of home adaptations of Japanese arcade games, Nintendo moved into the production of content for arcade games. The result was *Donkey Kong* (1981), a game often credited with transforming the video game industry through its introduction of story lines (Warren Robert's *Adventure* is another candidate). Where previous Japanese arcade games had made character design and even character expression central to the game experience, Miyamoto Shigeru, the designer of *Donkey Kong,* added elements of story to them. Significantly, he claims to have drawn inspiration from manga: "Thinking back, I would say that although it wasn't done consciously, I ended up designing *Donkey Kong* like a traditional Japanese four-panel *manga* comic strip. That way of telling a story in four distinct parts seemed natural to me, so I created four separate screens from the opening to the conclusion. The programmers were able to do this, but they told me at the time that I was essentially asking them to make four separate games."[21]

While Miyamoto's comments encourage us to look specifically at four-panel manga for the basic story patterns of his game designs, it is worth recalling that as a result of long-standing conventions for adapting manga into animated films and television series, such story patterns might be more broadly considered to be elemental compositional forces. They are not only properties of manga but also orientations for composing that were already at work across manga and anime at the time of *Donkey Kong,* and were later extended to other media forms such as console games and visual novels. As such, when Miyamoto says that his use of such fourfold movement was not conscious, he may be taken at his word. We might think of it as a nonconscious compositional force—a mangalike feeling operating on an infraindividual level across media. As such, although *Donkey Kong* is often singled out for its contribution to storytelling within video games, it also poses a challenge to received understandings of narrative.

The structural analysis of narrative introduced a fundamental distinction within narrative itself: story versus narrative discourse, or fabula versus *syuzhet* (subject), or the "what" versus the "how" of narrative.[22] Typically, the fabula or story is a series of events, which remains open to serialization, but discursive or subjective effects tend to introduce a sense of closure, even if that sense of closure is held in suspense (nonclosure or closure under erasure). In the case of *Donkey Kong,* the end of the game comes when Mario defeats Donkey Kong to rescue his girlfriend. Yet this story line happens across a four-level process that is at odds with received notions of narrative closure. While *Donkey Kong* allows for a story arc with a definitive end (moving progressively from levels 1 to 4 in order to win the game), this end does not necessarily function as a closure, for the four-level process makes for other possible paths without a definitive end (getting stuck at level 2, returning to one level, remaining at level 3, maybe because you like level 3, and so forth). As such, play pervades narrative, opening it to different series. The "how" or the "subjective closure" of the game comes of how you play through it. In effect, play takes the place of narrative discursiveness and subjectivity. Play provides the subjective technology, so to speak. Terms such as "fabulating" and "story-playing" better describe this arrangement than storytelling or narrative. It feels closer to myth, epic, and folklore (with slapstick) than to the bourgeois novel or bildungsroman.

A game like *Donkey Kong* makes the four-panel manga, which commonly entail gag setups, retroactively feel akin to story-play in television games. Yet this kinship or semblance is more a matter of intra-action between media forms such as manga and games than it is a matter of resemblance at the level of interaction. It is worthwhile trying to spell out the concrete intersections between manga and video games: character design, use of archetypal figures, generic conventions, multiplanar space, surface depths, voice acting, sound and music loops are a few possibilities. Yet because it occurs at the level of infraindividual intra-action as well, story-play conjures forth a media ecology—a plane of composition that comes prior to media individuals—that allows for their ongoing individuation. To use Simondon's terms, this plane is preindividual, activated in a transindividual manner. It explains how games may accommodate themselves to the conventions of television mentioned by Triclot, and how television programs in turn will accommodate themselves to games.

In their account of *Donkey Kong*, Uemura Masayuki, Hosoi Kōichi, and Nakamura Akinori devote a good deal of attention to the discrepancy players experienced between the arcade and console versions of the game. They find evidence that adults who already had experience with arcade games were the first to appreciate the console version of *Donkey Kong*, while children felt greater discrepancy between the arcade and the home console versions. Nonetheless, all the players thought that although the console game looked the same as the arcade game on the screen, the experience was quite different.[23]

Nick Monfort and Ian Bogost's study of the Atari Video Computer System comes to mind in this context, for they call attention to how, in the early days of video games, because Atari's VCS (Video Computer System) did not provide services for graphics rendering, the "programmer must draw each frame of a program's display manually to the screen."[24] As such, the mechanism of the CRT screen at once constrained programmers and facilitated certain forms of design, for designers were composing with the movement of the electron gun or scanning finger as it composes the TV image: "This task requires that the programmer write carefully timed code that fits the motion of the television's electron beam," which Monfort and Bogost beautifully sum up with the phrases "pacing the beam" and "racing the beam."[25] Thus we return to the stuff of blink. As game programmers and designers work with the affordances or orientations of the CRT TV screen, they are cutting out and composing with strips of blink. The result is a specific kind of movement built of blinky stuff, and the figures that carry out that movement—beginning with the Ping-Pong balls of *Pong* and extending into the snapping mouths of *Pac-Man*—come to embody that blinking. They are folded strips of blink with their flickering, jiggling, pacing, flipping, gobbling forms. It is surely no coincidence that the chomp-chomp or *paku-paku* of *Pac-Man* evokes something like the flash effects or *paka-paka* associated with the Pokémon Incident. It is also worth recalling in this context that photoepileptiform seizures were first associated with arcade games, then handheld games, and then animations—above all, those of Nintendo.

New Media TV (1980s–1990s)

By the late 1980s, "new media" had become a buzzword in Japan. In an influential account, television historian Shiga Nobuo established 1984 as the year of new media, referring to the use of this term in a 1983 essay by American scholar Martin Robert.[26] Shiga also notes that Japanese electronics makers were initially responsible for the widespread use of the term. But scholars of television and media opened the question of new media beyond the domain of electronics or media platforms such as the television set, the VCR, and the game console to pose broader questions about media environments due to the advent of satellite, cable, and global television networks. These discussions merit attention in this context for two reasons. First, they provide a strong reminder that transformations in the household or domestic television ecology were not confined to the household but were linked to global transformations in telecommunications infrastructures. Second, because they do not posit a rupture between television and new media, they contribute to a genealogical understanding of broadcast television.

In a 1989 book on the contemporary state of broadcast television, *Gendai terebi hōsōgaku* (Studies in contemporary television broadcasting), for instance, Watanabe Midori includes a final section entitled "Broadcast and New Media." She begins by exploring definitions of the term "new media," drawing on Shiga's discussion. Watanabe notes that although the term "new media" may initially seem to refer primarily to "medium" in the plural, it takes on broader connotations because it addresses what would otherwise be called "new technology" in English. Watanabe here cites directly from Shiga's essay, in which he writes, "As the plural form of medium, media takes on such meanings related to mediation, medium, materials, and life environments. As such, it is not enough to interpret new media in terms of new mediums. It would be more fitting to interpret new media in the broader sense of a new complex living environment [fukugō teki na seikatsu kankyō]."[27]

Following Shiga's lead, Watanabe takes issue with current trends in research that tend to divide the field into "broadcast-type" (wireless) media and "non-broadcast-type" (wired) media. Although she agrees that new media go beyond the confines of contemporary broadcasting, she calls attention to the overlap of wireless and wired networks: "'Broadcast-type' media, such as television and radio, that make use of airwaves are distinguished from 'non-broadcast-type' media that utilize wires, and yet it is impossible to definitively separate them since the two show so much overlap."[28] This is why she thinks that Shiga's notion of a complex life environment—or a sort of ecological complex—best describes the combinations of wired and wireless media that fall under the rubric of new media.

When it comes to how the wired and wireless are combined or assembled, however, discussions of new media become rather vague. Watanabe's discussion shifts into a presentation of the components of the media ecology rather than how it is put together. Generally discussions of television and new media tend either to treat the two kinds of infrastructure separately or to make a list of components. Evaluation thus dwells on the advantages and disadvantages of each infrastructure or component thereof, leaving open the question of how they interact. This is how Hidaka Ichirō proceeds in the final section of his 1991 book, *Nihon no hōsō no ayumi* (The advance of broadcasting in Japan), which is also entitled "Broadcast and New Media."

Hidaka situates television at the forefront of the development of information society. The teleaudiovisual for him is not merely a matter of connecting sound and image and transmitting them but of interweaving streams of multilayered audio and multilayered video. Yet when Hidaka turns his attention to technological transformations related to two new infrastructures, satellite TV and cable TV, he drops qualitative concerns about information in favor of more quantitative description. Instead of focusing on problems that might arise with combining wireless satellite TV and wired cable TV, he calls attention to the difficulties inherent in implementing these new infrastructures individually. Satellite TV demands satellite launches, for instance, which makes Japan dependent on American launch facilities until it develops its own. He also speaks of the 1977 World Administrative Radio Conference for the Planning of the Broadcasting-Satellite Service in Frequency Bands. In other words, satellite broadcast requires new forms of world planning. As for cable TV, it calls for building new girders for wires and laying underground lines, which in turn requires permission to use privately owned roadways.[29] Finally, when Hidaka weighs the advantages of the two infrastructures, he focuses primarily on the quality of image resolution and the number of channels.

Unlike Watanabe, who proposes to move beyond the distinction between wireless and wired media as well as between broadcast and nonbroadcast infrastructures, Hidaka seems to shore up the distinction by treating wireless satellite broadcast and wired cable transmission separately. Even in his account, however, there are signs that the wired world is coming to the fore, and not primarily in the form of cable TV. Hidaka's account of satellite TV includes diagrams, which, unlike other illustrations and tables in his book, present networklike flow sequences that are difficult to parse and are not explained in the text. Watanabe's account makes a similar gesture, as does Shiga's, in the presentation of satellite TV.

Such diagrams are calculated to differentiate satellite television from "old" broadcast television, which was commonly rendered with drawings of broadcast towers and wavelike signal transmission. Where diagrams of the old broadcast television entailed a strategy of visualization geared toward the ascendency of its one-to-many tendency, diagrams of satellite television look decidedly like networks, a series of nodes and relays without center. Satellite diagrams thus signal that satellite TV belongs to the era of a wired world and new media ecology. Hidaka includes such diagrams, but without comment, to reaffirm that satellite television is an information-age computational system. Thus new media are diagrammatically associated with the point-to-point tendency, while broadcast is by default aligned with the one-to-many tendency. The question then is, how is the relation between them changing?

Interestingly, even though he continues to contrast the wireless nature of satellite with the wired nature of cable, Hidaka ends up treating the two as analogous in their information network effects. Ultimately, although his account initially reinforces the distinction of the wired versus the wireless, the transformation in their relation ultimately cannot be understood in such terms. Almost as an afterthought, Hidaka introduces an entirely new distinction, one seemingly intended to supersede the distinction between wired and wireless, between nonbroadcast and broadcast—a distinction that we saw previously in the context of video game studies—between hardware and software, or in Japanese *hādo* and *sofuto*. This distinction actually makes things even more complicated. While the hard/soft distinction mobilizes computational terms and concepts, it is a fuzzy distinction, moving away from a simplistic oppositional stance and approaching the logic of relationality and ecology. At this point, however, because Hidaka does not discuss the hard and the soft in much detail, I will turn to Shiga Nobuo, who makes the hard/soft distinction central to understanding the transformation of broadcast television into new media.

In the concluding section to his 1990 book, *Shōwa terebi hōsōshi* (A history of broadcast television in the Shōwa era [1926–89]), entitled "The Relation between New Media, Satellites, and Computers," Shiga introduces the hard/soft distinction when considering how broadcast television is becoming more like telecommunications.[30] He often returns to this analogy: "Telephones offer a clear distinction between soft and hard, in which the people speaking to one another might be called extremely soft. This is because the hardware being used is leased from some sort of transmission enterprise."[31] In the old days, Shiga later explains, broadcast television differed from telecommunications because broadcast stations actually financed the production of content or programs, which would be exclusively aired by particular stations, at least initially. Now, however, on the contemporary scene, a new business model is making an appearance, in which content is to be produced independently, then sold or licensed in bundles to various providers in order to be deployed on their "hardware." In other words, the distinction between hardware and software, which is usually associated with running software on computer hardware, has been generalized into a paradigm for understanding how media infrastructures work in terms of their overall ecology, which is grounded in a media economy.

In empirical terms, the hardware/software distinction might be called into question. Media content such as videocassettes or video game cartridges are arguably different from computer software. As Masuyama notes in his book on television games, the concept of media is generally thought to indicate a system in which content and the playback system are differentiated, but in the case of television games in Japan, hardware and software were initially the same thing.[32] Content was later associated with software, which potentially collapses a distinction between something like an application and what it runs, converts, or plays back. Still, in light of its impact on the production, distribution, and reception of new media in Japan, the hard/soft distinction merits careful consideration. It may also productively trouble received ways of understanding of television media.

It should be emphasized that Shiga associates the emergence of this hardware/software ecology with the larger transition to new media. He initially depicts this transition in terms of a subsuming of broadcast television within telecommunications, for it seems that anyone can set up a network anywhere: "if you can set up a transmitter and a receiver, you can construct a network."[33] Apparently hardware is becoming so ubiquitous or accessible that networks capable of delivering television programs will be relatively easy to produce simply by leasing access. Of course, things are never so easy, and a number of factors worked against a proliferation of providers and networks in Japan. But Shiga's observation is prescient in its emphasis on how television will be unbundled into telecommunications. It thus seems that broadcast television is being or will be subsumed by telecommunications. Shiga indeed suggests that television was originally part of the larger formation of telecommunications, but was separated from it and granted some autonomy. (Recall that the moment of separation occurred in the 1950s, when responsibility for telecommunications was accorded to NTT, and NHK took charge of broadcast.) In this respect, Shiga's argument runs in the reverse yet complementary direction to Sheila C. Murphy's: television does not invent new media, but rather new media present a return of television into the fold of tele-communications. Television is the outside of the inside of new media, as it were.

Ultimately, however, Shiga vacillates on the issue of whether television is being subsumed within telecommunications. Into his moment of vacillation I would like to reintroduce the problematic of the assembling of polarized tendencies. The emergence of new media makes it obvious that, while telecommunications cannot fully or totally subsume television, television cannot sustain its former autonomy. The discussions of television and new media gathering steam in 1980s Japan indicate the emergence of new sites and moments of effective subsuming—or more precisely of assembling—of polarized tendencies. In the late 1980s and early 1990s in Japan, a new trend toward point-to-point network tendencies became visible and tangible through the rise of new telecommunications media. But the point-to-point tendencies could not (and did not) subsume the one-to-many tendencies. Consequently, one-to-many tendencies will persist into the age of networks, even within software production, and for historical reasons. The history of broadcast has effectively situated point-to-point network tendencies as an internal limit, as a site of potentiality. As such, even when point-to-point networks arise beyond the purview of broadcast television, that is, with a good deal of autonomy from it, broadcast television is potentially configured to profit from them, economically and technologically. This priming of broadcast television for new media brings us to the second challenge of Shiga's account.

Conceptualizations of media mix (transmedia serialization or multimedia franchising) were quick to adopt the distinction between software and hardware. OVA (animation released on videocassette) were dubbed "anime software" *(anime sofuto),* and video game cartridges were styled "game software" *(gēmu sofuto).* Even today, media content in Japan is often called soft, that is, software. This is how the business of media mix production came to be called the "contents industry," to distinguish it from the production of electronics or hardware, while putting them on an equal footing. This also explains how Japan, a country noted for its electronics industry, would gradually be transformed into a place renowned for its contents industry. The answer lies in the production of distribution. The very notion of a contents industry assumes an ongoing priority of investment in the production of distribution over and above the production of content. The idea is that, just as broadcast television entailed a built-in multiplication and proliferation of channels and providers, so too would the expanded television–telecommunication ecology of personal computers and mobile phones stimulate the demand for content. The contents industry thus presumes a continuous expansion in the production of distribution. There will always be more frequencies, more channels, more slots, more ports, more bandwidth.

Under such conditions, the one-to-many tendency associated with broadcast

TV reappears in new guises. Take Nintendo, for instance. Although the home console video game industry fairly exemplifies the regime of new media in which the hardware/software distinction is supposed to do away with the broadcast-style mediation of the relationship between them (in which shows are produced only for specific channels), Nintendo found itself in the late 1980s faced with suits charging it of illegally locking competitors out of the market, "squeezing supply and jacking up prices" to monopolize the market.[34] Atari, for example, filed a lawsuit alleging that "Nintendo has monopolized the video game market by preventing creators of games licensed for Nintendo systems from selling those games for use on competing video game systems, such as those made by Atari."[35] In response, Nintendo objected to Atari producing games that could operate on the Nintendo system, calling it "an illegal appropriation of the proprietary technology in its game systems."[36] Questions thus arose about their strategies for producing closed platforms: "Keeping Nintendo's offerings in demand through rationing supply is one thing. But far more in dispute is the company's other tactic: building the hardware system in its games with a special 'lockout' computer chip, so that only licensed Nintendo software can be played on the system. Mr. Main said that feature is essential to make sure that poor-quality software does not taint the Nintendo name. But other software publishers cannot tap the lucrative Nintendo market without Nintendo's permission."[37]

Interestingly, one of the points of reference for such complaints was the need to produce a free and open relationship between hardware and software within the computer world. In contrast, in the context of broadcast TV, it would be un-imaginable to produce a media platform only capable of receiving signals from one or two broadcasters. But if the point of reference had been cable TV, where it was possible to wire a box to the TV to deliver only one provider's bundle of content, the sense of the situation might have been very different. In any event, Nintendo had to change its business practices based on controlling the relationship between platform and content, which was in effect a new variation on the one-to-many tendency that once characterized broadcast television.

With the advent of new media, Japan's powerful key broadcasters—NHK, NTV, TV Asahi, TBS, TV Tokyo, and Fuji TV—naturally strove to prolong the effective subsuming of point-to-point tendencies. In the 1990s, the key broadcasters were in a financial and governmental position to profit from satellite infrastructures by funding satellite broadcasts; they thus run the major satellite channels today. These key broadcasters led the transition to digital terrestrial TV (DTTV or *chideji*) in the 2000s and 2010s. As of 2011, broadcast in Japan switched over to DTTV, largely through the efforts of Japan's major broadcasters, which have subsequently developed into holding companies, providing "a good example of a legal oligopoly."[38] Associated with the switchover to DTTV was the completion of the Tokyo Sky Tree in 2012, the tallest structure in Japan and the tallest such tower in the world. It is the symbol of the importance of one-to-many broadcast in the digital era.

While cable TV has gradually come to enjoy greater success in urban areas, it never became as prevalent in Japan as it has in North America and Western Europe, for instance. Indeed, Japan's key broadcasters have been quick to dismiss and undermine it. In its presentation of basic knowledge about television in Japan published in 2006, for instance, NTV actually gives a cultural nationalist spin to explain the lower penetration rates of cable television business in Japan:

> Compared with the United States and Europe, Japan has a greater number of relay stations built for broadcasting over public airwaves. Anyone who sets up an antenna can see quality commercial television programs for free, and the custom of paying for television programming has not taken root. In the United States and Europe where paying for television has been well established, however, everyone knows that you cannot watch popular sports, movies and other programs without subscribing to cable television. In multi-ethnic, multilingual societies like the United States and Europe, multichannel services are needed to cover the diverse number of languages spoken. This is generally not the case in Japan. These are some of the major causes for the difference in the pervasiveness of such services.[39]

Needless to say, such a presentation ignores reception fees for NHK and advertising revenues from commercial broadcast while suppressing linguistic and ethnic difference within Japan. It feels like a defensive position: because Japan is a homogeneous public, it does not have any need for the smaller, more privatized, and exclusive "wired communities" of cable. Nonetheless, in her account of how bureaucratic control of television in Japan has historically worked against the formation of public spheres, Chalinee Hirano has noted profound changes in the 1990s: "Technological changes in the 1990s have made it clear, however, that it will be more difficult for the Ministry to sustain its level of control within the rapidly changing environment."[40]

With such examples, I do not wish to give the impression that something unique and unusual is happening in Japan with broadcast television or with one-to-many tendencies. Japan has its specificity, of course, but it is that specificity that should allow for the production of general concepts instead of isolating Japan in its uniqueness. Above all, I do not wish to imply that broadcast television is a bad formation with monopolistic or oligopolistic tendencies that will in time be swept away by new media networks, which will flatten and equalize matters once and for all. On the contrary, the point of looking at the relation between television and new media genealogically is to avoid such simplistic oppositions, which encourage narratives of historical overcoming and transcendence. Such oppositions and narratives make it difficult to understand the contemporary situation in which concentration of media ownership into fewer and fewer hands is occurring alongside increasingly heterarchical and environmental media networks. It is as if we keep expecting one tendency to totally subsume the other. But such total subsuming does not happen. This is because the priority of the production of distribution, both in broadcast and in new media, introduces a gap, a generative interval, between distribution capacity and production capacity, which makes for a polarization of tendencies in dealing with this interval. The point-to-point tendency and the one-to-many tendency emerge together, polarized, introducing a charge and a resistance that makes for a field at once medial and social. If one tendency were really to triumph, to totally subsume the other, the field itself would vanish.

The challenge of accounts of television and new media in late 1980s and early 1990s Japan is that they do not posit a rupture between television and new media. Shiga Nobuo's emphasis on a sort of living environment or media ecology is particularly interesting. Although his notion of ecology remains vague and spontaneously naturalistic, it is clearly intended to avoid categorical oppositions between media formations, such as wireless versus wired, or broadcast versus information or computation. Significantly, when Shiga considers the relation between television and telecommunications, his account vacillates, offering a more complex historical movement, in which telecommunications does not seem able to subsume television, or vice versa. His account therefore opens possibilities for an exploration of assembling of polarized tendencies instead of linear historical overcoming.

The new media ecology can thus be imagined as something other than an inert deterministic environment. Media ecology may be considered in terms of a "charged" topology, charged with polarities arising where forces of distribution encounter relations of distribution. This is precisely where Williams situated the social technology of broadcast television in its heyday—where the distributive capacity of television was being harnessed and redirected into social formations through procedures of centralization, segmentation, and allocation. This chapter has focused on the ways in which new media—at the level of both platforms and infrastructures—transformed broadcast television in Japan from the 1970s into 1990s. Those media transformations did not break with broadcast television but began to open an outside on the inside. Likewise, as the next chapter will show, new media would not result in a break with the social technology of broadcast television but would begin to expose and exacerbate its inner psychosocial tendencies.

8

SOCIALITY OR SOMETHING LIKE IT

HOW DO NEW MEDIA PLATFORMS SUCH AS VCRS AND GAME CONSOLES, AND NEW MEDIA INFRASTRUCTURES SUCH AS satellite and cable affect the social technology of television? In the context of cultural studies and media studies in Japan, this question has been primarily addressed through discussions of media mix and the sociality of otaku.[1] Indeed, discussions of otaku fan cultures emerged in the late 1980s and early 1990s, about the same time that discourses on new media had reached their peak. But before I take up questions about media mix and otaku cultures, I wish to review some of the previous lines of inquiry in order to situate my approach.

Focusing on the Pokémon Incident of 1997, Part I showed where the assembling of television and new media that began in the 1970s and 1980s is headed: toward the emergence of the screen–brain apparatus that treats media use in the manner of substance abuse, shifting discussions of the social impact of media away from concern over how content influences psychology toward concern over how media act on brains. I called this formation media care, but it might equally well be called neurocare or neuronal media care.

Part II has centered on the genealogical backstory for this formation of media care. The goal of looking at this form of power genealogically is to expose its fault lines and to understand the complexity of its anchoring in daily practices as a social technology. Thus chapter 5 laid the groundwork for a genealogical inquiry into the relation between broadcast television and new media, establishing some of the parameters for an account of media ecology. Chapter 6 examined the social technology of broadcast television from the angle of establishment of broadcast television, drawing on Raymond Williams, Michel Foucault, and Yoshimi Shun'ya. Chapter 7 showed how broadcast television, even at the height of its movement toward a one-to-many system entailing transmission from centralized agency to a relatively undifferentiated mass audience, was already riddled with the point-to-point tendencies it had allegedly subsumed, most obviously in the form of peripheral devices such as the VCR and game console. At this juncture, before launching into a discussion of sociality, I would like to pull together these lines of inquiry to clarify my overall trajectory.

Media Care and the Household TV Complex

Williams and Yoshimi agree with the common wisdom that broadcast television takes shape as a one-to-many system. Yet unlike the caricatures of broadcasting common in many contemporary accounts of posttelevision, their accounts show the underlying complexity of procedures of centralization. Famously, Williams characterizes broadcast television in terms of mobile privatization, which bears comparison with Foucault's account of disciplinary power, in which "individuals are always going from one closed site to another, each with its own laws."[2] This is exactly what Williams brings to the fore in his account of broadcasting: people are always commuting to one centralized site or another for working, shopping, or education, each with its own interest, including commercial, legal, or political. But what stabilizes (or makes possible) this incessant movement from one disciplinary enclosure to another? For Foucault, it is the family. The family comes to serve as the relay between the emerging formation of disciplinary power and the waning formation of sovereign power. For Foucault, the shift toward the sovereign family (the nuclear family emerging through the dismantling of the extended family) is the key to understanding psychiatric power: psychiatric power assembles disciplinary power (the closed sites of production) and sovereign power (displaced onto the shrinking family).[3] Similarly, in Williams, the privatized household serves as a relay between centralized sites, but interestingly, in his account, broadcast television appears in the place that psychiatric care occupies in Foucault.

Although Williams brackets questions about psychology and television, his remarks about how television makes these new ways of organizing daily life livable provide some indication of how he might broach its "structures of feeling."[4] In any event, reading Williams's account of television alongside Foucault's account of psychiatric care makes the social technology of media care legible. If Yoshimi's emphasis on how television acts on families, as if from a retreating sovereign center, is also taken into account, we better understand how the family retains its sovereign hold in the heyday of broadcast television by operating as a relay between enclosed disciplinary centers associated with working, schooling, shopping. Broadcast television, then, is not simply in the household, even if that is where the family television set is. Television operates as a relay between the privatized sovereign household and disciplinary enclosures. In effect, it doubles the act of commuting, acting as its affective counterpart. It is not surprising that ambient television gravitates toward sites of resting in passing: the domestic-style TV sets in restaurants and other shops, the oversized screens at major intersections where pedestrians pause before crossing. Conversely, the domestic TV set underscores the status of the household as a relay, a site of resting in passing. As such, although listening to the TV often entails a high degree of immobility, this immobility is now relative to the commuter network, with family members going to school, to work, to shop, and so forth. The social technology of television is profoundly entangled with this differential social mobility.

Its role as relay puts considerable pressure on the sovereign family from within the privatized household, and on its organization of authority and sovereignty. As Yoshimi notes in the Japanese context, television programming was for some time structured to reinforce social hierarchies within the family: golden time was geared toward the father, centralizing his social authority within the household. Yet much as the formerly patriarchal emperor was transformed into a symbolic center for the nation, the authority and centrality of television father is largely symbolic. What is more, as stations, channels, and programs proliferate, there is a de facto flattening of hierarchies. Each member of the family has his or her television, even if they do not yet possess their own television set. Above all, it is the child who comes into question. For many reasons, children become closely associated with television: where today fuss is made about the digital generation, social scrutiny once fell on the "TV kid" *(terebikko),* who would undergo a series of mutations to become the "new type" *(shinjinrui)* and then the otaku. A more recent rubric, increasingly used in relation to female and male otaku, is *dempa* (or *denpa),* which literally means "electromagnetic wave" but which figuratively indicates those whose brains are especially receptive to information transmitted by media, including computers, tablets, phones, and television sets. It is almost like a return to the TV kid, but she is now fully grown and empowered by electromagnetic waves. The TV kid is a problem because television is directed toward children in a way that imparts sovereignty to them within the household in a de facto and technical manner, while the father (or parents) retains sovereign authority in both a de jure and symbolic manner. As such, there are two versions of the household: the ideal of paternal authority and patriarchal sovereignty, and the fact of the household as a relay between disciplinary closed sites, which fragments and flattens household hierarchies, whereby children and youth begin to exercise a kind of televisual prowess that imparts to them an aura of technical mastery and authority. Thus, in its capacity as relay, the household becomes what might best be called a complex. Instead of functioning primarily as a hermetically enclosed site organized in a hierarchal fashion, it becomes more like a set of interconnected and interdependent modes of resting in passing.

Thinking through the social technology of television helps to clarify what is at stake in all the attention paid to such phenomena as media mix and otaku cultures. The appellation "otaku" itself is telling: it refers to the allegedly excessive consumer of the products of multimedia franchises (media mix), who allegedly prefers solitude and isolation within his or her media world within his or her individual room in the household (or tiny apartment). This consumer takes on the name "residence" or "household" *(otaku)*. When the otaku ventures out into the city, it is, again allegedly, only to meet with other otaku in urban areas whose aesthetics recall the personalized media world of his or her room. The otaku is as much as discursive construction as it is an actual mode of social being, and the otaku is frequently treated discursively as something of a scandal, which is why I take care to qualify remarks about otaku with the term "allegedly." I wish neither to redeem nor condemn this social mode of existence in its diverse manifestations. Instead, from the perspective of the social technology of television, I think it becomes clear that the scandal of the otaku is precisely to reveal the role of the household as a relay between disciplinary power and sovereign power—which is today increasing the domain of neural media care. The otaku is the figure of a limit-experience of the social relay technology of television media. The otaku both consumes or consummates this social technology and threatens to push beyond its limits and ruin it. The otaku thus exposes the basic question about the media ecology of the household complex wherein "one of household" is simultaneously a "household of one": how does television hold it all together?

Television's Media Mix

When manga editor, writer, and cultural critic Ōtsuka Eiji began to publish his pioneering analyses of subcultures (otaku) and media mix in the late 1980s, he posed the fundamental question that continues to perplex scholars: what holds the mix together? Over the subsequent decades, various responses have appeared, ranging from Ōtsuka's initial emphasis on narrative to Azuma Hiroki's account of characters and database, as well as to more anthropological and sociological accounts of fan cultures. While there has been a gradual shift in interest toward questions about media and social practices, questions of narrative have persisted, and indeed continue to provide the key to understanding the media mix. Here I wish to show how such questions lead back to television.

As discussed previously in the account of *Donkey Kong*, structural or formal analyses of narrative, or narratology, tend to rely on a distinction between the "what" and "how" of narrative: between what is told (a series of events) and how it is told (narrative discourseness); or between fabula and *syuzhet* in Russian formalism; or more simply between story and narrative discourse.[5] A number of commentators have signaled the key problem of this approach: it subordinates story to narrative discourse and fabula to subject. As such, narratology introduces a bias toward discursive or subjective enclosure, which runs the risk of turning story into a subjectified object.

Ōtsuka Eiji adopts a similar perspective in the context of transmedia serialization. He argues that it presents a situation in which consumers encounter "small narratives" *(monogatari)* that function as parts to be assembled and understood within a large narrative. Ōtsuka's notion of a small narrative is analogous to fabula, while his large narrative recalls the subjective and narrative discursiveness evoked in narratology. But he introduces a significant twist: in media mix, the large narrative is not presented directly but only implied, yet it imparts a sense of overall unity to the serial components, to each of the media instances. Ōtsuka thus finds a sort of narrative closure under erasure at work in media mix, which he calls "world."[6]

Ōtsuka's transformation of the notion of narrative discourse into world makes clear that narrative alone can no longer be assumed to provide closure or subjective enclosure—at least not in any usual sense. It fell to Azuma Hiroki to expand on Ōtsuka's insights and to challenge the paradigm of subjective closure itself.

Azuma announces the end of "grand narratives" (and modern ideals and teleological history), positing in their place a postmodern database structure through which consumers make their own little stories, and nothing but little stories.[7] Azuma has also consistently argued that the resulting transmedia series do not lend themselves to a formal analysis in which story is subordinated to narrative; nor do they lend themselves to a Lacanian style of analysis in which the semiotic is subordinated to (or organized by) the symbolic. In this respect, Azuma's account recalls Derrida's challenge to the subjective privilege accorded to narrative subjectivity within narratology and psychoanalytic theory.[8] Derrida entertained the possible autonomy of story (or fabula) from narrative (or *syuzhet*), imagining a nonhierarchical relation in which each story would be a part of others, at once larger and smaller than itself, yet without subjective or narrative subordination of each distinctive part to any other.[9]

Ōtsuka, Azuma, and Derrida all call attention to the liberation of story from narrative discursiveness and subjective closure (albeit for different reasons), granting new autonomy to fabula and processes of fabulation. Ōtsuka and Azuma link this liberation of story concretely to the material conditions in which each media instance (manga, toy, video game, anime, movie, novel, soundtracks, drama CD) is always already inhabited by the other media instances, and in multiple formats. Such accounts of media mix also frequently evoke the paradigm of simulation. Baudrillard enjoyed great popularity in 1980s Japan, engendering both debates and new approaches to media, and in the context of media, it made sense to dispense with the logic of original and copy.[10] Each media instance is as legitimate as any other as a point of entry into the transmedia series. This is not to say that readers, viewers, gamers, and other users do not favor one media instance over others—in fact, they often consider one to be more legitimate. Ultimately, however, their claims present only one point of entry into and one possible pathway through the transmedia series. This is why Azuma's stance rings true: media mix has, in effect, concretely deconstructed the metaphysical tendencies of narrative. In recent work, Azuma has expanded his discussion to bring questions of play to the fore, much as I did in the prior section by styling fabulation in video games as story-play.

This is where questions about sociality arise, specifically about the social technology of media mix. After all, if fabulation or story-play is serving to integrate media mix, it is legitimate to ask to what sort of individualizing techniques and totalizing procedures are implied. Ōtsuka and Azuma take up the matter of sociality, especially vis-à-vis otaku. Both are exceedingly prolific and deliberately provocative writers, so I don't wish to reduce their interventions on the question of sociality to simple, unified, unchanging positions. Nonetheless, at the risk of exaggerating certain tendencies in their thinking, I would like to highlight something of the general turn in their recent work, with the aim of engaging with their concerns.

Ōtsuka is increasingly concerned with the nationalism implicit in the governmental promotion of media mix business (or contents industry) and with the power of corporations evident in the contemporary mergers of media companies.[11] In other words, where he once dwelled more on individualizing techniques implicit in media mix, he has begun to direct his attention toward totalizing procedures. While his contributions to both sides of the media mix are significant, the middle ground between individualizing techniques and totalizing procedures—that is, the actual social technology of their assembling—tends to drop out of the picture. In effect, the otaku and the corporate executive (such as Kadokawa Haruki) appear to mirror one another: fans are totalizing instances of individualizing techniques, while the executive is an individualized exemplar of totalizing power due to the concentration of media ownership in fewer hands.

In his earlier accounts of otaku, Azuma developed a two-tiered model, speaking of "two images of the consumer: that of solitary animalesque consumer who withdraws into favorite 'small narratives,' cutting off communication with the outside world, and that of the humanesque consumer who actively intervenes in received commodities, constructing a flexible network of communication via the 'grand database.'"[12] What is striking about Azuma's account is how it posits totalizing enclosure happening at the level of individualizing techniques, while it is the larger or grander structure that promises to open into new kinds of networked sociality. Azuma has subsequently pursued both strands of this two-tiered model in various ways. At the individualizing level, where his account frequently hinges on a stimulus–response model of control, he has recently declared anime to be nothing more than advertisements for toys and thus not worthy of closer analysis. He evokes a pure attention economy at the level of individualizing techniques. On the other hand, with regard to the totalizing level, he has continued his inquiry into possibilities for collective will and common interest in the realm of new media.[13]

Reading across these trajectories running through the study of media mix in Ōtsuka and Azuma helps to clarify what is at stake in asking, "What holds the mix together?" while turning the question in the other direction: "What is the compositional force of media mix?" Across Ōtsuka and Azuma, tension appears both in individualizing techniques and totalizing procedures. On the one hand, individualizing techniques imply a tension between an attention economy that appears to totalize the situation by producing enclosures (Azuma) as well as an economy of play and improvisation that may allow for divergence and divagation (Ōtsuka). On the other hand, the totalizing procedures associated with governmental and corporate investment in increasing centralization (Ōtsuka) are tentatively countered by network tendencies toward collective will for the commons (Azuma).

This is where the genealogical perspective on the social technology of television and new media may offer a complementary trajectory. The strength of Azuma's account comes from its scrutiny of new media technologies and gaming. Ōtsuka's experience as a manga writer and critic, in combination with his firsthand knowledge of media mix companies, allows him to write persuasively about marketing and about the relation between manga and anime. Oddly, although television is arguably integral to media mix, it has not been directly addressed. Yet, because the constitutive moment of media mix relied heavily on the movement from manga (print media) to television (electronic media), television has played an significant role in integrating media mix, maybe the integral role, for a number of reasons: (1) television entails a shift in demographic, usually expanding it, but definitely addressing multiple constituencies; (2) revenues from television, based on advertisements, have historically been greater than those from manga, and big manga publishers have relied on anime to retroactively increase the profitability or market share of manga; and (3) the widespread circulation of manga provides a primitive accumulation of attention (sometimes at a loss for the publisher), which the television animation puts to work, buying and selling attention to produce surplus value. This is why even those media mix modes that today begin with toys or video games continue to pass through television animation, usually broadcast television, even if placed in late-night slots *(shin'ya anime)*. In effect, television plays a double role, which, following Williams, can be succinctly put in Marxist terms: it entails forces of distribution and relations of distribution. The forces of distribution make for a media ecology in that the distinct media instances of media mix (toy, manga, novel, film, music, anime) relate to each other through their relation to television's energy cascade. On the other hand, the relations of distribution bring into play the social dimension of media through the dispositions and apparatuses related to media platforms and infrastructures.

An account of television's media mix thus affords a trajectory complementary to Ōtsuka and Azuma, addressing the complex forms of sociality swarming over the attention-charged field subtending the relation between character and world. Addressing this social technology will first demand an account of (1) the attention economy of media and (2) the parasociality of characters, in relation to (3) the world or media ecology of the household complex. The aim is not to determine whether media mix is enslaving or liberating but to better understand the contours of this emerging power formation of neuronal media care and thus its possibilities for dissensus. Thus I will retrace the prior movement across the decades of television media—roughly from 1957 to 1997—with an eye to its social implications.

Attention Ecology

The rise of commercial television reinvigorated modernist anxieties about how the intensification of nervous stimulation threatened to destroy the rational individual.[14] Advertisements in particular, but also strategies for attracting the audience's attention in general, became indicative of a crisis induced by attention. In 1957, for instance, Ōya Sōichi launched his famous invective against television, which he declared was making Japan into a nation of a hundred million idiots: "Viewers," he argued, "were more often drawn by attention-grabbing lowest-common denominator programs that relied on shock or titillation, rather than by programs that appealed to quality thought."[15] Simply put, attention threatened to overwhelm reason and sensation to disable cognition. The logical outcome of such an interpretation of television is an attempt to reintroduce reason, to denounce attention, and to favor cognition, with the aim of promoting quality thought. In response to Ōya's tirade, for instance, came government initiatives to provide incentives for commercial stations to produce and broadcast educational public service programming. In this respect, Ōya's anxieties about attention and sensation did not result in a loosening of totalizing procedures of centralization. Instead, they spurred totalizing procedures—educating the masses, regulating production. Government initiatives to encourage educational programs on commercial television proved unsuccessful, however, and by 1973 such initiatives had come to an end.

Ōya's invective and the resulting government initiatives may be characterized as liberal in that the sense that they involve a moralistic argument about the destruction of the individual in conjunction with a bid for government intervention to protect the individual. Such a stance tends to rely on tacit norms for what constitutes an educated individual. The counterargument that emerged may be characterized as neoliberal in that its stance is to let the market decide: what is good for audiences (that is, what they like) is good for society. This was the general stance of commercial broadcasters in Japan, and Shōriki made remarks to such effect. Ultimately, however, as Foucault persuasively argues, these two stances work together. Because the neoliberal free-market stance will always confront instances in which its laissez-faire stance does not produce the promised social good, it must then argue that the problem is that something is blocking the desired free flow. Consequently, intervention is needed everywhere to allow for laissez-faire. The result is the *ne-pas-laisser-faire* of neoliberalism, which draws on liberal moral invectives in order to authorize intervention in the name of nonintervention.[16] From this point of view, government television initiatives and educational channels such as NHK are not necessarily alternatives to commercial broadcasting; they may readily serve as an ideal supplement to commercialism, and vice versa.

These governmental and commercial stances toward broadcast television, as they whirl around each other, culminate in a generative vortexlike social paradox: intervention is construed not as an intervention but a restoration or emancipation of reality, but if it does not prove effective in freeing flows, then its failure proves that it was, alas, an intervention. This cooperation explains why such liberal and neoliberal stances have proved so persistent in relation to electronic media. In the context of broadcast television, as Ōya's position attests, the social paradox begins with an opposition between attention and reason, between nonrational choice and rational choice. Faced with this opposition, the liberal moralistic stance strives to resolve the situation in favor of reason, to bring the Enlightenment back into the picture. In response to the Pokémon Incident, for instance, we have seen how Peter Entell's documentary film *The Tube* begins with an inquiry into the effects of television and ends with moral panic over Japanese televisual attacks on French Enlightenment values and on reason itself.

As *The Tube* gradually narrowed its focus on the ways in which television screens affect audiences, two attention effects came to the fore: the radiation effect (television projects or radiates at the audience) and the flash effect (the electron gun of the CRT screen fires only half the image at any one instant). Focusing on such effects, the film contends that television overrides human perception and reason. Television thus is first and foremost an influencing machine, a brainwashing device. Entell's investigative journalist, Luc Mariot, then concludes that the television experience "could be very totalitarian." A paradox arises, however, around the notion of immersion: a paradox of the self.

In one sequence, Marion asks Eric McLuhan to stage his famous experiment on projected light (television) versus reflected light (cinema). A movie is projected onto a screen. One group watches the movie from the side of the projector and experiences a reflected image, while another group watches the movie from behind the screen, experiencing projected images. McLuhan found that the group watching projected images experienced the moving images as something personal, as belonging to them, where the reflected images were experienced as a representation of things happening in the real world. His experiment thus gives credence to a hallowed stance vis-à-vis moving images yet attributes it to television: the experience of moving images is dreamlike and immersive, which makes for a self folded back on itself, an enclosure of self. Paradoxically, even as the attention effects of television override your rational cognitive responses and plant ideas in your brain, they lock you deeper within your head. So what is it? Are you completely in your head or totally out of it? Entell concludes that therein lies the neurological and social pathology of television. The total enclosure of self is construed as structurally identical to, or coterminous with, a total enclosure of society. You are too in touch with your head to be reasonable or rationally social because you are highly susceptible. Your skull has become Plato's cave, and someone else is projecting images on its walls.

In a book on the media-induced crisis of attention, Matthew Crawford lays out this social paradox in a more cause-and-effect manner: when advertisements and other attention grabbers crowd into your daily environments, you will tend to withdraw into some kind of activity to avoid the noise, pollution, and constant irritation. Retreating into your head is a protective response.[17] His argument has some parallels with Entell's film, but where Entell attributes the attention attack on reason to television, Crawford generalizes it into a modern condition, evident in a diverse range of social media, such as advertisement, e-mail, Internet pornography, and television programs.[18] Crawford's characterization of the ills of such media is equally severe: he submits that because media incessantly evoke your "orienting response" or "stimulus-driven response," they not only blunt your sense of the affordances of the real world but also prevent you from developing genuine relationships with others. As in Entell's film, the upshot is, you are too much in your brain; you are all skull-encased neuronal firing.

Crawford, however, does not launch into a rescue mission to save reason from attention. In contrast to Ōya who would reinstate education, or Entell and Mariot who would restore the French Enlightenment, Crawford's response to the crisis of attention focuses on skill (which he elsewhere styles as soulcraft), on learning and practicing an everyday skill—"everyday activities that structure our attention"—such as hockey and carpentry.[19] Instead of striving to liberate reason from attention, Crawford's recourse to skill is intended to rescue the soul from the brain, from what he calls "representations." Thus he states that his "philosophical project . . . is to reclaim the real, as against representations."[20] In his account, representations are characterized as personal and even proprietary (they are only in the head, as it were). Crawford finds an alternative to representation-based approaches in James J. Gibson's ecology of perception with its theory of affordances. Such an approach allows him not only to engage with "the world beyond your head" but to consider how "our experiences are not simply 'our own.'"[21] In this respect, his project is entirely consonant with mine. His project offers a compelling way to move beyond the received opposition between attention and reason by deftly showing that the basic problem is not an attack on reason by attention but rather the persistence of what I will call the attention–reason complex, which implies a stabilized configuration of the social paradox generated by the insistence on an opposition between attention and reason.

With respect to dealing with media, however, Crawford's account reaches an impasse, albeit an instructive one. It reintroduces a Neoplatonic divide between reality and representation: all experience of media is placed in the realm of representations, which invariably consists of manufactured realities and fake encounters. Learning and practicing a skill makes for a genuine encounter with reality, with external objects, via affordances. In contrast, media—ads, e-mail, television shows, websites, and so forth—are construed as internal objects, which cut off all relation to the external world, leaving you locked inside the world in your head. Thus Crawford characterizes video games in terms of autism and addiction as well as in terms of the production of self-enclosed worlds, suggesting that social media (texting) entails "a heightened instinct for self-protection."[22] The problem is that in the process of using such media examples to characterize the contemporary social condition, Crawford ends up reducing them to that condition. As a consequence, it becomes impossible to think of media in terms of affordances, skills, or a structuring of attention—that is, as an attention ecology. Media are just the modern condition, nothing more.

In a belated attempt to mitigate this Platonic divide between reality (external object, affordance, skill) and representation (stimulus, response, internal object), he eventually introduces a distinction between positive and negative affordances: "In the *Mickey Mouse Clubhouse,* as in many other manifestations of contemporary culture, dealing with reality through a screen of representation serves to make the world innocuous to a fragile ego and the self more pliable to the choice architecture presented by whatever functionary of psychological adjustment is in charge. The world in which we acquire skill as embodied agents is precisely the world in which we are subject to the 'negative affordances' of material reality."[23] But it is too late: displacing the Platonic divide between reality and representation onto the distinction between negative and positive affordances serves to reinforce the divide instead of calling it into question.

As Monfort and Bogost's study of Atari games attests, it is possible to look at media platforms from the perspective of affordances, even so-called negative affordances. Likewise, even if fan studies may appear too eager to invest any form of fan production with embodied agency and even subversive intent, it is none-theless clear that contemporary culture entails a good deal of skill acquisition, implying a genuine encounter with external objects via negative affordances. Unfortunately, Crawford is too quick to attribute a lack of skill to those domains in which he lacks skill: popular culture and media.[24]

If I have lingered on Crawford's account despite its impasse, it is because his project is in agreement with mine in two key respects. First, his conceptualiza-tion strives to move beyond the opposition between attention and reason, offer-ing glimpses of the formation of the attention–reason complex. Second, I wholly agree with the ethical direction in which his emphasis on affordances over repre-sentations leads: "Affection for the world as it is: this could be taken as the motto for a this-worldly ethics."[25] The world as it is, however, includes social media and popular culture. What would it mean to have affection for this world with popular electronic media as it is?

Here, with a nod to William James and Marx, and drawing on the prior chap-ters, I would like to make some propositions in hopes of advancing the discus-sion of the social technology of television and new media. I propose first to con-sider the contemporary condition in terms of an intersection of neoliberalism and media instead of speaking of only a media condition. As Brian Massumi eloquently demonstrates, instead of placing reason in opposition to affect, neo-liberalism involves a superposition of affect (nonrational choice) and reason (rational choice).[26] Discussions of broadcast television, and of social media or popular media more generally, lead to a similar paradox: attention and reason, although allegedly contradictory, turn out to be superposed. Neoliberalism and media formations intersect, then, on this generative paradox, in which attention-affect and cognition-reason are in superposition. This does not mean that neo-liberal ideologies and media are the same thing. But as their point of intersection becomes stabilized and prolonged, they form the attention–reason complex.

We might also call this complex a condition, but the term "complex" has the advantage of reminding us that this condition is not homogeneously determinis-tic; it is more like a field charged across polarities or contradictions. Superposition makes for a vortexlike field, charged with centripetal and centrifugal forces, with attention as gravitational attractor for flights of ratiocination. Where is reason? Reason lies at the eye of the storm, an experience of Apollonian calm amid the whirling storm, positioned right over the attention attractor. It is an effect of the storm, not its cause, and as such, it does not afford a position of mastery. In fact, it no longer feels so reasonable or transcendent. It feels more like a passing mo-ment of insight, of possible enlightenment.

The attention–reason complex allows us to reconsider the apparatus of media care. In relation to this vortexlike field of experience, the apparatus of media care calls forth individualizing techniques. These are techniques for keeping you in addictive motion while trying to keep you from falling into the black hole of over-dose, seizures, or blackouts, inciting you to find yourself in the process of modu-lating and regulating the relation between your brain and the screen. Needless to say, addiction is an abusive concept: it usually implies a normative perspective, yet the norms remain undefined. They are relative to a cultural and social situa-tion. Commentators generally refer to media as addictive to insinuate that media entail a kind of nonnormative, excessive behavior in which intoxication turns toxic and self-destructive. Everything thus comes to hinge on establishing norms for intoxication, introducing guidelines for safe doses for different populations of users. In this respect, responses to addiction call on disciplinary procedures of segmentation as well as flexible control.

At the same time, the paradigm of addiction introduces a wild card, a singu-larity, because within a population some individuals are more susceptible, and for such a variety of reasons that there appears to be no end to the cofactors to be taken into account. TV guidelines put into place after the Pokémon Incident, for instance, uniformly addressed a large social segment (children) precisely be-cause it is impossible to single out, in advance, those individuals who will be susceptible. At the heart of a segmenting procedure that appears rational and rea-sonable lies something entirely unpredictable and uncontrollable. What is more, the rational procedure not only depends on that nonrational something but also generates it, as it distributes and ramifies its effects throughout the social field. The Pokémon Incident thus provides some insight into the specific parameters for the attention–reason complex of broadcast television: reason takes the form of procedures of segmentation, and attention introduces a dark precursor, an attrac-tor or singularity that justifies the procedures of segmentation, yet gives a charge to the field that defies segmentation. It is, after all, a field of intoxication.

It is possible to consider this attention–reason complex from the angle of totalizing procedures: for instance, how the government allocates frequencies, how stations and channels vie for audiences, and how audiences are thus aligned with privatized commercial interests and national concerns. At the same time, because TV's attention–reason complex sets up a vortexlike charged field of in-toxication, individuals are enjoined to situate themselves. They have to act as self-intoxicating subjects. They have to become aware of their propensities and potentialities in relation to both the dark precursor (the black hole of toxicity) and segmenting procedures. This is how individualizing techniques become inter-nally polarized.

This is why I previously introduced a distinction between work on self and care for self. But now it is possible to speak with greater precision. On the one hand, there are procedures of work on self, which are rather like what Crawford calls representations. They are, in effect, totalizing procedures of self, not because they present a totalitarian overriding of reason through brainwashing attention grabbers but because they take the side of what seems reasonable in a normative, nichelike personalized simulation sort of way. Indeed, Baudrillard applied the notion of personalization to such procedures and situated them within a regime of simulation.[27] His account of simulation meshes with Crawford's discussion of representations in that both address the generation of an autonomous, sovereign, or enclosed self, taking the whirlwind of reason and attention to be its own perfect storm. This is a self-segmenting self.

On the other hand, there is care for self, a notion with Heideggerian overtones recurring in Foucault's discussions of practices of self and self-cultivation.[28] Here too it is now possible to be more precise: care for self is akin to skill in Crawford, for it entails a sense of the affordances of the field intoxicatingly charged with potentially toxic attention (what Crawford calls negative affordances), which allows you to play the television as you might play hockey, play the piano, or make a jig in carpentry. For his part, Baudrillard tries to capture such play in his conceptualization of the renewal of symbolic exchange via the anagram and poetry in contrast to simulation. Care for self entails an individuating process instead of personalizing procedures, which I will tentatively characterize as self-animating processes.

At this juncture, I must underscore that although the individuating processes clearly feel more felicitous than self-segmenting procedures, my aim is not to redeem or to rescue the former from the latter. Such a redemptive rescue mission would grant a degree of autonomy to individuating processes that would ultimately transform them into segmenting procedures. I wish instead to complicate how we look at individualizing techniques. Instead of treating them monolithically, I propose to look at transformations in the assembling of these two tendencies (individualizing and individuating, or self-segmenting and self-animating) as it happens within any particular set of individualizing techniques. My genealogy of broadcast television and new media thus focuses more on individualizing techniques than on totalizing procedures, but with the understanding that the former are also being assembled with the latter. Still, wherever possible, I will address the totalizing tendencies as well.

In the context of individualizing techniques, as Ōtsuka's and Azuma's accounts made clear, it is above all characters that come to the fore—anime characters and game avatars, but also television personalities, actors, personas, and masks—in relation to dramatizing, fabulating, or story-playing. Interestingly, this was precisely the field opened by Katō Hidetoshi in response to Ōya's invective against the nonrational dimensions of broadcast television.

Parasociality

Jayson Chun offers this description of Katō's take on television: "Katō based his essay on the premise of Horton and Wahl's 1956 theory of parasocial interaction, which claimed that because media like television gave the viewer the illusion of a 'face to face' relationship with the performer, the viewer interacted with people on television screens as real people."[29] What appealed to Katō were the ways in which parasocial interactions seemed to counter the received hierarchy of performer over audience, of producer over consumer. Instead of standing on a pedestal and pontificating over the heads of listeners, television personalities and characters appeared to be coming into the home, stopping by to chat, dropping in for a visit. As such, parasocial interactions promised to flatten and equalize relationships between audience and television.

Katō's emphasis on parasocial interactions follows directly from his general approach to cultural production at that time. In the same year Ōya declared television had made Japan a nation of idiots (1957), Katō published a volume of essays, *Chūdan bunka* (Middlebrow culture), in which he argued that the poles of highbrow culture (debates among intellectuals) and lowbrow culture (radio shows, dance halls, movies, and mass publications) had begun to merge in middlebrow culture in the form of weekly magazines and mass-market paperback books that made specialized knowledge accessible.[30] Indeed, as Simon Avenell explains, Katō thought that as a result of cultural developments, "the masses *(taishū)* could be understood as a new civic stratum *(atarashii shiminsō),*" whose politics lay in their strong attachment to ordinary everyday life, which they could be mobilized to defend.[31]

Katō's interest in cultural production thus lay in the possibilities it offered for new social formations based on ordinary citizens, allowing for nonsectarian social movements, which would make for truly democratic politics. Given his interests, Katō tends to look at broadcast television in terms of the opportunities it might afford for flattening received hierarchies (intellectual elites). He does not, however, wish to embrace so-called lowbrow culture; he takes care to situate the progressive potential of television in a sort of middle, potentially nonsectarian ground. Thus, when in the late 1950s and early 1960s he called attention to the ways in which television counters the hierarchies of highbrow culture, he rescued television from what Ōya sees as its only possibility: lowbrow, that is, attention-grabbing, culture. Katō thus drew attention to the ways in which the audience begins to talk back to television personalities, precisely because television has made them into ordinary domestic visitors. The promise of television, for Katō, came of how it brought messages down to a level where ordinary people could both understand and contest them—hence his promotion of media literacy for people to understand how media work.

Put another way, what Katō sought was a way to navigate the vortex of the attention–reason complex. He wished to avoid the pole of reason with its highbrow unintelligible proclamations while steering clear of the black hole of attention-ridden lowbrow culture. His middlebrow movement would draw momentum from each pole in order to equalize their differences along a nonsectarian pathway. His is an extraordinary vision of the power of the ordinary. Such a nonsectarian movement is difficult to sustain, however, because the assembling of polarized tendencies is continuously transforming as a result of the continuous production of television's distributive capacity, and the storm incessantly spirals onward, as if beyond human control. It is not entirely surprising, then, that the parasocial possibilities of television subsequently proved a disappointment for Katō. Rather than trying to navigate the storm, he began to batten the hatches and denounce television. His later denunciation is nonetheless of interest, for it reveals the social problems arising in the context of parasocial interactions.

In 1973, the year in which commercial educational TV initiatives disappeared and in which 88 percent of households in Japan owned television sets, Katō published an essay entitled "Kyozō no sekai: terebi to jinrui" (The world of virtual images: television and humankind). As the title suggests, the essay sets forth a stark divide between the image world and the real world. He writes, "The character on the screen is, needless to say, a unreal image, without any substantial reality. After all, it is nothing but an optical illusion constructed by points of light shone on a glass screen via cathode ray tubes. Television is fundamentally a physical phenomenon, and the creation of images is a matter of physical entities and light. The world of television is thus a world of 'things.' It does not belong at all of the world of 'humans.'"[32]

Katō's use of the term "things" to describe the unreal nature of television images is odd in that it seems to impart an illusory quality to physical phenomena. His point of reference is social interaction between humans, so his usage is in effect intended to debunk the illusion that characters are real. In manner reminiscent of Crawford, his emphasis falls on manufactured reality. The same paradox thus appears: the television image is entirely physical and substantial, yet also artificial or virtual. Indeed, if television images and characters did not possess such a paradoxical nature, they would not be a problem at all. If television poses a genuine problem, it is because its images are at once real (physically constructed) yet unreal (not actual humans). Its images result in a crisis in the distinction between things and humans. Thus Katō insists, "Television, before our very eyes, continues to ply back and forth between the world of 'humans' and the world of 'things.'"[33] As a consequence, television images of humans appear to be as real as actual humans: "A human face transmitted on a twenty-inch receiver, when viewed from below, is almost exactly as large as its actual size."[34] In sum, television does not allow for a distinction between fact and fiction, reality and artifice, actual world and video world.

Note how the affordances of the television screen come into play in Katō's discussion. Apparently, because early TV sets tended to convey smaller images, they could be considered to flatten the hierarchy of screen over viewer more effectively, rendering television personages and personalities accessible. With larger screens, however, the parasocial relation is changing, yet screens are not yet large enough to feel cinematic. In Katō's account, it is precisely the parity between human and image that proves disturbing.

In the contemporary moment, new media are commonly characterized in terms of their lightness, ephemeral values, accessibility, and mobility[35]—qualities once attributed to television—and although television was not so mobile, it was nonetheless deemed ubiquitous and pervasive, particularly in its ambient manifestations. In contrast, when television is today approached from the angle of home theater technologies, it feels like a combination of cinematic and broadcast affordances, which is surely a legacy of the video revolution. Situating Katō's observations in the larger genealogy of media helps to emphasize two points. First, the sense of the affordances of the screen, which makes for parasocial interaction, is not merely relative to other media; it is relational. Second, because parasocial interactions bring a relational field to fore, they are always sites of crisis for categories and oppositions associated with Platonic thought.

For Katō, this crisis becomes especially palpable when the human image enjoys parity with the human viewer, for parasocial interactions have taken flattening too far; the human itself is flattened. Where Katō had earlier embraced the parasocial potentiality of television, now, in 1973, he seems to have reversed his stance. Television, instead of breaking with received forms of sociality and opening the way for new ones, encourages people to spend more time with virtual humans than with actual humans. He writes, "Television in itself is a neutral technique for communication but when it leads us to neglect relationships with living human beings, we reach the point where it offers our minds nothing but unreal images. George Orwell's *1984* is then not so far away."[36] It is as if the old hierarchies and territories had disappeared, but instead of new forms of sociality, everything has turned into individual antisociality and total control. Indeed, Katō does not limit his discussion to television in Japan but speaks to "communications networks that today cover the entire earth."[37] Unlike genuine sociality, which implies material constraints and spatiotemporal limits, this parasociality spreads like a contagion, without respect for received boundaries. The result is the global antisociality of what Katō dubs the twisted self *(fukakai jiga)*.[38]

Katō's evocation of the term "virtual" *(kyozō)* bears comparison with Baudrillard's notion of simulation. For Baudrillard, simulation indicated a total collapse in distinction between reality and representation, to the point where representation actually became more real than reality. As a consequence, Baudrillard thought it was useless to try to rescue reality from simulation, that is, to denounce simulation from the perspective of reality. Calls for returning to reality, in his opinion, merely increased the capacious omnivorous grasp of simulation. Rather than reality, what stands in contrast to simulation for Baudrillard is symbolic exchange, which would be a genuine form of sociality. For Katō's part, while he seems more prone to denounce the loss of reality and the rise of antisociality, there are hints of something like symbolic exchange in his earlier vision of sociality that hinged on educating citizens and organizing nonsectarian movements, which is evident in his enthusiasm for cable radio, in contrast to his lack of enthusiasm for personalizing media such as the VCR in the late 1970s.[39]

In sum, Katō and Baudrillard both suggest that antisociality or nonsociality (Katō's virtual world or Baudrillard's simulation) has gained the upper hand over sociality (Katō's ordinary nonsectarian citizens or Baudrillard's symbolic exchange) to the point where sociality comes to feel impossible. What is more, like Crawford, Katō and Baudrillard associate antisociality with the production of enclosed sovereign autonomous selves due to personalizing or individualizing procedures, which prove to be utterly and irrevocably totalizing. If Katō and Baudrillard feel darker in outlook than Crawford, it is partly because they do not think it is easy to step outside the pervasive mediation of global media. Nonetheless, all three appear to agree that television media culminate in the total subsuming of daily life within the attention–reason complex, for they see individualizing procedures and totalizing procedures to be seamlessly aligned within the parasocial technology of television. Everything thus turns into antisocial automatism. The parasocial entity—the character or persona from the TV screen—is construed as a blockage, as a wall, which encloses the subject in a nonreal world, once again Plato's cave.

It is useful here to recall Foucault's remark regarding "a tricky combination . . . of individualization techniques, and of totalization procedures."[40] Likewise, in the context of broadcast television, Williams remained attentive to the ways in which forces of distribution remained active, even when relations of distribution (corporate, government, military interests) had all but subsumed them. In the same vein, I have introduced the term "complex" in hopes of allowing for a nonnormative perspective on enclosure. From the perspective of totalizing procedures, a complex may feel like an enclosure. It may even function as an enclosure. A complex, however, implies a conjoined series of spaces, which implies a relation to the outside. The relation to the outside may take the form of an actual opening, but the passage to it may nevertheless prove tortuous; or it may take the form of a sort of internal clearing, like a vast courtyard.

Parasocial interactions may feel like enclosures, like self-contained, hermetically sealed worlds, which isolate and imprison the subject, allowing her nothing more than flickering images on the walls—flickering images as walls—that block social interaction. Even in isolation, however, an individual is in relation to the collective. Even when parasocial entities isolate someone, there is still a relation to the real world; there is still a social relation. It may be deemed a bad social relation for various reasons, or a good social relation. In any event, unless the goal is to impose a normative view of the individual and of society by setting them in opposition, the sociality of the parasocial must be acknowledged. In fact, Katō's account, for all its emphasis on twisted antisocial behavior, nonetheless implies that the parasocial entity does not simply block or stop social movement. Let me suggest a specific kind of relation in parasociality: parasociality implies stopping on social movement. It is at once social and antisocial. It is an antisocial social complex, so to speak.

Katō's account provides a reminder that an ethical approach to media has to do more than weigh in on the degree of sociality versus antisociality. The underlying problem might be restated: servility. It is not easy to arrive at a nonservile relation to media and technology. Normative accounts of antisociality make it difficult to conceive of a nonservile relation to media, yet antisociality cannot be ignored. The field of fan studies often encounters this impasse. When fan studies addresses parasocial entities such as characters and personas, it has tended to insist on sociality, depicting any sort of media interaction as an active social relation, as social agency. Fan studies thus risks omitting antisociality from the picture. Yet if antisociality is not taken seriously, if everything is already sociality, then sociality itself loses meaning. Rancière's notion of aesthetic dissensus, which he considers more fundamental than consensus in producing equality, comes to mind. When every relation to media is deemed to be social and interactive, then the intra-active relation, with its implicit dissensus, drops out of the picture. Surely, however, it is impossible to talk about a servile or nonservile relation to media if dissensus is not taken into account. But how does parasocial existence, the television character or persona, imply something like aesthetic dissensus?

Gilbert Simondon's approach is useful in this respect, for his basic question was, how can we develop a nonservile relation to technical objects? For Simondon, placing humans above or below machines implied a servile relation to technology. The hallmark of his approach was to look at a range of individuals—technical individuals and human individuals, among others—from an implicitly nonnormative perspective, that of the process of individuation.[41] From such a perspective, the individual is always more-than-one; no matter how concretely individualized, it remains open to processes of individuation. When previously I referred to individuating processes that take place alongside individualizing or personalizing procedures, I was explicitly drawing on his conceptualization of individuation.

Significantly, because Simondon considers technology from the perspective of individuation, he draws attention to "obscure zones."[42] If the relation between human individuals and technical individuals entails an obscure zone, it is because, as Read puts it, such a relation "is not well grasped by the divisions into part and whole, form and matter, genesis and use." As a result, Read concludes, "The problem of technology, of grasping its specific essence, is then immediately related to another 'obscure zone,' that of the individual and society. These two problems, the relation of the individual to technology and of the individual to society, constantly intersect while obscuring each other."[43]

The phenomenon of parasociality, situated at the intersection of media technology, human, and society, also has its obscure zones, which appear to be forms of antisociality and dissensus (which are rather like the negative affordances evoked in Crawford's account of skill). But it is precisely in such obscure zones that we can begin to detect infraindividual intersections and intra-active entanglements. When we consider parasocial entities or modes of existence through the composite lens of Katō, Rancière, and Simondon, we begin to see how obscure zones of technoaesthetic dissensus emerge through the attention–reason complex. As the complex strives to pull everything into the vortex of reason and attention, new encounters and conflicts arise, which may be neither socially attractive nor reasonable.

Social Media Mix

Among the parasocial entities appearing on the television screen, animated characters are notoriously troubling because they tend to break the sense of a material connection between image and human afforded by photography. Of course, everyone knows that the image of a person on TV is not actually that person, but photographic capture allows us to prolong the reality effects of representation by seeking details about the off-screen existence of that person. Thus we may even feel we really know the people on the screen. Still, as André Bazin remarked in his early writings on television, "This intimacy can even become troubling, to the point of implying reciprocity. As for me, each time I meet one of the presenters of the TV news or even a TV actor in the street, I have to suppress a spontaneous urge to shake their hand, as though they knew me from having seen me daily in front of my screen."[44]

This take on the intimacy of television has proved remarkably stable. For instance, even in the era of television multimedia, Watanabe Takesato defines television in terms of intimacy and proximity: images of something distant are perceived up close, near to your body. He even compares it to virtual reality.[45] But what sort of proximity or intimacy is this?

With animation's characters, this so-called virtual reality effect becomes more pronounced, for it is difficult to find a unitary source, to encounter the person in the streets. Not only do the characters break with the photographic ontology implying contact with an actually existing (or once existing) person or thing or place but they also usually imply multiple sources. Cartoon characters, for instance, frequently combine human and animal traits as well as features of machines. Conventions of plasticity and metamorphosis in animation reconfirm the logic of multiple sources for the character—indeed, within the character. This is why the animated character seems to anticipate and mesh with the logic of the digital: it disrupts discourses on the materiality of photography (indexicality) and implies multiple interconvertible sources.[46] For the same reasons, animation characters would seem to heighten the antisocial tendencies associated with parasocial entities. You cannot find an actual unitary human behind the mask, as it were. There is no moment of encounter in the street with an actual person whose existence forces you to resituate your feelings of intimacy. What is more, with animation, you do not need to. The world of animation feels somehow self-sufficient. It does not demand that you explore the real world or connections between the media world and real world. Paul Wells puts it this way: "Animation . . . prioritises its capacity to resist 'realism' as a mode of representation and uses its various techniques to create numerous styles which are fundamentally about 'realism.'"[47] Animation, then, forms its own reality.

This departure from received photographic conventions that ground representation in reality may lead to an anxious compensatory drive to ground animation in some external reality—by lionizing the character's creator or creators (Disney), for instance, or by acquiring toys and other goods that seem to provide a real-world support for the animated character, or by making pilgrimages to locations that were a source of inspiration for animated series.[48] However, such activities tend to feed reality back into the character and world: the toy becomes a real world instantiation or incarnation of the media world, and when the creators come onto the scene, they appear to be on equal footing with their characters (Mickey and Walt Disney shaking hands). Likewise, even when pilgrimages are made to sites that provide a sort of indexical reference for an animated series, the location has to become populated with animated characters to serve its purpose. Ultimately, then, efforts to ground the animated character in actual places in the real world do not confirm the priority of the real world. On the contrary, as in Baudrillard's theory of simulation or Katō's account of the virtual worlds of television, animation seems particularly disposed toward placing the real world in a subordinate, ancillary, or simply redundant position. Calls for reality serve to feed reality into animation, not into the real world. This is how animation becomes characterized in terms of a production of self-contained artificial worlds or simulations, which are in turn easily characterized as antisocial, or at best as minimally social enclosures.

Media mix, with its serialization across media, prolongs and reinforces the sense of an enclosed yet capacious alternative reality. Each new media instance— manga, anime, novel, game, toy, and so on—adds to the reality of the artificial world. Serialization across media makes for a self-indexing world whose reality comes not of an indexical relation to the real world but to other media instances. It is not unusual for creators today to prepare overall planning and strategies for the release of a variety of media instances in advance of releasing even the first or principal instance. In the case of the *Pokémon* franchise, manga and anime versions were envisioned from the outset, as part of what Hatakeyama Kenji and

Kubo Masakazu call its presentation.[49] Media mix thus appears to confirm Katō's worst fears: parasocial relations seem to take precedence over social relations to the point of replacing them within these alternative realities. Not surprisingly, the paradigmatic consumer of media mix—the male otaku—was initially characterized in terms of extreme antisociality.

Significantly, in the 1970s, when Katō deployed the term *jinrui* (human type) to discuss how television had trapped humankind in virtual worlds, a new discourse was on the horizon, characterizing the new generation as *shinjinrui* ("new humans" or "new types"). Discourses on the new type referred generally to those born between 1960 and 1970, distinguishing them from the previous generation, styled in Japanese as *dankai,* or a "clump" generation, in reference to those born in the baby boom clump of the immediate postwar era, with 1949 as its peak. Discussions of otaku later transformed the new-type generation into the first generation of otaku.[50] Terms such as "new type" and "otaku" take on a range of connotations in different contexts, but generally speaking, by the late 1980s, "otaku" had come to refer to men of the new-type generation whose love for anime, manga, games, and related media had transformed them into antisocial types who preferred the two-dimensional characters of multimedia worlds, and who feared and shunned contact with actual humans. In such discourses, the new type and then the otaku came to exemplify the antisocial condition Katō associated with the parasociality of television.

The male otaku became characterized by his excessively detailed knowledge about nonexistent fantasy or media worlds, by his excessively charged relation to certain kinds of female characters, or—frequently—both. The erotic pole of attraction eventually would be characterized in terms of affective response, or *moe*. In other words, otaku implies a specific configuration of the attention–reason complex in which interaction with media is defined in terms of excess, both of reason and of attention. This is how the otaku inhabits the heady worlds of media mix, at once highly cerebral yet behaviorally conditioned, supremely knowledgeable yet enslaved to specific stimuli. The otaku combines the detached intellectuality of the scholar with the passionate attachment of the lover, the ultimate connoisseur in a world in which consumption is at once didactic and erotic. A similar conceit was gradually applied to the female otaku, eventually styled as *fujoshi* or "rotten girl," who becomes known for her conditioned response to *moe* stimuli as well as her intellectual mastery of a vast world of fantastical situations.

The ideal site for otaku formation is the individualized room, a place of your own. As the number of televisions in households proliferated, it became increasingly common for a TV set to move from the family space of the home into the child's room. From the perspective of TV, then, the household is starting to have multiple centers. It is becoming a household complex. In addition, because the individual room is generally where the child studies, the presence of television as well as toys and entertainment allow the individual room to be a site for superpositioning attention and reason. Indeed, the otaku addresses the object of passionate attention with the didactic impulse of the exceptional student. Manga and anime abound with stories about top students who are secretly otaku, living a second life in which they indulge in their passion for anime, games, or manga. In other words, in the otaku room, the realm of education (a detached studious stance) and the realm of entertainment (passionate attachment to media worlds) remain distinct yet are superposed on one another, fusing attention and reason into a complex set of practices in which their distinction becomes indiscernible. This is surely why the otaku quickly became an object of fascination in mass media in the late 1980s and has remained a paradigmatic figure in popular culture ever since. Sometimes abjected, sometimes admired, their practices make it impossible to separate attention from reason in order to regulate attention with reason. This is also why no one seems able to decide, once and for all, what their relation to neoliberal capitalism is: are they paradigmatic examples of it, or symptoms of it or prophets of its destruction? In any event, the scandal of otaku lies in the exposure of the affective operations of markets, which are either disavowed or embraced through discourses on otaku.

The scandal of otaku is also related to the household media ecology where they are incubated, hatched, and reared within individualized rooms. In 1995, self-proclaimed king of otaku Okada Toshio published book, *Otakugaku nyūmon* (Introduction to otakuology), which provided a retrospective account of the emergence of this new type of human. Okada divides the male otaku into three generations, those born between 1955 and 1965, 1965 and 1975, and 1975 and 1985, and offers a portrait of each respective room. What is striking about these rooms is the prevalence of computers and televisions, with the gradual enlargement and increased sophistication of their interconnections. The attention–reason complex of the otaku room dovetails with the emergence of a personalized wired world.

Okada characterizes the first generation of otaku in terms of a passion for "special effects" or *tokusatsu*, that is, the special filming techniques associated with live-action science fiction, fantasy, and horror fare such as *Godzilla* and *Kamen Rider.* Alongside the science fiction books, manga, and record albums (soundtracks and drama albums from anime and SFX shows), salient in the first-generation otaku room is the Mac or Windows computer (with its floppy disks) and the TV set, which is described as "a rather small model, but with a video cassette deck, Beta."[51] In the room of the second-generation male otaku, the anime generation, there are laser disks, fanzines, and boxes of *dōjin* ("amateur" or "coterie") manga from Comike (Comic Market). Striking are the three screens: personal computer (Windows 95) for making an Internet home page, an older unused PC, and a twenty-nine-inch TV, in which is plugged an LD player and double-deck VHS player and recorder, for making copies from laser disks and videocassettes. Also wired into the emerging system are audio speakers and an eight-millimeter video camera.[52] Finally, the third generation of male otaku is characterized for its fandom of anime characters, garage kits (kits for making your own version of a favorite anime character), video games, and voice actresses. Among the piles of weekly manga and various character goods, wires are now conspicuous, connecting controls to the home video game consoles (PlayStation) and connecting the consoles and a double-deck VCR to the single screen in the room—a TV now larger than twenty-nine inches. A wireless phone lies beside a couple of remote controls.[53]

With these diagrams for three generations of otaku, Okada brings us to the mid-1990s, to the eve of the Pokémon Incident, when the assembling of television and new media culminated in an individual room that presents, in condensed form, the new media ecology that had came to the fore in the late 1980s and early 1990s. Needless to say, these successive generations of electronics, media platforms, content, infrastructures, and domestic architectures all merit additional historical attention, as does Okada's dependence on generational discourse.[54] But my interests lie in what is happening both in a larger register and in a smaller one: totalizing procedures and individualizing techniques, which is where recourse to television is useful.

In a manner analogous to contemporary discourses on posttelevision, discussions of new media in the late 1980s and early 1990s often announced the death of broadcast television—and the death of certain sociopolitical formation associated with the nation. Yoshimi, for instance, equated the emergence of personalized mobile media—"the Walkman, cellular phone, portable computer, pager, and *tamagocchi*"—not only with the demise of the national domestic television formation but also with a complete loss of social mediation and political negotiation between citizens and nation. When the procedures of segmentation associated with domestic television disappear, citizens also vanish. The television audience becomes unified only on the basis of national emergencies and natural disasters. The result is in effect a television nation that only exists in a continuous state of emergency. Where Okumura Kenta, for instance, finds confirmation of the importance of television's reality in its new coverage of disasters and emergencies, Yoshimi argues for the death of the nation-citizen formation and the rise of biopolitical governance shored up with ultranationalist declarations of states of emergency. The television allows the government to act immediately and with impunity on its people, who are reduced to a sort of bare perceptual life, atomized and ensnared in the attention–reason complex.

While I largely agree with Yoshimi's account of the shift from a paradigm of national citizenry toward biopolitical states of emergency, his argument reveals just one facet of what is happening between television and new media. Let me try then to introduce some of the other facets.

Broadcast infrastructures are by and large national (or sometimes supranational) projects arising at the intersection of governmental, commercial, and military interests. As such, as is the case with Japan, they repeat the national project, that is, the project of nation building. The national ideal for broadcast infrastructures is commonly expressed in terms of what Benedict Anderson called flat, even sovereignty. The emitted signal is supposed to radiate to the edges of the bounded national territory, thus erasing distinctions between center and periphery, between the urban and rural, by folding everyone into the centralizing forces of national broadcast. Broadcasting thus puts a different spin to the drive for this ideal national sovereignty. Recall that in the era of novels and newspapers, Anderson showed how the fatality of language came to function as a sort of internal material limit on the deterritorializing drive of capitalism, which made national sovereignty orbit around the assembling of forms of speech with print media. As Yoshimi shows in the context of national domestic television, the technical problems of vernacular language identified by Anderson (standardization of speech and of scripts) turns into a problem of standardization of programming, of the temporal rhythms of daily life, hierarchized with reference to a symbolic center. At the same time, these technical problems become entangled with technical problems associated with electromagnetic signals (frequency allocation and relays). Broadcast signals invariably, and simultaneously, fall short or go too far. Pockets of people in remote areas, for instance, often prove too difficult and costly to reach with relay stations. One solution is to supplement broadcasting infrastructures with cable or satellite systems. But full access remains incomplete, and coverage never happens in a smooth, even, technological manner. A techno-differential emerges in relation to the signal. As the relation between center and periphery, urban and rural, undergoes profound transformations sociolinguistically, it undergoes equally profound transformations signaletically. Broadcasting introduces electromagnetic fatality into the ideal of smooth and uneven distribution, such that national sovereignty has to operate through the signaletic. The imagined community is transformed into an image economy, which comes to subtend it.

Considered from the vantage of the electromagnetic signal, broadcasting appears only ever poised to provoke a shift from the ideal of national citizenry by transforming putative citizens into signaletic modes of existence. This transformation can indeed take the form of a shift from the nation-citizen formation to a biopolitical formation in which the attention economy makes for a bare perceptual life (attention) always in crisis and emergency. This is what Yoshimi sees new media provoking in the late 1980s, which is surely the forerunner of so many of the alarming government initiatives being implemented today to transform would-be citizens into bare data life.[55] In its heyday, then, broadcast television may be said to allow for a sort of holding pattern between the ideal of nation-citizen sovereignty and the biopolitical state of emergency through a displacement of sovereign power onto the television family. Yet the sovereign power imparted to this television household served primarily to stabilize disciplinary power, that is, to stabilize the movement from closed to closed site. The television family might be better characterized as a relay for disciplinary power than as a genuine formation of sovereign power.

In relation to the national project, broadcast television has relied on the sovereign power of household to provide a relay between different power formations traversing the nation. On the one hand, the television household couples ideals of national sovereignty and citizenry with biopolitical forces, thus domesticating the biopolitical deployment of signaletic potentiality. On the other hand, the television household serves as a buffer and mediator between disciplinary sites. Broadcasting is not, however, an intermediate stage between historical formations of power, one of which replaces the other in succession. It was, and remains, a mediator or a relay between them. In its capacity as a relay, it is not nothing. Nor is it a vanishing mediator. It is doing something, which accounts of parasociality strive to capture. As it undertakes its task of mediator between sovereign, disciplinary, and biopolitical power formations, the relay patches into something of each formation as it incessantly spins out new TV characters and parasocial relationships. Let's call these spawn of the television mediator—signaletic life-forms or signaletic modes of existence. The signaletic mode of existence takes on something of the biopolitical insofar as these TV characters, personages, or personas are treated as actual life-forms. It takes on something of sovereign power in that anime, manga, and game characters are legally treated as autonomous entities with actual rights of usage. It takes on something of disciplinary power in that, as Bazin and Katō stress, it feels as if the TV personage was watching you, as attentive to you as you are to it, and at the same time the "no one" and "every one" of statistics-gathering on viewership is actually you, which makes the audience conscious of its status as something monitored. The result of this movement across disparate levels of the exercise of power on a multiplicity is a qualitatively different form of power, exercised at the level of the parasocial relation: ontopower.[56] Ontopower strives to capture the relation between the human life-form and the signaletic life-form—the affective relation that comes prior to and follows from their interaction. Which is to say, ontopower is exercised at the level of infraindividual intra-active potentialities arising through the formation of signaletic modes of social existence. As with the exercise of power generally, it works through a bifurcation of forces and relations; it strives to capture the potentiality of signaletic modes of existence by turning them into lifestyles via personalizing and individualizing procedures (work on self). But in the process it also spurs individuating processes (care for self) vis-à-vis signaletic modes of social existence.

Commentators have noted these effects in various scales of social life. Okada's schema of three generations of otaku implies a transformation of the sovereign family centered and hierarchized around the family TV set. In its role of relay, the household becomes more and more like a relay station; it becomes a complex, while the personal bedroom begins to look like a broadcast–relay station. Everything is in place for the mobile privatization of broadcast television to flip into the privatized mobility of new media, to flip back and forth again and again. As new media disclose the outside on the inside of broadcast television through peripheral devices that allow for switching between media functions, they also disclose the outside of the inside of the household. Morikawa Kaichirō has persuasively argued, for instance, that otaku zones or areas in the city of Tokyo such as Akihabara, to which I would add Otome Road Ikibukuro and Nakano Broadway, present a swarming of the otaku personalized home space into urban space. The individual room pervades the city, making for areas that are otaku-room-like. The result is the personalized city or polis, or "personapolis," inhabited both by otaku and anime characters.[57] In such zones, otaku and media mix characters from manga, anime, and games are on an equal footing. If this personapolis formation is invariably associated with television's media mix, it is because, among the TV personas who drop by the home for a visit, some of them (the animated ones) cannot be anchored in any known place or time or person. Although they have the same homey, cozy, or familiar quality as live-action television personas, they seem to come from a different dimension of reality. They are visitors from another world. Another dimension of reality based on signaletic modes of existence appears at the juncture between the domestic and the exotic—anachronistic English butlers, French maids, Goth girls, robot pets, animal aliens, engineered boyfriends, goddess girlfriends, and so on. Special zones must be created for them and for encounters with them, zones of intimacy that are like a combination of life-support facilities with special economic zones. These signaletic modes of social existence have arisen at the juncture of sovereign, disciplinary, and biopolitical powers.

Considering how ontopower arises at the juncture of sovereign, disciplinary, and biopolitical powers in the history of broadcast television affords a better understanding of the shift from psychiatric power to media care. As broadcast television began to function as a relay between sovereign power and disciplinary sites in the 1950s and 1960s, it is not surprising that accounts of television would linger on deviant behavior and try to cultivate rational uses of media. Gradually, in the 1970s and 1980s, as new media disclosed the network potentialities arising with and through broadcast television, there occured a displacement of sovereign power that felt like its demise, and at the same time the increasing demand for attention began to outpace its segmentation, which revealed new possibilities for biopolitical governance through media. By the mid- to late 1990s, the stage thus was set for the Pokémon Incident to precipitate a new set of relations at the juncture of these power formations, at the very moment when new media were becoming visible yet again. Media care emerged as an effort to capture the ontopolitical forces and relations already in play as a result of decades of media mix and generations of otaku.

Some commentators construe the otaku formation as a return to or renewal of the cultures of discernment associated with the townspeople or *chōnin* of early modern Japan—the floating world. Okada, for instance, ends his introduction to otaku on that note.[58] Yet there is something historically specific about this juncture of institutional arrangements of disciplinary society; the ongoing centralization of governmental, economic, and military power as well as media ownership; and the reduction of workers to a pool of flexible resources and the ongoing transformation of media usage into site of a primitive accumulation of data to be put to work elsewhere. It is hardly surprising to find deep currents of pessimism about social—or rather parasocial—relations flowing through the history of television and new media, from Katō and Williams, to Baudrillard and Crawford, to Ōtsuka and Azuma. The contemporary paradigm of media care exercised through media addiction and signaletic toxicity is hardly cause for optimistism, and care for self seems a thin thread for articulating social transformation, whether revolutionary or reformist. Because care for self appears inextricable from work on self and thus from neoliberal self-governance and sovereign autonomies, it may appear to be a simple compensatory mechanism, a fleeting moment of anarchy and collectivity. Nonetheless, in the contemporary media context, this is where we would have to seek something like Katō's and Rancière's "ordinary" or "nonsectarian" aesthetics—in parasocial movements, in the translation or transmigration of characters or personas between individuals' rooms and special urban zones as well as other sites.

To understand this transmigration, we cannot simply linger on, pathologize, or otherwise reify the relationship between consumers and characters. In the spirit of Williams's insistence on social technology, we need to address the media infrastructures that mediate this relationship. The mediation of infrastructures does not simply vanish into the background. It does make for a media environment that operates below the threshold of awareness and beyond our interaction, which nonetheless exerts pressure on users. Platforms, for instance, are points of access that exert a pressure on users, where one feels the pressure of the all of the infrastructure, as it were. This is where users also push back in various ways. Mediation, then, always implies immediation.[59] It is through this pervasive platform pressure (PPP) that affective relations arise. The characterization of media as addictive (PPP becomes *pipipi*) acknowledges the importance of affective relations, but only to harness that potentiality to pick up the ontopolitical slack between power formations. To conclude this genealogical account of the social technology of television and new media, I thus propose in the final chapter of this part to draw together the lines of inquiry in the prior four chapters into a closer look at the triangular relation between users, characters, and platforms: the platformative relation.

9

PLATFORMATIVITY AND ONTOPOWER

IN THE CONTEXT OF TELEVISION, ANIMATION, AND VIDEO GAMES, ONTOPOWER MAY SEEM TO BE ENTIRELY A MATTER OF a personalized, interactive relationship between the consumer and the character. Addressing ontopower entirely in terms of personalized interactions, however, invites a highly abusive account of consumers, as has so commonly been the case in accounts of otaku. Both male and female otaku have been discursively constructed through a combination of psychology and typology: they are imagined in terms of distinctive physical morphologies and various forms of psychological excess such as antisociality or social reclusion. This sort of treatment of otaku is a variation on psychiatric care, for it frets over the relation between disciplinary formations of labor and the sovereign power invested in the family. The emergence of media care, however, suggests that something else may be happening in the context of ontopower. Media care forces us to understand something like otaku behavior in relation to intoxicating, mind-altering substances that are as widely used, and as ordinary, as tobacco or alcohol, to which people have different responses, tolerances, and propensities, for reasons at once social, psychological, and physiological. The paradigm of media care demands that we think in terms of a triangular relation and thus an infraindividual plane of composition instead of a personalized consumer-to-object relationship.

In Part I, I showed how both physiological and psychological accounts of the relation between viewer and screen missed the mark, precisely because they eliminated the third term, treating it as a vanishing mediator. Accounts of the image (or content) such as Bordwell's formal analysis ignored the screen or platform, and accounts of the screen like Eric McLuhan's suppressed the functions of the image. In fact, what mediates the three terms—viewer, image, screen; or user, content, platform—is an underlying plane of composition (infraindividual intra-actions) that is being generated through their interaction. As scientific accounts of the Pokémon Incident amply demonstrate, this plane of composition doubles electromagnetic reality (plane of immanence) as it enables the patching, cutting, and stitching of the fabric of blink. As such, as the screen–viewer–image relation comes closer and closer to this electromagnetic reality, it reaches a limit-experience in Pokémon Shock.

Where Part I considered media care in its more ecophysiological and psycho-phenomenological dimensions, Part II turned to the question of television media as social technology. Part II adopted a genealogical approach to the relation between television and new media, opening each term of triangle: first, the image was opened into a three-way relation between character and co-constitutive narrative tendencies (fabulating and subjective enclosing); second, the screen was opened into a relation between platform and polarized infrastructural tendencies (one to many and point to point); and third, the viewer was opened into a relation between user and disjunctive social tendencies (sovereign power and disciplinary power). Thus, in Part II, each point of the triangle in Part I turned out to have its own triangular relation, which is where social relations emerge at an infraindividual intra-active level. Looking at the social technology of television in this manner allowed me to understand what is at stake in the relation between television and new media: ontopower.

The genealogy of television media revealed a television ontopower stretched across sovereign, disciplinary, and biopolitical formations, allowing them to work together even as they continue to function separately. This ontopower brings into focus a specific social triad—self, character, and platform—that doubles the eco-phenomenological triangle of eyes–image–screen (the animetic plane of composition). Ontopower emerges at the level of infraindividual intra-action between these three terms, which make for fuzzy, complex, tensile sets of relations akin to fields: self–subject, character–world, and platform–infrastructure.

By way of conclusion to Part II, then, I wish to consider this social triad of self, character, and platform, concretely and genealogically, with the goal of drawing together the prior lines of inquiry and by clarifying both the social interactions and intra-actions of television media.

Platformativity

The relation between you and a character feels like an interaction, a personalized relationship. You interact, for instance, with animated characters both on and off the television screen. You interact with and through animated characters in video games. Yet at the same time you also interact with and through platforms. As video game studies has stressed, there are skills and procedures entailed in play,

FIGURE 9.1. A young girl offers a flower to a robot rebuild of her grandmother in episode 2 of the NHK series *Wasimo* (2014).

which shape your relation to it. Relations to platforms may also feel personalized. In the 1950s and 1960s, for instance, instead of saying, "We bought a TV," people often said, *"Terebi ga yatte kita,"* or TV has arrived, as if television had come by for a visit. What is more, even if you are not watching the television per se, the TV set, like the radio, is often said to keep people company.[1] The company kept today with mobile phones scarcely needs mentioning. Both the platform and the character, then, are liable to become parasocial beings that entail a social mode of existence.

An NHK animated series for children, *WASIMO* (2014), based on the bestselling illustrated book for children of the same title, provides a perfect example. A young girl continues to grieve the loss of her grandmother. She bursts into tears whenever she watches television because she recalls watching it with her. So her father constructs a robot version of grandmother: a television-like monitor sits atop the grandmother-like body as a head (Figure 9.1). He adds a set of clacking dentures to impart the feel of grandmother. The family calls the robot Wasimo in memory of the grandmother's characteristic way of saying "me too." It is as if the sociality of television watching had been flipped inside out: instead of watching TV with grandmother, grandmother becomes a parasocial interactive and intra-active TV being. Thus begins a series of comic and heartwarming misadventures with the TV granny.

Oddly, however, we tend to treat the two kinds of parasocial interactions separately, to hold them resolutely apart. The pervasive pressure of platforms, whether the ubiquity of ambient television screens or the constant demand for attention on the part of our mobile phones, is considered in isolation from the pressure of the image that is commonly embodied in characters, which characters may run the gamut from human actors to animated characters and avatars. Even though the platform in your life may feel personal, personalized, or characterized, a conceptual language does not yet exist to deal with that feeling, other than acknowledging that the platform is an actor or actant. When it comes to characters, however, terms and concepts abound to address its personlike qualities and its status as a social actor. Still, the character is largely treated in isolation from the platform, and the concepts used to deal with one or the other are rarely applied to both.

A rare exception is Ian Condry's discussion of the anime character. Condry describes the character as a "generative platform," arguing, "One can think of platforms not only as mechanical or digital structures of conveyance but also as ways to define and organize our cultural worlds."[2] Condry focuses especially on the anime character in terms of its platformlike capacity to generate links across media forms. His account thus invites us to move beyond the received tendency to hold apart platforms and characters, which is a by-product of analyses methodologically based on interaction between individuals. Analysis has traditionally focused on the character as an individual who interacts with the consumer or user as an individual (subject), or on the interaction between an individual platform and an individual user. Infraindividual intra-actions drop out of the picture. But this is where platform and characters actually enter into relation and jointly take on form.

To embark on an analytics of the infraindividual intra-actions between self, character, and platform, we might think in terms of platformativity, which is say, a sort of performativity related to platforms.[3] Judith Butler's now-classic articulation of performativity concerned the human individual reiterating itself, with iterations bringing an affective infraindividual potentiality to the surface, enabling repetition with difference. In platformativity, both characters (or media content more broadly) and platforms (and thus infrastructures) actively exert pressure and play an active role, or more precisely an intra-active role. Platformativity, then, concerns the iteration of selves, characters, and platforms that generates the compositional plane underlying their interactions, thus giving a compositional force to them.

As attested by Butler's transformation of Lacan's account of the mirror stage into a theory of performativity,[4] we remain heirs both of Freud and Marx when it comes to thinking about nonhuman actors. In the Freudian and Marxist legacies, the logic of fetishism is usually evoked to explain the pressure that objects exert on subjects. From the perspective of ontopower, both legacies are of interest because they fill in different parts of the story. When the Freudian legacy deals with the fetish, it is largely sovereign power that is in question.[5] The fetishized object takes on power and even takes possession of its would-be master. Significant variations on the fetish are possible. Julia Kristeva, for instance, dramatically expands on the negative powers of the fetish, making it a source of horror—overcoming bodily control, defying efforts to secure corporeal containment, oozing, leaking, rezoning.[6] On a different tack, Nakazawa Shin'ichi offers a Freudian reading of the relation of the child to the pocket monster, reading the pokémon as a prime instance Lacan's *objet petit a*, which entails a fetishistic relation to the maternal body not yet challenged by any paternal or other social authority (the symbolic).[7] Nakazawa remarks that the strangeness of the pokémon fetish comes from its encapsulation within the pokéball. It enables "wilds in your pocket,"[8] which is in effect the inverse of Kristeva's powers of horror. Nakazawa links this drive for mastery through encapsulating to engineering—creative powers of involution. Another example is Marilyn Ivy's reading of the mash-up of cute and criminal in the art of Nara Yoshitomo. She focuses on how such art plays between both possibilities, showing how the manga and anime character flips between powers of horror (trauma) and creative empowerment of fans.[9]

When the Marxist legacy deals with the power of the fetish over humans, it is the disciplinary power associated with labor that comes into question, for the fetish serves to mask the underlying reality of social relations, covering over the transformation of human beings into free labor. In effect, because workers also socialize through fetish objects, they enter into their own disciplinization, governing their social behavior. Anne Allison's account of *Pokémon* adopts something of this perspective, exploring how participation in *Pokémon* games situates children within the field of postmodern capitalism.[10] They become both self-governing subjects and flexible workers. Insofar as ontopower is what stretches across and holds together the sovereign power of the family and disciplinary power of schools and workplaces, both the Freudian and Marxist accounts of the fetish offer invaluable perspectives. Yet we still have to consider how a third kind of "object power" arises, precisely to assemble the sovereign and disciplinary formations addressed in Lacanian and Marxist accounts, and in conjunction with biopolitical forces.[11]

The work of Bruno Latour comes to mind, for his varied accounts of nonhuman actors, actor–network theory, and more recently modes of existence have inspired deep and far-reaching reflections on the social pressures exerted by actants including earthworms, quarks, and ozone. What is more, where Freudian and Marxist lineages of thought have tended to dwell on "power over," specifically the power of humans over humans via objects, Latour leans toward "power to," the power of both humans and nonhumans to affect change, hence his call for a new settlement between them and the parliament of things.

Another trend in discussions of object power deserves attention in this context because it tends to undermine a sustained account of infraindividual intra-actions. The trend becomes pronounced in some of the work associated with object-oriented ontology (or speculative realism) that claims to liberate objects from the subject, to free them of the subjectivization (which is conflated with correlationism) expounded in Western philosophy. The proposed liberation of the object consists largely in eliminating all reference to the subject, usually by expunging terminology with apparently subjective implications.[12] As such, a range of subject-related distinctions becomes superfluous, such as those between subject and self, or between subjectivity and the subject, not to mention, affect, perception, and consciousness. In such accounts, as objects take on complexity, subjects and subjectivity appear to become increasingly unified and simplified. Thus, at a deeper level, because such accounts remain committed to grinding away at binary subject–object schemas, the proposed liberation of the object ends up reinstating the isolated and enclosed subject. Especially disquieting for those whose research is related to locations discursively situated outside the putative West, the familiar geopolitical divides are put in place without comment or question. The liberation of objects not only reinstates the West versus the Rest but also proposes to reinstate the West as if without the Rest. The apparent attack on Western metaphysics turns out to be a rescue mission, a restoration.

The concept of platformativity, then, is designed to address object power in a more Latourian fashion, but its goal is neither to expunge objects of all relation to other objects and subjects nor to declare a definitive break with Freudian and Marxist understandings of the fetishistic power invested in objects by subjects that returns as a power over subjects. Rather, the aim is to explore the entangled set of relations arising across three complex terms: platform, character, and self. Through their interactions, each of the terms takes on a degree of semblance with the other two. As the platform becomes both character-like and selflike, so the character becomes platformlike and selflike, and the self becomes platform-like and character-like. In Part III, I will highlight the complexity of practices of self as they emerge stretched across media tendencies embodied in platforms and characters.

Here I place the emphasis on the platform because "platform" (and with it infrastructures and media) is the term usually ignored or downplayed within the Freudian and Marxist traditions as well as in Butler's theory of performativity. In these theories, the platform is treated as a mirror, and the medium of the mirror is scarcely problematized (see chapter 13). In the context of television and new media, however, ignoring the role of the platform or subordinating it to the subject in advance can only lead to a general dematerialization and dehistoricization of operations of power. Without some emphasis on the platform, television ontopower might appear to consist of nothing more than the mass manipulation of minds through ideas. By the same token, if the role of the platform is not addressed, then the relation between self and character will appear to be nothing more than a personalized relationship. Platformativity is thus the key to taking seriously the pressure of platforms, screens, infrastructures. It allows for a more careful account of the self–character relation and thus of self–self and self–other relations—which is where ontopower is exercised.

The platformative angle of ontopower is especially evident when the apparatus of media care addresses screen addiction rather than, say, personalized obsession with characters or fetishization (which discourses on otaku tend to do). Platformativity encourages a different way of looking at the force of characters (or the power of the fetish) in manga, anime, and video games. It encourages a consideration of infraindividual intra-actions arising both before and after (actualized through) the personalized relationship between self and character. Personalizing, obsessing, and fetishizing do not occur without the stuff of blink. They are ways of fashioning a turban from a scarf, to evoke my prior analogy. Just as turbaning the scarf transforms it back into a strip of cloth with multiple destinations, so the personalizing of characters turns them back into blinky stuff with multiple incarnations. Consequently, a closer look at how platforms affect characters provides a way to consider the platformative relation. Such an approach may seem counterintuitive. Wouldn't it be better to provide an exhaustive account of the affordances of various television-related platforms in the manner of media archaeology or platform studies?

While I understand both the contribution and appeal of detailed studies of platforms and devices, it is the very wager of this book that the actualization of platform affordances through the third party of the character may tell us more about the social technology of platforms, infrastructures, and media than media archaeology does. Indeed, platformativity is intended to bring media genealogy to the fore instead of media archaeology. Weihong Bao puts the issue succinctly: "Genealogy is meant as a remedy for the archaeological method's inability to account for the causes of historical transitions as anything beyond a series of discontinuous discursive and epistemic formations."[13]

The two approaches are not incompatible, however, as Bao shows. They have different aims. The genealogical turn implied in the notion of platformativity is intended to address the ontopolitical formations emerging around the social technology of television media. Consequently, manifestations of the transversal force of television media (platforms and infrastructures) within anime and game characters are more to the point than an exhaustive accounting of platform parameters. The previous chapters in this part strove to delineate that transversal force. The assembling of one-to-many and point-to-point tendencies through the introduction of plug-ins and peripherals gives rise to, and comes to rely on, something before and after these tendencies: the alternately localized and nonlocalized point, the everywhere and nowhere point that appears, as if magically, to stitch together different electromagnetic gradations of the stuff of blink. Its limit-experience arrives at Pokémon Shock, in epileptiform seizures, with a population suddenly precipitated into a network at once social and antisocial in its implications—an electromagnetic multitude.

Needless to say, we cannot inhabit this limit-experience, but as commentators on the Pokémon Incident frequently remark, it is already embodied in the principal character of the *Pokémon* series: Pikachu. The *pika-pika* of Pikachu is like the *paka-paka* of transmitted light effects in animation, as is the *paku-paku* of Pac-Man racing the beam in console games. The facts of the television screen prove inseparable from the facts of animation for platformative reasons. They are platformatively entangled. As such, they cannot be psychologized or disciplinized all the way down, that is, in all registers and levels of their being, acting, and becoming. From the depths of the farseeing platform, the character reaches out. In the intimacy of the character, the platform pushes back. The points of this triangle—self, platform, character—are not connected by straight lines in a Euclidean fashion to form a geometrical figure. This triangle entails curvature, in a Riemannian fashion, to form a topological manifold, or something more like a tritone (the musical interval composed of three adjacent whole tones) than a triangle. Genealogy, then, is an inquiry into the historical transformations of that manifold.

Code Switching

Ōtsuka Eiji's and Azuma Hiroki's accounts invite us to consider media mix in terms of a relation between character and world that is mediated through story-play or fabulation on the part of the consumer. Ian Condry's account introduces a slightly different triad from the perspective of the producers of anime series: characters *(kyarakutā)*, premises *(settai)*, and worlds *(sekaikan)*, "specifically, the design of characters, the establishment of dramatic premises that link the characters, and the properties that define the world in which the characters interact."[14] Nonetheless, accounts of media mix generally gravitate toward the anime character, for the character is the point of the triangle where it is relatively easy to gauge the pressure exerted by the other two points: the world or worldview, and the dramatizing or fabulating. Indeed, the anime character appears to have incorporated world and story-play into its very being. Thus the anime character may be considered to be social technology. This is why Condry calls the anime character a generative platform.

Looking at the anime character from the angle of the media platform and its infrastructures introduces a different yet complementary perspective. The emphasis is less on interactions between producers and consumers and more on intra-actions generating them and generated through them—the productive force of distribution, and the distributive force of television media. Producers and consumers are generating and playing on the same electromagnetically charged field, but that field is only charged because they are not distributed evenly or equally. Thus we need to think about the media mix less as a combinatory system and more as media ecology (forces and relations entailed in the production of distribution). Let me begin by focusing on a fundamental tension between the basic structure of anime episodes and the ecology of their media reception. In this way, I hope to gradually reveal what I think is a more fundamental tension between code switching and media switching.

Hatakeyama Chōko and Matsuyama Masako provide a detailed analysis of the basic structure of the thirty-minute episode of animated television series, focusing primarily on the original 1963–67 *Tetsuwan Atomu (Astro Boy)* and its 1980–81 remake; the years 1985 and 1995 in the long-running *Doraemon* animated series (1979–2005); and finally *Pokémon,* which began broadcasting in 1997. Their central structural analysis thus roughly covers the four decades from 1960 to 2000. Particularly striking is the degree to which the basic structure of the internal segmentation for an episode remains in place. The basic pattern is as follows: commercial, opening, commercial, first half of the story, commercial, second half of the story, commercial, preview, ending, commercial.[15] Striking, too, is the degree to which the timing for the segments remains the same across four decades. As might be expected, there are some changes, such as a slight decrease in the story time and an increase in the time allotted to commercials. But these changes are minor. Consider, for instance, Hatakeyama and Matsuyama's parsing of two episodes from the *Doraemon* series (Figure 9.2).[16]

The segmentation of televisual flow within the anime episode is analogous to the overall segmentation of televisual flow discussed previously in terms of the emergence of daily programming schedules, which during the heyday of the national domestic television formation (roughly from the 1950s to the 1980s) was organized viewing around an idealized family formation in which children watched their programs (such as animation) as the mother prepared supper, and the later golden time for family viewing centered on the father's interests. Indeed, the three animated shows that Hatakeyama and Matsuyama discuss adhere to such a schedule, which remains in place even today, although it no longer bears the same social weight after successive waves have eroded its centrality, such as the multiplication of channels through expanded broadcast, satellite, and cable; the use of time-shifting playback devices (VCRs and DVDs); and the emergence first of video games and now streaming services.

Williams's emphasis on flow is useful in this context, for it reminds us that even though an animated television series may be carved out of the televisual flow—treated as a more discrete object and bought and sold as a property (a

DORAEMON	May 17, 1985	October 7, 1994
Opening	1'13	1'10
Sponsors (telop)	0'15	0'15
Program commercial 1	0'30	0'30
Program commercial 2	0'30	0'30
Program commercial 3	—	0'30
Story A	12'44	9'00
Program commercial 4	0'15	0'30
Program commercial 5	0'15	0'30
Program commercial 6	0'30	0'30
Program commercial 7	0'30	—
Story B	8'56	13'00
Program commercial 8	0'30	0'30
Program commercial 9	0'15	—
Program commercial 10	0'15	—
Ending	1'00	0'50
Preview of next episode	0'30	0'30
Sponsors (telop)	0'15	0'15
Ending (telop)	0'07	—
TOTAL TIME	28'30	28'30

FIGURE 9.2. Breakdown of two episodes from the *Doraemon* animated television series, adapted from Hatakeyama and Matsuyama.

possibility increasingly realized through videocassettes)—its content remains permeated with the distributive force of broadcasting. The anime series is as much an anime differential within an overall flow as it is a discrete anime object. Its mode of existence thus entails an oscillation between being discrete and nondiscrete. Indeed, media mix was historically built on this technical mode of existence in which anime is at once discrete and nondiscrete.

Hatakeyama and Matsuyama's structural analysis shows an analogous, almost isomorphic segmentation of televisual flow within the anime episode. Thus a similar anime differential arises within the episode: the animation as a discrete object comprises the story segments and the opening and ending song-and-credit sequences. By convention, when anime series are bought and sold (or pirated and circulated), the commercials are removed, making for the sense of a discrete object. Still, the nondiscrete side of its being remains tangible: how many viewers really treat the ending sequence as part of the anime? Probably some contemporary viewers will even slide over the opening sequence, going directly to the story. Also, the midway commercial break remains palpable, part of the experience. These are just a few obvious ways in which the nondiscrete nature of an anime episode, its relation to televisual flow, defines its mode of existence. Those who complain that anime for children is nothing but an extended advertisement for toys are simply insisting on one possible way of approaching the nondiscrete side of anime, taking its nondiscrete side as evidence of a failure to become an autonomous object of art. Similar complaints have arisen vis-à-vis cinema as an industrial art. This is familiar territory, and clearly it is not particularly useful to try to redeem or condemn everyday popular cultural forms. If the goal is to speak truth to power, then the very everydayness of anime gives as much to push with as to push against—and probably more to push with.

Complaints about the pervasive commercial flows within anime are instructive precisely because they force a confrontation with its nondiscrete existence, which is precisely what contributes to the platformative potential of the anime character. The anime character will of course appear in the story segments as well as in the opening and ending. As characters such as Atom (Astro Boy), Doraemon, and Pikachu attest, the anime character may increasingly appear in commercials and even in other programming. Because the different segments by design entail different audiovisual codes, as the anime character crops up in different kinds of segments, it comes to incorporate the nondiscreteness of anime and to embody it within what appears to be a discrete body. There are different ways of assessing this combination of discreteness and nondiscreteness within the anime character.

Azuma Hiroki calls attention to the increased tendency in anime-related games toward disassembling characters into bits and pieces for reassembly.[17] Such disassembling and reassembling of characters harkens back to the "cel banks" used to streamline the production of animation for television while meshing with the "garage kits" sold for making your own anime figurine.[18] Marc Steinberg notes the interplay between the material and the immaterial aspects of the anime property: as anime characters are marketed and licensed, bought and sold, their immaterial value increases.[19] Here too it is possible to link this production of the immaterial value of an anime character to the history of animation production: as limited animation brings the depths of the image to the surface, characters come to embody that surface depth. Characters become endowed with a "soul" inscribed into their very design.[20]

Looking at this multifaceted production (comprising animators, broadcasters, viewers, players, marketers, and other human actors) of "characters with souls" or "soulful characters" from the angle of television (production of distribution) draws attention to some factors that receive less attention when the focus is primarily on the production of animation (production of production). It becomes evident that it is the relentless pressure of televisual flow that generates the non-discrete, immaterial soul of the character. It is the pressure of televisual flow via platforms through characters that encourages the formation of parasocial relationships with characters, thus making for the ontopolitical capacity of television animation. Characters are thus platformlike at an infraindividual level: like media platforms, they channel televisual flow, that is, the audiovisual flow of television.

Both television and animation come into play in this process, so let me briefly address the relation between them, which will clarify what television brings to the process.

Looking at the character from the angle of television animation, it is the history of limited cel animation that comes to the fore. Cel animation has historically tended toward the production of an image composed of multiple planes. These planes may be composited in various ways to assure that the image holds together under conditions of movement. The strategies used for compositing in cel animation have been prolonged in contemporary digital animation, where compositing remains the overall problematic in imparting a transplanar compositional force to the moving image.[21] Thus different lineages of animation have arisen on the basis of different ways of managing the overall compositing of the multiplanar image, that is, imparting and maintaining a specific kind of transplanar force through it. In the case of Japanese animation, for instance, Tsugata Nobuyuki writes persuasively of two axes of animation, one characterized by the more classic cinematic or full animation of animated films such as those by Tōei Studios and Studio Ghibli (Miyazaki Hayao) and the other characterized by the highly limited television animation inaugurated by Tezuka Osamu's *Astro Boy*.[22]

Looking at animation in this manner, the genealogical relation between cinema and animation comes to the fore. Focusing on the multiplanar image and its transplanar force tends to call attention to the production of space in animation—relations of depth and surface (non-Cartesian space), weightlessness (non-Newtonian space), and exploded projection or the register in which animation becomes more tactile and tactical, encouraging assembly, disassembly, and reassembly across media (participatory cultures). In contrast, from the perspective of television and audiovisual flow, the temporal dimension comes in question—flashes of sound and light, rhythms of color and music, wavelike timing, racing the beam, characters popping on and off the screen, which is say, the affective interval arising from composition of the stuff of blink. If Pokémon Shock presents the limit-experience (the pure experience that is blink), then the basic unit is the temporal loop of affective feedback exemplified by jittering eyes in close-up. Such loops emerge from and remain close to on–off effects. In cross section, temporal loops imply wavelike signaletic rhythms.

This temporal composition (composing across temporal loops) runs in parallel, disjunctively, with the spatial composition (compositing across the multiplanar image). Because the anime character is situated at the spatiotemporal cinematic–electronic juncture between these two ways of composing the moving image, it becomes platformative, sorting out and interwinding the crosscurrents, much as the television set at once segments audiovisual flow and generates new linkages across segments. If television is often likened to musical experience, to jazz or polyphony, it is because the stacked rhythms and interlaced tempos of television codes are something you can indeed experience like music—listening to it or learning to play it.[23] Playing the TV is thus like playing an instrument. It is something that demands learning and practicing; it is an everyday skill, one that is not entirely incompatible with the "everyday activities that structure our attention," such as hockey and carpentry, that Crawford evokes.[24]

Hatakeyama and Matsuyama's study draws attention to the persistence of a fixed structure of segmentation, both externally (the relation of the anime series to other programs) and internally (the relation of segment to segment within the episode). Segmentation implies the spatialization of time, but it also introduces the possibility for temporal patterns across segments in ways that complicate the tendency toward compartmentalization and homogenization. What is more, within the episode, segments imply different codes for listening and viewing, decoding and recoding. As the anime character makes its appearances in segments with different codes, such as songs, stories, and commercials, it oscillates between discrete and nondiscrete existence in a specific manner: it becomes an embodiment of code switching. As a discrete object, it sustains a high degree of formal resemblance as it moves across segments with their different codes. Atom, for instance, always looks more or less like Atom in terms of basic character design. Yet at another level, Atom is a code switcher. Much as the television set continues to look the same even as it displays different shows, so Atom continues to look like Atom even as he switches between codes. At the same time, while characters are becoming platformlike through this infraindividual intra-action with television, the television set will increasingly feel like a character in its own right. Indeed, the semblance arising across switching channels and switching codes makes both the character and television set feel active, even sentient and potentially intelligent. Through code switching, the anime character becomes a subjective technology.

As Williams's and Yoshimi's studies of television amply demonstrated, seg-mentation is also part of the social technology of television. Their accounts show how television, as a social technology, works both on the side of sovereign power and on the side of disciplinary formations. As such, the social technology of tele-vision is situated in much the same manner as psychiatric power in Foucault: it relies on the sovereign power of the family to assure the possibility of pass-ing, with some degree of efficiency, from one site of disciplinary enclosure to another—factory, school, political offices, and economic centers. Discourses on the social effects of television have dwelled on the ways in which watching TV might prevent familial space from smoothly functioning as such a relay, as if domestic television presented a competing or inferring relay. Television thus be-comes the site of a socially constitutive doubt, for it remains unclear whether the subjectivities associated with television work with or against the behavioral and cognitive norms associated with disciplinary formations. Katō's initial in-terest in and subsequent disavowal of the parasocial effects of television are a prime example: is this society-like effect the forerunner of an alternative sociality with progressive possibilities, or is it the harbinger of deepening and widening circuits of control? Such discourses are as fixedly structured as is the segmenta-tion of television animation identified by Hatakeyama and Matsuyama. Likewise, across remakes and multimedia franchises, the anime characters implied in their account—Atom, Doraemon, Pikachu—have proved surprisingly stable, even if this stability requires ever more preposterous social and familial situations—situations convoluted beyond the dictates of genre and world building. Their code-switching powers are enlarged and enhanced in the process.

Media Switching

The code-switching capacity of anime characters makes them a site of continuity, which is related to highly stable structures (infrastructures) requiring significant resources to sustain their operations. If we look at the anime character from the angle of the media transformations implicit in Okada's influential account of three generations of otaku, however, sites of discontinuity become more evident. From an otaku point of view, recall that the decade between 1965 and 1975 may be loosely characterized in terms of what he calls the *tokusatsu* (special effects) formation, in which superheroes like Ultraman were at the center of transmedia ecologies comprising live-action television series, movies, and science fiction nov-els. Anime and manga did not begin to play a central role until the next decade, 1975 to 1985, as the generation that had watched series like *Astro Boy* as children began to organize their multimedia worlds around them. Okada thus dubs it the television animation or anime generation. Here the VCR plays a crucial role as fans begin to record and play back anime series like *Galaxy Express 999* and *Space Battleship Yamato* with epic narratives, which provided the linchpin for transmedia worlds including television animation, animated rebuild and spin-off films, and OVAs alongside manga and fanzines. Finally, Okada describes the decade of 1985–95, not coincidentally the heyday of new media discourses, in terms of the anime character, largely as a result of the impact of video games. Azuma confirms Okada's basic schema when he indicates the rise of character-centered media mix from about 1995.

Anime, and ultimately the anime character, came to play the pivotal transmedia role in conjunction with the transmedia expansion of the television set via media plug-ins and peripherals, such as remote controls, VCR and DVD playback, and game consoles. Within the transmedia ecology, the anime character not only switches between codes but also between media platforms. How does this media switching differ from code switching? First, it should be noted that media switching was already in evidence as early as 1960s-era *Astro Boy* anime: Steinberg has documented how the Atom character began to make an appearance in nontelevision media forms other than manga, such as stickers and toys.[25] Still, Okada and Azuma are surely correct to argue that the anime character truly moved into a central role between 1985 and 1995 as a result of new media environments. When the anime character is considered in light of its capacity to move onto the same television screen via different platforms, it is easier to understand what makes media switching different from code switching. Where code switching followed from the segmenting procedures associated with broadcast television, media switching relies on the new capacity of the screen to flip between platforms. It was at this historical juncture that anime videocassettes came to be called software, while the platform was hardware. As such, media switching is neither a matter of segmenting nor codes. It is closer to computational paradigms such as software. In its capacity as media switcher, the anime character is still platformlike, but now the platform is like hardware capable of running software. The anime character now functions at once as software (code switching) and hardware (media switching). It thus provides a reminder of how tenuous the hardware–software distinction can be.

In historical terms, the seemingly softer code switching is more evidently a site of structural continuity, while the putatively harder media switching implies greater discontinuity. The result is an assembling of soft structures and hard processes. As odd as such a characterization may sound, it is a good one, for it forces us to look at the inverse side of new media, which are so often treated in terms of hard, inflexible structures versus soft, pliant processes. It also helps explain how broadcast television was only ever transforming into new media. Before addressing the social implications of code switching, however, I need to recap some basic points.

First, a genealogical account of the anime character will center on the tension between code switching and media switching. Because codes and media are not the same thing, they present a fundamental disparity, but that disparity proves generative because its "resolution" remains problematic. Second, both code switching and media switching are in evidence from the beginning of television animation, which is also the constitutive moment for media mix and transmedia storytelling. Third, considered from the angle of ecology (and media genealogy) rather than mix or convergence (and media archaeology), it becomes clear that what is called new media or posttelevision is indeed arising with and through broadcast television: broadcast television remains the structural side, and the inverse side (process) does not escape its gravitational pull. Likewise, it is impossible to liberate or isolate media switching from code switching in the context of platform-delivered animations.

These three points help elucidate some of the social stakes for thinking about new media and the entanglement of social media and television media. New media do not break or dispense with the social technology associated with the broadcast television formation. New media have not moved beyond either the sovereign power invested in the family (and the nation-state) or the injunctions for self-governance associated with disciplinary enclosures. They continue to stretch across them in a manner that at once troubles and assures passage between them. New media have, however, introduced new wrinkles, ones related to the biopolitical crises Yoshimi associates with the deathlike living on of broadcast television in the contemporary state of geopolitical emergency. Yet at such a juncture, television also begins to realize its ontopolitical capacity, continuing to allow links (both actionable and operative) between sovereign power in its authority crises and disciplinary formations in their ongoing multiplication. This is not to say that nothing has changed. There are indeed significant qualitative shifts, but they prove difficult to address if they are taken for radical breaks or ruptures. What is more, if we wish to consider how transmedia linkages can become actionable, that is, sites for activism, then we need to address how they have become operative in the first place.

In Part III, I will look at the complex negotiations occurring within media ecologies as they tend toward the formation of (operative) complexes, but with an eye to possibilities for activism. First, however, I would like to complete, in a somewhat cursory manner, this genealogy of the platformative character in order to spell out the implications of its social technology that play out in greater detail in Part III.

The Anime Character as Social Technology

In platformative terms, the Atom boy-robot character of the 1960s anime series is prototypical of television in its first two decades. A range of factors conspires to make him into an uncanny double or semblance of the television set: the TV is an engineered technology, yet it communicates with you in an entirely human capacity. Actually, much like Atom, the feelings the TV set conveys may feel more real than those of human beings. Atom's robotic functions include sending and receiving signals, and he seems highly susceptible and attentive to all forms of communication. Because Atom appears to be a boy but is a robot, questions arise about where to situate him socially. Abandoned by his creator "father" who made him in the image of his dead son, Atom, in his capacity as a boy, requires a family and even wants to be treated like a human boy. Yet he is not the usual sort of child, for he may be put to work in his capacity as a robot, which usually means responding to various threats to humanity. As such, his relation with his guardian, Professor Ochanomizu, is like that between father and son; but it is also like work. Atom is thus situated, oddly and uncomfortably, in relation both to the sovereign power of the family and to disciplinary formations of work, primarily in experimental sciences and engineering. For Atom, such work largely takes the place of the usual disciplinary situation for children, school, although he finds school attractive in his capacity as a humanlike boy. Significantly, when Atom is at home, he is most often depicted within the home's common spaces—living and dining rooms. As Atom blurs the distinctions between boy and robot, he creates a relay between domestic and disciplinary formations.

In sum, Atom is television-like in a number of registers, and as with television, it remains uncertain, even to him (hence his powerful dramatic appeal), whether he is holding the family together or tearing it apart. Still, although (or because) absent, the father symbolically sustains the sovereign power of the family, which allows the boy-robot to to function as a relay between domestic space and disciplinary space. In addition, because his primary vocation is to respond to emergencies, Atom imparts a biopolitical charge to the family–work relay. The crisis in the family is thus matched by a crisis in the nation or the world. Dramatic possibilities unfold from the uncertainty of Atom's relation to crisis: is he the problem or the solution? Atom oscillates between feeling his potentiality as he becomes technologically enhanced and dashes to the rescue, and mourning the affective bind implicit in his mode of existence. Atom is thus operatively stretched to provide a relay across the sovereign power of the family, disciplinary enclosures, and biopolitical crises in geopolitical sovereignty.

His character design meshes with this relay function. As a boy, he is evidently human, yet his neotenous features allow him to fuse with the nonhuman animal, and at the same time he is an atomic-powered, high-tech machine. As an animal, he appears biopolitically exposed and exceedingly vulnerable. As a boy, he appears entitled to state-backed familial protection as a sovereign being with rights. As a machine, he is put to work and is expected to act as a self-governing subject. He is animal, human, machine. He is at once bare life, sovereign citizen, and self-governing subject. These formations intra-act on an infraindividual basis within Atom. They must be fused and self-modulating at that level to serve as a relay. No wonder children and adults alike gravitate to the Atom future: this intra-action promises either to afford a highly operative and functional existence within a technocratic state in which sovereignty is forever deferred and compromised, or to inspire an activist insurrection to liberate one formation from the other two—or maybe to liberate the world from all three formations. Likewise, this is surely what drew everyone to the television in the living room: to cultivate social relations with the creatures spilling forth.

Because Atom is so platformatively entangled with the television of the 1960s, it is difficult to alter the character, world, or setup of the first animated series. While the 1980s remake proved fairly successful as a result of its faithfulness to the 1960s series, other efforts to transform or to enlarge the world have not met with much success. If the Atom series demands replication and reiteration even as it resists reformation and innovation, it is surely because its platformativity has become so fundamental for subsequent modes of platformative iteration. It cannot be changed without pulling the earth out from under the platform.

The next anime series in Hatakeyama Chōko and Matsuyama Masako's account, the *Doraemon* series, might be said to work through an interval implicit in the Atom character by splitting the animal-boy-machine into a boy (Nobi Nobita) and an animal-machine, a cat-robot named Doraemon. Instead of a resolute break, the *Doraemon* series presents a loosening and retying of the basic knot of sovereign, disciplinary, and biopolitical formations implicit in the television relay. It shakes the earth under the platform, moving the action from the living room to the world of boy's bedroom. Everything happens on the same earth, but that earth is now both looser and easier to cultivate. Indeed, the *Doraemon* world has proved more cultivable and adaptable than *Astro Boy*.

Fujiko F. Fujio's *Doraemon* manga began serialization in 1969. An animated television series aired for one season (twenty-six episodes) in 1973. With the second anime series, which went on the air in 1979 and ran until 2005, *Doraemon* exploded into a powerful multimedia franchise. During its twenty-five-year run, the anime series spawned a series of feature-length animated films, released on a yearly basis, as well as a plethora of character goods, OVA releases, and TV specials, alongside the ongoing serialization of the manga (completed at forty-five volumes in 1996). The next anime series, which began in 2005, follows directly from the previous series, featuring new voice actors, and sustaining and expanding the multimedia franchise. The series centers on a likeable but lackadaisical boy, Nobi Nobita, and the rotund blue humanoid (yet vaguely catlike) robot, Doraemon. Doraemon has been sent from the future to prevent Nobita from failing at his studies, becoming a washout, and thus ruining the family's future.

In keeping with Doraemon's muted animal traits, the biopolitical crisis here concerns the sovereign power of the family, but with a broad wink. Even when Nobita finds himself in crises extending well beyond the family to include the nation, the world, or other planets and eras, the series revels in comedic possibilities. It offers a series of light-hearted apocalypses, de-escalating large-scale crises by combining them or alternating them with small-scale concerns. The scale of reference remains Nobita's room, and everything revolves around this confined space, in which the schoolboy is supposed to be studying. Although his room does not include a television set, Doraemon plays a platformative role akin to it. Each time Nobita, lazy and distracted, turns from his studies, he finds himself in some kind of trouble, and the cat-robot offers a seemingly endless variety of technomagical gadgets. It is hard to determine whether the gadgets are the cause of trouble (Nobita often uses one without permission and creates havoc) or the solution (another gadget is produced to help resolve the situation). It is equally uncertain whether the cat-robot from the future is the source of his distraction or the answer to it.

Doraemon thus takes the place of the TV set in a context in which the television platform is undergoing media expansion. One of the more delightful recurring devices is his *doko de mo doa*, or "door to anywhere," which wonderfully captures the feeling of television, and especially television animation, as a mode of transportation to anywhere and everywhere. It also uncannily anticipates the *docomo*, or "anywhere," used to characterize one of Japan's major mobile phone services. Gadgets spill out of his pockets like software applications.

Considered in terms of its social implications, Doraemon's performance is situated where biopolitical crises (entertaining distractions built into the attention economy) threaten to disrupt disciplinary spaces and the relation between them (cognitive labor and reason: Nobita will fail school and thus fail to obtain a good job). Again, however, Doraemon is both the distraction from and the goad to study. Like television, his mode of existence implies a superimposition of attention and reason, generating a vortex. It is no wonder, then, that his protégé, Nobita, is often claimed to be a prototype for the male otaku. The cat-robot platform pushes Nobita's world toward a knowledge formation poised between education and entertainment, cognition and passion, wherein entertainment may be approached studiously while education takes on affective connotations.

As for Nobita, above all, he is the site where the sovereign power of the family is directed and invested. He thus enjoys a certain privilege, yet he does not really have autonomy. He is like his room: removed from the center of the household yet inextricably connected to it, implying vicarious or proxy sovereignty. In this respect, the household complex appears to resolve crises by reference to the sovereign power of the father precisely in the manner of television: it introduces multiple channels and time slots, precursors to websites. Golden time, which reinforced the father's authority by centering on his interests, may lose its hold, but centralizing effects still hold sway in the multiplication of proxy interests. The time loop conceit reinforces the point: Nobita is in a sense fathering himself. The question is, how to introduce genuinely disparate autonomies?

In this respect, the *Doraemon* series does something that the *Atom* series could not. Where the Atom character fused three formations into one body, the *Doraemon* series splits them across two bodies, those of Doraemon and Nobita. This splitting gives greater latitude to the platformative process of stretching across and holding together sovereign, disciplinary, and biopolitical formations. The greater latitude given to platformative effects enables a transformation that did not occur in the *Atom* series. As a robot, Doraemon is more obviously platformative, television-like, than Nobita. While his platformlike nature is not as visible as that of Atom in terms of hardware, Nobita takes on a platformative capacity akin to what is usually deemed to be software. It is as if, in deploying various technomagical gadgets, he were running a series of applications. As such, he is neither a machine to be programmed (educated or entertained) nor an autonomous agent.

As discussed in chapter 7, this is also the moment when anime is being characterized as software. Although anime is clearly not a computational platform, neither is it merely a message or content to be played back. Its content is like software in that it affords linkages with other content in other formats and media forms. Now, however, the software–hardware becomes so complicated that it is only possible to think in terms of software–hardware complexes, like the Nintendo complex, with its efforts to close its platform by limiting usage to its own game software, as discussed in chapter 7.[26] As hardware and software become increasingly entwined, what takes on greater importance is a relation between platforms—or, more precisely, different forms begin to interact as if they were platforms; they intra-act platformatively. This is precisely the relation arising between Doraemon and Nobita. This is surely why the *Doraemon* series has been able to prolong itself through its multimedia explosion. Once the platformative relation begins to affect all modes of existence, a vast array of beings may be held in relation—evident in the proliferating cast of motley characters in the *Doraemon* series. The platformative relation allows the transmedial forces of distribution coursing through the television to be channeled across a vortex. With transmedia ecology, organisms and environmental components come into relation via the energy cascade. Likewise, the Doraemon–Nobita duo only emerges once the vortex has started to gather, stabilizing pathways of multimedia serialization or transmedia storytelling across it.

As for the third series in Hatakeyama and Matsuyama's account, the *Pokémon* series seems to follow directly from the *Doraemon* series, both in its structure of segmentation and in its protagonists. With Satoshi and Pikachu, *Pokémon* also uses as its basic premise the relation between a boy and a kind of animal-machine. Until summoned, Pikachu and the other pocket monsters reside within the trainer's spherical pokéball, which is like a handheld platform. In platformative terms, then, the animal-machines of the *Pokémon* series recall the handheld platform with which the franchise was launched in 1996, the Nintendo Game Boy.

One of the novel features of the first *Pokémon* games was the use of cables to connect one platform to another. It was billed as the first game allowing players to connect one to one with each other rather than via a console plugged into the television. Indeed, the *Pokémon* creators were keen to stress that these one-to-one cables were "communication cables" rather than "combat cables."[27] Whether or not players actually used this feature, it is indicative of the overall orientation of the franchise toward creating a sense that players are at once building a network and dwelling within it. The *Pokémon* series thus mobilizes and intensifies the potential of handheld games to form a networklike structure similar to yet distinct from online networks. Another characteristic feature of the franchise, its equally popular card games, enhances the sense that its world is an off-line world that is like online worlds. All of its components begin to function as communication technologies, and the cards themselves are like platforms, with powers to be differentially activated in response to the powers of other cards.

To promote the series, a *Pokémon* manga began serialization in *KoroKoro Komikku* (Corocoro comic) in same year, often including bonuses, that is, special cards to be used in the card game. The anime series quickly followed, airing in 1997. Although the anime series proved as popular as the card and handheld games, it might seem as if broadcast television was no longer playing a central role in the transmedia ecology, because the *Pokémon* series appears to be predicated on a bid to form a network that effectively bypasses any physical wired connection to the television set. The series initially appears intent on autonomy from television both as delivery medium and as media platform. Indeed, in light of the recent popularity of the *Pokémon Go* game app for mobile phones, which moves its players into the streets in pursuit of pokémons, the *Pokémon* series appears to be a prime instance of posttelevision new media that breaks with broadcast television.

Even the domestic space associated with broadcast seems to disappear. Although its boy hero, Satoshi, has a family, he is usually traveling from town to town, from adventure to adventure and combat to combat, with media platform in hand and only a tenuous connection to his household. Satoshi is becoming fully platformative, like one of the pokémon animal machines, summoned and transported from place to place. Communication and transportation feel nearly synonymous. In this respect, the *Pokémon* series confirms Yoshimi's remarks about the disappearance of domestic television with the rise of mobile and social media that began in the late 1980s and early 1990s. As procedures of segmentation associated with broadcasting wane, the sovereign power of the family also seems on the verge of disappearing. The sudden resurgence of massive governmental, scientific, and familial concern for television in the context of the 1997 Pokémon Incident also jibes with Yoshimi's assessment of the morbid, undead afterlife of television: biopolitical emergency replaces the sovereign power of the family in organizing national life. Indeed, throughout the series, especially in the feature-length animated movies that contributed to its first global peak in the early 2000s, the larger story arcs within the *Pokémon* series concern planetary disaster and ecological crises. Socializing with and through cute electronics and animal platforms becomes increasingly associated with saving the planet from environmental disaster. Another kind of question thus emerges around the *Pokémon* series, a question about the relation between media environments and natural environments, and between ontopower and environmental crises. Let me address this question via the genealogy of platformative characters, which offers insight into the complex forces historically summoned and ordered within transmedia ecologies, which continue to exert pressure on the present.

Thus far I have focused more on the continuous nature of the ontopolitical transformations occurring across Atom, Doraemon, and Pikachu. Bifurcations also occur. We have seen that, in platformative terms, where Atom is like the (closed) television set of the early broadcast decades, Doraemon is like a television set open to expansion via peripherals. Pikachu is like the mobile phone, or *keitai,* as it is called in Japanese, a term that Mizuko Ito glosses as "something you carry with" in order to highlight its intimate connection with the user's body over its mobility or its technical infrastructure.[28] The pocket monster thus appears to conjure up an entirely different media formation than that of expanded television. Yet the pokémon does not present a resolute break with broadcast television in order to usher in a postbroadcast or posttelevision era. It follows from a bifurcation arising within Japan's television new media.

The easiest way to grasp this bifurcation is to consider the contrast between the cyborg and the pokémon, which is related to the bifurcation of electronic games into the game console and the handheld game, whose representatives are, respectively, the aptly named Famicom, or family computer, known outside Japan as the Nintendo Entertainment System (NES), and the Game Boy.

Although the first media mix cyborgs are roughly coeval with Atom (the *Cyborg 009* series), the cyborg took on new functions in 1980s Japan, riding high on the waves of OVA releases and reaching a peak around 1995 with Oshii Mamoru's *The Ghost in the Shell.* This cyborg was above all a creature of the wired world. To hook up to the net, their body had to have plugs or jacks for the insertion of cables or wires, a setup that looked and acted exactly like the jacks and cables used to plug VCRs and game consoles into the television set. The *Matrix* series expanded on this aspect of *The Ghost in the Shell*: characters have jacks in the back of the neck for wiring into the matrix. In platformative terms, the cyborg is like the television peripheral or plug-in. But the peripheral device is feeling increasingly autonomous, which explains the existential crises in cyborg identity: they are like peripherals roaming free of their home or base platform, looking for something to plug into in order to figure out who they are and what they are supposed to do. It's hard to be a VCR or game console without a TV set to direct you. They try plugging into one another, but, much as physical sexual intercourse holds less attraction for them than virtual sex, they really want to plug into something larger, that is, the matrix or Web. This Web and matrix turn out to be more than the sum of their wires. They have wireless effects. It is like they are able to broadcast signals right to the cyborg—which is to say, the wired world is dreaming of something wireless, but that nonwired effect now seems to arise within it. In effect, the wired world appears to have subsumed or incorporated wireless broadcasting, computationally.

In contrast with the pokémon world, the cyborg world may appear darker— and thus to be a world decidedly for adults. This distinction may have held through the mid-2000s. But as numerous failed attempts to reboot previous cyborg worlds as well as the broad demographic reach of games like *Pokémon Go* attest, the pokémon has ended up feeling truer to the current mobile and social media situation. The *Pokémon* series allows the handheld device to serve as an intimate parasocial companion. Unlike the jacked-in cyborg who risks becoming a puppet to a master, the pokémon feels unburdened by wires and infrastructures yet is somehow connected to friends. The pokémon is not mastered but trained, in a relation like that described by Donna Haraway for companion species.[29] It is as if the parasocial possibilities of the wireless revolutions of radio and television have been fully realized.

The bifurcation between cyborg and pokémon effectively repeats that between Atom and Doraemon, but with a difference. There is an analogous separation of animal-machine from the human, which opens the platformative relation across existences instead of collapsing it into an existence placed in opposition to mind. Thus with pokémons, the robotic problem of the matrix largely disappears, wherein wiring threatens to subsume mothering within engineering, which poses a challenge to the sovereignty of the human body, manifest in crises of personal and political sovereignty. With pokémons, mechanism and organism no longer appear ontologically different; nor do natural environments and media environments. Physical scale thus ceases to matter in the same way. The result is indeed "wilds in your pocket."

Because the production of these platforms is clearly contributing to the planetary depletion of resources and the global exploitation of labor, it is fair to ask whether the infraindividual intra-action of platform and cute animal simply serve to conceal this unpleasant truth.[30] Are we just pasting a cute image on the platform to hide its ugly reality? There is no doubt that associating platforms with cute animals can function in this manner, yet focusing exclusively on that kind of ideological function is too limited in its notion of ideology. It stops short of addressing the ontopolitical field of rationality emerging around the platformative character and its double, the characterified platform.[31] The ontopolitical field emerging through platformative characters is more than an ideal supplement to biopolitical crises of the environment. The genealogy of television media shows how it plays a broader, active, nonsupplementary role.

First, the genealogical approach suggests that as the sovereign power of the family is compromised, television sustains it by dividuating it, sharing it with individual family members. Second, individuals, thus endowed with their share or part of sovereign power, take on the family's relay function of assuring the smooth articulation of different disciplinary enclosures. The otaku becomes the exemplary figure because he is one of the family and a family of one. The family is no longer an individualized group; it is dividuated, making for distributed relays. To evoke Deleuze's account of societies of control, the relay of this "family-dividual" takes on a function of modulation across disciplinary sites. Third, even as this dividuation and modulation tends to leave dividuated human relays exposed to environmental disasters and biopolitical states of emergencies such as the Tepco disaster at Fukushima, it also situates human actors among nonhuman actors in a manner that may spur new kinds of collective experimentation and ethical relations.

In sum, as Latour, Stengers, and Haraway have all proposed, albeit in somewhat different ways, the ontopolitical is distinct from yet in relation to the biopolitical. The value of paying greater attention to television and new media lies in the light it sheds on the genealogical connections of ontopower not only to biopower but also to disciplinary and sovereign forms of power. It also urges us to consider the ways in which the contemporary overproduction of companion species, happening both in media and scholarship, may afford new frameworks for understanding the current juncture. How do we push against but also with and through these parasocial companion species, these platformative characters and characterified platforms?

This is precisely the question addressed in Part III. Having laid the groundwork for understanding the social technology of television media in Part II, I now turn to the third point of the triangle: self. Through four case studies of multimedia franchises, each of which implies a distinctive media ecology, I propose to explore different possibilities enabled by these ecologies for practices of self, for work on self and care for self. Part III thus presents a shift from the social technology of television to its psychological technology, but in keeping with overall genealogical focus of this study, I consider the social and psychic to be two faces of the psychosocial coin—which coin does not respect the Euclidean laws of geometry. It is more like a psychosocial Möbius strip. If you travel along the social side, you wind up on the psychic side, and back again.

Part III

INFRASTRUCTURE
COMPLEXES

10

THE FAMILY
BROADCAST COMPLEX

THE POKÉMON INCIDENT OCCURRED AT A TIME WHEN A SERIES OF DRAMATIC TRANSFORMATIONS IN TELEVISION MEDIA were becoming increasingly tangible and visible, culminating in a sense of crisis by the end of 1990s. First, at the level of infrastructures, the new media announced in the late 1980s and early 1990s had significantly increased the number of channels, especially as a result of new satellite stations and channels. Once again, the distributive capacity outpaced the production of content, which made for new venues for broadcasting animation outside NHK and the big five Tokyo stations, not only on satellite but also through independent stations.

Second, at the level of media platforms, the national domestic television formation—the family around the TV in accordance with daily time slots—had all too clearly given way to a household media complex. On the one hand, the household television set now included VCR and maybe a DVD player as well as a game console. In conjunction with new plug-ins to allow for reception of satellite broadcasts, the television set had become computerized, permitting it to switch between different media functions. On the other hand, television media systems had also moved into individuals' rooms, making for a household with more than one media center—a veritable household complex. At the same time, the rise of portable mobile media, especially the widespread use of cell phones with Internet service by the end of the 1990s, also contributed to undermining the sense of the household as a domestic media center. The other lineage of Nintendo platforms, based on the transformation of the Game Watch (1981) into the Game Boy (1989), into Game Boy Advance (2001), and then into the Nintendo DS (2004), fed into the trend toward increasingly personalized and portable media, to be used at home or while commuting to school, going to work, or running errands.

Across these two transformations in media appeared a third one related to multimedia franchising or media mix. The publishing house Shūeisha, which had emerged as the most financially successful version of the manga-to-anime model with anime adaptations of manga published in its weekly boys' manga magazine *Shōnen Jump*, hit its peak of sales in the mid- to late 1990s. Even before the *Shōnen Jump* model peaked and began to wane, the multimedia model centered on the adaptation of manga into television animation had already begun to give way to new strategies of media mix. On the one hand, there emerged a tendency to plan for, and if possible to release, multiple media instances of a franchise at the same time. On the other hand, a variety of new source materials other than manga received greater attention, such as light novels and video games. As both Okada's and Azuma's accounts of media mix attest, a new strategy had clearly emerged by the mid- to late 1990s. The new media mix would have a strong game component, with increased emphasis on characters and play. It also built on another powerful current of media mix established in the 1980s: making animated series based on toys, particularly transforming toys.

The *Pokémon* franchise rode this new wave, releasing its games for the Nintendo Game Boy in 1996, with their special platform-to-platform cables allowing for point-to-point communication networks. The games' success, amplified by a Pokémon manga serialized in *Corocoro,* led quickly to the broadcast of the animated TV series in 1997. As such, the Pokémon media mix presents a new site and moment for the assembling of polarized tendencies within the expanded television media formation, with an increased emphasis on characters and play. The popularity of the card games enhanced this emphasis. Nonetheless, as the Pokémon Incident would make abundantly clear before the end of 1997, this new game media mix, for all its emphasis on point-to-point network tendencies, nonetheless depended on assembling with the one-to-many tendency associated with broadcast television. The Pokémon Incident did not mark a rupture between television and new media but rather signaled a genealogical transformation in the television media formation.

The unparalleled global success of the *Pokémon* animated series serves as a reminder that this television media formation remains profoundly connected to anime. The success of both the television series and the animated movies made Pokémon a household term around the world, and Pikachu became as familiar as Mickey Mouse. Indeed, the anime market in North America is sometimes said to have peaked with the first three *Pokémon* movies released there in 1999, 2000, and 2001. The Pokémon animations owe a good deal to the anime lineage of limited animation, at the level of form (line, color, character design, backgrounds, movement, editing, and a range of other formal features) and at the level of function (animetic plane of consistency). Here it is also useful to recall that the identifiable cause of the epileptiform seizures of Pokémon Shock, the 12 Hz red–blue flicker, lay not in the anime or in the television screen but in the transformation of the flash effect in the anime in the process of broadcasting it. It is the coming to the surface of this "media betweenness" that exposed the groundless ground of television animation, its limit-experience, that is, seizure and blackout.

The genealogical perspective reminds us that this media betweenness is related to larger and deeper historical currents in television and new media. What the Pokémon Incident brought to the fore, then, is not only the limit-experience of animation or of television screens but also the assembling of medial tendencies implicit in broadcast television—point to point and one to many. This is why the incident suddenly mobilized experimental sciences, government ministries, television broadcasters, animation producers, and households, catalyzing a new set of relations. The genealogical perspective thus returns us to our point of departure, the social injunction (or incitement) that emerged from the Pokémon Incident: "Don't get too close to the TV when watching anime, and please keep the lights on!" Now, however, we are better equipped to consider the polarization of social tendencies implied in this injunction, which is inseparable from the assembling of polarized media tendencies.

Infrastructure Complex

The response to the Pokémon Incident largely ignored or bracketed questions about anime content, that is, story structures, themes, narration, or figuration, although these were sometimes mentioned as contributing factors. The response focused attention on the impact of media themselves, both techniques (such as the transmitted light effect) and technologies (such as CRT screens). The overall impression is that media (rather than content) constituted a direct neurological danger (rather than a behavioral or psychological problem). Part I looked at how neuroscientific studies strove to understand the Pokémon Shock in causal terms, quickly isolating the 12 Hz red–blue flicker as the cause of the epileptiform seizures, which arose from an unexpected transformation of the animation frame rate during broadcast. Something escaped or exceeded this strict localization of the cause, however. Similar effects also occurred with other kinds of screens and other techniques of animation, and those affected often ceased to show signs of being susceptible to PSE, which suggested that other factors might have come into play.

The Pokémon Incident effectively placed television animation high on the list of dangerous media substances, that is, substances whose intoxicating effects might cross the threshold into full toxicity. The fuzzy relation between cause and effect also allowed the incident to cross easily into general discourses on media addiction, which are fuzzier still, precisely because the criteria for safety and toxicity remain wide open to interpretation. This fuzzy causality also explains why the injunction to watch television animation at a safe distance in a well-lit room has continued to appear with anime, despite substantial changes in animation techniques and screen technologies. The fuzzy relation between media cause and neurological effect has been translated into a fuzzy danger zone in front of screens in general: How close is too close? How much illumination is needed in the room to assure safe viewing? The fuzziness of this zone may also invite experimentation: How close can I get before passing out?

Now, due to its emphasis on a cause-and-effect relation, such a scenario gives the impression that media happen first and social responses follow, with a lag, belatedly. It thus encourages a deterministic stance vis-à-vis media and technologies, which tends to overstate their impact and thus to overlook the actual complexity of media configurations as well as their historical and genealogical depth. When the Pokémon Incident began to focus new attention on the fuzzy zone in front of the television set, for instance, it was building on and transforming a larger set of social and technological relations. Before exploring the complexity of this transformation, however, I would like first to revisit my approach, extend it, and render it more explicit.

Previously, when drawing on Raymond Williams's account of television, I have made reference to Deleuze's manner of thinking "determination" (three syntheses) and to Deleuze and Guattari's Marxist reworking of it. When Raymond Williams calls television a social technology, he reminds us that the social and the technological (and thus the medial) always appear entangled. It is impossible to separate them definitively, to give priority to one over the other. His notion of social technology is thus not a matter of social uses of technology, which is a variation on the scenario in which media or technology happen first, and social responses or uses follow. The social is entangled with the medial from the outset. We tend to think, for instance, of point-to-point tendencies as socially individualizing and one-to-many tendencies as socially totalizing. For Williams, the key determination of television as social technology lies in the production of distribution capacity over and above the production of content. Such a determination is not, however, simple or unitary. As in Deleuze's account of determination in *Difference and Repetition,* it might best be described as synthesis. Indeed, the production of distribution capacity in Williams's account has a synthetic function: it brings together point-to-point logistical tendencies and one-to-many centralizing tendencies. Although Williams sees a subordinating or effective subsuming of the former by the latter, he still sustains the sense of a synthesis determination across his analysis: flow and segmentation, mobile privatization, multiple centers. In other words, the production of distributive capacity is a determination, but it does not totally and deterministically turn television into segmentation, privatization, and centralization because flow, mobility, and multiplying forces are continuously synthesized with them.

Williams's emphasis on the production of distributive capacity as the key synthesis determination of television jibes with Guattari and Deleuze's reworking of the concept of disjunctive synthesis into that of production of distribution. Disjunctive synthesis is one of three syntheses that Deleuze introduces in *Difference and Repetition* in his account of the emergence of the subject: connective, disjunctive, and conjunctive. For Deleuze, the subject is the tentative outcome of these syntheses. In *Anti-Oedipus*, Deleuze and Guattari remap these three syntheses onto Marx's account of production (connective), distribution (disjunctive), and consumption (conjunctive). In keeping with Marx's insistence that circulation increases unevenness instead of generating equalization, equality or equity, Guattari and Deleuze see disjunctive synthesis (distribution) as the key to understanding processes of capitalism. Disjunctive synthesis produces the monstrous body of capitalism, its *socius*. Steven Shaviro provides this cogent summary:

> The socius is the matrix of surplus appropriation, and then of circulation and distribution. It operates what Deleuze and Guattari call a *disjunctive* synthesis, or a synthesis of recording, "of distributions and of co-ordinates that serve as points of reference." But such a process cannot continue indefinitely, all on its own. The disjunctive synthesis of capital is not a perpetual motion machine; it is not a closed, self-contained, self-renewing system. Contrary to the assumptions of neoclassical economics, it is not an equilibrium system. Rather, it is what Ilya Prigogine and Isabelle Stengers call a *dissipative structure*, a far-from-equilibrium conductor of flows of energy. If the socius were only able to feed back upon itself, and live upon its own resources, it would either suffer a short circuit and quickly burn out, or else slowly succumb to entropy.[1]

This is why, as Shaviro points out, the production of distribution demands, on the one hand, a continuous flow of production of production (connective synthesis), which provides fuel to power the expanding and intensifying processes of disjunctive synthesis. Indeed, the distributive capacity of television would collapse if not for the relentless production and reproduction (replicating, repurposing) of content. On the other hand, the production of distribution also calls for the production of consumption or conjunctive synthesis—"a spark of *self-enjoyment* that discharges tensions and reboots the entire reproductive process."[2] This is where the subject is synthesized, as a tentative outcome, a fleeting artifact of the feeling of release that comes from dissipating overstocked energies—burning up fuel, so to speak.

Deleuze and Guattari famously strive to grasp the anarchic possibilities implicit in the capitalist ascendency of the production of distribution in order to counter capital's axiomatic tendencies. They basically agree with Williams in their rejection of the privatized subject of consumption because the private subject constitutes an attempt to stabilize or reinforce the production of distribution by introducing norms for consumption and by identifying and denouncing excessive forms of consumption or expenditure. Guattari and Deleuze also seek a kind of nonsectarian movement of subjectivity, akin to Rancière's distribution of the sensible, and not unlike Katō's bid for noncitizen movements. Ultimately they may differ from Rancière and Williams in their emphasis on belief in a new world (a revolutionary overturning of the subject, a recomposition of subjectivity) instead on the revolutionary production of a new subject. But that is another story. What matters in this context of the social technology of television media is the general perspective opened by the emphasis on the production of distribution in Williams, Guattari, and Deleuze.

This general perspective makes clear that media determination versus social determination is a false abstraction, for the entanglement of the social and technological (or socius and media) comes of a determination, albeit a complex synthesis determination—specifically, disjunctive synthesis, the production of distribution. This socius/media problematic may also be likened to Foucault's conceptualization of power/knowledge. This is why I have addressed the socius/media problematic—the social technology of television—genealogically in terms of the polarization of tendencies within disjunctive synthesis, harkening to eventfulness at specific moments and sites of assembling of polarized tendencies.

Another dimension of this problematic then emerges. As specific instances of disjunctive synthesis (assembling) are prolonged into a conjunctive synthesis, a spark of subjectivity bursts forth as assembling burns through fuel to make the polarized tendencies mesh and operate. When a specific assembling is stabilized and prolonged, that spark may become a series, and that series of sparks may take on a form or pattern. The subjectivity persists, sparks on, serially. Such patterns and series lend themselves to regulative functions. Guattari uses the term infrastructure complex to discuss this technoregulatory serialized subjectivity.[3] An infrastructure complex is analogous to a psychological complex, like the Oedipus or Electra complex, with similarly normative or regulative implications. Guattari coined the term to sustain an expanded view on socius/media entanglement (rather than a narrow view based on the family) and to avoid positing the subject prior to its synthesis. It is to this socioaffective dimension of television media that I turn in these chapters.

Previous discussion has paved the way for my discussion here. Part I showed how the Pokémon Incident catalyzed the formation of a screen–brain apparatus, which mobilized scientific, governmental, aesthetic, and domestic concerns to deal with the neurological effects of media. Across the social history of television media, Part II explored the gradual emergence and intensification of parasocial relationships in the context of television and new media. Some commentators (Katō and Crawford) characterized these relationships in terms of a thoroughly enclosed, fundamentally antisocial sovereign self that is at once fully personalized and entirely totalized. They described what is in effect a highly rationalized stimulus–response machine, one without feeling, enjoyment, or relation—the ideal subject of rational choice theory. If we consider this ideal subject in terms of the superpositioning of nonrational choice (attention stimulus) and rational choice (response), we begin to see a complex rather than an enclosure, a whirlwind stirred up around these two attractors. What Katō and Crawford describe is the production of distribution in its immediacy (the groundless ground of its monstrous body) without the production of subjectivities, histories, worlds, or relations, that is, ways of feeling self-enjoyment.

The term "production of distribution," awkward as it may seem, reminds us that there are always two sides to distribution: what produces distribution (media infrastructures and platforms) and what distribution produces (feelings, nonpersonal affect, socius body). Put another way, different ways of navigating the monstrous whirlwind body arise—ways of plying its currents, of feeling its affordances to find your path. These manners of feeling your way do not rely on, or necessarily result in, fixed subject positions. To use Deleuze and Guattari's terms, it is a matter of feeling or affect, which arises through disjunctive synthesis (attention–reason complex) where reason and attention are at once fused and separated (superposed), while conjunctive synthesis remains in the offing. Some paths become well-worn routes, seemingly complex yet highly regulative—infrastructure complexes, subjectivities of the media socius—holding onto the whirlwind where the assembling of polarized tendencies introduces an eddy in its vortex. The infrastructure complex is thus reminiscent of what Williams calls structures of feeling, but with greater emphasis on technologies of distribution, medial arrays, and assembling.

In the wake of the Pokémon Incident, a diverse set of techniques and relations was drawn into the vortex of the media brainstorm, striving to define an eddy amid the dangerously flashing and flickering currents—the pool of light radiating from the flickering television set. It can prove difficult to dwell in an eddy; it may demand great resources, strict disciplinary or regulatory measures, and a mind-set. This is where television animation comes into play, and it matters how you play it. For there are different ways of relating to this eddy, this pool of light, this charged field. What is more, the pool of light itself is changing as television sets undergo transformation, becoming wired with recorders, players, and consoles, shunted into play and computation, and hooked into satellite networks. In this part, I propose to look at four examples that present different paradigms for playing with television's charged field, which advance the genealogical perspective on the relation between television and new media. I begin with a rather basic, even classic, scenario: a little boy watching television in the living room under the eyes of his mother and father, ignoring parental advice, acting out, and acting up.

The boy is Shin-chan, of the media franchise centered on Utsui Yoshito's manga *Crayon Shin-chan* or *Kureyon Shin-chan,* which began serialization in 1990.

Broadcast Media Ecology and SFX Media Mix

When you read or hear "Stay back from the TV, and keep the lights on!" from the screen, who is addressing you? If you assume that it is the voice of some great authority beyond the screen, telling you how to use the TV, you would not be entirely off the mark. After all, this is how government regulators and broadcasters seem to imagine the warning message. They apparently think that television has the authority to tell people how to use it—or at least that television can be used to tell some people (parents) how to tell other people (children) how to use it. If the message bears authority, it is due to the conventions associated with broadcast television. The ascendency of the one-to-many tendency appears to give the one the authority to dictate to the many who are to follow. Television appears to be a tool of instruction, propaganda, and even domination. It bears the words of an absent master. This dream of broadcast media to indoctrinate the masses is one of the great fantasies of fascism.

This vision of television has proved tenacious, whether in theories of overt indoctrination (say the same thing over and over; omit dissenting ideas), subliminal indoctrination (distract them with bright lights and movement while smuggling in unnoticed messages), or addiction (use flashing lights to intoxicate children). The fundamental vision is one of passive reception of an active message. A muted version of it persists in the discredited theory of the persistence of vision used to explain the illusion of moving images in cinema. Film scholars adopting a more ecological approach to perception grounded in scientific studies have aptly objected to the continued use of the persistence of vision theory within psychoanalytically oriented film theory. Yet it is worthwhile to recall that theoretical reliance on the persistence of vision introduced temporal lag in hopes of complicating our notion of the spectator's reception of images. Such a theory posited a passive recording of images in the unconscious, which spurred a more active process of psychological working through (condensation and displacement), which in turn exposed basic psychic or ideological dispositions (such as patriarchy), but in a cryptic form (say, fetishism). But there are other ways of complicating the audience body.

Considering the reception of television messages more actively in the context of the Pokémon-inspired warning, you may conclude that it is reasonable to obey it, because television animation may harm your brain or your child's. You are situated as a rational agent, albeit a vulnerable or fragile one, whose reasonable response would be to avoid harm, to protect you and yours. This scenario evokes a mitigated politics of fear based on rational choice, which assumes minor, reasonable compliance to assure safety. It shows affinity with the psychoanalytic scenario, by which you internalize the authority of the message, the voice beyond the screen, applying its regulations to yourself or your child. You are normalized, subjectified under the sign of the One, as it were, as you acknowledge and compensate for your fragility or vulnerability vis-à-vis media.

A now-venerable line of media theory, beginning with Friedrich A. Kittler, heads in this direction: the technological functioning of technologies and media becomes so efficient and flawless, so superior to human bodily capacities, that you cannot fail to feel your fragility, vulnerability, disability. Such a stance often heralds a crisis in European reason (centered on the white man's able body), which is reminiscent of the Pokémon-induced crisis of French reason presented in Entell's documentary, *The Tube*. Needless to say, dwelling on the technology-provoked crisis of the average body nonetheless serves to sustain Europe as some kind of global center, if only that of the afterlife (or half-life) of reason.

But what if you are a five-year-boy like Shin-chan, somebody who cannot read the message, who refuses to listen his parents, and who feels energized and empowered by what's on the tube, everything from exercise videos to family smackdowns and children's shows, but above all else SFX action heroes such as Action Kamen?

As it turns out, Shin-chan is not just another kindergartner. His behavior swings wildly and hilariously among needy manipulative toddler, lewd old man, and horny teenager. Despite the age of its protagonist, the *Crayon Shin-chan* manga is definitely not for children only. It was serialized in *seinen* (adult male) venues, initially in *Weekly Manga Action* (1990–2000) and subsequently (until Utsui's death) in *Manga Town* (2000–2010). The image of a line drawn in crayon suits this fare perfectly, for it is somewhat childish and overtly crude, yet potentially powerful in its sketchiness. It is perfectly suited to Shin-chan's signature gesture in which he whips down his pants, wiggles his butt, and chortles with glee (Figure 10.1). Such a body defies those discourses on media and technologies centering on (and reifying) its fragility, its failure, its constitutive lack. It also runs counter to a politics of media based on hurt, harm, and damage.

In the course of the multimedia series, the perverse little Shin-chan increasingly displays an obsession with Action Kamen. Action Kamen is a transforming hero in a special-effects TV show (Figure 10.2). The transforming hero evokes a male archetype that contrasts sharply with needy toddler, precocious kindergartener, horny teenager, and dirty old man, not to mention Shin-chan's easygoing, easily pushed aside father. Indeed, the male action hero feels like the antithesis of the male phases associated with Shin-chan. Gradually, however, in the *Crayon Shin-chan* series, the SFX hero's ability to transform or alter his body in order to command higher powers *(henshin)* runs parallel to, and even begins to appear analogous to, Shin-chan's talent for wiggling his butt, slurring his speech, and

FIGURE 10.1. Shin-chan's signature
butt wiggle from the eighteenth
Crayon Shin-chan animated film.

playfully deforming his body in order to command its "lower" powers *(hentai)*,
much to the embarrassment of his parents. As the series unfolds, and as the
manga crosses into a still ongoing anime series (from 1992), an ongoing series
of feature-length films released yearly (from 1993), and a number of video games
for different platforms (from 1993), the art of *Crayon Shin-chan* settles on exploring different scenarios in which these two lines of transformation—*henshin* and
hentai—come to intersect. For instance, the perverse little boy comes to adopt the
role of the upright hero himself, or to assist the masked hero, or even to travel
through time to save his future self, who turns out to be a transforming hero like
Action Kamen. In sum, Shin-chan is not a boy but a transformative body that
implies multiple functions and gradually takes on the capacity to switch between
modes of transformation (from *hentai* to *henshin*).

Shin-chan's obsession with Action Kamen appears early in the manga se-
ries and gradually becomes a trope. In the anime series, from the first episodes,
Action Kamen takes on greater importance, becoming the organizing conceit
for first animated movie, *Shinchan: Akushon Kamen tai Haigure Maō* (Crayon
Shin-chan: Action Kamen versus Leotard Devil, 1993), which was directed by the
series director for the first season of the anime series, Hongō Mitsuru. Hongō
Mitsuru then directed the next three movies (1994, 1995, 1996), while Hara
Kei'ichi moved from episode director to series director for the second season of
the anime. Hara Kei'ichi, who took on the direction of the next six *Crayon Shin-*

FIGURE 10.2. Shin-chan is often featured in front of the television mimicking what he sees, particularly the stunts of his hero, Action Kamen.

chan movies (1997–2002), also made Action Kamen central to one of his films, the eighth in the series, *Kureyon Shin-chan Arashi o Yobu Janguru* (Crayon Shin-chan whips up a storm: the jungle, 2000). Hongō returned to direct the sixteenth movie to celebrate the anniversary of the manga series's publishing house, centering it again on Action Kamen, *Kureyon Shinchan chō arashi wo yobu: Kinpoko no yūsha* (Crayon Shin-chan totally whips up a storm: the hero of the golden sword, 2008). In addition, the eighteenth movie, *Kureyon Shinchan: Chōjikū! Arashi o Yobu Ora no Hanayome* (Crayon Shin-chan super space-time! My bride who whips up a storm, 2010), directed by Shigino Akira, features a Shin-chan who travels into the future to save his future self, who is a version of Action Kamen. These movies supply the major point of reference for my account here, especially the first and eighth films. But let me first introduce Action Kamen and his relation to the SFX media mix and the broadcast TV ecology.

The character of Action Kamen in *Crayon Shin-chan* expressly builds on the media mix model that Okada Toshio deemed characteristic of the first generation of otaku (those born between 1955 and 1965). Shin-chan's creator, Utsui Yoshito, was, in fact, born in 1958. In this media mix model, special effects *(tokusatsu)* television shows that featured transforming heroes played the key role, such as the *Ultraman* series (begun in 1966) and the *Kamen Rider* series (first aired 1971–73), which two series serve as models for Shin-chan's beloved *Action Kamen* series. Shin-chan's media habits prove entirely consonant with those of first-generation otaku. For instance, his beloved Action Kamen TV show also promotes Shin-chan's favorite snack, little chocolate-filled nuggets called Chokobi (or Chocobees), which are a play on Kamen Rider snacks promoted in the early 1970s.[4] The first animated movie, after its teaser and the title and song sequence, opens with Shin-chan and his friends buying Chokobi to acquire Action Kamen cards (Figure 10.3). Building humorously on the media mix model associated with *Kamen Rider,* the *Crayon Shin-chan* series also reprises the media ecology from which this SFX media mix derived its distributive effects. It is a media ecology in which broadcast television played a key role for three reasons.

First, the television set sits in the common family room of the household where family members watch broadcast programs at prescribed times. *Action Kamen,* for instance, is shown in a particular time slot on a particular channel. When Shin-chan's mother scolds him for coming home late (good boys should come home by 5 PM), Shin-chan agrees, but for a quite different reason: *Action Kamen* comes on at five![5] Even if the hero show is targeted to the boy in the family, other family members may well watch, because there is only one TV. What is more, even if they do not watch it, it permeates their household experience in various ways. Shin-chan's mother, in an attempt to punish him for coming home late, steals the remote so he cannot turn on *Action Kamen.* Shin-chan simply resorts to the monitor controls instead, and a channel-switching war ensues between mother and son.[6] This is but one of many ways in which a television show targeted to one demographic comes to reach a wider, cross-demographic audience. Weekly manga magazines, as a result of their ubiquity, entailed similar effects, but the greater ubiquity, centrality, and commercial clout of the broadcast television within the national domestic formation made its effects more powerful and general.

Second, the television also serves as a site of code switching, both within and across programs, dramatized in the channel-switching war between Shin-chan and his mother. Animated TV series, for reasons discussed previously, proved especially adept at embodying and amplifying code switching. But special effects or *tokusatsu* also turned out to be quite effective for code switching, and the *henshin* hero in particular provided a way for shows to condense this switching within a character. *Henshin* fare thus paralleled and complemented the operations of limited cel animation, which contributed to the expansion and generalization of animation into animetic plane of consistency. It does not feel strange, for instance, that Action Kamen is rendered as an animated character in the *Crayon Shin-chan* series.

Third, in the 1970s, although the television set was not yet significantly wired with plug-ins to become a multifunctional platform with computational capacities, it had begun to anticipate its future role in media switching. Indeed, it had

FIGURE 10.3. The first animated movie opens with a riff combining the *Kamen Rider* media mix of the 1970s with the Bikkuriman chocolates media mix of the 1980s: Shin-chan and his friends buy Chokobi to acquire Action Kamen cards, meeting with disappointment when they do not wind up with the super rare card they desire.

already become the key medium for composing across media forms. In fact, Ishinomori Shōtarō's manga version of *Kamen Rider* appeared in serialization after the broadcast aired, which makes the television show into the pivotal media instance in the mix. The *Kamen Rider* series presents a logical permutation of the television-animation–centered media mix that exploded onto the scene with Tezuka's *Astro Boy,* a permutation in which *tokusatsu* operates as a variant of limited cel animation. The fact that Okada construes *tokusatsu* as the defining feature of the first generation of otaku provides a powerful reminder of the centrality of the broadcast television in the media mix.

The *Crayon Shin-chan* multimedia franchise, however, did not adopt the SFX media mix model. Its pattern centered instead on the adaptation of manga into television animation. This model began with Tezuka's *Astro Boy,* gathering steam in the 1970s to become the dominant model for media mix in the 1980s. Although this pattern peaked in the 1990s, it remains important today. Various factors have contributed to the astounding success of this pattern of manga-to-anime serialization: the ubiquity and centrality of television in daily life, greater investment in marketing and advertising, the increasing importance of manga weeklies and of the subsequent sales of manga books within major publishing houses, and, later, the revenue from videocassette rentals and sales. In this pattern, the animated television series or anime becomes the key instance, the pivot or linchpin, within the media mix, for economic reasons (imparting value retroactively to cheap manga published at a loss), for demographic reasons (crossing or seeping across market niches), for material semiotic reasons (code switching), and for mediatic reasons (media switching). This manga-to-anime pattern had become so dominant by the mid-1980s that Okada sees anime as the defining feature of the second generation of otaku (born 1965–75).

The *Crayon Shin-chan* series adopted this classic anime media mix model of the 1980s and 1990s. The popularity of weekly serial manga had already led to its publication in book form (thus accruing greater profits) by the time the anime series went on the air in 1992. If successful, an anime series not only spurs the sales and increases the value of the manga but also broadens its demographic. But another problem appears in conjunction with increased distribution: divergence. The manga and anime series start to diverge in a number of registers. For instance, the *Crayon Shin-chan* anime aired between 7 and 7:30 PM, during TV Asahi's golden time, which meant that its *seinen* (adult) content had to be reconsidered in light of viewing by children, adolescents, and families. In addition, while the manga consists largely of three- to four-page gag sequences, a thirty-minute anime series demands other forms of continuity and sequencing. To sustain the gaglike comedy while adding a new layer of continuity, many sequences and episodes rely on the parody of popular genres, of popular movies or programs, or of current events as a general setting for the gags. In this context, it is not surprising that Shin-chan's hero, Action Kamen, began to play a more important role, as did other characters, such as Shin-chan's neighborhood gang of friends.

With the production of feature-length films, divergence increased. Here too the character of Action Kamen was used to impart a greater sense of narrative consistency to the movie format. Yet he changes in the process. The anime series often takes a parodic tone vis-à-vis Action Kamen, which the English dub strove to capture by calling him "Action Bastard." In the feature-length films, the tone of parody persisted, yet because such films are even more obviously geared toward audiences comprising a family with children, Action Kamen gradually took on more recognizably heroic and righteous qualities. Shin-chan himself began to play a variety of heroic roles, albeit in a tongue-in-cheek manner, grounded in large-form genres such as the spy movie, the western, or the samurai film, as well as genre remix (for example, time-travel samurai films).

In the course of multimedia serialization, divergence is inevitable. Manga, television anime series, and animated films are necessarily unfaithful to each other. In the case of the *Crayon Shin-chan* series, it is the anime that allows these different media instances (manga and movie) to communicate with one another. The manga series and movie series feel like entirely different media worlds; they are almost incommensurable. The movies use the characters and the stock gags from the manga, but these characters and gags have already been filtered through the anime. In this respect, the TV anime plays a pivotal role, producing the link between the manga and the movies.

Let me briefly introduce some of the factors contributing to the play of similarity and difference across manga, anime, and films in general. On the one hand, various factors have contributed to the increased entanglement of manga and anime. First, as a result of the prevalence of manga-to-anime adaptations, each media form began to take on some formal features of the other from the 1960s onward.[7] Thus, by the late 1980s, manga characters even began to look more like anime characters. Second, the *dōjin* production of manga in the 1980s contributed to a sense of the manga world as somehow smaller and more intimate than anime, while because of the broader demographic reach and increased profits associated with anime adaptations, it also began to feel as if manga aspired to become anime.[8] Such factors contributed to the sense of a deep connection between manga and anime, connections deeper than formal resemblance or shared stories—infraindividual intra-action.

On the other hand are the factors that conspired to make feature-length animated movies look like television animation. First, when anime series first began to move onto the big screen, the movie was often an abridged, reedited version of a few episodes or an entire season of the anime series, sometimes with some new footage added. Second, the rise of video and then DVD meant that the big-screen animated film would actually receive its widest distribution and largest number of viewers on the household television set, as if the animated film was fated to be folded back into television animation through its distribution. Finally, although the animated films are feature-length movies and often depend on parody of well-known film genres, their aesthetic harkens back more to anime than cinema. As early as the 1970s, for instance, it became common practice to release an abridged and reedited film version of popular TV anime series. The aesthetics of such anime films owed nothing to the cinematic animated film but drew almost entirely on techniques and effects associated with TV anime. However, their popularity proved that audiences neither expected nor demanded a cinematic experience from these anime films.

This trend paved the way for television anime directors to move into the production of animated films. In the case of *Crayon Shin-chan,* for instance, the directors for animated movies first gained experience working on the anime series. Hongō served as series director for the first season before directing the first four films. Hara Kei'ichi worked on storyboards, as an episode director, and then as series director before taking on the next six animated movies. Subsequent directors, such as Mizushima Tsutomu (movies 11 and 12), Masui Sōichi (movies 19 and 20), Hashimoto Masakazu (movie 21), and Takahashi Wataru (movie 22) first gained experience working on the anime series and then on the animated movies in various capacities before directing films. The twenty-second movie, *Kureyon Shin-chan Gachinko! Gyakushū no Robo Tō-chan* (Crayon Shin-chan all-out! Robo-Dad strikes back, 2014), which was the highest grossing Shin-chan film since the first two were released in 1993 and 1994, had Takahashi, one of the oldest hands from the TV series, at the helm. Directors frequently step back into other roles. Hongō and Hara often supplied storyboards or supervision when not directing. For a variety of reasons, then, the hold of the original anime series team over the film productions has been significant.

In sum, as the different media instances (manga, anime, movies, games) diverge, it is the anime series that allows them to communicate with one another for a combination of reasons—aesthetic, economic, demographic, semiotic, and medial. The result is not media convergence, at least not in its usual sense, associated with the work of Henry Jenkins. First, where Jenkins's model of media convergence gives a central role to the Hollywood blockbuster film, this sort of media mix, in contrast, pivots on television animation. Second, television animation is able to serve as a communicator or mediator across a range of media forms (not only manga but also light novels, toys, and games, to name some major sources) because it comes to embody the distributive capacity of television as expressed in code switching and media switching. Television animation or anime ceases to be a form or set of forms; instead it becomes a set of functions and a plane of composition for multimedia serialization. Third, because it is television animation that serves as the communicator between media forms, this sort of multimedia serialization is grounded in (or folded within) a specific media ecology: broadcast television and its ongoing new media intensification. This broadcast ecology provides a sort of eddy within the whirlpool of distribution capacity, and strategies of media mix are strategies to dwell within this eddy, where it seems possible to channel and harness the force of the surrounding currents. For these reasons, as discussed in chapter 5, transmedia storytelling is nothing new in Japan, and certainly not a posttelevision phenomenon. The economic power of the publishing industry and the distributive capacity of television came together profitably in the production of anime adaptations of manga, which led to an expansion and refinement of the manga–anime encounter, including transmedia storytelling.

In the context of the early 1990s, when the transformation of television into new media was already well underway, the reliance of the *Crayon Shin-chan* media mix on the 1970s SFX mix and its broadcast ecology may seem odd, anachronistic, and possibly nostalgic, especially because its major trope is the transforming-hero show airing on a television in the living room. Indeed, the extent to which the paradigm of broadcast television media remains central to the vision of media in the series is startling. Even the more recent films return time and again to Action Kamen, and the *Crayon Shin-chan* world remains one of broadcast towers and household television sets. It is also, by extension, a world in which media are transmitted from the one to the many.

It is worthwhile to recall that the *Crayon Shin-chan* creators who shaped the multimedia franchise were all born in the late 1950s: manga-ka Utsui Yoshito was born in 1958, Hongō Mitsuru and Hara Kei'ichi in 1959. (The other director who centered a film on Action Kamen, Shigino Akira, was born in 1953.) These three creators, whether they would consider themselves otaku or not, are contemporaries of the first generation of otaku media. Their generation was coming into its prime in the late 1980s. Their use of the broadcast ecology only appears behind the times if histories are reduced to a single, simplistic linear movement from one medium to another. As the layering of different generations of media mix within *Crayon Shin-chan* attests, however, historical movement is never simple or linear. Shin-chan watching Action Kamen on the household TV captures the past (SFX media mix), channels the present (anime media mix), and anticipates the future (character-centered, game-soaked media mix). It is precisely because the underlying broadcast ecology is an assembling of polarized tendencies that its temporality may be at once anachronistic and right on time. The franchise remains highly popular today. Consequently, instead of asking whether broadcast ecology and SFX media mix are old-fashioned, the crucial questions are these: How do you dwell with this sort of television ecology? How do you inhabit its assembling?

Shin-chan wiggles his way toward one solution. Sometimes he sits and watches television quietly enough, but gradually the manga shows him mimicking the movements on the screen, mostly of human figures but sometimes of nonhuman figures as well. The charged field in front of the TV becomes a zone for a particular kind of play—the kind Walter Benjamin evokes in his accounts of semblance and the mimetic faculty: the child mimicking the windmill or imitating the passage of clouds. So do the movements on the television screen course through Shin-chan's body. He does not internalize its messages. He may not even hear them, and if he did, Shin-chan would not grant them any more authority than he grants any other figures of authority—parents, teachers, shop clerks, which is to say adults in general. Consequently, as a result of his general rejection of authority and hierarchy, Shin-chan introduces a tentative split within the one-to-many tendency of broadcast television, a split between a hierarchical tendency (centralized authority) and a unidirectional tendency. The result is a very different way of understanding (and performing) the effects of television.

Because Shin-chan separates out and refuses everything that constitutes authority, his relation to television runs counter to the propaganda model, thus stymying any attempt at the imposition of a univocal message. This refusal is part of Shin-chan's mode of being. The humor of *Crayon Shin-chan* comes from how deftly Utsui sets the stage for Shin-chan to outwit adults, to get his way despite their efforts to thwart his wishes, and to expose adults as idiots in the process. The setup never loses its punch: adults speak to Shin-chan as if they are reasonable, as if they might implant reasonableness in him. In retort, Shin-chan always finds the gesture or phrase that punctures this show of reasonableness, thus exposing adult behavior as somehow unreasonable, and usually downright contradictory and even hypocritical. Adults confirm his stance by turning nonplussed and then losing their temper. In effect, Shin-chan's sense of timing shows that adult behavior is not rational but affective—as affective as any child's behavior. His retorts introduce a lag within reason, from which affect bursts forth. He thus rejects the hierarchy of reason over affect, preferring to stick to his bodily functions, like pissing, shitting, wiggling, and cooing—and because Shin-chan is drawn to pornography and any sort of female display of sexuality, fucking feels as if were on the horizon as well. This is why, as a media entity, he is perfectly endowed to depose the hierarchy of the message and elevate the bodily functions of media.

Shin-chan's ability to depose the hierarchical message continues to be a central trope in the anime series. In the animated movies, it often becomes prolonged into a narrative thematic: Shin-chan deposes dictators, monarchs, propagandists, and a range of other villains who seek to monopolize the message, to render it univocal and authoritative. In the eighteenth film, for instance, Shin-chan travels to the future to battle the corporate despot, Kaneari, who holds sway over the city of Neo-Tokio, proclaiming his rule from large television screens tacked on the sides of skyscrapers to impose his will on the populace (Figure 10.4).

In the world of this film, giant meteors struck the earth and clouded the skies when Shin-chan and friends were about five years old. Business mogul Kaneari acquired unprecedented power by developing a monopoly on electricity. The result is a city strictly divided into energy haves and energy have-nots. The futuristic megalopolis of Neo-Tokio, surrounded by moatlike rivers, abounds in soaring skyscrapers, brilliantly lit against the sky. On the outskirts of Neo-Tokio, however, the homes in Shin-chan's suburban neighborhood have become dilapidated and impoverished. The Shin-chan of this future city has adopted the guise of Action Kamen to combat the evils of Neo-Tokio, chief among them Kaneari.

Kaneari has encased the future Shin-chan Action Kamen within a statue, not only to stamp out his rebellious influence but also to prevent him from marrying his daughter. The daughter travels to the past, however, to bring the five-year-old Shin-chan (and accidently his friends as well) into the future to save the day.

FIGURE 10.4. In the eighteenth *Crayon Shin-chan* film, Shin-chan travels to the future to battle the corporate despot, Kaneari, who holds sway over the city of Neo-Tokio, proclaiming his rule from large television screens tacked on the sides of skyscrapers to impose his will on the populace.

Thus our diminutive *hentai* hero is called upon to fulfill his destiny as a full-size *henshin* hero. The imposition of the villain Kaneari's will on the city repeats in the familial register: at one point, he broadcasts commands to his daughter from television screens throughout the city. The result is an obviously Oedipal scenario: the future groom must defeat the girl's powerful father to win her hand in marriage. This Oedipus complex becomes thoroughly mangled and enmeshed with the media matrix: the little boy Shin-chan must confront and defeat the towering broadcast system that empowers the masterful voice of the energy monopolist in order to take on his full heroic manhood as Action Kamen. In classic psychoanalytic fashion, the stage is set for an internalization of the force of broadcast television on the part of the little man-child to compensate for his lack.

Ultimately, however, the Oedipal displacement of male authority does not take place in the classic fashion because of Shin-chan's propensity toward splitting the signal into two tendencies, hierarchical and unidirectional, in order to reject the hierarchical tendency. As such, what Shin-chan internalizes is not authority or hierarchy. Instead, he internalizes and embodies the unidirectional tendency. Put another way, he individualizes the totalizing tendency of broadcast television and becomes like a tiny self-powered automated TV. Big TV is shattered into a thousand tiny TVs, myriad little screens without messages as such.

Similar gestures occur across the audiovisual surfaces of the screen: small cartoon characters appear against giant hyperreal backgrounds; graphic bursts of color and line confound any sense of depth of movement; the large image frequently splits into smaller screenlike geometric fragments, which take on distinct temporal flows and sometimes distinct forms of action; flashes of light crackle across the image or pulse through sequences; sound applies not only to diegetic sounds but also extends into screen effects, as if to make media themselves part of the action; and musical sequences crop up, inserting smaller media genres into the overall show, creating side attractions. A nicely condensed example of these aesthetic tendencies appears in the eighteenth movie, when corporate despot Kaneari takes control of a giant robot to crush Shin-chan as well as his friends and family. A screen on the chest of the robot shows a music video of Action Kamen singing and dancing with cartoon animals, while Shin-chan climbs onto the robot to put out one of his eyes (Figure 10.5). The ultimate would-be Oedipal showdown in which the boy pokes out the father-despot's eye is shattered by incongruous audiovisual overlays that conjure up seemingly incommensurable tropes and themes as well as media forms and functions. The experience, needless to say, is not cinematic in any received sense. It is like television and animation gone wild, anime shattering and carrying off fragments of cinema and its big screen while amplifying and intensifying small screen effects to the point where they scatter into autonomous signals whose intermittent intersections and entanglements become the show.

These schizoid effects are potentially egalitarian in their aesthetics, not only because they tend to level hierarchies within the image but also because their origins are humble, deriving from techniques of limited cel animation used to streamline anime production to meet weekly programming schedules. What is more, in the process of deposing or overturning the despotic villain, Shin-chan's antics mobilize a motley crowd with diverse affiliations: alongside his increasingly eccentric friends and family appears a gamut of neighborhood crazies, secret societies, underground organizations, special ops, and genuinely wacko groups spanning the spectrum from religious cults to exercise fanatics to ecoterrorists. Is Shin-chan at the center of a new nonsectarian movement that takes root in the demotic, leveling, parasocial aesthetics of daytime television to furl into nonaffiliated or weirdly affiliated "groupuscules" posing a genuinely alternative worldview? Or does this series tend to align the family and the neighbor with the received social order, to affirm what already is? And if Shin-chan does succeed in stripping away any traces of an authoritarian disposition within the one-to-many

FIGURE 10.5. In the eighteenth
Shin-chan movie, the villain
Kaneari mobilizes a giant robot
to attack Shin-chan and company.
As if to anticipate the victory of
the little screen, the robot's chest
plays a dance video featuring
Action Kamen and cute animals.
In this image, Shin-chan has
climbed onto the robot and
has blocked his eye, literally
screening the robot's perception
and making it malfunction.

tendency of broadcast television, is there something that replaces broadcast television? Is there another possible TV formation?

While such questions make for an overly stark contrast, as if the *Crayon Shin-
chan* series could be definitively placed into one camp or the other, they do help
to situate the challenge of the series. Its challenge comes of its bid to split off
(and reject) the hierarchical tendencies of the one-to-many tendency of national
domestic broadcast television formation while retaining its unidirectional force
and shunting it into a multitude of ones (throngs of outrageous beings) or into
a multitudinous, multiplicitous one (Shin-chan). As the broadcast signal passes
through Shin-chan's wiggling body, there is a movement from univocity (univocal message) to multivocity (multivocal signing).

Similarly, it was the hallmark of early cultural studies of television, as in the
work of Umberto Eco and Stuart Hall, to reject the notions of a univocal broadcast

message and a passive audience. Their pathbreaking work on codes and semiotics called attention to the ways in which receivers actively decoded and recoded television, and even refused its codes outright. Such work paved the way for thinking about angry, irritable bodies and disgruntled, disenfranchised, even combative audiences. Eco's early work on television offers an especially good point of reference for considering the challenge posed by the *Crayon Shin-chan* series, for it similarly strives to dispense with the univocal authoritative broadcast message and develop other ways of using television.

How Children Have Bad Effects on TV

Eco invites a departure from the questions that have, in his opinion, dominated the study of television, namely, "What do mass communications do to audiences?"[9] Instead, he directs attention to what audiences do to or with mass communications. His approach is opposed to the neurological studies explored previously, in which the focus is consistently on the harm media may inflict on brains. Hence his provocative question: do audiences have bad effects on television? Or, we might add, do brains hurt television?

Eco's focus is on content analysis, on the message, and on what audiences do with the message. What interests him are those moments when people fail to understand the message in accordance with the senders' intentions.[10] Yet failure to understand the television message does not signal for him a simple error that can be corrected by educating the audience or making the message clearer. Rather, he reminds us that the message is in fact "a text on which converge messages based on different codes."[11] Sending a univocal unambiguous message is impossible. Failure to understand on the part of an audience is not a passive misunderstanding. Eco calls attention to a dimension of misunderstanding that is potentially active. Active refusal resides tacitly in the failure to understand.

Active refusal is, of course, Shin-chan's general strategy with messages from figures of authority. When his mother scolds him that he is to be home by 5 PM like a good boy, he hears something entirely different: it's time for the Action Kamen show! Shin-chan always fails to understand messages that run counter to his single-minded, or rather nonminded, bodily desires. He can extract from any message a meaning that suits his wishes, turning the inherently multivocal quality of language to his advantage. But what is it that he fails to understand about TV? Above all, he actively fails to understand that Action Kamen is not real. Or, more precisely, he refuses the received logic of representation, whereby the actor playing the role is real but the role (representation) itself is not real. The first movie, for instance, adopts Shin-chan's point of view, positing that Action Kamen is indeed real. Action Kamen has come from another version of earth to this one in order to play the role on TV. To bypass the logical divide between reality and representation, the movie resorts to multiple possible worlds. There is thus a world in which Action Kamen is real and not a mere representation or fantasy. Gradually everyone is pulled into Shin-chan's multiple worldview, although to some of them it continues to feel somehow unreal. His parents remark at one point that it feels like they are in a cartoon film *(manga eiga)*. Shin-chan's failure to understand thus appears to be somewhat different from Eco's account.

In the failure of certain audiences to understand television's messages, Eco sees not passive inability or incompetence but rather nonconscious yet active refusal, an act of self-exclusion, which implies potential for the formation of a self-conscious, critical subject who may take a political stand in the world. Eco builds on Paolo Fabbri and Walter Benjamin to characterize television reception in terms of "detached involvement," a combination of distracted noncognitive daydreaming, combined with the "reticence of someone who doesn't feel involved."[12] This is Eco's way of avoiding the attention–reason complex, in which constant distraction (attention) encloses the audience within a world of mental representations. Instead of focusing exclusively on the immediacy of stimulus (attention and distraction), he allows for a temporal lag, for affect—a feeling of reticence.

In contrast, in the case of Shin-chan, the temporal lag is not a feeling of reticence but an outgoing, extroverted, overly involved, communicative feeling. Shin-chan feels he communicates with Action Kamen, as do the other children. For instance, the villain arrives from the other earth and steals the action stone in Action Kamen's belt, which is needed to travel between worlds. Because Action Kamen leaves to recover his action stone, the producers of the TV show replace him with another actor. Shin-chan feels so attached to Action Kamen, so in touch, and so in communication with him that he can instantly detect the impostor. Shin-chan is rarely reticent or detached.

For Eco, it is the institutionalization of affect, of the feeling of reticence or detachment, that transforms it into something socially and politically generative. When reticence is institutionalized, it turns into a mechanism of self-exclusion ("this doesn't concern me!"), which may give rise to institutionalization of refusal and factious interpretation,[13] which in turn would pave the way for "a community which has stopped regarding itself as an object of surveys, and is, instead, a subject that discusses and brings into the open its own rules of competence and interpretation, discovering in the meantime, those of others."[14]

Eco insists on this movement of institutionalization precisely because he wishes to avoid a neutral stance vis-à-vis the question of how audiences use television. In effect, he wishes to avoid a neutral stance because the neutral stance "could end up with a 'free market' theory according to which *the audience does what it wants with the message.*"[15] Consequently, his emphasis falls on the possibilities for the emergence of communities linguistically marginalized within the nation-state.

Although the *Crayon Shin-chan* series does not side with the self-determining movement of any linguistically (or otherwise) marginalized communities in Japan, it does not allow audiences to make whatever they want of Action Kamen either. It is not a neutralized free market free-for-all. Shin-chan himself introduces rules of interpretation or of competence vis-à-vis TV, with one crucial rule being that Action Kamen is real. This rule implies a more basic stance: fantasy is real and has real effects, because desire is something. In this way, the *Crayon Shin-chan* series entails a kind of institutionalization of its basic temporal lag, the gaglike reversal built into Shin-chan's reply to authoritative stances. If the *Crayon Shin-chan* series builds in a mechanism of self-exclusion, it entails excluding oneself from stances relying on reason, positing a foundational divide between reality and representation. Such stances ultimately marginalize desire, for they assume that desire is always for something, for an object. In contrast, in the *Crayon Shin-chan* series, desire is something, with a reality in itself.

Where Eco wishes to transform linguistically marginalized groups into self-determining politically active communities, Shin-chan strives to prevent the marginalization of his libido. In the same vein, the *Crayon Shin-chan* series works to institutionalize the libido, or rather the libidinous, which has been marginalized by the adult world with its reality despotism and representation police. The result is a libidinal politics, which addresses broadcast television at an entirely different level than Eco's semiotic analysis of content with its linguistic orientation. Yet the two stances are oddly, uncannily alike at another level.

In semiotic terms, Eco assumes that a univocal message is impossible even as he assumes that television is unidirectional in medial terms. His gesture is analogous to that of Shin-chan: he splits off the hierarchical tendency in order to challenge and reject it. However, Eco completely ignores the unidirectional tendency associated with media. This is precisely where Shin-chan tries to adhere (in an effort to cohere): to the slippery surfaces of the monstrous body of television's distributive capacity. He hangs onto the very reality of TV's fantasy as it moves beneath him like a whirlwind, carrying him along. One line of fantasy is that Shin-chan and Action Kamen are the same person and not the same person. They are a couple that are not a couple. There is an Oedipal solution to this paradox, namely that Shin-chan grows up to be Action Kamen—a development scenario culminating in a full substitution, or at least a socially stabilizing substitution. The eighteenth movie flirts with this scenario. Yet the movie reverses the logic of substitution using time travel: the bride seeks out the boy and the boy must rescue his adult self; then duplicates spill onto the scene—duplicates of friends and family. The *Crayon Shin-chan* series delights in the liberation of doubles. These doubles are not ghostly apparitions in the sense of revenants but rather harbingers of possible worlds, avenants, and futures.

Still, the question highlighted in Eco's account remains: how does the uni-

FIGURE 10.6. The villain in the first *Crayon Shin-chan* movie erects an insane-looking robotic "high-leg" broadcast tower atop a high-rise in Shinjuku, which sends out signals compelling people to don high-cut exercise leotards while chanting *"haigure, haigure"* or "high leg, high leg."

directional tendency of broadcast television also serve to constrain (even as it liberates) the process of multiplying and proliferating possible selves? The first movie clearly sets the stakes for Shin-chan's doubling of Action Kamen, and in a manner that sets the stakes for libidinal politics of the entire *Crayon Shin-chan* series.

In the first movie, the univocal or hierarchical tendency of broadcast television is embodied in the villain. The villain has taken control over the other earth by erecting a tower in Shinjuku that sends out signals that compel people to don high-cut exercise leotards while chanting *"haigure, haigure"* or "high leg, high leg" (Figure 10.6)—hence the villain's name, Haigure Maō or "Demon King High-Cut Leotard." The model of control is that of broadcast propaganda or advertisement, which somehow transforms individuals into an identically uniformed mass of people chanting slogans and exercising in unison. The absurdity of this scenario lies in the sense of embarrassment provoked by the ridiculous-looking costumes. It is especially hilarious and humiliating for the men forced into servitude to this broadcast craze because they appear shamelessly feminized. Indeed, the scandal of feminized men is what holds the movie together. In the final scenes, it turns out that the villain is not a man, or rather not a manly man, but one who proudly announces himself to be *okama,* derogatory slang applied indiscriminately to transvestite or homosexual men. One of his minions, T-Back, is also homosexual, a muscular, bearded biker who sports a thong and oscillates between roaring savagely and mincing. These men are but two of the many ridiculously homosexual types who populate the *Crayon Shin-chan* series.

Nonetheless, heterosexuality does not emerge as a norm which with to pathologize queerness. While the series consistently plays homosexuality for laughs as over-the-top behavior, it is exceedingly liberal (albeit coy) in its application of homoeroticism. It slyly extends it to men who are positioned as straight, that is, neither feminine nor outrageously manly, such as Action Kamen himself. How manly is that Kamen outfit anyway? Near the climax of the first movie, when Shin-chan confronts Haigure Maō, Shin-chan ends up with the action stone, which he stuffs into his pants. He then summons Action Kamen, who bounds out of his crotch, in the manner of a fantastical erection or queer birth. When a man is born so vibrantly from a boy's crotch, it is difficult to say what exactly is happening (Figure 10.7). This is precisely the point. At the close of the film, this weird incident is cause for embarrassment on the part of Action Kamen, who asks Shin-chan not to tell the other children. Shin-chan asks, with a blush of embarrassment, if that is what is meant by a secret among men. This exchange seems at once to evoke homosociality to contain homoeroticism and homosexuality, and to make those distinctions impossible. If everything is libidinous, then, to everyone's embarrassment, every gesture is potentially erotic, like Shin-chan nibbling sensuously on his father's ear; every exchange harbors pan-sexual possibilities, overtly, even publicly—like Action Kamen coming out of Shin-chan's pants.

Instead of a dirty little secret, sexuality in the Shin-chan world is more like masturbating in public, sexing yourself and everyone else in the process. It is like broadcasting practices of self-stimulation in a bid to make them into a group activity: *haigure, haigure!* Shin-chan and Haigure Maō are the same in this respect. Ultimately, however, Shin-chan differs from Haigure Maō, and from other adults for that matter, in that his autoerotic propensities are defined as prepubescent. Orgasm, then, does not happen, or, if there is something like orgasm, it has a meaning not readily comprehensible from the perspective of adult sexuality. Consequently, Shin-chan's fascination with his penis and with its potential enlargement may be read in two conflicting ways.

On the one hand, the libidinous is defined in male terms, and transformative possibilities are consistently mapped onto the weird deformative capacity of the penis. Female deformation is difficult to imagine, unless it is allied with normative heterosexuality or male homosexuality. As such, it is easy to read *Crayon Shin-chan* as nothing more than an autoerotic enlargement of the sphere of the

FIGURE 10.7. Toward the end of the first movie, Shin-chan summons Action Kamen, who springs into action from his crotch.

male libido, reinforcing a familiar homosocial fantasy with potentially normative implications for gender roles in the household and the workplace. In this respect, the recent success of the nineteenth movie, the first anime film centered on Shin-chan's father, Hiroshi, provides a new litmus test for the gender politics of *Crayon Shin-chan,* for Hiroshi is transformed into a robot and is led into a battle against a conspiracy on the part of a secret society to restore the authority of the family father in Japan.

On the other hand, even though just about anything arouses Shin-chan, as if he were a horny teenager or dirty old man, he is not depicted or described as having erections, and even if he has them, his mode of erotic enjoyment—orgasm, as it were—remains out of focus, intense yet diffuse. Also, when Action Kamen is born out of his shorts, it implies generative force, a semblance of giving birth. It evokes an experience Lacan attributed primarily to women, and to saints and mystics in particular—a spiritual yet profane experience of the Absolute, an out-of-body experience, a nonpersonal orgasm.

The first *Crayon Shin-chan* movie culminates in a climax that arrives as an extended series of flashes, an eye-searing effect produced by the rapid alternation of three images (the baseline scene; sketches of the scene on a white background; and a white screen with intensely transmitted light), to the point where they cannot be distinctly perceived as they are experienced. Thus the Shin-chan world strives toward a nonpersonal orgasm of animation, a pure experience of the stuff of blink. If they wish to sustain the more radical possibilities of the series, fans of *Crayon Shin-chan* need to ensure that this experience does not become an ideal complement to the male libido. This blinky experience is the profane reality of the Shin-chan world in its bid to harness the unidirectional force of broadcast television while rejecting its hierarchical tendencies. It is the stuff that a nonsectarian libidinal media politics might be made of.

11

THE HOME THEATER COMPLEX

HIGHLIGHTING THE SOCIAL IMPACT OF TELEVISION ON THE NUCLEAR FAMILY FROM THE PERSPECTIVE OF A PRECOCIOUS five-year-old, the *Crayon Shin-chan* multimedia series showed how the one-to-many tendency of broadcast television could be split into two tendencies, hierarchical and unidirectional. The hierarchical tendency is totalizing. It strives to impose a univocal message on an entire population from a centralized source. The unidirectional tendency can be individualized in that it implies a tendency to stick to a single-minded pattern of reception, based on an invariant and impersonal interval, to the point of nonmindedness. In the case of Shin-chan, this single-minded tendency entails introducing a gap between message and meaning, twisting and rejecting apparently reasonable demands in favor of pursuing libidinal bliss.[1]

Rather than promulgate a new message, Shin-chan's pursuit of meaning is less about delivering content than about enacting an experience of libidinous affect. The result might be described as a tendency toward privatization without centralization, individualization without totalization. As he splits, individualizes, and embodies the one-to-many tendency of broadcast television, Shin-chan ends up oscillating between two possibilities: tiny male tyrant (a little privatized central authority) and anarchic quasi-orgasmic dissipation of received social hierarchies. In subjective terms, the broadcast media complex of *Crayon Shin-chan* oscillates between an Oedipus complex and an anti–Oedipus complex vis-à-vis television infrastructures and platforms. It jibes with Guattari's and Foucault's insistence that psychic complexes (or subjectivities) are not autonomous of material formations; nor are they products of them. They cling to the monstrous whirlwind distributive media body from the outset, adhering and cohering when and where possible.

In the instance of television media, as prior chapters have shown, the broadcast one-to-many media complex of the *Crayon Shin-chan* series is only half the story. The other half is the point-to-point tendency. To explore this other tendency, this chapter turns to another successful multimedia series, *Meitantei Konan,* styled in English as *Detective Conan* or *Case Closed.* The two series are comparable in many ways. The protagonist of *Detective Conan* is roughly the same age as Shin-chan (Conan is declared to be about age six), and its creator, Aoyama Gōshō (born Aoyama Yoshimasa in 1963), is about the same age as Shin-chan's creator. The *Detective Conan* manga began serialization in 1994, only four years after *Crayon Shin-chan,* also in a weekly manga magazine backed by a powerful publishing house, Shōgakukan's *Weekly Shōnen Sunday.* Like *Crayon Shin-chan,* it was also adapted into an anime series within two years, which started airing in 1996 on major networks in a thirty-minute slot during prime time. It was broadcast on the Nippon Television Network System (NNS) in the Kansai area and on Yomiuri TV (YTV) in the Kantō area, both organized by NTV. Likewise, one year later, in 1997, animated *Conan* movies began to appear each year, with the first seven directed by the series director of the anime, Kodama Kenji.

In its historical moment, in its creation, publication, and media mix model, the *Detective Conan* series is largely analogous to the *Crayon Shin-chan* series. *Detective Conan* has enjoyed even greater commercial and critical success than *Crayon Shin-chan,* with both its manga and anime ranking among the top all-time favorites and winning various awards. The *Detective Conan* series differs somewhat from *Crayon Shin-chan* in that its identified demographic is boys *(shōnen)* rather than adult men *(seinen),* and its publishing house (Shōgakukan) is more powerful, two factors that have surely contributed to its phenomenal success. Its media mix has also taken some different directions—for instance its serializations as live-action television dramas and CD dramas. Still, these are not shocking differences, and the series are comparable.

A greater discrepancy appears at the level of their media complex, however, and that is what interests me here. While its media mix and media ecology also conspire to make broadcast television function as the linchpin, the *Detective Conan* series tends to treat broadcast television as one medium among others at the level of its audiovisual tropes, themes, motifs, stories, and narrative play-through. It thus approaches broadcast television media from a very different perspective, one that brings the point-to-point tendency to the fore. At the same time, the *Detective Conan* series splits this tendency into two tendencies, environmental and heterarchical. For these reasons, the *Detective Conan* series provides a good point of reference for considering how the point-to-point tendency becomes subjectivized, and how it splits and twines into an infrastructure complex across the slippery surfaces of television's distributive capacity.

Mystery Otaku

For the detective, anything and everything may function like a recording medium. Wherever the detective looks, she detects traces of what has occurred, recently or over the course of years: she finds meaningful patterns in a person's gait, in calluses on the hands, in the scattering of crumbs, in splash marks on a wall, in the broken twigs of a rosebush. There are many different ways of capturing a movement, and the world abounds in indexical signs. Such is the poetry and science at the basis of detection—a world of signatures. The world affords incessant opportunities for narrating across or playing through an endless series of possible stories. But something else happens in detection, something that casts its shadow on poetry and science. A particular event, a disturbance of the social order, a crime, often a murder, becomes the point of reference. A closed domain replaces the world. Deduction steps in. As she reads the signatures of the world to establish their temporal order, the detective also must reach a conclusion: whodunit. She considers the list of possible suspects, reasons deductively, and rules possibilities out until only the guilty party is left. This is why the detective is said to be ruled by reason, not emotion.

In keeping with the genre, the *Detective Conan* manga highlights the work of detection and deductive reasoning. It introduces a new wrinkle, however. It opens with a young man, a senior in high school, Kudō Shin'ichi, who is quickly gaining renown as a detective, solving crimes beyond the abilities of the police. Also a gifted soccer player, he is rather arrogant about his intellectual and physical prowess. When it comes to his girlfriend, Mōri Ran, however, his abilities put him at a loss. When the two go on a date to an amusement park, Shin'ichi is utterly distracted: everything grabs his attention, and as a result, he seems completely locked into his thoughts and world. His conversation returns obsessively to explaining how he deductively detects patterns and reasons.

Shin'ichi is trapped within a variation on the attention–reason complex. He is at once distracted and locked in his head. What is more, although he longs to break out of his shell and to open up to Ran, events conspire to heighten his enclosure. A murder occurs on their ride at the amusement park, and Shin'ichi is compelled to solve it. While Ran feels the murder is frightening and unusual, it is the world as usual for Shin'ichi. Ran even remarks that he must live in a different world. Indeed, he does: he lives in a world composed of mysteries. Ran frequently refers to him as *suiri otaku* (mystery otaku).

Because Shin'ichi's father is a famous mystery writer, Shin'ichi has grown up reading mysteries, quite literally dwelling within a library of them at home. Yet his love of mysteries has not instilled in him a desire to become a mystery writer. He wishes to become a real detective. Oddly, however, his example of a real detective is Sherlock Holmes. Ran is quick to catch the contradiction, pointing out that Holmes is a fictional character. This contradiction does not bother

Shin'ichi. What matters for him is that Holmes is the greatest detective ever. He wishes to be the Sherlock Holmes of the 1990s. Ultimately, then, Shin'ichi is content to live in fictional world. He is intent on producing a mystery world in which he may become the greatest detective. He is indeed an otaku—but one in the negative sense of the term, trapped in his fictional world and shut off within his attention–reason complex.

In this way, deftly and subtly, with his delineation of a mystery otaku, manga creator Aoyama Gōshō puts his twist on the detective genre by opening up a set of associations between detective work (detection and deduction) and the attention–reason complex (an otaku mystery media complex). What sets the *Detective Conan* series in motion and lends it depth is the basic polarization in seventeen-year-old Kudō Shin'ichi's desire. On the one hand, he wants to become the world's greatest detective, that is, to remain within the otaku-like attention–reason complex. On the other hand, he wants to break out of the attention–reason complex in order to be closer to and more intimate with Ran. Aoyama's manga offers him an opportunity to do both at once.

After Shin'ichi solves the case at the amusement park, he trails suspicious-looking men who meet with other members of their crime syndicate, the Black Organization. The men discover Shin'ichi, and, aware of his work with the police, they opt to kill him with a recently synthesized and untested poison that will leave no trace. The toxin does not kill Shin'ichi, however. It acts on a cellular level to transform his body into that of a six-year-old boy while his mind remains unaltered. The names of the two men who poison him—Gin and Vodka—invite us to think of this transformation in terms of drunkenness, a sort of prolonged hallucinatory intoxication, in which the clarity of reason is folded into an unreal condition where it cannot achieve its ends directly. Indeed, our detective now embarks on an unusual kind of double life. He will remain a detective in pursuit of criminals, especially the Black Organization, but he lives undercover, for he is also a fugitive fleeing the Black Organization. Thus Shin'ichi comes to live as a six-year-old boy named Edogawa Conan.

Shin'ichi chooses this name under pressure. He has retreated to the home of an inventor, Professor Agasa Hiroshi, when Ran makes an appearance. Agasa has already persuaded Shin'ichi that he has to hide the truth and that he must work undercover as he pursues the Black Organization, because the Black Organization may do harm to him or to those close to him if they know he is still alive. When Ran appears, Shin'ichi must introduce himself. In a panic, he chooses his name from some books on the shelf: Edogawa Conan. His first name, Conan, comes from the author of the Sherlock Holmes mysteries, Arthur Conan Doyle. His last name comes from Edogawa Rampo, an author renowned for his tales of mystery and the uncanny, whose pen name is itself a play on Edgar Allan Poe. In name Shin'ichi thus becomes precisely what he said he did not want to become: a mystery writer—and not just any mystery writer but a combination of two of the most celebrated. He has transformed not only from Kudō Shin'ichi into Edogawa Conan, but also from a mystery otaku (who longs to become like a famous character in mysteries, Sherlock Holmes) into a mystery writer.

In the wake of this transformation, although Shin'ichi's mature mind solves the mysteries, Conan must close the case. Because his diminutive, immature body makes adults ignore or discredit what he says, Conan can only close the case by working behind the scenes. He becomes a sort of stage director, setting up a drama and working with those around him as if they were actors, or like an author who works with different characters in order to bring a situation to a satisfying conclusion. Indeed, in name, fictional characters surround Conan. He ends up living with Ran and her father, a detective whose name, Mōri Kogorō, evokes that of Edogawa Rampo's fictional detective, Akechi Kogorō. The police inspector who appears on the scene in all the initial mysteries is named Megure Jūzō, evoking Georges Simenon's fictional detective, Jules Maigret (pronounced "megure" in Japanese). Significantly, only the name of Conan's accomplice, Professor Agasa, evokes a mystery writer, Agatha Christie ("Agatha" is pronounced "Agasa" in Japanese). Agasa helps Conan write his stories with the fictional detectives around him.

The doubled detective is at once a consumer of fiction (Shin'ichi uses deduction to read or interpret the mystery) and a producer of fiction (Conan works with and through characters invisibly in order to close or write the case). This doubleness becomes the characteristic feature of the manga. The delight of reading *Detective Conan* comes from its double story line: seeing how Shin'ichi solves the mystery while seeing how Conan shapes the story from behind the scenes. This double story line also suits the format of the serialized mystery. While each case is generally closed in the course of three chapters (longer cases tend to be multiples of three), Conan's duplicitous situation provides an overarching story. He must, for instance, continue to explain Shin'ichi's absence to Ran; he even contacts her as Shin'ichi by telephone. He wants to tell her the truth, but he enjoys the proximity to her afforded to him as a child. What is more, Ran and Kogorō occasionally become suspicious of Conan, and he must stage new dramas to prolong the deception. Later in the series, Conan becomes able to revert to Shin'ichi, but only for a few hours. Thus an overarching story appears across the cases, a blend of melodrama and romance. Readers share in authorizing the duplicity: although they know from the conventions of the genre that Ran and Shin'ichi are destined to end up together in the end, they do not want the series to end, so they must side with Conan's duplicity, thus serializing the suspense of romance across the series of suspenseful mysteries.

This doubleness also imparts a distinctive tone and trajectory to the *Detective Conan* series. Shin'ichi is a better person as Conan than he is as Shin'ichi alone.

As Shin'ichi, he is admirable for his athletic ability, intellectual prowess, and dedication to justice, but he is not entirely likeable, and surely not loveable or adorable—at least not compared to Conan. As Shin'ichi, there are two paths he expressly wishes to avoid: that of his father, the successful writer, and that of Ran's father, an entirely imperfect and maybe even incompetent detective. Ran's father, Mōri Kogorō, often provides the comic relief in the *Detective Conan* series. A former policeman become detective, Kogorō smokes and drinks, struts and preens, gambles, flirts shamelessly, even lecherously, with young women, speaks loudly, arrogantly, and thoughtlessly, and above all, craves and demands attention. Shin'ichi is his opposite, which surely explains Ran's attraction to him, even though Shin'ichi's success is the ruin of her father's detective business. Not surprisingly, Shin'ichi sees only Kogorō's flaws.

When he becomes Conan, however, he gradually comes to feel a degree of affection and admiration for Kogorō. While Conan mutters and grumbles darkly to himself as Kogorō proudly and oafishly takes the credit for solving crimes that Conan has in fact solved, Conan comes to see his potential through the imperfections—precisely because he is forced to work with him, around him, or through him. Early in the series, Agasa fashions a voice-altering device and installs it in Conan's bow tie. This allows Conan to knock out Kogorō (literally) at the crime scene and to speak to the assembled adults in Kogorō's voice. Kogorō becomes known as the "sleeping detective," for he does not appear to be awake when he comes up with his astounding solutions to mysteries. In a comedic and opportunistic way, Conan comes to depend on Kogorō. At the same time, as six-year-old Conan, Shin'ichi also experiences a sense of vulnerability because he no longer has the strength to defend himself. Although Agasa provides him with various contraptions to compensate for his physical limitations, Conan nonetheless feels his limitations and frequently depends on Ran's skills in karate to save him. All in all, as Conan, the perfect, invulnerable, autonomous Shin'ichi comes to understand flaws, vulnerability, and dependency—not only his own but also those of others.

This tone and trajectory extend to the family. Like much of boys' manga, the *Detective Conan* series tends to break the family apart in order to give the young protagonist sufficient autonomy to undertake various adventures. Shin'ichi lives alone to finish school in Japan while his parents live abroad. Ran's father and mother have separated, apparently as a result of Kogorō's brash behavior, and she lives alone with her father. These situations allow Conan, Ran, and Kogorō to become family. The breaks in family thus do not become obstacles to family. Rather, they become a new kind of extended family or adopted community. Generally speaking, in the *Detective Conan* series, invulnerability and autonomy give way to vulnerability and dependency, and it is the former, not the latter, which comes to appear as an obstacle to the formation of a family-like community. Conan's path, however, is inevitably a contorted one, weaving between dependency and autonomy. As the cover illustration to the first volume of the manga shows, the character design for Conan captures something of the weirdness of his twofold trajectory by condensing modalities: he appears dressed as Sherlock Holmes in a manner that simultaneously evokes an adorably diminutive yet worldly man of action and a humiliated household pet.

The *Detective Conan* series sets up a tension between the closed system of the independent mystery otaku (attention–reason complex and detachment) and the open family-like community of the dependent little boy (affective exposure and attachment). Needless to say, if given a normative status, this family-like community and its reliance on affective exposure and attachment (vulnerability, dependency, care) may prove exceedingly oppressive. I do not mean to endorse the affective dimension of the *Detective Conan* series as such. What interests me is how affect implies a pathway through or around the attention–reason complex, which engenders a more specific kind of complex from it. Put another way, what interests me about the *Detective Conan* series are its moments of improvisation. While the cases to be solved in the series tend to form deductively closed story systems, there is always a moment of improvisation when Conan has to act quickly behind the scenes to produce a little drama or improvise another story line. Improvisation is, of course, not a matter of doing whatever comes to mind. It requires a highly cultivated sense of situation.

Although Conan's moments of improvisation are scripted in the manga, there is a sense of the manga story being held temporally in suspense between two kinds of closure—between solving the mystery versus closing the case, as it were. In the moments of improvisation, Conan has to consider everyone present in terms of their potential, each in terms of his or her not-yet-expressed abilities and capacities. He acts with any eye to what others are doing or may do in order to act with them, even through them. Simply put, improvisation demands a sense of the infraindividual.[2] Such moments flatten hierarchy and unevenness but avoid neutralizing individual and social differences.

The *Detective Conan* series is also a media mix franchise, and as such, the question arises of what happens across media instances in the series. Does such improvisation continue to work effectively across media, and how? Or does the media mix and its implied media ecology undo these moments of infraindividual operations?

From Pervasive to Immersive Media

In keeping with the detective genre, the *Detective Conan* manga does not privilege broadcast television over other media. Solving a mystery relies on detection (reading material traces across media) and deduction (eliminating possible interpretations within a closed domain), a process that proves readily compatible with the closed otaku-like world of attention, distraction, and cognitive representations.

In keeping with the detective genre, when television makes an appearance in the *Detective Conan* series, you would expect it to be with an eye to the information or documentation it provides, relative to the closed domain of the mystery. In addition, because the resolution of a mystery typically hinges on indexical traces or documentation, the detective genre tends to address broadcast television from that angle, without according it any greater ontological weight than other media. If the detective genre has a medium preference, it is for photographs, and indeed in the cases in the *Detective Conan* series, photographs play a pivotal role more often than television does. The series attributes an indexical function to photography: the photograph affords a capture of what was present to it at a specific moment in the past and thus offers a material record of undeniable evidence.[3] In contrast, broadcast television is generally situated in and of the present. It commonly serves as a source for current news relative to the case at hand.

Consequently, unlike the *Crayon Shin-chan* series, in which emphasis consistently falls on the hierarchical and unidirectional tendencies of broadcast television and thus on its stupendous capacity for brainwashing its audience, the *Detective Conan* series does not dwell on the one-to-many tendency of broadcast TV. Nor does Conan strive to embody television as Shin-chan does.

Because anime, as an audiovisual media form, prefers to provide information in an audiovisual fashion, the *Detective Conan* anime series is fond of having televisions pop up on the fly in order to fill in whatever facts are needed. In the second episode, for instance, after a visit to the Ueno museum, Conan and three primary school friends (Ayumi, Genta, and Mitsuhiko) find a sheet of paper bearing a list of strange symbols. This proves to be a coded message that sets them on a hunt for hidden treasure. As they dash through the streets of Tokyo, television sets flicker from the window of an electronics store (Figure 11.1). They remain unaware that a group of three men, sharply dressed in dark suits, have seen them with the sheet of paper and are on their tail. No sooner have the kids, with the sinister men in pursuit, passed the store than the scene cuts directly to a television broadcast. A news report announces that police have just arrested a mob boss but have lost track of his henchman, as well as a huge stack of golden coins they had recently stolen. It is as if the scene has simply cut to one of the TV sets in the store window.

This device of situating television sets in the city wherever needed to fill in information necessary to the story builds on the genuine ubiquity of television in urban space, relying on television sets to make an appearance not only in homes but also on the streets and in restaurants, shops, and a variety of other public places. This device reinforces the feeling that television is pervasive, for television appears anywhere in the city you can pick up a signal, which is, practically speaking, everywhere. This strategy tends to downplay the one-to-many tendency of broadcast TV. Indeed, in episode 2, the pictographic symbols on the list lead

FIGURE 11.1. As Conan and his
friends run past an electronics
store, the screens of the
television sets flicker blankly,
yet as soon as they stop to look
at the television, it shows images.

the children to Tokyo Tower, but, in contrast to the *Crayon Shin-chan* series, the broadcast tower is not treated as a centralized source radiating messages down upon the populace. The broadcast tower figures simply as a prominent recognizable landmark in the city, one easily rendered as a pictogram, and its centralizing role in television transmission is unimportant to the story. The pervasiveness of ambient television, however, plays a key role.

The image of television in *Detective Conan*—pervasive, ambient, public, yet not centralized—recalls Yoshimi's discussion of *gaitō terebi*, or street TV. Street TV operates as a sort of point-to-point event-based network. People pick up an item on TV in one part of the city, in the ramen shop, at the hairdresser's salon, or from a shop window, and develop the event as they discuss it with other people throughout the city. As people pick up the signal here and there, street TV turns into an urban network, a sort of mobile telecommunications network before the fact.

As for telecommunications, the *Detective Conan* series relies a good deal on telephones and mobile phones, not only as a neutral form of communication but also as a dramatic device, for Conan uses the telephone to stage Shin'ichi's presence. Typically, when Conan is speaking in Shin'ichi's voice on the phone, Shin'ichi's image appears, sometimes looming behind Conan, sometimes replacing him entirely, as if the telephone voice had the power to convey the speaker's image as well. The *Detective Conan* series is fond of using audiovisual fill-in techniques in conjunction with media devices, which contributes to and meshes with a more general tendency toward situating media platforms and audiovisual flow within a point-to-point mobile telecommunications network. Its use of ambient television is part of this tendency toward a world of all-around pervasive audiovisual signaling.

In the second episode of the anime series, however, there are already signs of a strange wrinkle in the point-to-point, anywhere-and-everywhere signal reception. The episode shows the mob henchmen in the real world of the story: they are in front of the museum searching for the coded message they dropped, and they see the children pick it up. Oddly, when the scene cuts to the television news broadcast and shows the same men on the screen, they do not appear any differently than in the real world. The screen world is not marked as different in any way from the real world, and as a consequence, humans and images appear equally real; they appear to have the same ontological consistency. In such moments, the anime series reinforces the parasocial tendency of television. The beings who appear on the screen appear as real as the beings who reside in the real world. The distinction between real world and screen world vanishes.

This is an effect easily produced in animation because the same images are used to render the on-screen and off-screen worlds. In fact, it takes more time and effort to mark the screen world as distinct from the real world: a layer must be added to the image on the television screen to make it appear separate from the everyday world. Generally, the *Detective Conan* manga takes care to separate the television world from the real world, drawing fine bands across the television image to indicate scan lines—an artifact of the ray gun scanning half the image in lines across the screen at a time. The *Detective Conan* anime, however, avoids using scan lines to differentiate the television screen. The people who appear on the television screen in the anime series thus look as real as people in the everyday real world. This opens the possibility for characters to move back and forth, unimpeded, between the everyday and television worlds. Potentially, then, any sort of entity or being may emerge from the television set and take up dwelling in the real world.

The *Detective Conan* series avoids this possibility, relying on conventions associated with a photographic ontology. The series sticks to characters who can be established as real people rather than having cartoon characters or machines swarm out from the TV set. The series relies on and reinforces a feeling that the images of people on TV are precisely *images of.* The images on TV are photographic captures of actual people and are derivative of them. Images are treated as of something; they are not treated as something in themselves. Such a gesture is in keeping with the detective genre, which depends on indexical traces serving as clues, evidence, and documentation. In this respect, the manga does introduce something of a source effect, which implies both a unidirectional and a hierarchical tendency, but instead of a centralized source, the source lies in the world around us.

Nonetheless, although the *Detective Conan* manga generally strives to differentiate real world from screen world and to assure that images are derivative of reality, there are, even in the manga, peculiar moments in which the hierarchical divide and unidirectional movement between reality and image break down. At the opening of the third case, for instance, Kogorō, whose lack of skill as a detective has left him at home drinking beer, smoking, and watching TV while waiting for business, reveals his infatuation with an idol singer, Okino Yōko. He presses his face close to the television set to ogle her as she sings, talking to her and whistling in approval. If Conan expresses a somewhat droll contempt vis-à-vis such behavior, it is because Kogorō's display of fandom appears excessive, particularly undignified for a grown man. Again, as with the characterization of Shin'ichi as a mystery otaku, the *Detective Conan* manga presents otaku activities in a negative light, characterizing such behavior as not only excessive but also as trapped within a mental fantasy.

It is also at such moments that the manga loses its grasp on reality—or, more precisely, on its photographic version of media reality. As Kogorō sits with his face close to the television, the doorbell rings, and there is Okino Yōko at the door. It is as if she had stepped out of the television into the real world. Suddenly the regime of photographic realism, with its firm sense of a line drawn from real world to image, threatens to break down. Kogorō, however, knows just what to do. He swiftly transforms his appearance into that of a dapper Lothario (Figure 11.2). Whereupon Conan asks dryly, "Who are you?"

This is the problem that arises when the unidirectional force of photographic capture is reversed: a new reality emerges in which images on the screen are as real as allegedly real people, which opens the possibility that no one need remain who they are. You may become someone else. It is in such moments that the pervasive media ecology transforms into an immersive media ecology. A tentative horizon appears, precisely because it is impossible to sustain a completely neutralized relation to the world or a completely indexical relation to media. Something intervenes to produce an event. In the context of the detective genre, that something is a crime, usually a murder. The *Detective Conan* series is equally fond of another eventful something: an otaku-like obsession with mysteries, with detectives or writers, or with idol singers, among other possible obsessions. The series introduces an affective charge that catalyses the formation of a specific media environment out of the larger media world.

FIGURE 11.2. While scenes of improvisation stick to the conventions of genre, as with this rapid transformation of Kogorō into a handsome suitor, they make use of techniques of light and movement, of flash and flicker, which are intended to impart an experience of something nonhabitual, akin to the electromagnetism of television.

The general point-to-point network tendency (the media world allows for interaction with signals anywhere and everywhere) thus splits into two tendencies. One tendency is toward the tentative formation of a horizon for an immersive world or an individualized environment, which might be called an environmental tendency. Such a tendency is to some extent implicit in the detective genre, at least in the detective fictions that gravitate toward larger-than-life personalities, celebrities, and the lives of the rich and famous, such as athletes, actors, singers, models, popular writers, or millionaires—people who are likely to make an appearance in the mass media. Such characters introduce obvious motives for crime (money, fame, reputation) and make the abundance of information about them feel plausible. The *Detective Conan* series enhances this tendency, pushing it to the limits in its very premise: a mystery otaku, who has gained his unparalleled skills in detection by reading fiction, is transported into a reality populated by a remix of fictional detectives and actual writers. In this way, the *Detective Conan* series produces its distinctive world: it puts a twist on detection that carves a distinctive media-saturated ecology from the detective genre.

Despite its reliance on a photographic ontology to impart a sense of neutrality or objectivity to detection, the *Detective Conan* manga introduces a split into the unidirectional force underpinning that brand of all-around pervasive realism, folding it back on itself to form a media environment. The series is as much about being obsessively drawn into fictional worlds as it is about solving mysteries and closing cases. It is about individualization, but its techniques differ from those of the *Crayon Shin-chan* series. That series divided the one-to-many tendency of broadcast television, making for a self that appeared to generate its own reality, a totally personalized world, like an action figure springing from Shin-chan's crotch. The self thus appears to be sui generis, as if it might exist prior to its production. It verges on becoming the subject. Of course, in *Shin-chan,* this self is equally prone to dissipate its energies into nothingness. In contrast, in the *Detective Conan* series, it is the formation of an environment that summons forth a self. Or rather, the self and its environment emerge together, and practices of self are geared toward sustaining the environment that sustains the self.

The result is like what Isabelle Stengers calls an "ecology of practices," for a concern or a problematic serves to gather together a set of practices relative to it, practices that engage directly with knowledge formations and truth-effects.[4] Indeed, it might be argued that both Stengers and *Detective Conan* imply a photographic ontology as their point of departure, that is, a unidirectional capture going from nature into image-effect or truth-effect, precisely in order to ground the possibility of knowledge, that of the scientist and the detective, respectively. Moreover, the *Detective Conan* series, surely because of its commitment to dramatization, calls forth another dimension within the ecologized horizons stemming from image-effects or truth-effects: that of improvisation (which is not unlike experimentation for Stengers). In the manga, improvisation takes place largely in the juncture between Shin'ichi solving the mystery and Conan closing the case. In the anime, improvisation occurs in another register, through media experimentation, which is teased out of the manga to be prolonged in animation.

Video Media Mix and the OVA

In the *Detective Conan* manga, the television screen appears striped with scan lines. Scan lines commonly appear when photographing the television with a movie camera. The movie camera captures images at a frame rate different from the frame rate or refresh rate of the television image. It thus picks up what the human eye does not usually perceive on the CRT television screen: cathode rays fire half the image at a time in alternating rows at a rate faster than the human eye can detect. The movie camera, shooting at a faster rate, catches the interlacing of the two images, and the result is a striping effect of darker and lighter bands across the image. Scan lines thus result from an encounter between two different media rates or media temporalities. It is from the (temporal) perspective of the movie camera that we see the television screen's frequency.

Scan lines became associated especially with video media, with the camcorder or video camera and the VCR, for a couple of reasons. First, as video cameras became widely available in 1980s and enthusiasts and filmmakers began experimenting with them, they started filming images from the television screen, only to discover, upon playback, scan lines striping the image. Second, when something recorded at one rate is replayed at a different rate, scan lines can also appear, covering the entire image. Such an effect is so commonly associated with video playback that in movies, surveillance camera footage is usually presented with scan lines to indicate a discrepancy in resolution between two platforms. In addition, the first game systems used a noninterlaced signal and introduced frames with 240 lines for compatibility with television screens, yet the resulting difference in frequency produced scan lines on the image, which today are associated with classic video games. In other words, scan lines become common effects with the advent of expanded television, that is, television with peripherals such as the home game console and the VCR.

When the *Detective Conan* manga presents a television screen with scan lines, it conjures up this expanded home television media ecology, which become prevalent in the 1980s and reached its peak around the time *Detective Conan* began serialization in the mid-1990s. The series feels continuous with this media ecology. The standard cases, which run for about four files, already feel like a television episode, and the longer cases feels like a double episode, or a TV movie, or a movie shown on television. Creator Aoyama's comments on his sources of inspiration, included on the jackets of the paperback editions, confirm this feeling. He speaks of his favorite television detectives, such as Columbo, as well as his favorite movie heroes. It is easy to imagine him as a mystery otaku, not only reading books but also sitting in front of the television screen, watching runs and reruns of TV series on broadcast channels as well as videos of movies and shows. This mystery otaku has an audiovisual library, a video archive. As such, because *Detective Conan* already feels continuous with expanded television media, the transformation of the manga into an anime series does not feel particularly jarring. Each case seems poised to become a stand-alone episode.

A major shift occurs in the sequencing of episodes. The anime series puts the cases in a new order, thus creating a story arc different from the manga. The first season, for instance, begins with the three cases in the first manga volume, jumps to volume 4 for the fourth and fifth episodes, offers an original case not found in the manga for the sixth episode, and proceeds to draw cases from volumes 3, 4, 7, 6, and 9 before returning to volume 2. Shuffling the order of the cases, however, does not significantly affect the individual mysteries or the overarching story. The changes in sequencing serve primarily to introduce the major characters in a straightforward fashion and tend to reinforce the general trajectory of the series rather than alter it. The difference in tone between the manga and anime is primarily a result of differences in manga and anime conventions. Three shifts in tone are salient.

In the anime, Conan becomes cuter and more adorable (if possible), with his childlike voice, saucer eyes, and rounded lines. The anime Conan rivals in intensity the cute cover illustrations of the manga each time he fills the screen. The parasocial quality of Conan is thus enhanced. In addition, with its opening song, ads, and story segments, the anime series amplifies effects of code switching, which at once seem to permeate and emerge from its techniques of limited animation. Finally, the anime series brings media switching to the fore.

In the manga series, media switching is palpable primarily in the use of scan lines on television screens, which highlights the gap between platforms, in particular between television set and video media (camera, player, recorder). In the anime series, media switching comes to the fore in the presentation of television screens. Instead using scan lines, the anime series oscillates rapidly between two techniques of presentation. On the one hand, there is the technique discussed above, in which the real world and the screen world appear to be at the same level in terms of their reality effects. On the other hand, this sort of screen quickly turns into another kind of screen—a flickering, blinking screen that glows whitely without presenting any images. When the children run past the electronics stores in episode 4, for instance, the TV screens in the window flicker brightly but show nothing but bright, blinking light. Likewise, in episode 3, when Kogorō is watching TV, the screen first appears at an oblique angle as a sheet of flickering light (Figure 11.3). Such effects also derive from the ascendency of video cameras, and the television glows brighter and flickers as a result in differences in frequency between the television set and the camera.

The *Conan* manga and the anime use different techniques to express the force of the television screen. Where the manga expresses the temporal frequency discrepancy between media platforms in the form of scan lines, the anime expresses it by switching between two modes—a figurative mode of expression in which images on the screen appear, and a nonfigurative mode of expression in which the screen is a glowing, flickering sheet of bright white light. Thus the anime amplifies and prolongs the temporal discrepancy between media platforms already evident in scan lines, which imparts an uncanny, almost supernatural force

FIGURE 11.3. In episode 3, although Kogorō is watching TV, the screen appears to viewers as a sheet of flickering light because no one is paying attention to it.

to the television screen. The television no longer feels like a realm apart from the everyday world. It either pulses with electric life, as if to surge into the real world, or its images appear to exist on the same plane as things in the real world. In either case, television exceeds its function of offering relevant information and documentation. It operates as a force, even a life, in its own right. A distinction between modes of existence of different media platforms (their temporal life, as it were) starts to displace a distinction between real world and media world.

Because such effects come to the fore in conjunction with the widespread use of the VCR, the impact of the VCR on anime merits a brief digression. Previous chapters discussed how VCR and the home video game console appeared in the 1970s as peripherals or plug-ins for the television set, becoming familiar, even standard, features by the end of the 1980s. Such plug-ins, often developed and manufactured in Japan, effectively suspended the broadcast receiver function to permit the TV set to be utilized in more interactive and computational fashions. The result was a household media complex centered on the television set.

The VCR affected the experience of anime in a number of ways. Because it allowed for repeated viewing and for stopping the moving image, anime fans began to consider its construction in detail, focusing as much (or more) on information retrieval. By the mid-1980s, animated series could be recorded from broadcasts, rented, collected, shared, even subtitled and distributed outside Japan. While the home theater experience differed greatly from the cinematic experience, it gave new life to cinema. Miyazaki's 1985 film, *Castle in the Sky (Tenkū no shiro Rapyuta)*, is sometimes credited with saving the animation cinema industry, yet its success depended as much (or more) on videocassette sales as on box-office receipts. Finally, the VCR gave birth to a new form of animation: the original video animation, or OVA.

In his account of the first fifteen years of OVA, Tokugi Yoshiharu tells a story of the great promise of the OVA and of its failure to live up to that promise. I rely heavily on his account in this context because, as the OVA critic for the famous anime fan magazine *Animage*, he provides a strong sense of his criteria for evaluation. In addition, because his criteria build on his hopes for the OVA to become separate from the commercial TV market, his account highlights the ways the OVA remained poised between cinematic animation and television animation, remaining a sort of in-between form instead of emerging as an more independent "third generation media" form beyond the first generation of cinema and the second generation of television.[5]

The promise of the OVA lay in its potential to produce animations geared more toward adults, of higher quality than television animation, with stories of a (generally shorter) length than standard seasonal runs for television animation, with less budget than animation cinema. This was the case with the first OVA series, *Dallos,* directed by Oshii Mamoru and released in 1983. Oshii had previously gained experience in television animation as an episode director on various series, but he really came to the attention of anime fans upon the release of his first animated film, *Only You,* an offshoot of the *Urusei Yatsura* anime based on Takahashi Rumiko's *Urusei Yatsura* manga. Because his film, released in February, had won great acclaim, fans eagerly awaited the release of his OVA series in December of the same year.[6] In other words, like director Oshii himself, the *Dallos* OVA was strategically poised between big-screen cinematic animation and small-screen anime series. There were high hopes that Oshii's OVA would bridge the gap between them, that it would build on the strengths of both kinds of production and open a movement beyond their constraints. But in Tokugi's opinion, such hopes were dashed. Oshii directed a number of OVA and animated films related to TV or OVA series in the 1980s, only to move almost exclusively into feature film production in the 1990s. Yet the impact of the OVA is tangible in his films: his animation techniques remained close to video animation aesthetics, particularly in his use of video footage. His 1995 anime film, *The Ghost in the Shell,* released in the inaugural year of the DVD, may be seen as the culmination of this period of video-inflected animation.[7]

Although in Tokugi's opinion *Dallos* did not live up to the promises of the OVA, the following year saw the release of three kinds of OVA that effectively established the three basic tendencies for subsequent OVA production. The first, *Machikado no meruhen* (Street corner fairy tale, 1984), was original in both design and subject. The second, *Bāsu* (*Birth,* 1984), gave free reign to a well-known, well-loved animator and director, Kanada Yoshinori, to pursue his craft. Finally, the third, *Mahō no tenshi Kurumīmami: eien no wansumoa* (Magic angel creamy mami: eternal once more, 1984), was a follow-up *(afutā mono)* to a highly popular animated television series. To the disappointment of Tokugi, it is this latter tendency that gradually came to dominate OVA production.

On the one hand, in Tokugi's account, the OVA failed to live up to the promise of producing autonomous works to rival cinematic animation. For instance, the impulse to produce animation of a higher quality than television anime gradually diminished in favor of rapid and cheap production of "what you can't do on TV," namely sex and violence, as in Kawajiri Yoshiaki's *Wicked City* (*Yōjū toshi,* 1987).[8] In addition, although OVA production allowed animators to experiment with mecha designs independent of the toy manufacturers who dominated the television market, this trend gradually shifted toward OVA featuring fan-targeted parodies of special effects films *(tokusatsu eiga)* or well-known anime. Anno Hideaki's *Gunbuster* or *Toppu o nerae* (1988) is a prime example.[9]

On the other hand, because the pattern of adapting manga series into televised anime series had come to dominate the market, it was simply easier to position an OVA release as a follow-up, a side story, or alternative story within a series whose key instance was the broadcast animated series. This pattern made it difficult to have the OVA serve as the core and nucleus for a series.

In sum, although Tokugi does not dismiss the genuine achievements of the OVA and makes note of significant exceptions, his overall assessment of the OVA as of 1999 remains somewhat negative, precisely because, for economic and aesthetic reasons, instead of becoming a third generation or third wave of animation, the OVA remained largely within the orbit of television anime, like a satellite or a peripheral device. The relation between OVA and anime was entirely analogous that between the VCR and the TV set.

With regard to the television anime media mix, then, video affects broadcast animation in several ways. First, as the anime series goes into circulation on videocassette, it accrues new profits resulting from sales and rentals, complementary to the advertisement revenues of broadcast yet increasingly more important than them. Indeed, the trend is such that the broadcast may even serve as an advertisement for the video sales (and later the DVD sales). Second, the video release is often used as publicity for the manga and other products. In the context of *Detective Conan*, for instance, its weekly manga magazine, *Shōnen Sunday*, began in 2000 to release an OVA episode each year, whose sale was limited to magazine subscribers, which served to promote its circulation. The episodes were subsequently compiled for general release on DVD under the rubric "Secret Files." Third, video allows the anime series to be experienced in a different way, often watched repeatedly, sometimes scrutinized in its details, not to mention purchased, possessed, collected, and archived. This intensity also extends to the other media instances in the mix, spurring encyclopedic forms of detailed knowledge. At the same time, such a knowledge formation places increased emphasis on the quality of the animation and its reproduction on video or disk. Thus, as digitally remastered versions of *Detective Conan* anime began to air in the mid-2000s, another OVA series, styled the *Magic Files,* began to appear on DVD. The first DVD, released in 2007, consisted of four remastered episodes of the anime, while the subsequent *Magic Files* releases were original animation DVDs or OADs. In sum, as Tokugi stresses, the *Detective Conan* OVAs, like its video releases, remain in orbit around the broadcast anime formation; they are offshoots, follow-ups, or technically enhanced rereleases.

Still, it is interesting that the *Detective Conan* OVAs are styled as "secret files" and "magic files." Without overstating the matter, such terms insinuate a different relation between the TV series and the OVA series—magical action at a distance, inexplicable depths, uncanny semblance—rather like the relation of the character Magic Kaitō (Majikku Kaitō) to Conan and Shin'ichi. Kuroba Kaitō, whose nickname is Magic Kaitō, is a gentleman thief, albeit a young one. He is the title protagonist of another of Aoyama's manga series, only sporadically serialized to date. Magic Kaitō has a strange relation to Kudō Shin'ichi and Conan. As a thief, he is, of course, an opponent. Yet he also has strong affinity with Shin'ichi and Conan. Magic Kaitō, who is nearly identical to Shin'ichi, successfully impersonates him without disguise. He also possesses insider knowledge. In the *Detective Conan* films, for instance, he knows that Conan is Shin'ichi. Odder still, episodes featuring Magic Kaitō, without any connection to the *Detective Conan* series, have aired in the *Detective Conan* time slot, as if they were in fact part of the *Detective Conan* series. In sum, Magic Kaitō not only crosses between series but also takes on different functions in different media forms. Magic Kaitō at once appears overly related to Conan and the *Detective Conan* series, and not related to them at all. There is a magical relation, an action at a distance, which may serve to call attention to another dimension of the interaction of video series and broadcast series within media mix.

Previous chapters underscored how the VCR, although an add-on or plug-in, intensified a polarization within television media, functioning as an outside of the inside, giving greater play to what seems to be subsumed within broadcast television, namely, point-to-point network tendencies. Thus, although Tokugi is surely correct to signal how broadcast anime tends effectively to subsume the OVA, the OVA might nonetheless be considered in light of its potential to induce an "internal" intensification of television animation, which occurs with the transformation of the television screen into a multifunctional operator capable of switching between broadcast receiver and computational monitor. It is a magical relation in the sense that platforms appear to communicate across a distance. Although the means of communication can be explained (cables, antennas, or modems), the communication also feels deep or secretive, instantaneous and magical. This is precisely what comes to the fore with the techniques used to render television screens in the *Detective Conan* series, especially with the glowing, flickering screen effect. In such instances, communication across media platforms implies an effect that exceeds and thus intensifies the platform on which it appears: the TV screen.

The OVA contributed greatly to the general tendency in Japanese animation to render television and computer screens as sheets of glowing flickering light, using techniques of transmitted light whose *paka-paka* came to the fore in the Pokémon Incident. The OVA initially strove for a darker, more adult tone, gravitating toward darker, more adult settings—the nighttime underground city, with seedy bars, sinister streets, and rooms submerged in shadows. In this darkened world, and in conjunction with the emergence of cyberfictions, television and computer screens came to be the preferred source for eerie illumination, akin to the angular neon glare of noir worlds but attuned to vast shadowy interiors. At the same time, to enhance the quality of animation on a tighter budget, OVA directors began to film with video cameras, using video footage as an inspiration for animation backgrounds and sequences, to impart a sense of a gritty, video-real world. Again, Oshii Mamoru was something of a pioneer in this respect, and by the time of his *Patlabor* films (1989 and 1993) and *The Ghost in the Shell* (1995), he had developed a signature style with slow, almost elegiac movement through darkened rooms, illuminated only by the light of flickering television screen striped with scan lines (Figure 11.4).

The same effects were extended to computers. It is worth recalling that the screen refresh rates for computers were modeled on those of the CRT television screen, which meant that the computer screen showed identical effects of glow, flicker, and scan lines. A prime example occurs in a relatively early OVA, *Digital Devil Story Megami Tensai* (*Dijitaru debiru sutorī Megami Tensai*, 1987).

The publisher, Tokuma shoten, whose publication of science fiction series and the anime magazine *Animage* had won a wide fan base (not to mention their support of Miyazaki Hayao's manga and animated films), backed the *Digital Devil*

FIGURE 11.4. Oshii Mamoru's animated films frequently dwell on the pulsing glow of television screens, as in this scene from the first *Patlabor* movie (1989), which makes for ghostly figurations whose videolike reality refuses to recede or to give way to the actual world.

Story OVA to develop a media mix franchise around the highly popular novels by Nishitani Aya. After the release of the OVA in March, a role-paying game (RPG) for Famicom appeared in September. While not generally deemed a great success commercially or aesthetically, the *Digital Devil Story* OVA does nevertheless use flickering computer screens in darkened rooms to good effect in the context of its story. The glow and flicker of the screens become so intense that they impart new powers to the computer itself, which paves the way for demons to swarm into the real world and for humans to be engulfed by the screen world (Figure 11.5). I will discuss such effects in greater detail in chapter 13 in the context of *Persona 4*, which is a more recent entry into this game and anime media mix series. Suffice it to say at this juncture that the *Digital Devil Story* OVA is a prime example of a media mix that appears to bypass broadcast television, yet only by flanking the TV set with peripherals: the VCR and the NES. It thus provides a powerful reminder that it was in the context of the internal intensification of the capacities of the television screen that screens in animation, especially as imagined within

the worlds of OVA, began to express this weird communication across platforms within a platform, with the TV receiver-monitor becoming like an uncanny energy life-form flickering into the everyday world.

By the time of the *Detective Conan* anime in the mid-1990s, such effects were largely a matter of convention, part of expressing the look and feel of television, in much the same manner that the force of the OVA had been pulled into the orbit of broadcast anime. In the wake of the Pokémon Incident, however, something of the force of expression buried in those conventions for intensely flickering screens comes to the fore, renewing a sense of the magical communication occurring across media platforms enhanced by the legacy of video. As such, the

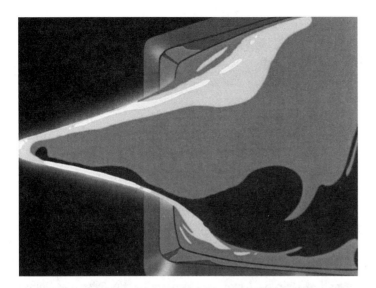

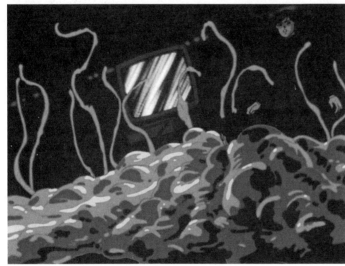

FIGURE 11.5. This sequence shows how the 1987 OVA *Digital Devil Story* brings such intensity to computer screens that their glow and flicker transform into actual demon powers that swarm into real world, engulfing humans in this screen reality.

implications of those screens definitely merit a closer look in the context of the *Detective Conan* series.

Between Personating and Nonpersonating Modes

The "Pro-Soccer Blackmail Incident" *(Puro sakkā senshu kyōhaku jiken)* is the tenth case (episode) in the anime series, based on files 68 through 71 of volumes 7 and 8 of the manga. The case centers on a televised event, the broadcast of the final match in an important soccer tournament, pitting a Tokyo team against an Osaka team. The case also presents numerous instances of impersonation, beginning with a young woman who arrives at the Mōri Detective Agency, Akagi Ryōko. She solicits the Mōris' assistance in locating the missing Kudō Shin'ichi, providing a photo of him and claiming to be his girlfriend. Ran is at once incredulous and jealous. Conan, who does not know this Akagi Ryōko, wonders who she really is. He pretends to receive a telephone message from Shin'ichi to the effect that Shin'ichi will call Ryōko at her home. Ran insists on going to Ryōko's apartment in case Shin'ichi makes an appearance there. Conan tags along. While Ryōko pretends to be Shin'ichi's girlfriend, Ran pretends not to be.

At Ryōko's apartment, Conan finds evidence of deception: Ryōko clearly does not live there, and a child's room has been ransacked. He finds a photo of a boy with a young man. Piecing together the clues, he deduces that the boy is Akagi Mamoru and that the young man is Akagi Hide, the star player for the Tokyo soccer team. At the kitchen table with Ran, Ryōko has now turned on the big match, in which Hide is playing. Once the match has begun, Conan must solve the mystery and close the case before it ends. As often happens in the *Detective Conan* series, the television broadcast is very much of the present, creating a sense of urgency, ticking like a clock on a countdown. In contrast, the indexical markers of the crime are of the past, traces of what has already happened.

Concealing himself in the toilet, Conan uses his secret mobile phone to call Ryōko, revealing that he knows that someone has kidnapped Hide's little brother, Mamoru, in order to force Hide to throw the match. He asks Ryōko to send the kidnapper's note to his mobile fax. Ran, jealous to see Ryōko crying as she speaks with Shin'ichi on the phone, grabs the phone and shouts into it—so loudly that she can hear her voice echoing from somewhere in the apartment. Ran now becomes the detective, deducing that Shin'ichi must be there. As Ran pursues Shin'ichi, Conan barely manages to stay one step ahead of her. Meantime, in response to Hide's scoring a goal in the match, the kidnapper sends another note by fax to the apartment, threatening that Hide may never see his brother again.

While poring over the video games in Mamoru's room, Conan finds traces of another important person in Mamoru's life: Hide's teammate, Uemura Naoki, who cannot play in the match because of an injury sustained during practice. Again hiding in the toilet to call Ryōko, Conan tells her that Naoki is the kidnapper, while Ran, hearing Shin'ichi's voice, pounds on the toilet door. Conan–Shin'ichi, however, manages to give her the slip yet again.

As it turns out, Naoki is indeed the culprit; he has only staged the drama of a kidnapping. He invited Mamoru to his apartment to play video games, then impersonated a kidnapper in order to force Hide to throw the game. His goal is to exact revenge on Hide for injuring him during practice. Jealous of Hide's superior natural abilities, Naoki has persuaded himself that Hide injured him deliberately in an attempt to take all the glory of winning for himself. Ryōko and

Mamoru speak to Hide on the phone; then, free of anxiety, Hide quickly wins the game. Mystery solved, case closed.

As this quick summary indicates, this case mobilizes a variety of media. Mobile phones and faxes play a major role in acts of deceptive impersonation— Naoki impersonating a kidnapper, Conan impersonating Shin'ichi, and Ryōko sustaining her impersonation of Shin'ichi's girlfriend, almost despite herself. The case itself centers on the television set, calling a good deal of attention to the TV both as a receiver of the soccer broadcast and as a monitor for video games. Let me begin with the role television and then turn to mobile telecommunications.

In the manga, as expected, the television screen is marked by scan lines as well as bold *kana* to indicate its clamor—"wa-a!" There are some interesting moments when the television screen begins to fill the panels, to the point where characters appear to be layered into the television world. Yet it is in the anime in particular that the television screen begins to exhibit truly strange effects. Oddly, when no one is watching the television, it turns into a plane of bright flashing white, without figures or figuration, as if intent on attracting attention. Often in anime television screens seen from the side will flicker, while screens seen head-on will show images (Figure 11.6a). In this instance, however, the TV screen flashes and flickers when seen from the front. When Ryōko enters the room in Naoki's apartment where Mamoru is playing a video game, as Mamoru turns to look at her, the television goes into flicker mode (Figure 11.6b). When Mamoru turns his attention back to the video game, the screen shows figures and images (Figure 11.6c). In other words, the screen flashes and flickers when no one is looking at it—or at least when no one can be seen looking it at. The TV screen thus appears to go into a base mode when ignored—a flicker mode.

This flicker mode implies a nonpersonal mode of address, for the screen is not addressing anyone in particular. The screen is simply doing its thing; it is doing whatever it does when it does not have to show anything to anyone. But it may be trying to address some*thing*. As discussed above, this nonpersonal flicker mode is related to the interval between media platforms operating at different frequencies and in different temporalities. As such, in its baseline mode, the television screen is communicating, or trying to communicate, with other media platforms. In effect, it is addressing humans nonpersonally, communicating with them as if they were media platforms, in a grab for their attention.

On the other hand, as this episode highlights, as soon as somebody looks at the TV, the screen offers images—and not just any kind of images. These are images as real as you are. The humans on the screen are not substantially different in any way from humans in the world. The result is a highly personal mode of address, which episode 10 of the *Detective Conan* anime utilizes in order to bring about the emotional closure of the case. In an interview after the match, Hide expresses his special thanks to his teammate Naoki, for even though Naoki

a

c

b

FIGURE 11.6. This sequence in the *Detective Conan* series exemplifies the oscillation of the television screen between modes. (a) Seen from the side, the screen glows and flickers because the audience cannot see the images. (b) But it also goes into flicker mode when no one in the room is watching. (c) It returns to showing images when Mamoru turns his attention to it.

could not play, it was Naoki's constant efforts to improve his abilities in practice that pushed Hide to improve his own skills. Because there is no marked difference between the screen world and the real world, as Hide expresses his heartfelt gratitude, it is as if he were speaking directly to Naoki, face to face. Indeed, the episode highlights this effect, making it seem as if Hide and Naoki were looking squarely into each other's eyes across the distance (Figure 11.7). It is the ultimate parasocial moment, a moment of localized transcendence in which media affectively fulfills its communicative capacity. Tears stream down Naoki's face, and he collapses. Naoki's personal drama has come full circle. In the end, although

Conan solves the mystery and closes the case rationally, it is television that closes the case emotionally, through a moment of affective communication.

This personal mode of address results in the formation of an immersive environment by building on the environmental tendencies implicit in the point-to-point tendency internal to television. Here broadcast is not a matter of imposing a univocal message on a mass audience. It enables one-to-one communication, a network effect that cuts across and flattens the hierarchical implications of the one-to-many tendency. In contrast to *Crayon Shin-chan,* in which the hierarchical tendency is evoked and rejected, the *Detective Conan* series breezily bypasses it, precisely because it has already situated broadcast television as one medium among others. The resulting personal mode of address nonetheless implies a different tendency toward totalization, shunting it into an immersive personalized media environment—the formation of otaku-like enclosures and affective feedback loops. While characters in the *Detective Conan* series (primarily Ran) may denigrate otaku-like worlds, the series itself cannot live without them. This personal mode of address might best be described as a personating mode, in that it does not merely address preexisting persons but also personalizes them, constructs their personas.

Episode 10 of the *Detective Conan* series dramatizes the act of flipping from the personating mode into the nonpersonating mode of address that occurs when the TV screen suddenly turns into a flickering plane of light. Both personating and nonpersonating modes run counter to the one-to-many tendency of broadcast, embracing its internal point-to-point tendencies. Where the personating mode constructs personalized environments, the nonpersonating mode tends toward a radical individuation: its flashing implies a process of seeking to establish a connection with another platform. It wants something, or rather somebody, to link to it, in whatever capacity that body can muster. Each body is invited to contribute to the network in its capacity, and there is no hierarchy among bodies. This mode mobilizes a heterarchical tendency. Connections between bodies or nodes are nonhierarchical, and because elements are unranked, there is potential for the emergence of diverse ways of relating or ranking them. This mode embodies the potentiality implicit in media switching, that is, the ability of the television platform to switch from broadcast receiver to video and game monitor.

The rapid oscillation of the television screen in this *Detective Conan* episode, between a thoroughly parasocial mode and a flickering media-switching mode, presents in condensed form the larger media ecology operating across the *Detective Conan* series. The series dramatizes a tension between two medial tendencies: the environmental and the heterarchical. Both tendencies are generally associated with point-to-point media tendencies, such as networks, telecommunications, and new media, including mobile phones, social media, and video games. In *Detective Conan,* the television screen, even in its broadcast

FIGURE 11.7. Animation often presents images on the screen as if at the same level of ontological reality as the actual world, which allows for an intensification of parasocial effects, as here, where the soccer player on the screen seems to speak directly to his friend.

capacity, is configured as if it were continuous with new media. Consequently, broadcast media loses any sense of one-to-many tendencies. Still, the *Detective Conan* series does not champion point-to-point tendencies at the expense of one-to-many tendencies. Partly for reasons of genre and partly for reasons of media mix, the series simply sets to work with the point-to-point tendency. This is why the series so effectively locates and dramatizes a tension within it.

The *Detective Conan* series dramatizes the tension between two ways of dwelling in the point-to-point tendency: you may become personated to the point where you live enclosed within an otaku-like world in tune with affective feedback, or you can become nonpersonated to the point where you function almost exclusively as a link or node in a network, one platform among others, whose singular potentiality remains anonymous. Conan becomes more and more personated, for instance, while Shin'ichi lends his skills largely in anonymity, as if nobody. Between Conan and Shin'ichi comes impersonation. Everyone in the *Detective Conan* series is caught up in impersonation, with dramas of wearing masks, adopting disguises, and taking on personas. The dramas are always petty and personalized, yet with pronounced streaks of anonymity (no one knows) and noninterest (someone else benefits). The dramas inevitably hinge on acts of improvisation with media.

In the end of the "Pro-Soccer Blackmail Case," for instance, the drama of Hide and Naoki is closed, rationally and affectively, and yet the drama of Conan-Shin'ichi and Ran remains open. To live as an indulged little boy within his adopted family, which he increasingly enjoys, Conan must not only refine his impersonation of a boy but also find ways to impersonate Shin-ichi with various media devices. Thus he is constantly improvising with whatever gadgets come his way. At the end of the episode, with Ran in pursuit, Conan must finally confront her. Conan ducks around a street corner, stands on a box, and uses the streetlights to project an enlarged Shin'ichi-like shadow on the building opposite. He speaks through his bow tie device to project Shin'ichi's voice. Thus he improvises a silhouette animation, an experimental animated short, on the fly. In these moments of media experimentation, as in those with the flickering screen, the *Detective Conan* series digs deep into the animetic plane of composition to weave the stuff of blink into improvised animation.

In the *Crayon Shin-chan* series, the experience of nearly photoepileptiform flashing verged on a quasi-mystical experience of bodily communion with the Absolute. In the *Detective Conan* series, the experience of the flash affords an instance of localized transcendence, a momentary experience of immanence, an affective loop introducing a pause or hesitation into the headlong rush of dramatic impersonations. It is in that moment that your body becomes like a media platform, switching between media platforms, individuating on the animetic plane underlying those media. In keeping with the detective genre as well as its video media mix heritage, however, the *Detective Conan* series pushes such instants toward a kind of indexical capture, following material traces only to eliminate some possibilities on the list of suspected causes in order to close the case. Ultimately it often feels as if the *Detective Conan* series resolves the tension between environmental and heterarchical tendencies in favor of the environmental and immersive: case closed. Still, it leaves open a possibility that will be pursued in the emerging media mix movement between console games and television anime—a host of animated entities, a veritable pantheon of animist deities and spirits, swarming forth under the spotted sun of broadcast television.

12

THE GAME PLAY COMPLEX

THE TWO KINDS OF INFRASTRUCTURE COMPLEXES EXPLORED IN THE PREVIOUS TWO CHAPTERS GRAVITATED TOWARD opposite poles of broadcast television media. The family broadcast complex of the *Crayon Shin-chan* series was orientated toward the one-to-many tendency, which hinges on domestically privatized reception of transmission from a centralized source. The home theater complex of the *Detective Conan* series was turned toward the point-to-point tendency, which situates the television as a monitor. As a monitor, television appears to be one media platform among other media platforms, yet it plays a special role in that other platforms tend to circle around it. It thus becomes an attractor instead of a centralized transmitter.

Each of these infrastructure complexes introduced a split into its general media tendency, a bifurcation into totalizing and individualizing tendencies. The *Crayon Shin-chan* series split the one-to-many tendency into a hierarchical tendency (which was continually enthroned and deposed) and a unidirectional tendency (which was joyously embodied and dissipated). The *Detective Conan* series divided the point-to-point tendency into an environmental tendency (immersive personalization) and a heterarchical tendency (nonpersonalized improvisation to which each body contributed in its capacity as an expressive medium). It is because these general tendencies bifurcate yet remain entangled that they transform into complexes, at once psychic and medial. Indeed, it is through such bifurcation that subjectivity tentatively emerges, striving to adhere to the monstrous body of distribution at moments and sites where some of its energies may be dissipated or expended. This is how a specific experience of media distribution emerges—as a limited distribution due to limits happening across and arising through distribution. The experience of media is at once individualizing and totalizing, along specific pathways of bifurcation and entanglement, with specific patterns of dilation and contraction. Still, although experience is transformed into an experience, it is not an experience in the purely subjective sense, that is, purely internalized or interiorized.

In methodological terms, media mix affords some insight into the actual forms of distributive experience, but it is the media ecology that truly matters. Indeed, accounts of media mix tend toward an exhaustive and sometimes exhausting enumeration of items: first, there is the manga or the game, and then the toys, the anime, and the movie. The list dwells on how each one is produced, licensed, and marketed thus and so. Accounts of media mix make it appear to be a combinatory system. The media ecology offers a different perspective, for it concerns what runs across and through the specific media instances. It concerns what is expressed within them (for instance, how television media appear within a specific manga or anime series) and what is composed across the affordances of the different media of media mix (the television set, for instance, contributes in its weird capacity as receiver and monitor). In effect, the media ecology localizes and stabilizes the assembling of polarized tendencies inherent within infrastructures. The complex arises where the media ecology becomes subjectified—not only individualized but also totalized.

With these distinctions in mind, I would like to offer a diagram mapping the medial tendencies introduced thus far (Figure 12.1), repeating the caveat that these are tendencies, not categories. Nor does it offer quantitative scales in the manner of coordinate geometry. The point-to-point tendency and the one-to-many tendency appear on the same axis, the medial axis, yet these tendencies do not represent more or less of a certain measurable quantity. In the context of television media, moving toward the point-to-point tendency is like moving toward the inverse side of structure. As for the other axis, the psychosocial axis, it is surely clear that quantification is impossible in contrasting individualization to totalization, even if there is a pronounced yet mistaken tendency to think of society as a larger entity comprising smaller individual entities. Individuals and societies emerge together; individuals can be considered as societies, and societies as individuals. What happens along this axis, then, are intensive quantities related to the social, rather like measuring temperature. Finally, the point where the two axes meet is really a process, that of assembling. Any television media ecology, and by extension any television infrastructure complex, implicates all these tendencies as it cuts, folds, and stitches the stuff of blink, if given the flicker of a chance.

This diagram is useful in that it offers a convenient way to map the emergence of the next television infrastructure complex: the game play complex. The two prior multimedia series provided examples that tended toward one of the poles along the medial axis. What characterizes the game play complex is its tendency

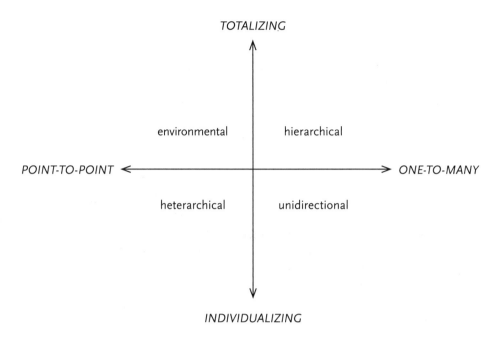

FIGURE 12.1. The polarized tendencies of television media may be schematized along two axes, which might be roughly characterized as psychosocial (totalizing versus individualizing) and technological (point-to-point versus one-to-many). As technological tendencies bifurcate psychosocial tendencies and vice versa, the result is a complex, an entangling of tendencies that becomes stabilized into a tentative holding pattern.

to pit one medial tendency against the other. It sets forth and starkly opposes two media ecologies—one centered on video games with a point-to-point tendency, and one based on the one-to-many tendency of broadcast television—and lets the battle begin. Of course, video games cannot defeat television, any more than television can emerge victorious over games. The outcome does not really depend on winning or losing, but on subjectifying a process of assembling polarized tendencies, producing a gamelike television media complex. A prime example is the *.hack* series, pronounced "dotto hakku" or "dot hack."

Meta–Media Mix

The *.hack* series is a multimedia series whose media instances or instantiations— manga, anime, PlayStation 2 (PS2) console games—center on characters who are playing an online game, "The World," which comes to feel increasingly strange and even ominous as they play it. This MMORPG (massively multiuser online role-playing game), or more simply MMO, appears some two years after a strange virus has resulted in the worldwide shutdown of computers and the Internet, in an alternative version of earth, with nearly apocalyptic consequences. After two years without any computer and network media, the launch of "The World," built on a massive scale, attracts millions of players. It now runs on an operating system immune to the virus, Altimit OS, and yet something strange begins to happen in "The World." You enter the game amid rumors that players are blacking out and remaining in a comatose condition in the real world. For whatever reason, maybe hackers, maybe a new outbreak of the virus, "The World" poses a genuine danger to its players.

Difficulties are compounded for you as a player because you do not know exactly who you are, and you do not know whom to trust within the game. Because "The World" is somehow damaged, your experience of role-playing is not one of expressing and shoring up a preexisting sense of self. Instead, it is only through an experience of losing your self that you arrive at a sense of self. Because of the analogy established between "healing yourself," "fixing the game ('The World')," and "saving the world," the role-playing and action adventure within the game takes on a decidedly existential therapeutic tone. The game action turns into a voyage of self-discovery or self-awakening, which self-awakening in turn affects the game and the world.

The characteristic feature of the *.hack* series is this paradigm of the game within the game, which affords metaperspective on game play. You do not simply adopt a player character and play through the game. In order to figure out what is happening with the game, you also have to discover who or what your player character is, and who and what other characters are. The metaperspective is most palpable when playing the *.hack* video games, and indeed, the conceptualization of the *.hack* franchise begins with its games.

The games are designed to afford an experience of online gaming without being online. In the first *.hack* project, for instance, which ran roughly between 2002 and 2006 and consisted of a series of four PS2 games released sequentially over the course of a year, *Infection* (released June 20, 2002), *Mutation* (September 9), *Outbreak* (December 12), and *Quarantine* (April 10, 2003),[1] you take on a player character named Kite who is playing the MMO called "The World." Within the *.hack* game, you can log into or log out of "The World," and "The World" itself is modeled on popular sword-and-sorcery MMOs, which reinforces the sense of playing an actual online game, although you are in fact playing on a PlayStation console plugged into the television set.

At the level of its media ecology, the *.hack* franchise consists of an online game within an off-line game. The global computational network (Internet) is situated as if within the home media network that is centered on the television set with its peripherals. As such, the *.hack* franchise intensifies and amplifies the point-to-point network tendencies implicit in the home media system, as if to say you do not need the Internet to experience network effects, for they are already implicit in your home media system, awaiting intensification. The home media system provides a metamodel of online networks. By offering the experience of an online network within an off-line network, it produces a network within a network.

Such a metamodel differs greatly from usual definitions of metamedia.[2] Building on Guattari's conceptualization of the metamodel, Massumi comments, "'Meta-' is to be understood here in its etymological sense of 'among.' It refers not to the on-high of the ideal, but on the contrary to the spontaneous remingling of acquired regularities of practice with the emergence-level chance and indeterminacy from which they evolved."[3] This is precisely what the *.hack* games strive to do: instead of looking at online games from on high, from a transcendent or ideal perspective, these consoles games situate you among the regularities of practice or play acquired within online games. The console game becomes a metamodel for online MMOs by mapping out an experience of them, not by telling you what they are or how they work.

What is more, "The World" is not operating in an ideal fashion. It is causing players to become comatose. With Kite, you have to figure out what is going on, or at least how to put an end to this situation, which requires working with an AI program evolving within the game, appearing in the form of a girl named Aura. In other words, potentialities immanent to the MMO are emerging, but not with ideal effects. You have to come closer and closer to the plane of immanence—to the stuff of blink, where toxic and intoxicating potentialities of media mingle and merge, spawning a range of possible nonpersonal experiences, including ecstasy, enlightenment, addiction, and blackouts—the flicker of a chance.

Such an experience cannot, however, be achieved through the PS2 alone. The network effect of the home media system, its point-to-point tendency, must be drawn out. This is where media mix comes into play. Each of the four games in the first *.hack* project came bundled with one episode of an OVA series, *Liminality*, which recounts events happening concurrently with the game action, largely in the real world (whereas the video games focus on "The World"). In fact, the first *.hack* project was developed with the capacity of the PS2 to play DVDs in mind. The *.hack* project invites you to switch between media modes on your PS2, to experience different media functions of the television platform—an expanded and intensified TV network.

In addition, an anime series entitled *Sign* began airing on TV Tokyo before the release of the PS2 games and OVA. The anime series follows a player character, Tsukasa, who awakens within the game not knowing who he is and finds himself trapped within the game. Being trapped within the game turns out to be as much as a psychological problem as a medial problem, and as Tsukasa overcomes various obstacles and advances in the game, he gains greater awareness of who he is. As it turns out, he is the player character of a girl in the real world who has succumbed to the game and gone into a coma. Only when Tsukasa wants to log out in order to meet with someone in the real world does the game end.

The first *.hack* project also included a manga series, published in *Comptiq* (short for "computer boutique"), a monthly game magazine published by Kadokawa, which carries advertisements for and information about new games as well as manga. The manga series, *Legend of Twilight (Tasogare no udewa densetsu)*, began serialization in January, before both the anime series and the PS2 and OVA series. While its advance publication in *Comptiq* positions the manga at the same level as advertisements for games, the manga series proved popular enough to continue into serialization well past the first anime series and the PS2 and OVA series, until April 2004. The manga even received an anime adaptation, which aired between January and March 2003. This series follows the adventures of twins, Shūgo and Rena. Aura sets up a contest in the real world, in which the twins win special avatars to play the MMO. Shūgo also receives a mysterious bracelet from Aura that both aids and hinders his ability to play the game. The twins thus embark on a quest to find Aura not only to resolve the mystery but also to overcome the disquieting situation.

The *.hack* series is thus centered on the production of games, and the games serve as the source material or concept for the other media instances. It may seem that the manga serialization, the anime broadcast, the OVA series, and the other media instances are ancillary or supplementary to the console games. One of the series producers, from Bandai, speaks in this manner, as if media mix were primarily a business strategy using multiple media in order to promote the games and make their attractiveness apparent.[4] This manner of speaking makes sense coming from Bandai. Bandai began as a toy company that gradually expanded into the production of video games and plastic model kits as well as *tokusatsu* series and anime. Although they did not invent the toy-centered media mix in which the anime series is launched to promote toys (such as transforming robots), such a strategy became prevalent in the context of the *Gandamu* or *Gundam* series, for which they are the primary licensee.

On the other hand, while the series creators started by conceptualizing the multimedia franchise around the video games, they clearly wished to create a cross-media effect, particularly across games and anime, selecting prominent creators of anime to work both on the games and animations.[5] Matsuyama Hiroshi, president of the development studio (CyberConnect2) and the *.hack* series director, selected for his character designer Sadamoto Yoshiyuki, well known for his work on the anime series *Neon Genesis Evangelion*. He also chose Itō Kazunori, renowned for his work on *The Ghost in the Shell* animations, to write the scripts. The idea was to generate a powerful experience across games and anime. In addition, the decision to produce a series of four games was couched in terms of deploying the narrative patterns of four-panel manga, harkening back to Miyamoto Shigeru's conceptualization of *Donkey Kong*.

Such tactics owe something to another media mix strategy, generally associated with Kadokawa Publishers, whose major innovation in the late 1980s and early 1990s lay in licensing all the media instances in advance while moving closer and closer to simultaneous, or at least strategically synchronized, releases across multiple media.[6] The *.hack* creators are obviously relying on such strategies, releasing the *.hack* manga in a Kadokawa magazine and broadcasting the anime series just before launching the first game. But they also transform these strategies into a metamodel—an online network experience within an off-line network. Multimedia serialization is used to induce a network experience at the level of media switching. Switching between game and OVA on the PS2, and switching between monitor and receiver on the TV set make for network tendencies within the off-line game, intensifying the point-to-point tendencies inherent in home media systems. The off-line game becomes capable of taking on the worldwide network, thanks to its position within the paradigm of media switching.

The paradigm of media switching is in turn grounded in code switching within media, evident in the evocation of manga patterns in the serialization of games, in the serialization of the manga alongside advertisements, and in the different styles of animation used to render the real world and the game world, both within the anime and the games. The real world is decidedly thinner and duller. Such code switching is not exclusive to animation, of course. But in the history of television and media mix, animation emerged as the prime code switching media form.

In sum, by highlighting the work of animation creators and using animation to bridge the gap between games and television anime, the *.hack* series perspicaciously situates animation both as a multimedia form and as the multimedia ground (or, more precisely, animetic plane of composition). This is how media mix strategies are used tactically to produce a metamodel of global media networks, the pure experience of which is one of blink, of an utter loss of self. But how can such an experience be sustained, and for how long? If it is sustained, does it become just another recognizable brand, just another media mix, just another model?

Guattari presents the metamodel as the very vocation of his schizoanalysis, as "a discipline for reading *other modeling systems*," that is, "not as a general model, but as an instrument for deciphering modeling systems in diverse domains, a meta-model."[7] At the same time, he signals the risk: "One might object that the limit between a model and a metamodel does not appear to be a stable frontier. And it is true that in one sense, subjectivity is always more and less an activity of meta-modeling."[8] The risk is that the metamodel will become a model and that the process of crossing between domains will turn into an actual structure, complete with subject position. Such a risk is endemic to multimedia franchises. The challenge for the *.hack* series is that of prolonging its metamodel, staving off its collapse into a model.

The *.hack* franchise adopts an unusual pattern in its bid to prolong and renew its metamodel. It comprises a series of projects without narrative continuity across them in any usual sense of the term. In November 2005, on the heels of the success of what would retroactively be known as the first *.hack* project, its creators launched an MMO version of their game, called *fragment,* which featured identical game play to the PS2 games, but with online capabilities. When the MMO, despite its popularity, was being phased out in late 2006, the second *.hack* project had already made an appearance, centered on a revised version of "The World" known as "The World R:2." This revision of "The World" comprised three games (*Rebirth, Reminisce,* and *Redemption*), an anime series as a prologue *(Roots),* a manga series, a series of light novels, and an OVA (*Trilogy,* 2007).

The games of the first project take place largely in 2010 in the alternative world timeline. In this *.hack* timeline, the MMO "The World" was launched in 2007, reaching over twenty million subscribers by 2008, when players began to experience blackouts. The anime series *Sign* takes place in 2009, setting the stage for the PS2 games and the *Liminality* OVA in 2010. The games and anime series of the second project, however, take place in 2017 of the *.hack* timeline, within an MMO ("The World R:2") completed in 2016. A third project (begun in 2010 of our timeline) hinges on another revision of "The World," called "The World R:X," completed in 2020 in the *.hack* timeline. This project comprises the *Link* PlayStation Portable (PSP) games and the *Quantum* anime. Yet another *.hack* project appeared in our 2012, centering on the game "The World Force:Era." In this fourth project, a computer virus within the MMO begins inducing blackouts in the year 2024 of the alternative earth.

With each project's revision of the "The World," the series advances chronologically in the alternative timeline, yet in every revision the story revolves around the virus-induced destruction of global computer networks and the advent of an MMO called "The World." The series is predicated on cycles of shutdown and rebuild, which does not allow for linear progression or chronological accumulation. The result is a multiplication of worlds operating on different frequencies, and yet these worlds communicate with one another in the manner of media platforms: across a temporal gap, autonomous yet capable of connecting. Player characters sometimes recur, bringing with them a certain mood, and sometimes moods recur, connecting projects at the level of their worldview. Thus "The World" of 2024 may feel like "The World" of *Legend of Twilight.* But it is a matter of semblance instead of resemblance. It is in this way, with these revisions of its world, that the *.hack* series tries to sustain its metamodel of the anime–game media mix.

Of course, the success or failure of the metamodel also depends on the extent to which we can remain in its perspective and prolong the experiment. With this challenge in mind, I wish to take a closer look at a fairly recent entry in the series, the animated film *Beyond the World (Sekai no mukō ni)*, released in theaters January 21, 2012. This animated film inaugurated the fourth project in conjunction with the serialization of a manga in *Comptiq* from January to July of the same year. Initially, this animated film may seem an unlikely example because it was released as a film rather than an OVA or television anime series. Yet the film was actually articulated in a noncinematic way and geared toward the television set: it was produced with a technical upgrade in home media systems in mind. Its animation, known as high-density-resolution computer-generated animation (HDCG), was designed with an eye to the PS3 and its capacity to run both games and Blu-ray disks on an HDTV screen. To this end, a PS3 game, *Versus*, was bundled with the Blu-ray release of *Beyond the World*. Cinematic release was used as a springboard for selling an OVA–game bundle. Cinema was thus included within the home media network, playing a role analogous to manga vis-à-vis the media mix centered on television console games and television animation. In this respect, *Beyond the World* recalls a previous *.hack* entry in the second project, called *GU Trilogy*.

GU Trilogy was envisioned as an OVA series, and yet before its OVA release in March 2008, it appeared in movie theaters, with a screening in December 2007 and then a two-week theatrical release in January 2008. Here, too, the idea was to address (or exploit) technical upgrades in home media systems. The HDCG animation for *GU Trilogy* was drawn largely from the *GU* games, enhanced with techniques of tone rendering or cel shading. Cel shading flattens the volumetric feel of CGI by applying contour lines and shading to animated characters. It thus imparts something of the look and feel of traditional cel animation to computer-generated imagery. With such techniques, the *GU Trilogy* aimed to produce an experience across games and animation while upgrading its technical specifications to assure cinema-quality resolution for PS3 consoles plugged into HDTVs.

Beyond the World likewise aimed at a technical upgrade in the anime–game media mix. Like prior *.hack* projects, its creators bridged the domains of animation production and game production. Its director was Matsuyama Hiroshi, director of *.hack* projects and president of the development studio (CyberConnect), generally associated more with game production than with animation. Itō Kazunori, better known for his work in animation production, again provided the script. As with *GU Trilogy*, the cinema release of *Beyond the World* served as demonstration of its HDCG animation, with release of the anime–game bundle for PS3 in mind. As such, *Beyond the World* provides a highly condensed and thus relatively handy example for considering what is at stake in the *.hack* bid to transform media mix strategies into a metamodel for global media networks.

Social Media Ecologies

In keeping with the *.hack* vision, the *Beyond the World* animation introduces a divide between the real world and game world, yet at the same, since the MMO is called "The World," the impression is that the game world may function as the world, that is, may potentially replace the real world. Depictions of the two "worlds" reinforces this impression: as with other instances in the series, in the *Beyond the World* animation, the real world appears duller and thinner, less vibrant and vital, and less real than the game world. In other words, there is a tentative inversion of the received priority of reality over representation: the game world is potentially realer than the real world. As such, the animation invites reading it in terms of simulation in the manner of Baudrillard. Because simulation is realer than real, it not only replaces the real but also absorbs reality effects, making recourse to representation in the usual sense impossible. As Baudrillard says, try simulating a bank robbery, and you will find how real simulation can be.

The notion of simulation, however, does not entirely describe the relation between game world and real world in the *.hack* series, or rather, it only seems to address the relation from one side of its movement—how the game absorbs reality, sucks the life out of representation. The *Beyond the World* animation offers another kind of movement, too, in which the real world comes to surround or encompass the game world. To address this double movement, we do indeed need to go "beyond the world," that is, beyond the notion of one world absorbing or encompassing the other. In fact, if we consider how the animation sets forth

FIGURE 12.2. The real-world sequences of the *Beyond the World* animated movie present a big-screen ecology in which screens cover walls and crop up in streets.

FIGURE 12.3. Within the home, advertisements dominate the imagery on large flat-screen TVs, not only highlighting the segmentation of television programming but also the commercial publicness of the big-screen ecology.

these two worlds, we see that they are not so much enclosed worlds as they are media ecologies, two distinctive sets of media practices distributed throughout urban space.

The real world is in fact a media ecology structured around screens of varying shapes and sizes, but with general emphasis on large ones that appear through-out urban space. One screen covers the side of a building, another fills a wall in a shopping center, and yet others crop up on walls along the streets, like billboards (Figure 12.2). This big-screen ecology extends from the streets of the city into private homes equipped with flat-panel HDTVs. In the streets and in homes, the screens of this media ecology generally display news reports in formats ranging from evening TV news programs to bloglike Web news and public service an-nouncements. Occasionally advertisements appear within programs, providing a reminder that this sort of programming is segmented into slots (Figure 12.3). In other words, this big-screen ecology is that of broadcast television, but expanded to include Internet-derived materials and distributed throughout public space, as ambient news.

While this ecology may thus feel environmental and even immersive, the messages that catch the eye and further the action are public service warnings. For instance, near the start of the animation, as four teenagers walk home from school through this urban space, a government warning about media addiction is prominently displayed on billboardlike screens: "Internet addiction at the highest

ネット依存症、過去最大に

Internet Addiction Hits All-Time High

ネット依存症の患者の数が、20年前の調査開始以来、
最大になったとNGOが発表。
この依存症の主な特徴である「常にインターネットに
接続・閲覧できないと不安や孤独を感じる」といった
症例は、現在、発症の低年齢化が問題になっており、
とりわけ小中学校においては深刻化している。
とある中学校を対象とした調査では、40％以上の生徒
が授業中に隠れてインターネットに接続した経験があ
ると答えている。

11月23日(土)9時27分配信

AMAMI

FIGURE 12.4. In the *Beyond the World* animated film, the publicness of large screens extends to service announcements, with the government posting warnings about media addiction on billboardlike screens: "Internet addiction at the highest level ever."

level ever" (Figure 12.4). Governmental warnings about the dangers of the Net and online games (*netto gēmu,* or Net games) appear frequently on big screens within this broadcast formation, with increasingly urgency. As such, *Beyond the World* imparts a strong sense of the dominance of the one-to-many tendency within the big-screen ecology, of transmission from a centralized source for privatized reception, especially in homes. Indeed, the teenagers in the streets do not pay attention to these big screens—until they reach home. The heroine of *Beyond the World,* a fourteen-year-old girl named Sora, for instance, returns home to watch HDTV with her grandfather and grandmother.

In sum, this big-screen ecology is an almost paradigmatic example of the procedures of social segmentation that Raymond Williams highlights in his account of television. There is a multiplication of centers with movement between them. The teenagers commute from homes to their school and back home again, with daily life organized around disciplinary procedures of segmentation—now you are at home, now you are at school, now you are at work; you are a minor or an adult, a student or teacher, a child or adult, a man or woman—which procedures of segmentation are echoed and reinforced in the segmentation of audiovisual flow into frequencies, channels, stations, programs, and audiovisual codes (ads, news, stories). Significantly, Sora's family is slightly broken or dispersed: she lives with her grandparents while her father has been transferred to work else-

FIGURE 12.5. As players of the online game "The World" don their augmented-reality glasses, it is as if they drop out of the real world, or rather the big-screen ecology.

where. Sora initially clings to domestic space and social segmentation, resisting her friends' invitations to enter "The World."

"The World" presents a different screen ecology, revolving around the small screens of mobile phones. In contrast to their general indifference to the big-screen ecology, the teenagers are passionately engaged with these small screens, which are devoted to social media (texting) and online games, above all "The World." Seen from the perspective of the big-screen ecology, this small-screen ecology does indeed appear to entail some kind of addiction or loss of self-consciousness. The animation shows students in various sites throughout the city, on trains and park benches, with their mobile phone in hand while wearing augmented-reality glasses to play "The World." They appear completely oblivious to the world around them, that is, heedless of the big-screen ecology (Figure 12.5). They are totally immersed, intoxicated as it were, in the small-screen ecology. These players, scattered in little groups here and there, also appear to have a different relation to procedures of social segmentation. They are no longer commuting between school and home, between enclosed sites, but are stopping along the way, stopping amid the segmented flow, stopping on segmentation. This gesture extends into "The World."

When Sora enters "The World" and takes on an avatar, she identifies and quickly meets up with two of her classmate girlfriends. The appearance of her grandfather, however, comes as a surprise: he appears as a dashing young man, maybe an echo of his younger self. In other words, social segmentation is still in evidence, and avatars can be situated in terms of their real-world segment, yet those segments are slightly scrambled and modified. Instead of eradicating real-world social segmentation altogether, "The World" cuts across them, pulling individuals out of their segments and making new groups with them (Figure 12.6). Thus Sora enters into a little society comprising her two girlfriends and her grandfather, as well as two boys from her class at school. She confuses the identities of the two boys, however. One appears as Balder, a paladin, and the other as Gondo, a berserker. Her confusion makes for a romantic twist: when Okano Tomohiko declares his love for her within the game, she thinks it is Tanaka Kakeru. Her error, however, produces truth. "The World" allows Sora to fall in love with Tanaka although she had initially (mistakenly) pinned her affections on Okano. In sum, by stopping on social segmentation, the small-screen ecology releases potentiality, affective reality, and expressive or generative truths. In social terms, instead of positing a radical break with the big-screen ecology, the small-screen ecology transforms it, primarily by loosing the hold of its procedures of segmentation in such a way as to flatten the hierarchies associated with the one-to-many tendency.

The *Crayon Shin-chan* series offers a useful case for comparison. Recall how that series ridiculed authority and dethroned despots, splitting off and embracing the unidirectional tendency implicit in the one-to-many tendency of broadcast television while rejecting its hierarchical tendency (univocal messaging and propaganda). Like the *Crayon Shin-chan* series, *Beyond the World* holds onto the one-to-many tendency, shunting it away from its hierarchical tendencies into unidirectional tendencies. As with Shin-chan becoming Action Kamen, the individual appears to be turning into its truer self, naturally, spontaneously, and joyously. Grandfather becomes a virile swashbuckler. Each person becomes a privatized center, personified. At the same time, *Beyond the World* brings to the fore a tendency only implicit in the *Crayon Shin-chan*. "The World" releases the potentiality of socially segmented individuals by situating them within contingently segmented and thus truer forms, such as wavemaster, paladin, or berserker—truer to their potentiality for creative play, contingent on the unfolding action. "The World" thus allows players to experience something of the contingency buried within procedures of social segmentation that have come to weigh on bodies like an immoveable immutable structure—at the price of adopting another kind of segmentation. Grandfather, for instance, takes on a recognizable archetypal role within the game.

Taking on an avatar or player character thus has two sides. On the one hand, adopting an avatar feels like a process of personalization, in the form of self-segmentation. On the other hand, it feels like a process of potentialization, in which you contribute in accordance with your capacity, nonpersonally. The moment in which Sora enters "The World" is a prime example. She retreats to the privacy of her bedroom, effectively segmenting herself, to don the VR glasses. Entering the game, however, is like stepping through Doraemon's "anywhere

FIGURE 12.6. Instead of eradicating real-world social segmentation altogether, "The World" cuts across them, pulling individuals out of their segments and making new groups from them: Sora's grandfather, for instance, is the young man, while the other avatars are school friends, whom she does not always identify correctly.

door." Sora leaves behind her bedroom and the national domestic television formation, to find herself in the cosmopolitan domain of "The World." What is more, her avatar seems to select her, and through a series of mysterious encounters, it is as if she is entering the game as someone other than herself, who may be herself (Aura). But once she finds her way to the vast forum where characters assemble, her friends recognize her as Sora. In its contingency, taking on an avatar pivots between these two possibilities: self-segmenting (personalization) and self-animating (potentialization). Therein lies the drama of *Beyond the World*.

What initially appears to be a clash between worlds (game world versus real world) turns out to be a contrast between media ecologies, and then the drama lies in finding a way to move between ecologies without becoming trapped in either of them, that is, without falling from the metamodel into one model or the other. As the interactions among avatars make evident, the challenge comes of the fact that the social technology of the big-screen ecology, with its procedures of segmentation, permeates, informs, and threatens to overwhelm the small-screen ecology. It is thus no easy matter to give equal time or equal weight to self-animating processes, to potentialization.

In the *.hack* series, animation techniques are used to shift the balance toward potentialization, to compensate for the pull of the big-screen ecology. Animation is used to make "The World" brighter, livelier, and more colorful than the real world. It is a space of animation, whose actual places run the gamut from vast horizons to intimate and intricate passageways. Its people are diverse and motley, often hybridized with nonhuman beings, albeit in a highly iconic manner (the palette is geared toward familiar sword-and-sorcery hybrids from myths, legends, and folklore). Where cel shading for the real world imparts a flat, drab two-dimensional texture to characters, the volumetric feel of computer-generated figures is more palpable in "The World," moving beneath the brighter colors and contour lines, like a soul stirring beneath the skin. Finally, in contrast with screens in the big-screen ecology, which, however large, appear with frames, "The World" appears without any edges. This effect of total immersion can be explained by the use of VR glasses to enter "The World," but in fact such glasses have edges. Rendering "The World" without frames or edges is calculated to enhance a sense of total immersion. But this is precisely where the small-screen ecology risks becoming a trap and where self-animating processes risk lapsing into a model.

Ultimately, then, the great experiment and the challenge of the .hack series lies in its commitment to sustaining a metamodel. In the case of *Beyond the World,* for instance, even as it calls on various techniques for imparting greater affective weight and animating force to the small-screen ecology, it avoids the trap of setting up the game as an autonomous alternative reality, as a self-sufficient model for the world, for being in the world. This is why the game world itself must break or fail, again and again, if .*hack* is to succeed in moving "beyond the world" (both the game world and the real world) and sustaining a metamodel of our contemporary multimedia ecologies. In its commitment to the metamodel, the .*hack* series not only offers a challenging gamic perspective on contemporary television media but also provides a perspective on games and gaming that runs counter to some of the received wisdom about them. The challenges of this twofold perspective built into its metamodel deserve closer consideration.

Gamic Realism

A good deal of the initial scholarship on video games in North America strove to ground analysis in the medium specificity of video games, distinguishing games from other media forms and from other forms of interaction with media. As Nick Dyer-Witheford and Greig de Peuter sum it up, "Much of this literature is concerned with delineating the specific properties of games as media, describing their genres and conventions, and forming a lexicon with which to describe them. When the literature does look to games in their larger context, the assessment is often positive, asserting the creative empowerment of game players compared to the audiences of the broadcast media."[9]

In early scholarship, video games were generally characterized in terms of the activity and creativity of gamers, in contrast to the passivity and lack of inventiveness on the part of cinema and television audiences as well as readers. Such an opposition has proven too stark to be sustained, and one line of inquiry has gradually transformed it into a distinction between participation and interaction. In his account of cybertext, for instance, Espen Aarseth distinguishes the interactivity of games from other forms of participatory engagement, such as those associated with radio and television shows.[10] Still, the characterization of games in terms of interaction did not resolve the issue. Alexander Galloway, for instance, rejects the notion of interactivity: "One should resist equating gamic action with a theory of 'interactivity' or the 'active audience' theory of media. . . . I avoid the word 'interactive' and prefer instead to call the video game, like the computer, an *action-based* medium."[11] Nonetheless, although Galloway rejects the theory of interactivity, his reasons for rejecting it do not put him on a completely different footing from Aarseth. The basic idea is still to distinguish gamers from audiences, however those audiences are characterized (passivity, participation, interactivity).

A similar concern arises in the context of distinguishing video games from other media forms on the basis of play versus narrative, or ludology versus narratology. Gonzalo Frasca, for instance, situates himself among theorists "who claim that videogames should not be viewed as an extension of narrative, literature, theater or cinema."[12] Interestingly, yet perhaps not surprising in light of how he groups together narrative, literature, theater, and cinema, Frasca also rejects the notions of interaction and interactivity. He proposes a distinction between simulation (games) and narrative. His conceptualization of simulation sustains a sense of action versus passivity but at the level of playing with (or within) a simulation (and thus creating with what is presented to you) versus taking in a narrative, that is, receiving something re-presented to you. In this respect, probably unintentionally, his distinction is not unlike Baudrillard's distinction between simulation and representation. Yet where Baudrillard associated simulation with totalizing procedures, Frasca seems to envision some sort of creative empowerment for individuals in the act of playing with simulation.

In sum, as Dyer-Witheford and de Peuter are keen to point out, accounts of the medium specificity of video games that emphasize activity over passivity tend to rule out questions about totalizing procedures in the context of game studies, and thus they avoid the urgent question of neoliberal takes on individuality and creativity. To counter this tendency, Dyer-Witheford and de Peuter call attention to the totalizing procedures at work in the world of video games, with an emphasis on economic determinations related to game production. In the context of media convergence, for instance, they call attention to "a world of fiercely bargained properties" in which "games are increasingly integrated *with* films, music, and other media."[13] In other words, even if games entail some sort of medium specificity, that specificity does not remove them from the operations of Empire. Likewise, but in a different register, Galloway has also focused increasingly on questions of power in the context of games and software, finding totalizing procedures in software protocol, that is, fine-scale medial determinations.[14]

Accounts of games and media mix in Japan encounter a similar set of questions. Yet Japanese accounts of video games have generally not belabored the question of the medium specificity of video games or tried to separate games from other media forms. As discussed previously, because of the historical prevalence of the manga–anime media matrix, transmedia storytelling became a force to be reckoned with as early as the 1970s. By the late 1980s and early 1990s, when the paradigm of media mix started to impart new discursive and economic force to the production of multimedia franchises, critics and commentators directed their attention to the operations of media ensembles instead of treating media forms in terms of their specificity. As a result, as discussed previously in the context of the work of Ōtsuka Eiji and Azuma Hiroki, the tendency was to deconstruct and repurpose theories of story and narrative rather than to reject them. Recall that Ōtsuka looked at media mix in terms of a relation between "small narratives" and "world," moving away from a theory of narrative giving precedence to subjective or discursive enclosure. But it was Azuma in particular who made great efforts to think through the consequences of the liberation of story or fabula from narrative discursive enclosure in the context of anime and games. In his first book on otaku and postmodernism, in addressing media mix, Azuma introduced a two-tiered model based on a distinction between "little stories" and "grand database structure," with the grand database effectively replacing narrative structuring.[15] In his second book devoted to otaku and postmodernism, which centers on "the birth of gamic realism," Azuma looks at games from the angle of their interrelation with light novels, anime, and manga. This emphasis leads him to rethink his prior emphasis on database structure. In its place, he introduces the notion of metastory (meta-monogatari).[16] With the notion of metastory, Azuma develops something akin to Guattari's metamodel and Deleuze's conceptualization of fabulation. Instead of implying a underlying or overarching structure for a set of stories, the notion of metastory addresses the process of expressing and taking on a relation across a set of stories, which Azuma describes in terms of world lines. Put in Deleuzian terms, the metastory expresses, captures, and prolongs the "virtual" of storytelling or of story series, that is, their relationality, even—especially—across media.

The metastory thus does not entail a formal or structural distinction between play and narrative. Nor does it rely on an opposition between activity and passivity. Instead, the metastory attends to difference in expressive function within the media mix. Recall how the creator of Donkey Kong, Miyamoto Shigeru, likened the form of his game to the form of four-panel manga, and how the creators of the first four .hack games similarly evoked the form of the four-panel manga to explain their series of four games. Also, by the time of the GU games of the second .hack project, there is a good deal of formal overlap between the games' animation and that of the OVA. Yet no one imagines that the game is identical to the OVA. Resemblance occurs between games and other media at the level of form and content—or, to be precise, the form of content. Dissemblance arises between games and other media at the level of expression, that is, the form of expression. The metastory composes with resemblance and dissemblance, generating an experience of semblance across media instances. Azuma glosses such an experience of semblance with the phrase "gamic realism" to account for non-game gamelike media, such as gamelike novels in addition to the genre known as novel games. But he makes clear that this realism is not a matter of representation or resemblance.[17]

The .hack series strives to impart the experience of an online MMO within an off-line game. To do so, as we have seen, it constructs a metamodel of online games by using media mix to draw on the network potential implicit in its media ecology (the home media system). Azuma's notion of metastory explains how the .hack series may be devoted to the specific experience of games and gamic media and at the same time not be averse to using anime, manga, and novels to generate that gamelike experience. The .hack series must do two things simultaneously: it must both evoke and transform the medium specificity of games. Its metastory, then, is the story of this transformation of the medium specificity of the game into a metamodel, into the gamelike or gamic. Like some of the game scholars cited previously, the .hack series tends to locate the specificity of games in action and interaction. But it must at the same time problematize and move beyond the notion of interactivity, beyond the interactive world, beyond "The World," into the realm of infraindividual intra-action and metastory.

Beyond the Interactive World

What exactly is the problem with interactivity? Brian Massumi offers these guidelines: "What interactive art can do, what its strength is in my opinion, is to take the *situation* as its 'object.' Not a function, not a use, not a need, not a behavior, exploratory or otherwise. But a situation, with its own little ocean of complexity. It can take a situation and open the interactions it affords."[18] The problem is that interactions tend toward instrumental function. Massumi writes, "Inter*action* is just that: a going back and forth between actions, largely reduced to instrumental function. . . . I use the word *interactivity* to designate an instrumentally contracted dynamic for that tends to shrink to the parameters of its objectively instrumental function. . . . That's what has happened when we hear the comment, all too common, from interactive art participants that experience felt like a video game. You often feel there's a trick you need to find and to master."[19]

Massumi is careful not to rule out interactive art, or video games for that matter, but he wishes to pinpoint the troubling tendency of interaction to turn into an instrumental functioning, that is, a closed system of signs and actions, which you are invited to master. Interaction thus loses interest as soon as you master the trick. The .hack series similarly worries about this instrumental functioning in context of role-playing games. You know, for instance, what it means to play the role of a berserker, paladin, or wavemaster, and you know how the quest unfolds and even how it probably ends for that role. What is more, as the example of Beyond the World makes clear, this interactive functionalism tends to repeat disciplinary procedures of segmentation. The game threatens to turn into just another site of discipline, one in which you engage in practices of self-segmentation, work on self. The game ceases to take a situation as its object, ceases to open its interactions. The game becomes just another enclosed site of work, to which you commute at certain times of day.

This is surely why dramas about being trapped within games, such as Sword Art Online or Overlord, are so prevalent today. Such a gesture is one way of trying to combat the functional enclosure of interactivity, not only by concretizing the tendency of interactivity toward enclosure but also by stopping movement in and out of the game, that is, putting an end to commuting—when flows are stopped, segmentation loses its hold. This is one way of stopping on segmentation. The violence of disciplinary society is laid bare, fully exposed. If you fail to work on self and power up, if you are killed within the game, you die in reality. This sort of drama runs the risk, however, of endorsing a simplistic, primitive view of power as something that is held at the point of a sword or in an avatar, when in fact something else is at stake: the transformation of disciplinary procedures into a continuous retooling to acquire new skills and abilities, in keeping with the incessant modulations of markets and opportunities characteristic of neoliberal modes of control.

The .hack series also dramatizes entrapment within the game but doubles it with entrapment within your body, within your head. As the computer virus advances, players lose consciousness and enter into a comatose state. As we have seen, from the perspective of big-screen ecology, this physical, neurological loss of consciousness is associated with addiction. In other words, the game is breaking down for medial reasons (computer virus) that are simultaneously neurological reasons (blackout, coma). The advance of the virus is dramatized as an enclosing of the game world. When the game world breaks down, the vast, open spaces begin to crack and fissure. What looked like an expanse of sky now looks like a ceiling; buildings topple and shatter, revealing gridlike walls; crackling electricity buzzes all around. Also, the big-screen ecology seems to become larger

FIGURE 12.7. The big-screen ecology tends to function best during crises when large screens in the streets and in homes offer news updates and displays of data in large-scale monitoring of trends.

and more powerful. As the danger of the virus increases, various organizations and institutions in the real world mobilize, relying on data from giant banks of screens inside control rooms, monitoring viral effects with an elaborate array of scientific equipment. Large screens in the streets and in homes also offer news reports and displays of data, to allow people to track the situation wherever they may be (Figure 10.7). The world of the game thus feels confined and constrained as techniques are mobilized to make what is happening knowable and controllable. In effect, the big-screen ecology starts to enclose the small-screen ecology.

Hierarchies are more evident in the big-screen ecology, yet the overall focus (and solution) is on the game and individual bodies affected by the game. But the big-screen ecology cannot pull rank on the small-screen ecology. It cannot stand over and above it as an absent master, for the game has the potential to bring down the big-screen ecology as well. The game has become, in effect, the outside operating on the inside—the brain within the big-screen body. The real world is on the brink of a black, a coma. The totalizing procedures of the big-screen ecology are thus directed in a unidirectional manner (instead of a hierarchical manner), applying pressure to the game and its individual players. It thus falls to individuals—Sora and her cohort—to fix the game and save the world, to save both worlds. The fix, however, is not a simple matter of action or interaction.

Generally the *.hack* series paints a negative portrait of interactivity and of action within the game. When you find yourself trapped within the game, as Tsukasa does in *Sign* or as Haseo does in *GU Trilogy*, you are in fact trapped within repetitive, unthinking cycles of action, doing the same thing over and over, moving within the game without actually going anywhere. You are trapped within instrumental function, as Massumi puts it. For the video game to take the situation as its object, it must hamper or impede this sort of activity and interactivity, which is associated with simplistic psychological motivations, such as revenge, fame, or desire for recognition. Put another way, the video game must break with immersion and addiction because these conditions prevent the game from developing any inner distances. Under such conditions, game space is just space. It is just distance to be covered. Still, because interactivity is essential to the game, you cannot simply eliminate it. You must complexly transform it.

The fix of the .hack series is to introduce pauses and hesitations, moments in which interaction with the game fails for some internal virus-related reason. In effect, the game stops on itself. The game stops on RPG action and interaction. The game now appears to be something other than what seemed at first, that is, a sword-and-sorcery RPG. It becomes a situation. It turns toward a different sort of quest or journey, away from immersive addictive interaction.

The usual way to stop gamic action and interaction within the RPG is to introduce cinematics—that is, movielike sequences, usually animation, to be watched rather than played—which are the bane of theories of medium specificity. Usually cinematics come as a reward for completing a level or unlocking a bonus. They thus feel different from the game, as if they come from without. The .hack series, however, troubles this neat divide between game play and animation sequences. What if at some point in the game you pushed a button that switched you from the game into the OVA, or vice versa? What if you could not really tell the difference? Or rather, what if the experience of switching between them felt gamelike, if it felt interactive but somehow disrupted interactivity? This is precisely how the .hack series begins to generate its metamodel: switching between media starts to feel gamelike. But the series does not remain content with such a large, potentially gross gesture. It introduces the feel of switching into the game such that as you become immersed in the game, you begin to feel that you may have been switched, maybe into another kind of game, maybe into another kind of medium, maybe to another sort of media platform. This is how the .hack series embarks on the story of its metamodel, which actualizes the metastory.

Switching is basically a matter of moving from one frequency to another, whether you are switching from channel to channel on the television set, or whether you are switching from one media platform to another—hence the scan lines that appear on classic console games, or on TV screens shot with a camcorder, or on video footage played on the TV. Aptly, then, it turns out that Sora is able to save the world as a result of an unexpected unpredictable resonance of frequencies. Equally aptly, her friend shows her this unusual resonance of frequencies on a cell phone (Figure 12.8). Sora is, by chance, in resonance with Aura, an intelligence that is a chance effect of the game, evolving with the game,

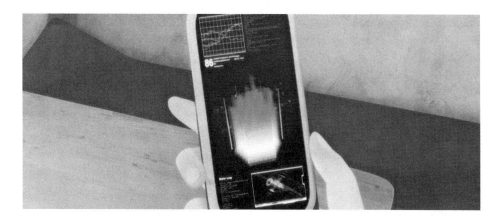

FIGURE 12.8. Because Aura's waveform perfectly matches Sora's brain synapse response, Sora has taken on abilities within the game that will allow her to save the game world. Appropriately enough, it is a mobile phone screen that conveys this unexpected resonance of frequencies.

as a result of a sort of positive discrepancy or potentiality within it. To play Aura, however, is to go beyond the immersive world of interactivity, to open the situation of interactions, to experience an aura or distance in proximity that resonates with switching between media forms and platform frequencies, crossing media ecologies. It is an experience of an internal switching, of a self-animating process. This is how you go out of the game, how you move beyond "The World," without ever leaving it.

All in all, the game of the *.hack* series might be summarized as one that plays both ends against the middle. Its metastory relies on a conflict between two media ecologies: the small-screen ecology of gamelike networks versus the bigscreen, broadcast-derived ecology. In other words, it sets the point-to-point tendency against the one-to-many tendency, emphasizing the differences between them. If this conflict is to the advantage of the middle, however, it is because at the same time it produces a new assembling of totalizing and individualizing procedures. Figure 12.1 makes this situation clear. At the big-screen end, the *.hack* series focuses on individualization, bringing procedures of segmentation to the fore. At the small-screen end, it emphasizes totalizing tendencies implicit in immersive worlds. In effect, the *.hack* series plays both ends against one another— unidirectional versus environmental, segmentation versus immersion—to the advantage of the middle, that is, to the advantage of assembling them in a new way. The experience of the avatar in *Beyond the World* gives a sense of this assembling of polarized tendencies.

On the one hand, the avatar is experienced as if someone is behind it, as if it were the projection of someone in the real world—say, your grandfather projecting himself as a dashing young hero. As such, the avatar may be treated as a symptom of his personality, as a way of working through his limitations, for instance, dealing with old age. The avatar is thus a mode of work on self, a mode of self-segmentation that strives to resolve the strictures of disciplinary society by individualizing and psychologizing them. On the other hand, the avatar is experienced not as a psychological projection with someone's personality and hang-ups behind it. The avatar is experienced as its own truth or reality, as an affective reality, as an enactment and transmission of nonpersonal dispositions (dashingness and youthfulness). The avatar is thus a mode of production of self, of self-animation. The experience of the avatar tends to work in both ways at once, albeit with different consequences. For instance, Sora's avatar looks like Kite, the avatar of a fourteen-year-old boy from a previous version of "The World," yet because Aura wishes to mobilize Sora, it is as if Kite selects her.

In sum, the avatar is the site of assembly of polarized tendencies, which makes it also feel able to produce something new, a middle that is both and neither. The avatar mobilizes immersion to stop on segmentation (the self-animating mode) and draws on segmentation to stop on immersion (the self-segmenting mode). Between the two arises the possibility of a care for self, yet this care for self remains contingent on switching, that is, contingent on a radical loss of self, blackout. Consequently, care for self does not emerge as a model, much less a subject position. It does not side entirely with self-animating or self-segmenting. It hovers over both models. It produces the soul of the metamodel, which takes in the process of media assembling, thus affording a perspective on it.

It may seem odd that media mix enables the emergence of a gamelike soul. After all, media mix is fundamentally a business model. Yet it is not the business model that generates the soul of media mix. In the *.hack* series, for instance, the corporation is generally responsible the virus and for the operating systems immune to it. In fact, in *Beyond the World,* a corporation called CyberConnect is even alleged to have introduced the virus, apparently hoping to profit from treating it. The business model thus generates problems and solutions even as it generates yet more models. But the soul is something else. It is what is busy among the models, trying to get a feel for where we are and where media are taking us. Still, for the soul of the metamodel to have the ghost of a chance, it would need to ally itself somehow with improvisational forces, with the heterarchical possibilities offered by networks.

13

THE PORTABLE INTERFACE COMPLEX

IN THE WAKE OF THE POKÉMON INCIDENT, GOVERNMENT AGENCIES, BROADCASTERS, AND PRODUCERS MOBILIZED TO ASSURE the safety of animation audiences, especially children. In addition to the recommended advisory messages, broadcasters like TV Tokyo introduced an "animation checker," that is, a flicker analysis machine for checking episodes before broadcast to guard against infractions of the new production guidelines (Figure 13.1). Producers of daytime and prime-time animation showed new restraint in their use of flashy effects. In addition, the presentation of television audiences within anime series, especially of children and families, took care to reinforce the ideal parameters for using the television. Children are typically shown sitting at a proper distance from the television screen in well-illuminated rooms (Figure 13.2).

But what would happen if you deliberately ignored the viewer advisory for television animation? What if you refused to keep the room well illuminated or to keep your distance from the TV screen? What would happen if you turned off all the lights and walked right up to the TV screen to watch animation in the middle of the night? Would you immediately go into convulsions and black out? Or would the transformation be subtler, yet potentially vaster? Would your relation to government authority, family structures, medical institutions, scientific knowledge, police forces, and your brain be altered? To what extent would your relation to the media care implicit in the screen–brain apparatus be transformed? Would you become a rebel or an addict, an outlaw or a victim?

These questions are wonderfully dramatized in *Persona 4: The Animation (Perusona fō ji animēshon),* a 2013 anime series based on *The New Rebirth of the Goddess: Persona 4 (Shin megami tensei: Perusona fō),* the fourth RPG console game in the *Persona* series, released in 2008 for the PlayStation.

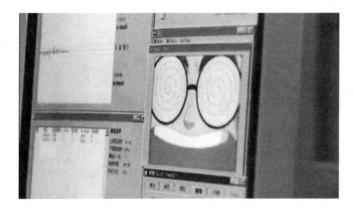

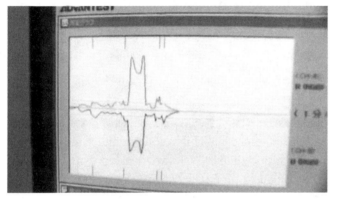

FIGURE 13.1. In one sequence in *The Tube,* personnel at TV Tokyo play clips of the notorious episode 38 of *Pokémon,* measuring the frequency of flicker for red and blue, which is mapped alongside the footage. The second image shows the measurements for the 12 Hz red–blue flicker scene, which jumps well outside the safety zone.

Persona 4 follows a young man, Narukami Yū, who has transferred from Tokyo to a high school in a small town near Mount Fuji, supposedly in the middle of nowhere. Each night, the local "midnight TV" station *(mayonaka terebi)* broadcasts scenes of people who have been kidnapped and somehow imprisoned in dungeons within the television. Narukami discovers that when he approaches the television screen late at night in a darkened room, he is sucked into the television world. As he enters the television screen, the effects even recall those of *Pokémon's* "Dennō senshi Porigon" episode, with psychedelic whirling concentric patterns filling the screen (Figure 13.3) as well as transmitted light effects, flashes, and flicker. The Pokémon Incident would surely be a solid point of reference for the targeted audience of *Persona 4*: the children in the group sensitive to PSE (ages six to twelve) at the time of the 1997 Pokémon Incident would have been roughly ages seventeen to twenty-three in 2008 when the *Persona 4* game was released, and about twenty-one to twenty-eight when the animation was broadcast.

"Midnight TV" is a sly reference to the time slot for *shin'ya anime,* or "late night" series, like *Persona 4.* As Mitsuyo Wada-Marciano puts it, "Instead of aiming for high TV ratings, these past-midnight anime production began to play a different role in the new format of media mix, acting as promotional spots for

FIGURE 13.2. After the Pokémon Incident, television animations made sure to show the correct way to watch TV, as in this scene from episode 3 of *Persona 4: The Animation*.

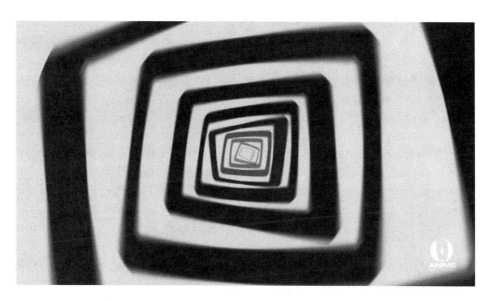

FIGURE 13.3. When three teenagers fall through the TV screen in episode 1 of *Persona 4*, the experience of movement into the TV is rendered in a manner that recalls episode 38 of *Pokémon*.

repackaged DVDs or to encourage follow-up sales of computer games."[1] In the wake of the Pokémon Incident, these slots also afforded sites of experimentation with anime effects that might not make it past the flicker analysis machines. The *Persona 4* anime series thus places itself and its viewers in a potentially harmful nonbroadcast yet broadcast television situation.

Within the television world, Narukami and his new friends subsequently explore dungeons, confront the dark side of their selves (their shadows), acquire powers (called personas), and combat demonic entities in order to save the victims and to solve the mystery, that is, to figure out who is responsible for these abductions. In sum, in *Persona 4*, something like Pokémon Shock becomes entangled with a game scenario in which you summon powers within yourself, or "power up," in order to defeat demons, solve mysteries, and save the world. In this scenario, the charge of the screen releases some sort of potential within you.

As with the examples in prior chapters, *Persona 4* belongs to a larger multimedia franchise. It is the fourth game in the *Persona* series, which is a spin-off series from the *Rebirth of the Goddess (Megami tensei)* series, which was reconfigured in 1992 as *The New Rebirth of the Goddess (Shin megami tensei)*. Let me use the fan abbreviation and call it the *MegaTen* series for the sake of convenience.

Like the *.hack* series, the *MegaTen* series also stages an encounter between two worlds, a daytime world of ordinary humans versus a nighttime world of demons and of humans who can summon demons (or other special powers such as personas) in order to engage in combat with demons. Typically a conflict breaks out in which the demon world threatens to supplant and destroy the ordinary human world. The demon world is often a gamelike world, into which you enter via some sort of gamic media. Thus the *MegaTen* series, like the *.hack* series, offers a metamodel of gamic media.

At the same time, however, as *Persona 4* attests, where the *.hack* series concentrates its attention on creating an off-line experience of online networks, the *MegaTen* series tends to focus on the experience of the screen itself, the experience of the user–screen interface. Its basic concern is that of how you can summon and embody the demonic, shock-inducing, mind-altering charge of the screen. It is because the metamodel of the *Megami* series tends to settle on the screen interface instead of on networks that Pokémon Shock becomes a perfect trope for exploring the effects of screens in *Persona 4*.

In the *MegaTen* series, as I will show, the screen commonly turns out to be a site of bifurcation, where two distinct kinds of user–screen experiences are at once held apart and held together. Because of its articulation of the screen interface as the site of bifurcating media tendencies, the *MegaTen* series presents yet another manner of dwelling in (or striving to adhere to) the polarized tendencies assembled within new television media formations, which I propose to call the interface complex. *Persona 4* is an especially good example in the context of this study, both for its focus on broadcast TV and its evocation of Pokémon Shock.

Significantly, when Narukami in *Persona 4* approaches the TV screen late at night, he implicitly defies the quasi-disciplinary apparatus of media care that coalesced in the wake of the Pokémon Incident. He surrenders to the charge of the screen, falling under its spell. As he and his friends embrace the shock of the screen, they experience a kind of media intoxication. They also adopt something of an outlaw position. Still, they are not best described as addicts or outlaws—or victims or rebels, for that matter. Instead, they become detectives, but detectives whose exploration of mystery leads beyond the everyday human world, turning into a spiritual quest entailing initiation rites, combat with dark forces, and, most importantly, psychic, therapeutic self-transformation. *Persona 4* thus casts a different light on the relation between media and detection seen in the *Detective Conan* series, and it puts a different spin on the relation between self and media highlighted in the *.hack* series. As with the prior examples, I will track how its media mix provides a point of entry into its media ecology, which is the key to understanding how the series works across media and strives to inhabit the distributive force of the ever-expanding new media television formation.

Portable Media Mix

With the *MegaTen* series, the paradox of media mix comes to the fore anew. On the one hand, each media instance is supposed to be equivalent to other instances as a point of entry into the series. It does not matter if you enter the *.hack* series, for instance, via the manga, the anime, or the game. Media mix does not rely on a hierarchy of media. On the other hand, however, it generally does matter that the source for a series, or the overall emphasis of a series, is a game, manga, or anime series. That source imparts a distinctive tone to it as well as a trajectory. With the *MegaTen* series, for example, the source for media mix is console video games (and more recently iOS games), and its overall strategy is to develop other media products after or around the release of the games. Games are clearly the source and even the center of the *MegaTen* series, and there is a gamic tonality that imparts a distinctive feel to *MegaTen* media mix. Nonetheless, its gamic feel does not necessarily place manga, anime, or other media instances in a lesser position as merely secondary, ancillary, or derivative. Other media instances are supposed to communicate with the gamic feel of the series in the literal sense of communicating as "building with." They become gamic co-munitions.

The *MegaTen* series began in a manner that seems to anticipate the media mix model later formalized in the Kadokawa model, which relies on the simultaneous licensing and release of different media instances, and which introduces a new wrinkle into transmedia storytelling. The *Digital Devil Story: Megami Tensei* OVA appeared early in 1987, its title drawn from the first volume of Nishitani Aya's series of novels, published in 1986. The *Digital Devil Story: Megami Tensei* Famicom (NES) game appeared later in 1987, with a follow-up Famicom game in 1990. While Atlus (a subsidiary of Sega) produced the games, Namco published them, for it had acquired the rights to Nishitani's novels. Initially, then, *MegaTen* seemed poised to become a multimedia franchise with novels, anime, and games. But the series then took a different multimedia turn.

As Atlus began to produce and to publish the games, the series largely turned away from the paradigm of simultaneous tie-in media. It distanced itself from Nishitani's novels and from anime adaptations. Instead, Atlus renamed the franchise *Shin megami tensei (The New Rebirth of the Goddess)* and developed a number of spin-off game series. (The moniker *Shin megami tensei* is now applied to all the spin-off game series.) In 1992 and 1994, it released *Shin megami tensei* and a sequel, *Shin megami tensei II,* for Super Famicom as well as a spin-off game, *Shin megami tensei if . . .* (1994). But it was not until 2003 that the third game in the series, *Shin megami tensei III: Nokutān* (or *Shin megami tensei: Nocturne* in North America), appeared. In the intervening decade, Atlus launched two spin-offs. The *Devil Summoner* games began with *The New Rebirth of the Goddess: Devil Summoner (Shin megami tensei: debiru samanā)* for the Sega Saturn in 1995, followed by *Debiru samanā: sōru hakkāzu* in 1997. The *Persona* games began with the release of *Megami ibunroku persusona* for the PlayStation in 1996. *Persona 1* (as it is sometimes called retroactively) was also the first North American release in the series, under the title *Revelations: Persona,* also in 1996. The success of *Persona 1* led to two new entries: *Persona 2: Innocent Sin (Perusona 2: tsumi)* in 1999 and *Persona 2: Divine Punishment (Perusona 2: batsu)* in 2000.

The *Persona* series quickly became the most popular and profitable in the *MegaTen* franchise. Its success may be attributed to a variety of factors. It may be explained in terms of the appeal of its specific features within the franchise: the *Persona* games take general features of the *MegaTen* world, such as role-playing dungeons and battling demons, summoning demons to power up in combats, and adapt those features to the specific context of local high schools where students unlock personalized special powers called personas. *Shin megami tensei if . . .* is commonly considered the precursor for the general focus on high schools in the *Persona* games. The high school scenario served to clearly distinguish these games within a market that was at the time dominated by *Dragon Quest* and *Final Fantasy,* role-playing games unfurling vast fantasy worlds. The focus in the *Persona* series on high school, in conjunction with its other-dimensional demon battles, has also allowed the *Persona* series to incorporate different styles of game play, for instance by using aspects of everyday simulation games in conjunction with RPG. What is more, the *Persona* series could count on the distributive force of Sony's PlayStation, which spread like wildfire. In contrast, the *Devil Summoner* games, developed for Sega's Saturn, did not enjoy the same platform advantages in the global market. The first *Devil Summoner* proved popular in Japan, spawning two live-action television series in 1997 and 1998, and yet as the

Saturn system lost ground to the Nintendo and Sony systems internationally, its games could not keep pace with the *Persona* series.

A variety of factors conspired to push the *Persona* series to the fore within the *MegaTen* franchise, and its success pushed the other spin-off game series toward the PlayStation. It was because of the popularity of the *Persona 1* and *Persona 2* games on the PlayStation that the third *Shin megami tensei* game *(Nocturne)* was developed for PS2 and released in 2003.

What comes to characterize the media ecology of the *MegaTen* series, then, is porting games—developing and releasing new games for multiple platforms as well as reworking and enhancing already released games for other platforms, usually newer ones. Such a strategy is not unusual in the video game industry. The *MegaTen* series moved into porting as early as 1994, when the first two *Shin megami tensei* games for Famicom were reworked and rereleased for Super Famicom. Similarly, the Sega Saturn games were enhanced and released for PlayStation: *Devil Summoner: Soul Hackers* (1997) appeared for PlayStation as early as 1999, and *Shin megami tensei if . . .* was ported in 2002. But it was from the mid-2000s that the process of porting intensified to the point where it started to take on a reality of its own, especially under the impetus of portable media.

The year 2004 saw a convergence of these trends within the *MegaTen* series. Atlus continued to produce spin-off console game series, creating the new series, *Digital Devil Saga,* for PS2 in 2004. At the same time, the ubiquity of cell phones spurred experimentation with mobile games. In 2004, Atlus created a mobile game for FOMA 990i phones, a prologue to *Shin megami tensei if . . .* entitled *Hazama-hen (Hazama's Chapter)*. This venture encouraged another: in 2007 Atlus developed a cell phone app *(keitei apuri)* of the first *Persona 2* game for mobile phones, *Persona 2 tsumi: rosuto memorīzu,* first for use with NTT's Docomo i-app service and subsequently for Softbank and KDDI. Finally, 2004 saw the release of two new portable game platforms, Sony's PSP and the Nintendo DS. The first *Devil Summoner* game was ported to PSP as early as 2005. It was with some delay, however, from around 2009, that the *MegaTen* series truly registered the impact of these new portable platforms.

The first game in another new spin-off series, *Devil Survivor,* was created for the Nintendo DS in 2009, and *Devil Survivor 2* quickly followed, in 2011, for Nintendo 3DS. On the other hand, the widespread popularity of the *Persona 3* and *Persona 4* games, released in 2006 and 2008, respectively, encouraged the porting of *Persona 3* to PSP in 2009 as well as the porting of an enhanced version of *Persona 1* to PSP, also in 2009. The PSP version of *Persona 1* bore the new title *Shin megami tensei: Persona,* to encourage fans of the more recent games to see them as part of a larger series. The success of these PSP editions led to the PSP release of *Persona 2: Innocent Sin* in 2011 and *Persona 2: Divine Punishment* in 2012.

These ports to portable platforms (or "portable porting") paved the way for an even more ambitious porting project in the context of *Persona 4*. Initially the game was slated for a PSP release in the manner of the *Persona 3* game, but the development of the PlayStation Vita allowed the game producers to expand the *Persona 4* game to include a host of new features as well as wireless networking. The portable porting of *Persona 4* thus received a new title, *Persona 4: Golden*, to reflect its enhanced status. Where it had been common practice to enhance and to some extent expand older games when porting them to new platforms, the portable port of *Persona 4* marks something of a new moment in its media mix in that its porting to the portable platform entails an enhancing and expanding of the game.

In sum, in the course of the 2000s, the media ecology of the *MegaTen* series becomes characterized by two kinds of movement. On the one hand, the movement of games across media platforms becomes more pronounced than the movement of the game sources into other media. While certain games had previously inspired adaptations into other media (manga, anime, and television series), the *MegaTen* series did not arrive at a consistent strategy for serialization across media forms before the 2000s. Movement across media platforms, however, gradually became the site of greater and greater attention, as games were continually enhanced and ported to newer platforms. As such, the feel of the *MegaTen* series is different from that of the *.hack* series. The *.hack* series consistently focused on imparting an off-line experience of online play, drawing on the network feel of the home media system and on the capacity of the TV set to switch from its broadcast receiver function to its computer monitor function to interact with different media. In contrast, although the *MegaTen* series also relies on an experience of switching, it relies more on serializing across game platforms and thus on an experience of switching across media platforms.

The *.hack* series belongs to the wired world and the *MegaTen* series to the world of wireless. Emerging in the early 2000s, the *.hack* series called on the wired media ecology of the home media system that had transformed domestic media space and spurred the cyber imagination in the 1990s. In contrast, emerging in the late 1980s, when discourses on new media emphasized expansive infrastructures allowing satellite and cable networks to interface with home media systems, the *MegaTen* series was poised to leap over the wired world of the 1990s into the wireless world of portable media of the 2000s and 2010s. Indeed, in 2009, as many of its console games were being ported to portable media, Atlus moved decisively into developing portable games. An ambitious RPG for the Nintendo DS, *New Rebirth of the Goddess: Strange Journey (Shin megami tensei: sutorenji jāni)* extended the *Shin megami tensei* line into portable media, and Atlus launched the new spin-off series, the *Devil Survivor* series, also for the Nintendo DS. Significantly, in the *Devil Survivor* series, the act of summoning demons to

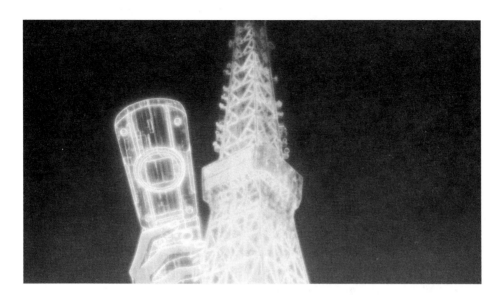

FIGURE 13.4. *Devil Survivor 2,* within the *MegaTen* franchise, focuses on the media platform of the smartphone. As shown in this image from episode 8 of the anime series, to combat demonic invaders who descend into cities via telecommunications towers, players point their phones at the same towers to acquires their abilities.

do battle with them occurs through mobile phones, that is, *keitai denwa,* an appellation that aptly highlights the portable and personal qualities of such phones.

The increasing emphasis on personal and portable media in the recent entries in the *MegaTen* series gives it a more contemporary feel than the *.hack* series and than console games more generally. Take, for instance, the use of portable media in *Beyond the World*: players access the game via their *keitai* wearing VR glasses and tap at its screen (see Figure 12.5). These games thus feel like a transformation of the setup of console games, with glasses wirelessly connected to the portable platform, yet the platform appears as a high-tech variation of the joystick. In contrast, in *Devil Survivor,* players point their phone skyward, usually at a telecommunications tower, to summon their personal power directly (Figure 13.4).

Nonetheless, despite the differences in their media ecology, the *MegaTen* series and the *.hack* series are equally contemporary. They simply strive to inhabit or adhere to the contemporary media ecology in different ways. Likewise, because the *Crayon Shin-chan* and *Detective Conan* series derive from media mix models popular in previous decades, they may appear to be grounded in older media ecologies. Yet their continued popularity provides a powerful reminder both of their contemporaneousness and of the ongoing viability of prior media mix models. Taken together, these four series signal not merely the persistence of broadcast television (though it is incredibly persistent as such). More importantly and precisely, these four series demonstrate the persistence of the underlying polarized media tendencies that broadcast television, in its heyday, was thought to have done away with once and for all. As such, these series might all be termed neotelevision media, posttelevision media, or expanded television media. As discussed in chapter 5, because the term "posttelevision" in particular is currently used to impart the sense of historical rupture that makes normal the condition of American or European worlds of media production, I have tended to avoid such terminology. Given that theories of metamodeling and metastory have greater explanatory force in the context of media mix and transmedia storytelling, the term "metatelevision media" would surely be preferable, provided meta- is not taken to mean "beyond" but rather in its original sense of "among," as discussed in the previous chapter.

In the context of the increased porting and portability of games in the 2010s within the game-centered media mix of the *MegaTen* series, what appears to be a new media formation is in fact a complex transformation of the assembling of polarized tendencies—the point to point and the one to many—that might be called metatelevision. It also implies a complex combination of individualizing and totalizing procedures that follow genealogically from television media. Characteristic of the *MegaTen* series is the use of some sort of media platform to summon personal powers. *Persona 3* has the most disturbing variation: you point what looks like a gun (an evoker) at your head, pull the trigger, and apparently die in order to be reborn. A suicidal gesture serves to empower you. This variation dramatizes what commonly happens with media platforms in the *MegaTen* series: death and rebirth of the self. Time and again, the series dramatizes a total loss of self as a way to awaken individual powers. Considered in isolation from the assembling of media tendencies, such a gesture may be easily simplified, psychologized, or misconstrued. In fact, the scenario may appear downright fascistic—as a desire for submission to totalizing forces in order to take on a share of their authority, or as a path to self-empowerment.

In the *MegaTen* series, the site of this loss of self and acquisition of powers is frequently the screen. At the opening of *Devil Survivor 2*, for instance, two young men in the subway watch their own deaths in a train accident on a *keitai* screen, but once they exit the subway station, evidently alive, they find themselves in a world at war with demons descending to earth through telecommunications towers—and their phones now endow them with new powers when directed at the same luminous towers. The example of *Persona 4*, however, proves to be the most interesting and challenging in the context of this study because the site of loss of self is the television screen: in a scenario reminiscent of Pokémon Shock, a whirlpool of light sucks the media player into the television world where the player first encounters his or her shadow, a repository of negative attributes that must be killed. The use of the screen as the site of self-transformation tends to mitigate the overtly suicidal use of the gunlike evokers in *Persona 3*. Still, as its evocation of photoepileptiform seizures attests, *Persona 4* is equally keen on staging a total loss of self, or total self-annihilation, but through broadcast television.

Keeping in mind how the general media mix ecology of the *MegaTen* series has come to focus its metamodeling on the screen interface, I propose now to turn to *Persona 4: The Animation* to consider more carefully how the television screen becomes the site both of the assembling of polarized media tendencies and of the assembling of individualizing and totalizing procedures.

How the Screen Bifurcates

A venerable tradition of media analysis begins with the notion of the medium as mirror. In film studies, especially in its psychoanalytic turn, the process of watching a movie was likened to looking into a mirror. But you were not simply looking at yourself, neatly and accurately reflected. Cinema was not taken simply as the neutral experience of an undistorted reflection. Because the screen presented a series of characters in a series of settings engaged in various actions, the movie screen did not present the spectator with a stable or neutral image of herself. The film image introduced distortion, and rather than looking at yourself nicely mirrored in cinema, it is as if you were looking for yourself, seeking a stable configuration of movements in which you might dwell, however temporarily. Faced with such inevitable distortion, you had to go great lengths to develop a stable relation to the ideal image of yourself, the imago. This is what Lacan calls the imaginary.

In other words, looking in the mirror gives rise to a complicated relation of self to self. What makes the mirror relation complicated is the difficulty in determining with certainty which self comes first. The "real world" self appears to come first, and yet the "mirror world" self, presumably second, produces such a profound transformation in the real-world self that it cannot really be discounted or discarded as secondary. Indeed, the psychoanalytic turn concluded that the two selves emerged at once, together, making for a subject internally polarized between the imaginary and the symbolic. The imaginary was construed in terms of desire for an idealized image of the self, which allowed you feel omnipotent and omniscient, in control of yourself, while the symbolic referred to the social forces acting to constrain or limit your mastery.[2] The imaginary was frequently downgraded to the status of a bad form of desire—a desire for omnipotence predicated upon a disavowal of social constraints and demands.

In the context of film criticism, the psychoanalytic turn encouraged looking at how films staged anxiety-inducing scenarios that threatened the viewer with an experience of the loss of omnipotence and omniscience (or the stable, idealized image of self) through an encounter with the symbolic. Movies could thus be evaluated in terms of the degree to which they afforded an experience of the symbolic, which experience amounted to an undercutting or undermining of the imaginary. Some films, however, and popular Hollywood films in particular, were deemed ultimately to reinforce the sense of omnipotence and omniscience, at least for certain audiences (above all white male bourgeois viewers). Such movies could thus be held accountable for not sufficiently allowing the forces of the symbolic to challenge received imaginary positions. Thus, in the psychoanalytic turn, apparently bad objects turned out to be teachable objects. Needless to say, this way of reckoning with the power of the moving image depended primarily on an analysis of visual and narrative structure.

In psychoanalytic terms, the death and rebirth of the self in *Persona 4* may initially appear to be an almost paradigmatic example of a bad (yet potentially teachable) object. Although *Persona 4* stages an encounter with the negative aspects of the self (shadows), it does so only to overcome them, which allows for the acquisition of individualized special powers (personas), which are presented as mythological forces and spiritually higher states of being. In this respect, *Persona 4* seems to be intent on staging fantasies of omnipotence—transcending your bodily limitations, acquiring idealized selves, and taking on superpowers. In this register, *Persona 4* is sometimes characterized as Jungian. Indeed, in addition to using Jungian terms such as "shadow" and "persona," the series makes reference to Carl Jung's *Red Book,* especially in the character of Philemon. What is more, if the overall arc of the series is considered in structural terms, it feels like a paradigmatic example of the narrative structure that Joseph Campbell, drawing on Jung, called the monomyth.[3]

Across the twenty-six episodes of the anime series, for instance, the mystery scenario gradually turns into a spiritual quest. As Narukami and his friends enter the television world to solve the mystery and apprehend the criminal, the enigma not only conjures forth supernatural or mythic beings but also tends toward psychological mysticism: if you are to conquer the enemy, you must first conquer your self. At one level, the story presents a mystery to be solved; at another level, it recalls the archetypal monomyth: the initiation of a hero, who confronts various trials, encounters spiritual guides, and acquires new powers, which allow the hero to return to his or her community and to restore stability to the world. On such a journey, you are supposedly discovering who you really are, learning to see yourself without distortion, and thus overcoming your limitations.

In sum, *Persona 4* seems intent on overcoming distortion in two registers: first, solving the mystery and setting the record straight, and second, arriving at a higher spiritual state. To overcome distortion, however, *Persona 4* must first introduce distortion, or at the very least establish where distortion arises. Suddenly matters become more complicated. Does it matter how distortion happens?

The *Persona 4* anime opens with a scene intended to replicate the act of adopting and naming the avatar in the RPG. Two characters in a black stretch limousine, Igor and Margaret, address the audience as you *(anata)* with connotations of the singular (not *anata-tachi*), offering you a contract to enter this place that lies between dream and reality, mind and matter *(yume to genjitsu, seishin to busshitsu no hazama ni aru basho)*. Indeed, the limousine is surrounded by fog that obscures all signs of location and motion. Thus you are invited to enter placeless place, a utopia poised between mind and matter, dream and reality. The scene quickly cuts to a wavering, hissing image on a television screen (which we later learn is midnight TV), and we hear voices calling "Narukami." The voices come out of nowhere, or anywhere, or maybe from the television. The scene cuts on these voices to a young man sleeping on a train who seems to awaken to the call, which implies that "you" are now Narukami, the central protagonist of the series, Narukami Yū. The name Narukami implies becoming *(naru)* a god *(kami)*, or a god-becoming. Thus your godlike avatar has precipitated out of fog, buzz, and cacophonous voices, like water condensing into a bead on glass. The animation then immediately cuts to the opening sequence with its song and credits.

Already there are two possible ways of interpreting distortion in this scene, and indeed the series itself consistently unfolds along two distinct pathways for distortion, which imply different ways of understanding the relation of self to self. For the sake of convenience, let me characterize one as Lacanian (or psychoanalytic) and the other as Foucauldian.

On the one hand, as soon as these voices call Narukami in existence, *Persona 4* has introduced something of a Lacanian perspective, for it appears that some sort of powerful agency is working behind the scenes. Narukami is not present to himself in the sense of being in control of himself. This sense of an absent master, to use Lacanian terms, will recur with increasing frequency throughout the series. It tends to undercut the omnipotence or mastery of the person called Narukami. In the context of game play, this is not an unfamiliar experience, for you are never entirely in control of your avatar. A lack of complete control is a banal fact of game play: there are always forces at work in the avatar beyond your control, ranging from programmed features to contingencies of play. As such, you do not own or control the avatar any more than you control or own the game when you buy it. But you may possess it. You may take partial possession of it, so to speak, hence the possessive pronoun: your avatar, your self. The opening scene of *Persona 4* thus sets up a fundamental tension reminiscent of the Lacanian distinction between imaginary (you are in control, your mastery feels expanded) and symbolic (there is an absent master, a voice bidding you to do its will). The series gives Narukami a range of persona powers but also posits a deity working behind him, conferring special abilities on him.

On the other hand, the same mirrorlike encounter may be read in terms of what Foucault calls the production of utopia: "In the mirror, I see myself there where I am not, in an unreal, virtual space that opens up behind the surface; I am over there, there where I am not, a sort of shadow that gives my own visibility to myself, that enables me to see myself there where I am absent: such is the utopia of the mirror."[4] In the context of game play, for instance, the avatar may be considered a sort of shadow that permits you to be where you are not, in an unreal, virtual space behind the screen. In this respect, Foucault's notion of utopia recalls the Lacanian imaginary: it entails a play of perceptible space where you are split between two possible selves, but the overall effect is to amplify your range of actions and field of influence. The psychoanalytic turn tends to see in this moment the dangerous advent of a narcissistic fantasy of omnipotence and omnipresence that must be challenged by social constraints that effectively negate it. In contrast, although Foucault does not settle for utopia, he is interested in how utopia may be socially and historically transformed. Thus, where Lacan sees the mirror as the hinge between the imaginary and the symbolic, Foucault sees the mirror as the hinge between utopia and heterotopia:

> But it [the space in the mirror] is also a heterotopia in so far as the mirror does exist in reality, where it exerts a sort of counteraction on the position that I occupy. . . . The mirror functions as a heterotopia in this respect: it makes this place that I occupy at the moment when I look at myself in the glass at once absolutely real, connected with all the space that surrounds it, and absolutely unreal, since in order to be perceived it has to pass through this virtual point which is over there.[5]

These two accounts of the mirror present two distinctive trajectories for thinking about what happens when you perceive yourself in a media space, effectively traveling back and forth between real world and media world. When the relation of self to self is abstracted from where it takes place as in the Lacanian scenario, everything gravitates toward the paradigm of the absent master, a godlike force behind the scenes. When attention is paid to where and when the relation of self to self takes place as in Foucault's account, it is the relation between actual sites that comes to the fore, affording a topological perspective.

Naturally, it is possible to opt for one of these perspectives, but what interests me about *Persona 4* is how it keeps open not only the Jungian scenario but also the Lacanian and Foucauldian scenarios. Television media are thus working in three ways at once when it comes to the relation to self to self. As it turns out, because *Persona 4* gives so much latitude to different understandings of self and subjectivity, the notion of heterotopia ultimately comes closer to the overall tonality of series, particularly when the gamic milieu is taken into account. Nonetheless, because *Persona 4* does not begin or end with an obvious endorsement of media heterotopia, it is the actual processes of producing or enacting a media heterotopia that merit attention. With that in mind, let me sum up the three perspectives or scenarios running through the series in a schematic fashion.

First, there is the Jungian scenario, which entails the spiritual quest or monomyth and self-transformation through an encounter with archetypes or archetypal forces. In effect, it assumes that the encounter with the shadow self in the mirror allows you to confront your negative attributes and to overcome them. It implies a movement of self-transcendence—you travel into the mirror and then come home again to bestow boons on your community. Lacan and Foucault would characterize this scenario as imaginary and utopia, respectively. Second, there is the Lacanian perspective, in which the shadow self is not an archetype that enables a self-overcoming; the shadow self presents an encounter with a force of negation of the self that must be acknowledged and internalized: you are called on to constrain, or more precisely encrypt, your hero fantasies in order to live with others socially. The result is the internally divided subject. Third, there is the Foucauldian take on heterotopia in which the encounter with the shadow self cannot be abstracted from where it takes place, that is, from the world within the television in *Persona 4*. At stake is not the subject but a sociohistorically specific formation of subjectivity arising where different kinds of space are at once held together and held apart, topologically.

With reference to the effects of distortion that are highlighted from the outset in *Persona 4*—buzzing noises, cacophonous voices, wavering images, blurred locations—the three trajectories may be summed up even more succinctly: the Jungian scenario entails transcending distortion, the Lacanian scenario hinges on internalizing and encrypting distortion, and the Foucauldian account grapples with inhabiting and embodying distortion. Let me now return the anime series with these angles in mind.

After the opening song and credits, Narukami arrives in a small rural town in the middle of nowhere, Yaso-Inaba.[6] Because his parents are working abroad for a year, he has come to live with his uncle in Inaba, where he will attend the local high school. His uncle, Dojima Ryūtarō, a gruff yet affable detective on the local police force, meets him at the train station, together with his young daughter, Nanako. As his uncle drives Narukami to his new home, the car radio buzzes with speculation about an affair between a female television announcer, Yamano Mayumi, and the Inaba city council secretary, Namatame Tarō, who is married to singer Hiiragi Misuzu. This information, while integral to the story, hovers on the threshold of perceptibility: it weaves through the dialogue, coming to the surface during silences and then retreating into the background again. When they stop at a gas station, the attendant chats with Narukami and then shakes his hand. A few seconds later, a buzzing and ringing noise suddenly seizes Narukami like an intense migraine. His uncle hurries him home, and as Narukami settles into his new room, he slips into a dream. A voice hails him, asking if he wants to know the truth.

Already the animation has established a threshold where noise turns into signal, where buzzing and ringing sounds transform into intelligible speech. In the Jungian scenario, this moment might be said to anticipate the basic structure of the series as monomyth: through a rite of initiation or trial (passage through a painful ordeal of noise), the hero comes into contact with a higher being, a spiritual guardian. The hero is already preparing to transcend distortion, to hear signals above and beyond noise.

In the Lacanian scenario, the emergence of a deep masculine voice from the buzz of distortion is indicative of an absent master. The voice feels authoritative, but its source remains invisible, unidentifiable, enigmatic. You do not yet know who is hailing you. This is precisely what Žižek calls the *acousmaître,* a pun combining "acoustic" and "master."[7] This *acousmaître* is a paradigmatic example of Lacan's absent master—the invisible authority that organizes the linguistic and semiotic field, that structures desire by transforming sensation into symbol. In this scenario, Narukami is not so much transcending distortion as he is internalizing the authority that lies behind distortion in order to read symbolic meanings.

Finally, in the Foucauldian scenario, distortion itself has meaning—not meaning in the symbolic sense, but in terms of material practices and affective orientations; even when you push distortion into the background in order to hear the voice, distortion nonetheless is equally important to the overall field. Indeed, it may prove more important to understanding the actual distribution of agency and power. In the Foucauldian angle, it matters how the voice is transmitted and received: Narukami begins to hear the mysterious voice when he adjusts his body to receive it, as if tuning a radio or television to receive a broadcast signal, or tilting a phone to receive a wireless signal. He is inhabiting and embodying a signal–noise topology.

Looking at the opening of *Persona 4* from these three perspectives paves the way for considering the complex negotiations that arise in the context of confronting your shadow and taking on your persona power.

Between Archetype and Platform

The next day at school, Narukami meets the classmates who will become his companions on his journey: Satonaka Chie, a friendly, outgoing girl; Amagi Yukiko, a rather shy and proper girl; and finally, Chie's friend, Hanamura Yōsuke, a goofy boy with a quirky sense of humor. As Narukami gazes at the fog swirling outside the classroom windows, the episode cuts to a girl who discovered the body of

FIGURE 13.5. The scene in which a female classmate discovers the body of the first victim impaled on a TV antenna later appears again in the credits, where it is framed within an old-fashioned television set, to underscore the multimedia components of broadcast TV infrastructures.

television announcer Yamano Mayumi impaled on a TV antenna (Figure 13.5). Narukami's uncle, Detective Dojima, appears at the crime scene with his rookie partner, Adachi Tōru. Back at school, as the kids prepare to go home, an announcement is made about the weird crime. After school, Narukami ends up in the company of Chie and Yōsuke, and as they are eating in a *yakisoba* shop at Yōsuke's father's electronics store, Junes, Chie talks about the mysteries of midnight TV: on rainy nights, at midnight, images mysteriously appear on the air, and whoever appears on the screen is fated to be your mate or partner *(unmei no aite)*. Her tone implies romantic bonding, but "fated partner" could also be "destined rival."

That rainy night, after Narukami watches television with his uncle and Nanako properly—that is, in a well-lit room at a good distance—he retires to this room, where images appear on the television at midnight. A wavering image appears on screen of a girl (Figure 13.6), the ringing in his ears starts again, and a male voice intones, "I am you, and you are me." Narukami begins to experience symptoms like those associated with the Pokémon phenomenon: severe headache,

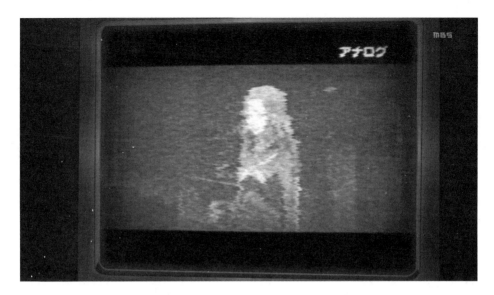

FIGURE 13.6. On the midnight TV channel, Narukami sees the next victim to be kidnapped and trapped in the TV world. The series plays with various screen types and broadcast formats, here CRT and analog.

blurred vision, vertigo, and shaking, hinting at an onset of convulsions. Instead of experiencing a seizure per se, however, Narukami's loss of self takes the form of the television taking over his body: the TV set seems to be pulling him closer, and as he approaches and stretches out his hand, his arm goes right through the screen (Figure 13.7). The television is seizing him, as if to absorb him into the screen, at the urging of the voice of some unknown master. He resists pulling his hand out of the screen, and the television goes black.

The next day at school, Narukami tells his three new friends about what happened. Although they too have seen strange images on the screen, they have never been pulled into a television. Narukami expresses his fear that he wouldn't fit into such a small TV, so Yōsuke suggests that they try out the large-screen televisions at his father's store, Junes. On one of the TVs at Junes, Narukami sees the girl from his midnight TV experience being interviewed on the news: it is their classmate, Konishi Saki, who found Yamano's body. Narukami reaches out for the screen, and his hand goes into the television. Chie and Yōsuke freak out, but Narukami tentatively reaches deeper into the TV. His friends stumble into him, and all three fall through the wide screen (Figure 13.8). They find themselves in another world, largely obscured by fog, with architectural elements suggesting a vast warehouse or studio set.

FIGURE 13.7. In the first episode of *Persona 4*, a voice calls to Narukami Yū, and as he reaches toward the television, he begins to enter the TV world. The series was simulcast on the Anime Network in America and on MBS in Japan, hence the different station logos on the images.

Out of the fog appears a short, bulbous creature making weird noises. Fleeing the creature, the three friends find themselves in a room with a noose and with movie posters of an actress pasted on the walls, her face torn away. The bulbous creature turns out to be a cute, highly sociable but querulous humanoid with vaguely bearlike ears and a high-pitched voice named Kuma (Bear). He hands Narukami a pair of glasses, fearfully warning them of the shadows coming. Gruesome, surreal entities begin to flow in the room around them, transforming into snail-like shapes, with tongues protruding from their striped shells in the place of a snail's foot. Narukami becomes paralyzed with fear as they attack, and the same voice rings in his head: "I am you, and you are me." In a blue halo of light, a card descends into his hand, and he utters the word "persona" (Figure 13.9). In flashes of light, a large warrior (Izanagi) materializes above Narukami, and Narukami, his glasses blazing with blue light, directs the warrior's movements with his own gestures, dispelling the creatures with a flashing sword. The episode ends with Yōsuke looking in awe up at Narukami, who replies, "Kore ga ore no chikara" (this is my power).

In sum, in the first episode, in keeping with general approach of the larger

FIGURE 13.8. In the Junes electronics store, Yōsuke trips into Chie and Narukami, knocking the three of them into the TV world.

MegaTen series, *Persona 4* stages an almost paradigmatic Campbellian monomyth scenario in which a hero leaves home, undergoes initiation, receives powers, and combats demons who threaten the community. In the end, the hero will presumably save the community and return home. Yet this monomyth is staged within or through an actually existing media formation. In this instance, the media formation is broadcast television, but from the opening, it is clear that broadcast television is being situated within a larger problematic of wireless screen media that includes radio and has some affinity with mobile phone service. In effect, Narukami is both a Campbellian hero and a media platform capable of receiving signals out of thin air. Indeed, therein lies the lure of the series: it is effectively dramatizing the process of taking on a second self, an avatar. The avatar is at once like an archetype and like a media platform. In this scenario, media platforms, such as the television set, also begin to feel somehow archetypal or mythical; they are portals into alternative worlds.

Yet a paradox arises: although the monomyth is predicated on transcending the world, it cannot take place without the media formation. It requires the passage of the hero into the television set, which mimics the passage of the gamer into the video game, and as everyone knows, no game, no life. As a result, friction arises between the ideals of monomyth and the realities of media. Again, this friction is part of the fun of the game, part of its life, allowing for a proliferating, highly inventive series of archetype–media hybrids in the form of shadows,

FIGURE 13.9. Narukami's first persona card descends into his hand, summoning forth his persona power, Izanagi, near the end of episode 1 of *Persona 4*.

personas, demons, and helper entities like Kuma. Still, this friction and these hybridized beings point to an underlying paradox in the Jungian scenario: transcendence is localized; the nonplace or utopia turns out to be an actual place and not truly utopian at all. The Jungian bid for self-transcendence bifurcates, or more precisely it turns out to be internally bifurcated in advance—that is, paradoxical. What is interesting about *Persona 4* is how it pushes that paradox into a bifurcated understanding of the self and media. On the one hand, the series entertains an understanding of the relation of self to self that feels consonant with the psychoanalytic emphasis on the absent master (and the internally divided subject). On the other hand, the series allows for a more topological understanding of the relation of self to self, wherein the taking place, the media formation itself, is what produces localized effects of mastery and subjectification.

This bifurcation plays out in subsequent episodes, in which each of Narukami's friends is psychologically tested, one by one. Within the television world, an ignored or repressed aspect of their personality appears in the form of an evil double or doppelgänger, which is called a shadow. In the second episode, for instance, Yōsuke's shadow loses his cool, expressing his anger over living in the countryside. When Yōsuke denies his double's claims, the double turns into a shadow who attacks him and Narukami. As they battle the shadow, Narukami succeeds in convincing Yōsuke not to deny his double's statements. They are thus able to defeat the shadow, which transforms into Yōsuke's persona, Jiraiya. In episode 3, it is Chie's turn: she has to confront her suppressed feelings toward her best friend, Yukiko. Yukiko has been imprisoned in a castle within the television world, and Chie's shadow enters the scene to mock and torment Yukiko. When Chie rejects her double's feelings, it transforms into a shadow that Narukami and Yōsuke battle. Only when Chie accepts that she feels jealous of Yukiko does she gain her persona (Tomoe Gozen). Similarly, in episode 4, Yukiko meets a double who expresses her secret fear of being trapped, unable to escape taking over management of the family inn. Her denial of these fears turns the double into an attacking shadow, but a successful battle produces her persona (Konohana-Sakuya). In sum, one by one, the characters must each undergo a psychological test or trial in which a repressed negative aspect of their personality must be accepted and in effect integrated into their everyday selves. When what was disavowed is avowed, the character takes on a persona, a special power with mythological connotations.

These examples also demonstrate one of the persistent problems of the Jungian approach: although archetypes are not supposed to be stereotypes, they are often indistinguishable from stereotypes. As such, while archetypes are supposed to allow for an overcoming or transcending, they run the risk of endorsing received social categories. The fine line between archetype and stereotype is evident in the presentation of gender and sexuality in the initiation sequences of *Persona 4*. Among the negative feelings that overwhelm girls are feeling jealous (Chie), feeling powerless (Yukiko), wanting attention (Kujikawa Rise), and disliking their boyfriend (Konishi Saki). Negative feelings for boys present a quite different scope and intensity. The hero, Narukami, apparently gains his persona without any internal struggle, and later, as he enters into battles and helps his friends gain personas, he takes on a series of personas and learns to combine them. Yōsuke, however, has a repressed negative side: losing his cool, his cheerful composure. Generally speaking, girls are presented as prone to disavowing their feelings of jealousy, powerlessness, and narcissism, while boys are inclined to deny their fear of appearing weak or lacking in composure. This way of gendering emotions is so banal and predictable as to feel normative: girls are crippled by emotions, boys by their lack of emotions. But the most spectacularly and disturbingly normative trial is that of tough guy Tatsumi Kanji. Kanji is afraid of being rejected if he appears sensitive or girly, so, as if naturally, his psychological trial hinges on a series of stereotypes pathologizing gay men as weak and effeminate. It turns out that Kanji is not homosexual, but *Persona 4* appears so intent on disavowing homosexuality that the bid for Jungian transcendence shows itself to be militantly normative, like an echo of Jung's embrace of German fascism.

Nevertheless, only dwelling on the moments when archetypes repeat stereotypes runs the risk of mistaking the overall impetus of the series, which is as

FIGURE 13.10. When the series reaches episode 10, five characters have already acquired persona powers, manifested in the forms standing behind them.

much toward queering relationships as it is toward normalizing them. Kanji, for instance, ends up falling for a girl (Shiragane Naoto) who disguises herself as an archetypal boy detective. Because it is not clear whether he knows that Naoto is a girl when he falls for her, the scenario oscillates between reinforcing heteronormative ideas about couples and allowing for alternative ways of pairing. This oscillating, this athwart-ness, may be read as queering. In addition, the overall tendency of series is toward the formation of alternative social groups based on mutual assistance. Indeed, what is striking about the staging of the relation of self to self in *Persona 4* is its tendency toward group sessions and societal therapy. Although each psychological trial is individual, the individual has assistance from friends, and the series insists that that the initiation into persona powers strengthens social connections with others (Figure 13.10).

This gesture of *Persona 4* is the most challenging and the most worthy of careful attention: individual powers are not associated with personal sovereignty. Although personas entail a sort of personalized identity, that sense of an individual self is not placed in opposition to society; nor does society begin with the negation of the individual. In this respect, the series departs not only from the Jungian scenario but also from the psychoanalytic scenario, for the sense of self in *Persona 4* does not depend on a paradigm of sovereign enclosure, in which the individual psyche is posited in advance as a bounded entity that is wounded when its walls are breached. Affective relation comes to the fore instead of the traditional Freudian paradigm of sovereign enclosure.

Wounds and Powers

In his discussion of Freud's notion of trauma, Pheng Cheah draws attention to Freud's emphasis on a breakdown of protective walls and secure barriers between the autonomous self (ego) and the world: "Trauma occurs when the ego's capacity for security is compromised, when the protective shield it erects against the outside world is penetrated. This is the first step of the ego's loss of self-mastery, when its system of defense begins to break down."[8]

Cheah persuasively argues that Freud's use of such terminology is "not merely metaphorical." Rather, he sees in Freud a model of

> psychical security as a pre-positive form of security that precedes and grounds any historical form of social or political security and the loss of self-mastery and autonomy in traumatic neuroses as a form of pre-positive domination by another that can function as an opening and foothold for social and political domination. In other words, the security of an *individual* psyche's interiority in its interaction with the external world and its management of internal excitations is the template for historical forms of sociality and political community. Conversely, psychical insecurity or trauma is also the basis for violence and domination qua the determinate negation of community and belonging.[9]

The model of the defensive wall, security shield, or protective barrier tends to see any form of physical and psychical vulnerability in negative terms such as wounds or trauma. Thus, in Thomas Hobbes, for instance, as Shiloh Whitney reminds us, corporeal vulnerability presents a definitive danger for the formation of personhood in terms of autonomy, for in "our corporeal specificity we encounter an inexhaustible danger to the independence we desire."[10] It is to overcome our vulnerability that we come to cooperate, to consent to the social contract, to protect ourselves. "In normative reasoning like Hobbes's, domination is easily identified and easily denigrated as trespass by the normative independence of personhood: all dependency and heteronomy is domination, dangerous to our autonomy."[11] In Hobbes, then, Whitney concludes, "Because personhood is normatively independent, any *dependency is always domination,* and corporeal vulnerability always signifies an *opportunity to wound.*"[12]

It is precisely this normative psychic model that *Persona 4* calls into question. When individuals go into the television world, they confront the negative side of their personality, their corporeal vulnerability. Instead of rejecting or overcoming vulnerability, however, they accept and avow it. It might be thought that when they gain their persona powers, these individuals have, in effect, overcome vulnerability. Yet that shadow, that vulnerability, stays with them. Not only is it integral to their sense of self and their persona power, but it also makes for dependency on others. In sum, the persona powers in *Persona 4* make for a sense of personhood that is not at all like the Hobbesian or Freudian models, in which physical and psychical vulnerability must be overcome to gain autonomy.

As such, *Persona 4* feels compatible with Whitney's take on vulnerability. She reminds us that many of our most highly valued relationships are ruled out when vulnerability and dependency are framed exclusively in negative terms: "Over the course of a life and across collective life, dependency relations are often not avoided, secured against, or overcome, but instead embarked upon as integral to the valued experience and development of personhood."[13] Such dependency entails an open-ended set of relations in which it remains impossible to establish equivalency or symmetry between giving and receiving care. Consequently, Whitney strives to conceptualize collective life via vulnerability and dependency rather than security and autonomy, that is, normatively independent personhood. Her shift in emphasis—"Vulnerability signifies a *need for care* instead of an *opportunity to wound*"—leads her to affirm "the opportunity to care and to be cared for."[14] This need for care is what is at stake in *Persona 4*: becoming a hero, taking on persona powers, means accepting vulnerability, which lead to opportunities to care for others and to be cared for.

Once vulnerability and dependency are brought to the fore, however, a new risk arises: that of making vulnerability and dependency normative. This risk may be addressed in different ways. Cheah, for instance, sees exposure to prepositive flows of capital as constitutive of the social, but he does not treat such exposure or vulnerability as normative. His aim is to show that although protective barriers and sovereign walls should not be given a prepositive or normative status, they may nonetheless prove desirable under conditions of finance capital. One of the underlying implications of Cheah's account is that making vulnerability normative tends to produce an alignment with flows of capital.

Lazzarato states the case more forcibly, suggesting that if we simply endorse the need for care, we wind up, however unwittingly, endorsing "work on self" within the debt economy. He writes: "The increase in psychologists', sociologists', and other 'self-help' experts' interventions, the creation of 'coaching' for better-off workers and obligatory individual monitoring for the poor and unemployed, the explosion of 'care for self' techniques in society—these are symptoms of the new forms of individual government, which include, above all, the shaping of subjectivity."[15] In the debt economy, as Lazzarato describes it, individuals are empowered both to express their need for care and to become their own caregivers, which allows social institutions and employers to download all responsibility onto individuals for their welfare. It would seem that as the nonnormative personhood implicit in the need for care is rendered normative, it may readily be mobilized to fuel the debt economy.

In effect, however, Lazzarato's account of the debt economy echoes Hobbes's take on vulnerability: it assumes that people need to come together to overcome their individual debt by entering into agreements for collective protection. Autonomy emerges through a process of overcoming vulnerability. What distinguishes the debt economy is its denial of collective autonomy in favor of placing the ultimate responsibility for overcoming on the individual. Discourses on media addiction, as shown in Part I, adopt a similar take: it is assumed that you are always already exposed, vulnerable to electromagnetic flows, and no one but you can overcome this exposure. As such, even if there are psychologists, sociologists, and other experts to offer assistance, such assistance focuses on you, not on the formation of new kinds of society.

Such a stance is made manifest in the warning message on anime: you take care of yourself. This is where *Persona 4* begins: mystical experts speak to you, enjoining you to take care of yourself under conditions of exposure to inscrutable forces at work in media infrastructures and platforms, where received forms of social protection—the police, teachers, parents—mean well but prove ineffective at best. Yet for all that you may enter the game as an individual with the potential to take on individualized powers, the acceptance of vulnerability in *Persona 4* does not mobilize it for the production of isolated autonomous individuals. Its solution is similar to Whitney's: she proposes to undermine the very dichotomy of vulnerability and power, insisting on relational and adaptive *"powers that are consistent with vulnerability,* even complicit with vulnerability: powers whose development is inseparable from the adaptation and cultivation of specific vulnerabilities."[16] The result is not a debt that is to be mobilized or a weakness that is overcome, but equity. Equity, in contrast to debt, implies a sense of equilibrium, that is, something that is fair, balanced, or impartial; at the same time, the term "equity" implies a sense of positive value or worth.

Now it is clearer what is at stake in the juggling of three different ways of treating the relation of self to self in *Persona 4*. The series juggles three perspectives in order to avoid losing its sense of equilibrium, and to avoid the normative implications of Jungian self-transcendence and Freudian self-alienation. In effect, the series entertains both possibilities, thus transforming them into topologies or fields whose juxtaposition makes for something like the Foucauldian heterotopia, the latter of which is more explicitly counternormative. The result is equilibrium, but this equilibrium, in which wounds are consistent with powers, is far from equilibrium. It is a metastable state, in a psychosocial register, generating equity, a sense of self-worth. The complex conflicts and negotiations arising between self, shadow, and persona during the individual trials or initiations play into the production of equilibrium far from equilibrium, that is, the psychosocial metastable state in which wounds are consistent with powers, and personalized powers are consistent with mutual aid. Sustaining such a charged equilibrium and relational adaptive powers across the entire anime series results in a highly convoluted story, with a series of false endings.

In episode 9, for instance, Narukami and friends catch a young man, Kubo Mitsuo, a die-hard fan who is stalking a local idol singer (Kujikawa Rise). Adachi (Uncle Dojima's rookie partner) holds Kubo for questioning but releases him. In episode 11, Kubo takes credit for the murders and turns himself in to the police. In the subsequent episode, however, Kubo's shadow in the TV world alters the timeline. Narukami and friends are moved forward in time. Only later, after a battle in which Narukami uses his newly formed social bonds to summon multiple personas to defeat this shadow, do signs appear that this was a false ending: Kubo confesses, but his defeated shadow does not become a persona. At the end of the episode, the teenagers find themselves back at zero—the point where the episode started.

In the wake of this temporal loop, which occurs roughly at the midway point in the series, the series shifts considerably in tone, and a new character appears among them, a boy detective named Shirogane Naoto, who claims that there is something wrong with the apparently concluded investigation (episode 16). The story gradually begins to focus once again on the murders in the TV world. Finally, as it approaches the final chapters of its twenty-six-episode run, the series returns to the characters and setup of the first episode. It is not until episode 21 that Adachi realizes that Namatame may be the culprit. (Recall that speculations about Namatame's affair with the first victim, Yamano, aired over the car radio at the beginning of the first episode.) When Narukami's gang pursues Namatame, Namatame kidnaps Nanako. Ultimately, however, when confronted by the teenagers, Namatame claims that he put people inside the TV world to save them. In other words, the temporal loop midway through the series seems to set the narrative in motion forward and backward at the same time, as if the entire series might turn out to be a giant loop.

Indeed, Namatame's capture turns out to be another false ending: after his arrest, fog billows from the TV world into the real world. Narukami and company realize that the real criminal is still at large. Ultimately, then, in episode 24, Adachi turns out to be the real culprit. Adachi is a criminal mastermind with a genuine master plan: to destroy the boring reality of the real world by breaking down the boundary between real world and TV world, which is tantamount to the destruction of humanity. Significantly, as he expounds on his plan to the kids, his image becomes charged with static and noise, as if he were only a television image; then, after he shoots himself, a voice takes over his body and a new force appears behind him: the orb of sight, which is basically a giant eyeball in the sky with a camera lens for an iris.

In terms of interpretation, these false endings leave the story open to all three perspectives. The story may be read in terms of an escalation of the Jungian scenario: the trials of the hero become larger, more arduous, and more demanding spiritually, hence the combination of ever-deepening quasi-mythic mystery and ever-enlarging battles. In the end, the hero successfully slays the evil entity and saves the community. What really matters, however, is neither the beginning nor the end, but the prolongation of the journey. The story thus remains open to new trials and adventures that can be inserted into it—akin to the abstract encyclopedic quality of the epic, as Mikhail Bahktin defined it.[17] Once the beginning and end are set, the series can weave new materials into it.

For instance, when the PSP *Persona 4* game was ported in an enhanced version for mobile phones, its title became *Persona 4: Golden*. As a result of the commercial success of the *Persona 4* anime, *Persona 4: Golden* also gave rise to an anime series. This follow-up anime series enhances the first anime series by tracking the same story while introducing new characters whose actions serve to add new perspectives and adventures into what is essentially the same endgame. In contrast to the traditional epic form, which tends to add new adventures around a single hero, this story form introduces new characters, new perspectives, and new adventures. In effect, the highly stable structure of the monomyth is transformed into a field for the generation of multiple story lines and worldviews. This is precisely what Azuma calls metastory and world lines.[18] Here it is clear that the metastory depends on exploded projection, use of multiple planes in the image to construct possibilities for traversing it along different story lines based on introducing the perspectives of different characters.[19]

At the same time, because the series of false endings makes the villain in *Persona 4* into an increasingly abstract godlike entity, it is difficult to rule out feelings of paranoia, the sense of a vast conspiracy, of someone running the show behind the scenes, which invite Lacanian interpretation. Particularly because the villain turns into a disembodied eye with a disembodied voice (and a deep, masculine voice at that), the scenario invites a more Oedipal interpretation: Narukami does not slay this force that would negate him; he accommodates and internalizes its (paternal) authority. Indeed, the disembodied voice of the final battle recalls the disembodied voice that hailed Narukami in the opening episode: "I am you, and you are me." What is more, the general relation to authority in *Persona 4* adopts a comfortably Oedipal trajectory. Narukami adopts the role of detective like his gruff and affable uncle, as if internalizing his authority. Similarly, the teenagers take on the work of the police force; they do not reject policing but rather encrypt it. They become new kinds of detectives, new kinds of police, new kinds of authority. Generally speaking, when the focus is on crime and detection, the story feels Freudian or Lacanian, and when the focus falls on spiritual journey, the story feels like a Jungian scenario, a Campbell-like monomyth.

If the Jungian and Lacanian scenarios are conflated or collapsed into one another, then *Persona 4* may appear to present nothing more than a transfer of authority—or the desire for a transfer of authority—from traditional sources (police and off-line detection, parents, broadcast television) to new bodies (gamers and online detection, teenagers, mobile phones). The story then appears to be about generational turnover, a transfer of power: the wound inflicted by the traditional source is internalized to empower the next generation. *Persona 4* adopts a different tack, however. It does not place wounds and powers in a linear temporal movement, a movement from wound to power, either in the form of transcending wounds (Jungian) or of encrypting wounds (Lacanian). What characterizes *Persona 4* is its emphasis on relational adaptive powers consistent with wounds. As such, the Jungian and Lacanian scenarios are held in disjunctive synthesis, at once held apart and together, to make way for a third scenario, in which the "taking place" between the two is what matters. Similarly, a third site emerges between the two generations.

The final episode returns to the first episode when Narukami shook hands with the gas station attendant. At that moment, Izanami, a goddess, conferred on Narukami the ability to travel into the TV world. Yet the very source of power turns out to be multiple and heterogeneous. Izanami bestowed the same ability on Adachi and Namatame, with quite different effects. These three characters—Narukami, Adachi, and Namatame—present different ways of dephasing the metastable source. What is more, although Izanami is in fact a goddess who appears in one of Japan's earliest mythological texts, *Kojiki*, her role in *Persona 4* does not follow in any direct way from that corpus of myth. Reading *Kojiki* will not help with navigating *Persona 4*. Because sources ultimately turn out to be multiple and heterogeneous, their effects cannot be reduced to wound versus power. It is not a matter of a wound followed by power, or vice versa. When a path is traced from the source, or when a story is told, the effect is provisionally one of linearity or causality. But then the story folds back, and back again, and yet again, precisely to prolong the metastable state associated with its multiple heterogeneous source.

In sum, departure from the source is like dephasing: there is a relation, but it is not causal in the usual cause-and-effect way. Dephasing retains something of the multiplicity and heterogeneity of the source: an individual emerges with (at least) three facets: self, shadow, persona. Because these three facets cannot be ordered hierarchically, the individual turns out to be internally populated with selves. Moreover, this apparently internal physic population is matched by an external social formation of friends and relationships. As it individuates, the individual brings forth a heterarchical society. I am aware that in describing the process with terms such as "metastable state" and "dephasing," the process may appear neat and tidy. On the contrary. As the twists and turns of the story line of *Persona 4* attest, the process entails a seemingly endless series of qualifications and complications, a veritable horde of nonhuman modes of existence, a hybridized throng of shadows, demons, personas, and persons, all of whom clamor for attention. Such a complex, messy situation calls for tactics of "lived distance," to use Merleau-Ponty's term, ways of living closely with diverse modes of existence while maintaining a certain degree of distance.[20] After all, you do not wish to get too attached to your wound or to your power.

Living between Platforms

Drawing on Merleau-Ponty's discussion of "childlike perception," Shiloh Whitney writes,

> The child's perceptual field is not yet organized around a qualitative distinction between private and public parts of perception—those that take place outside of bodies, and those that take place privately, inside bodies. The indistinction of self and other is for Merleau-Ponty a corollary of this indistinction of interoception and exteroception. . . . When the adult smiles at her, the child experiences not "an other person" in the adult sense of that expression, but rather a *conduct,* which is literally "transferred" from the adult to the child through "sympathy."[21]

Thus Merleau-Ponty and Whitney broach the problematic of affect through feelings of sympathy between child and parent. Sympathy entails indistinction at the level of perception: the child does not perceive a boundary between inside and outside, between self and other. The appearances and movements of others are felt as conducts that induct behavior in the child—hence the "dizzying proximity of others" that characterizes child perception.[22] A smile induces a smile. A smile affects our conduct. What interests Merleau-Ponty is the persistence of such affective indistinction in adults, who are nonetheless prone to make self–other distinctions. "As adults, what we see others doing still functions to mobilize *feelings*—again in both the motor and affective sense—in our own bodies." Segregation does occur. "And yet this segregation does not abolish the indistinction between myself and other, for it is 'a process which, moreover . . . is never completely finished.'"[23] Ultimately, then, although Merleau-Ponty wishes to call attention to a dimension of experience that is usually neglected (indistinction), he is actually interested in the relation between distinction and indistinction. He sums up the experience thus: "I live somehow from a distance."[24]

Both Whitney and Merleau-Ponty focus on what happens between human selves and human others; they thus bracket questions about techniques and technologies. Yet in the context of television and animation, such questions are impossible to bracket. What smiles at the child, or at the child in you, is the animated character. That smile affects your conduct. Adults, of course, are supposed to make the proper kind of distinction between self and this anime other, but, as Merleau-Ponty persuasively demonstrates, feelings of indistinction remain in adult perception. Adults surely also feel the dizzying proximity of the anime other, even as they strive to segregate themselves from it. Adults are equally susceptible to have their conduct affected by the conduct of anime others. They are susceptible to parasocial relations.

The same may be said of the conduct of television others. Lazzarato, for instance, sees such indistinction as the central feature of television, one that he wishes to denounce: "In the 1970s Pasolini described very precisely how television has changed the soul and bodies of Italians, how it became the main instrument of an anthropological transformation that affected first and foremost the young. . . . [Television] operates through example rather than through discipline, imitation, or constraint. It is a conduct of conduct, action on possible action (of which also Foucault talks about)."[25]

Lazzarato's massive generalization about television recalls prior accounts of television that tended to pathologize its parasocial effects, but it also clarifies the underlying mistake that allows for such exaggeration and totalization. Lazzarato assumes a kind of automatic immediacy at work in the operation of conduct on conduct. Feelings and conduct are a site of immediate control in his account, because for him what lies below the threshold of perception or perceptual distinction in television remains inaccessible to political resistance or ethical engagement. In contrast, while Merleau-Ponty's notion of indistinction implies a vertiginous feeling of closeness, he does not equate affect or feeling with immediacy. On the contrary, he turns to indistinction in order to approach the process of differentiation between self and others without assuming the model of sovereign enclosures or bounded territories in advance. As such, as Whitney notes, the distinction between self and others is not given once and for all but must be lived and negotiated. Thus, she concludes, "It follows that the wall, the border or partition, is not the right model for all of our experience of intercorporeal difference. There must be an operation of differentiation in childhood and intimate adult relationships that is not finally or fully describable as the parsing of territories, the assertion 'this is mine, this is yours.'"[26]

This is precisely the stance of *Persona 4* in its treatment of the relation between human self and human others. Thus it avoids massive generalizations about television and takes care in its treatment of media platforms. And it proceeds in a manner similar to Merleau-Ponty: focusing attention on indistinction, on how the conduct of the other affects your conduct. Yet *Persona 4* does not limit feelings of indistinction to your relationships with human others. It suggests that it is through your experience of an affective relation with nonhuman others that your affective relation to human others is possible. Which is to say, the indistinction between human and nonhuman does not follow from the indistinction between human self and human other. It comes first. It is experientially prior, and it may be prior to the phenomenological relation itself. In the context of *Persona 4*, for instance, things do not begin with a "natural" relationship, such as the relationship between child and parent. They begin with what Foucault calls the counteraction of the mirror in his previously cited account of heterotopia: how does the conduct of the mirror (its generation of a virtual space) affect your conduct? Interestingly, Foucault is close to Merleau-Ponty on this point: the counteraction of the mirror affects not only you but also your space, your incorporeal topology, that is, the flesh of the world.[27]

In *Persona 4*, what Foucault calls the counteraction of the mirror happens through the screen interface. The anime and game series focus specifically on the television screen, but in keeping with the media ecology for the franchise, which is centered on porting games from platform to platform (console to console, console to smartphone), the behavior of the television screen is compatible with mobile phones and smartphones. This compatibility may seem surprising. After all, the screens of smartphones and television sets operate in different ways, and the actual platforms would seem to entail different kinds of experience. They diverge, technically and socially. The wager of *Persona 4*, however, is that whatever diverges communicates. The actual divergence of screens makes for a virtual unity, and this virtual unity becomes technically actualized within a media ecology, whose form of expression is media mix or multimedia franchising. In other words, the counteraction of the television screen, its pressure, bears with it the virtual unity of its media ecology. In the anime and game series, the TV screen is enacting the portable ecology based on porting media across platforms.

A concrete example occurs in the culminating episodes of *Persona 4*, where Narukami, who has the ability to take on multiple personas, confronts multiple versions of himself on television screens piled high (Figure 13.11). It is a perplexing, paradoxical scenario. The television set appears to be a vehicle for presenting multiple images of Narukami as if captured at slightly different angles. Yet it is impossible to figure out how these images are or were being captured. If they are live transmissions, a camera or some camera-like device should be visible. If the images were prerecorded, the effect would nonetheless be the same: the screens do not really represent Narukami but instead are transmitting his virtual unity. But then, conversely, the multiple screens are also enacting the virtual unity of television platforms, as if these televisions were somehow, somewhere connected. It is like a distorted version of the television studio, with its multiple cameras capturing the drama from multiple angles, or like a disjointed rendition of the broadcast studio. In any case, the overall effect is to produce a likeness or semblance between the virtual unity of Narukami (psychosocial) and that of the television screens (technological, infrastructural, or both). Suddenly it is as if

FIGURE 13.11. In the "true ending" of episode 26, Narukami feels alone and trapped within himself, which is experienced as multiple television images, in another combination of source and surround effects.

Narukami were a vehicle for multiplying the number of connections across platforms. Narukami is the key to the multiplication of screens and the connections between them. In sum, this scenario mobilizes the relation between distinction and indistinction: there is a perceptual distance and also a dizzying proximity between Narukami and the screen.

From Narukami's perspective, this experience of the relation to self might well be described in terms of the self as other. Yet this other self (or self–other) does not split along the fundamental divide of the psychoanalytic turn—between self-love and self-alienation. Instead it marks the advent of a media heterotopia in which media topologies (ecologies and infrastructures) associated with television and smartphones affect conduct in real world, becoming its flesh. The ethics of lived distance, then, happens with and through media platforms and infrastructures. In this ethics, exposure to the expanded television media ecology does indeed present a risk. But that risk is not to be managed through discourses on media addiction, for instance, which demand a constant suppression of vulnerability and dependency, a work on self to attain and maintain an autonomous relation to the screen. The gambit of *Persona 4* is that you must run the risk of media dependency because dependency on media is not essentially different in kind from dependency on humans. So you spiral down the rabbit hole, where you undergo training and learn techniques for living the distance between your self and others, both human and nonhuman. In this portable interface complex, television truly takes on its gamic dimension through the counteraction of the television screen on everyday life, which transforms daily space into a heterotopic field of play-through.

CONCLUSION
SIGNALETIC ANIMISM

METHODOLOGICALLY SPEAKING, MY INTERPRETATIONS IN PART III HAVE BEEN GROUNDED IN READING ACROSS DIFFERENT levels of encounter between television, animation, and games instead of relying on an analysis of the anime series alone. This is because the "affective solution" or "virtual unity" is neither in the anime series nor contained by it. The affective solution occurs through what Williams calls the social technology of television, through its technosocial machine, that is, the practices, habits, and techniques that arise in the context of engaging with or using television animation. Interpretation of the social technology of television animation thus must work across infrastructures, platforms, and transmedia franchises while considering specific media instantiations and individual series. When the analysis moves across these orders or gradations of complexity, it is above all the media ecology that provides the key to understanding the affective solutions of these different franchises and series. The media ecology is a holding pattern between television infrastructures, multimedia franchising, and the transmedia storytelling called media mix. It arises through the energy cascade: because each component or instance of the mix relates to the others via the energy cascade, their relations are as much infraindividual and intra-active as they are interindividual interactions. The ecology is the affective–material continuum that emerges intra-actively together with interactions: its solution is thus affective and its unity virtual.

My point of departure was thus to situate the anime series within its media mix franchise in order to delineate the media ecology that at once enabled and happened through that franchise formation. The affective solution might be considered a holding pattern hovering over another holding pattern, or coursing through it. In methodological terms, there are two sides to the media ecology, which, in the manner of William James, might be described as objective and subjective. The objective side is primarily a matter of components, that is, infrastructures, platforms, and media instances such as manga, anime, games, toys, novels, songs, singers, and voice actors. It offers a higher degree of extensivity, and thus we try to map and measure the interactions between individual components. The subjective side is usually addressed in various ways as psychology: feelings, moods, emotions, formations of self, subjects, subjectivity. Here intensity is the key.

In chapter 12, I offered a schematic mapping of these two sides of the problematic arrayed along two axes (see Figure 12.1). The psychosocial axis referred to the polarization of individualizing techniques and totalizing procedures, while the technomedial axis referred to the polarization of point-to-point and one-to-many tendencies within television infrastuctures. In a rudimentary and tentative way, such a schematization is intended to provide of a diagram of how technical tendencies become socially bifurcated, and conversely, how social tendencies may become technically bifurcated. As for the relation between the two axes, I first characterized them as two sides of the same coin, only to transform that coin into a Möbius strip, a non-Euclidean figure: when you travel along one side of it, you somehow wind up on the other.

When I speak of affective solutions or virtual unity, it is the traveling I am trying to address—the traveling in which you are continuously flipping between sides because you are moving along both at once. Objective and subjective are different ways of talking about that movement, not different realities. As such, affective solutions arising in different media ecologies cannot be neatly mapped onto the diagram, for they are not categories or positions. They are complexes— entanglements of psychosocial and technomedial tendencies. They occur through the "mangle of practice," to evoke Andrew Pickering's phrase.[1] They mobilize all the zones of the field to a greater or lesser degree, which serves to generate holding patterns or incipient zones of autonomy gathering across the field.

Although this study has avoided neat and clear-cut separations between the social, psychic, and technical or medial aspects of the technopsychosocial mangle of television-animation media, each part has had its emphases. Part I dealt primarily with the site and moment when the limit-exerience of that technopsychosocial mangle came to the surface: the Pokémon Incident. Part II adopted a more objective or technosocial perspective on the mangle through an inquiry into the genealogical relation between television and new media. It concluded with an account of the emergence of an ontopolitical field of television media stretching across sovereign, disciplinary, and biopolitical formations. Part III looked at transmedia ecology more from the subjective or psychological side of the mangle—media-mangled practices of self. Now the question is, what is the relation between the ontopolitical field disclosed in Part II and the affective solutions explored in Part III? This is precisely the question into which I wish to delve by way of conclusion. What are the ontopolitical implications of the affective solutions offered by the four transmedia ecologies discussed in Part III?

Affective Playback

Recall that the *Crayon Shin-chan* series played with the social bifurcation of the one-to-many tendency, highlighting a tension within one-to-many broadcasting between a hierarchical ordering of source over audiences and a unidirectional force to be embodied in the individual TV user. In contrast, the *Detective Conan* series lingered on the point-to-point tendency of television distribution, only to split socially into two tendencies: environmental and heterarchical. Figure C.1 schematically maps the movement of these two affective solutions. Such a mapping is rudimentary and inadequate because it looks more like Cartesian coordinate space rather than the Riemannian topology that informs my thinking. I venture it nonetheless in hopes of these coordinates may prove useful to readers

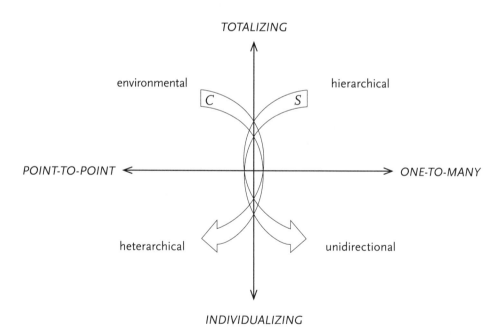

FIGURE C.1. In the *Crayon Shin-chan* series (S), the one-to-many technical tendency becomes socially bifurcated into hierarchical and unidirectional tendencies, with an affective solution that favors the latter in autoelectromagnetizing discharges. In the *Detective Conan* series (C), it is the point-to-point technical tendency of television distribution that becomes socially split, into environmental and heterarchical tendencies, in which improvisational moments continuously rupture immersion.

in understanding the basic argument, and with the expectation that readers are capable of imagining them topologically.

Figure C.2 offers a mapping of the affective transmedia movement of the *.hack* and *Persona 4* series. Like the *Crayon Shin-chan* series, the *.hack* series deals with the ways in which social tendencies become technically bifurcated, but it largely focuses on the totalizing end of the spectrum. It thus stages a conflict between environmental tendencies (the immersive world of the online game) and hierarchical tendencies (corporate and governmental ordering of the world outside the game). It was as if the series could only arrive at genuinely individualizing tendencies by staging cycles of mutually assured destruction in which "The World" destroyed the world, and vice versa.

Like the *Detective Conan* series, the *Persona 4* series also deals with the ways in which social tendencies become technically bifurcated, but true to the larger *MegaTen* series, it gravitates toward the individualizing end of the spectrum. In

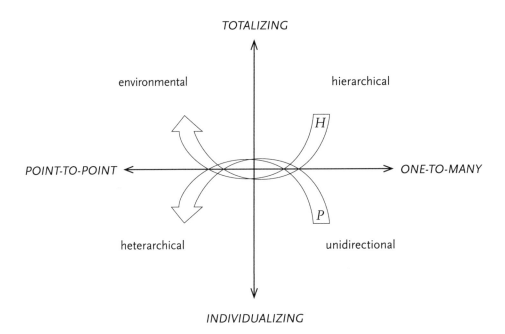

FIGURE C.2. The *.hack* series (H) dwells on totalizing social tendencies, which are bifurcated through the interaction of the online "World" and the real world into hierarchical tendencies (corporate governmental control) and environmental tendencies (complete immersion in augmented reality). Its affective solution comes of staging mutual destruction to release individual frequencies. The *Persona 4* (P) series is skewed between individualizing social tendencies, splitting them in order to map out heterotopological possibilities arising between source (unidirectional) and surround (heterarchical).

keeping with its porting media ecology, *Persona 4* strips the one-to-many tendency of broadcast television of its hierarchical implications, highlighting its unidirectional force—with a quest for the source of the signal. At the same time, the
source is constantly splitting into multiple signals, resulting in a field swarming
with diverse modes of existence—a thoroughly heterarchical field. The series
does not, however, envision a conflict between the unidirectional (signal from
source) and the heterarchical (multiple signals). Nor does it strive to contain the
signal within an immersive or environmental field. Instead, the heterarchical
tendency turns out to be somehow in the source itself: the source proves multiple, heterogeneous, metastable.

As I will explain below, the *Persona 4* series thus brings us closest to the ontopolitical possibilities of television media, precisely where (and when) broadcast
television is becoming entangled with mobile and social media via iOS games
for *keitai*. But this is not merely because the *Persona 4* series is more contemporary than the other three series. In fact, even though the *Crayon Shin-chan* and
Detective Conan series, for instance, may feel older than the *.hack* and *Persona 4*
series in terms of their technologies and media practices, all four are equally
contemporaneous. All are currently successful franchises. Their contemporaneousness provides a reminder of the complexity and diversity of transmedia
encounters between television, animation, and games. Interestingly, *Persona 4* is
arguably the oldest of the franchises, in that the first game of the *MegaTen* series was released in 1987, before the inaugural chapters of the *Crayon Shin-chan*
manga (1990) and the *Detective Conan* manga (1994), and well before the first
Pokémon game (1996) and the first *.hack* gamic media mix (2002).

If *Persona 4* feels more contemporary than the other three in its media ecology, it is partly because the *MegaTen* series has been the most heteregeneous and
openly structured of the four franchises, which has enabled it to branch into side
series like *Persona 4* that radically depart from prior series in their media ecology. It is partly because the *MegaTen* series emerges in conjunction with the new
media of 1980s Japan and thus speaks directly to it. In effect, *Persona 4* is both
the newest and oldest media ecology: it is a genealogical descendent of 1980s new
media, comprising the home television network (VCR, game console, PC) and
expanded distribution infrastructures that increasingly aligned television with
telecommunications (cable, satellite, video), and it is the forerunner in new gamic
ecologies moving across televisions and smartphones. The *Persona 4* series thus
puts a spin on the notion of posttelevision that agrees with Lyotard's formulation
of the postmodern: posttelevision transmedia are incipient in television media,
and as such, their emergence confirms that television is now irrevocable and
inevitable.[2]

This surely explains why the affective solution offered in *Persona 4* delves the
deepest into the production of distribution of television, dipping into its metastable

source to propose a wondrous and troubling manner of exploring the relation of self to self, and of self to others, in the era of new television media: all beings are modes of signaletic existence. Everything is becoming a signaletic being, potentially. Thus the gamic encounter between television and animation converges on a vision of signaletic animism. This is where the ontopolitical field of television comes to the fore—not for the first time, but as if to realize fully the parasocial possibilities debated in the early decades of television. Signaletic animism might be described as the inverse of the ontopolitical field, or as the resistance that sends a charge through that field.

To situate the ontopolitical implications of signaletic being and animism, let me reconsider the four transmedia ecologies in terms of their relation to the power formations discussed in Part II.

Ontopower Reboot

Insofar as the more subjective side (infrastructure complex) is the inverse or double of the more objective side (technosocial fields of rationality), the one may be tentatively mapped onto the other (Figure C.3). The hierarchical tendency is a double of sovereign power and the unidirectional tendency of disciplinary sites. The environmental tendency doubles the biopolitical, while the ontopolitical is the flip side of the heterarchical tendency. Such a mapping is not exact, or more precisely anexact. Yet it allows us to consider how the four infrastructure complexes are related to a field of rationality: sovereign, disciplinary, biopolitical, and ontopolitical.

When the *Crayon Shin-chan* series introduces a bifurcation into the one-to-many tendency, it is also generating a relay between the sovereign power of the family (invested in the father or father figure) and the disciplinary segmentation of space. The toppling of the hierarchical domination of source over audience is akin to overturning the sovereign authority of the father. But the father does not disappear. In fact, sovereign authority is invested into the tiny body of Shin-chan, where it cannot be fully accommodated, resulting in wriggling, jiggling joy and perversion. It cannot be fully accommodated because Shin-chan cannot function properly in disciplinary spaces (school, work, army, or political and economic centers). For the same reason, sovereign power cannot be eradicated. Television media are thus functioning in the social manner that Yoshimi and Williams describe: at once centralizing and segmenting, but at the same time multiplying and flowing. This is precisely what Shin-chan embodies with his transformative *hentai* and *henshin* powers.

What is more, because the father does not vanish from the scene even when overturned, the crisis in sovereign authority can be readily displaced onto and enlarged into biopolitical crises. Indeed, when the more diminutive TV-format

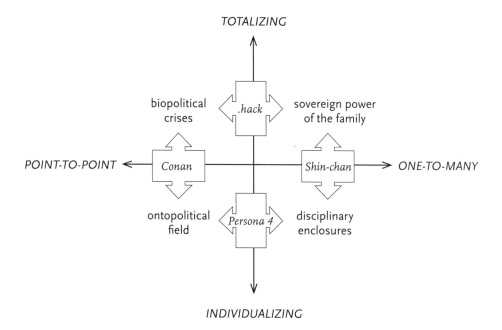

FIGURE C.3. The four transmedia ecologies can be mapped, anexactly, with respect to the technosocial fields of rationality, with an emphasis on their primary relay function. Thus the *Crayon Shin-chan* series, for instance, is primarily operative between the sovereign power of the family and disciplinary sites, which is also where its potential for activism arises.

Shin-chan is enlarged and prolonged for the big screen of theatrical release, biopolitical crises are introduced: the end of the world in some guise or another. These are always resolved, however, through the domestic scenario: father, mother, son, daughter, and pet dog working together. In sum, the arrow in Figure C.1 depicting the affective movement of the *Crayon Shin-chan* series is in fact a countermovement and a generative resistance to sovereign power (whose movement runs into the contrary direction). Consequently, although the *Crayon Shin-chan* series liberates ontopolitical forces in the form of diverse beings swarming onto the scene, these beings are usually articulated in contrast to the family: angry brides, evil patriarchs, and homosexual lone wolves or gay love couples, for instance. This multitude becomes shackled to the household to deal with crises in sovereignty.

Like the *Crayon Shin-chan* series, the *.hack* series presents a challenge to the hierarchical tendency and thus to the sovereign power of the household. It moves away from the family into an online world where household members may adopt quite different, radically nonhierarchical relations with one another. Such a move demands, however, an enlargement of biopolitical crises to the point where they encompass all relations. Thus the crisis in the online world registers immediately as a crisis of the off-line world. All the disciplinary sites—especially government and corporate operations—must be brought to bear on the biopolitical crisis wherein the end of the media world is synonymous with the end of the natural world. Ontopolitical forces are also enclosed within the game: the diverse avatars do not operate solely within the online world. Also, the only avatar who can save the world is synchronized with a game-generated AI. As such, although the ontopolitical affects the off-line world, it leads back to the household through its subordination to the biopolitical crisis. The affective solution of the .hack series thus consists of a countermovement or resistance to the movement that produces a relay between biopolitical and sovereign formations of power.

The Detective Conan series produces a relay that scarcely seems germane to television media at all, at least initially. It consists of a twofold eccentric movement in which closing the case follows from solving the mystery, but case closed occurs in a different register than mystery solved. Case closed requires improvisation, switching within one body between bodily potentials associated with radically different bodies (child, teenager, adult; and radio, telephone, television, print). Improvisation thus releases ontopolitical possibilities. The murder mysteries, which typically hinge on familial intrigues or workplace rivalries, imply biopolitical crises embracing both familial and disciplinary sites. The question is thus, to what extent does this ontopolitical field function autonomously of the biopolitical crises of sovereignty that pull disciplinary expertise into their fold? The delight of the Detective Conan series comes of its improvisation (how will Conan close the case once he has solved the mystery?), and its improvisation entails a countermovement to the more totalizing tendencies inherent in biopolitical crises of sovereignty. It tends to reach an impasse, however, in its tendency to personalize improvisation. Personalization is its internal limit, at once the condition for and the impossibility of improvisation.

The interest of the Persona 4 series lies in how it pushes more resolutely toward the production of heterarchical entities and thus comes closer to the ontopolitical field. The series does not dispense with crises in sovereignty, either of the family or of the biopolitical. Like Conan, the hero of Persona 4 inhabits a sort of extended family remix, and the murder mystery enlarges into a biopolitical crisis akin to the .hack series in which the media world threatens to destroy the off-line world. As with the other series, the Persona 4 series folds the four tendencies into its manifold. Yet it pushes more against disciplinary space: its teenagers are uncanny doubles of the officially trained and sanctioned police force. The police force embodies a biopolitical crisis to the extent that some officers are operating beyond the law as criminals. The teenagers, then, are doubling an extralegal disciplinary situation. In effect they present a countermovement to a situation that might be described as fascism or totalitarianism, in which forces operating outside the law are the rule of the land, with sovereignty invested in special opera-tions and extralegal contingencies—what Agamben calls the state of exception.

Collectively, these four transmedia ecologies help clarify what is at stake in the ontopolitical capacity of television media. They show the capacity of television to produce parasocial relations and thus to populate online and off-line worlds with a heterarchical multitude of human and nonhuman actors. With the *.hack* and *Persona 4* series, television-animation media appears so confident of its ability to serve as relay between sovereign, disciplinary, and biopolitical formations of power that it can now function in a metamedia or supermedia capacity. As such, ontopower is not merely a fourth possibility that emerges with the transforma-tion of television through new media. It is the key not only to what television has been doing for a long time but also to what it can be. New media have not broken with television media. On the contrary, new media have spurred television media to realize their ontopolitical possibilities, to enhance and intensify their para-social capacity. Put another way, television media are pushing toward a situation in which the plane of composition emerging through the infraindividual intra-action of self, platform, and character is becoming operative, more and more tangibly. As such, the affective solutions of these transmedia ecologies are wor-thy of careful consideration precisely because they indicate the sites of potential counteractualization. They gravitate toward the sites where the ontopolitical field of television media is increasingly becoming operative. But they do not simply reproduce ontopower. Their affective solutions imply the possibility for an activ-ism that confronts the operative capacity of the field on its own terms, by sticking to the resistance inherent to the field.

This sort of activist potential comes to the fore when the *Persona 4* series chal-lenges us to think of power consistent with vulnerability through a mode of sig-naletic being. Signaletic being in *Persona 4* is not simply an operative entity (an avatar you control). It becomes a platformative entity that situates you to act with and through nonhuman actors in order to raise infraindividual intra-actions to a different power.

Animism

I previously evoked a distinction between signal and noise, only to say that the two are inseparable, regardless of whether the medium is digital or analog. It would be more accurate to say that signaletic being involves a relation between signal and noise akin to the relation between wound and power for human be-ings in *Persona 4*: it is a matter of signals that are consistent with noise. Put another way, the power of transmission of a signal takes on consistency with or through noise. As such, noise is not external to the signal, something that can be stripped away. In fact, it is not noise at all. It might be called internal resonance, even though it is not really inside or outside, because such resonance occurs with other signals. It refers to the way in which the signal affects other signals, including how it is received. It is more like noise populated with signals, or vulnerability replete with potentiality. It opens into the infraindividual intra-active relationality implicit in media.

If *Persona 4* imagines human being and signaletic being in an analogous manner, it is because interactions among human beings take place within a media ecology that spurs and activates their intra-active relations. Like signaletic being, human being entails a sort of internal spreading, implying multiple bandwidths and frequencies, and it is these patterns of resonance that make for affective relationships. It is a matter of feelings that are always active in perceiving and acting—a dizzying proximity that subsists within perception occurring at a more comfortable social distance. For Merleau-Ponty, the point is not to say that everything is indistinct, that all relations are only ones of dizzying proximity, without distinction. On the contrary, indistinction provides a way to consider how self–other distinctions emerge and operate, how differences are negotiated and lived. In *Persona 4*, indistinction is expanded beyond the human–human relations in Merleau-Ponty's account to comprise nonhuman others, that is, character and platform. The smile or frown that affects your conduct is a smiling or frowning machine, which happens with and through a gamut of human, humanoid, and nonhuman bodies, including television platforms and anime characters. The flesh of the world thus includes media worlds and platform infrastructures, and differences are lived and negotiated through play, that is, story-play or gamic fabulation.

Two objections to such an approach frequently arise. The first is that this approach is thoroughly anthropomorphic; it implies an underlying analogy of platforms and characters to human beings.[3] The second objection is that humans are transformed into machines, and whatever makes humans distinctive is lost. I began to anticipate such objections in chapter 9 by addressing the ontopolitical implications of platformative characters in terms of a plane of composition formed by the intersection of three lines at three points: animal, machine, and human. This geometry is not really Euclidean, for such points cannot be located in a coordinate fashion, and the consequent plane is a technosocial topology, a field. It is the looser and stranger technosocial coordination of these points in anime characters that makes for their ability and capacity for serializing and for generating worlds of story-play. As such, a human is not turning into a machine. Nor are all beings turning into humanlike entities. Neither one needs to resemble the other. Something is crossing over from the platform to the character, and from the character to the user, and from the user to the platform during these interactions. These interactions are not producing resemblance. They are performatively iterating a set of infraindividual intra-actions: semblance. The ontopolitical field is precisely a field, not a unidirectional action on the part of humans upon machines, or machines upon humans, or for that matter nonhuman animals.

The technosocial topology of the ontopolitical field, then, recalls animism. For instance, Danny Naveh and Nurit Bird-David see in animism a shift in how we perceive things: "What may *appear* as a 'thing' to a mind infused with 'typificatory schemes' and nonimmediate considerations may *appear* as a 'person' more than a 'thing' to a mind available to perceive it in its outmost vividness."[4] Likewise, Kenneth M. Morrison notes that the animic mode organizes "indigenous life . . . around the existence of persons, human and otherwise, rather than around materiality."[5] This is precisely what is at stake in the *Persona 4* series: what matters is the person and relations among persons instead of distinctions between humans, machines, and animals. What comes to the fore is personation—the generation of persons (ontogenesis) in conjunction with careful attention to personness (relational epistemology).[6] The animism of television animation differs profoundly, to say the least, from the animism of indigenous peoples and the new anthropology of animism. Two differences in particular merit attention.

First, as the prior discussion of power formations attests, personation in transmedia ecologies always runs the risk of becoming normative and operative, or at least conventional and habitual. The question is thus, when, how, and to what extent do these habitual and conventionalized crossings turn back into techniques that reopen the relation of semblance? How or how much does it happen? How does the operative become actionable, open to activism?

Second, the animism of transmedia ecologies is related to the electromagnetic and signaletic, which is to say, elements or instances within transmedia ecology relate to one another through their relation to an electromagnetic energy cascade, which might also be called, in the manner of William James, a "little absolute," something nonrelational at the heart of relationality. Everything is composed of blink. The personness of signaletic beings occurs in relation to electromagnetic realities through composing with blink. How, then, are we to proceed with this signaletic animism?

Thinkers of the ontopolitical such as Latour, Massumi, Povinelli, and Stengers come to mind, as well as Donna Haraway. During the heyday of Japanese discourses on new media, Haraway began to consider such questions by proclaiming to her preference to be a cyborg rather than a goddess, embracing a figure that N. Katherine Hayles has aptly referred to as "contaminated to the core, making it exquisitely appropriate."[7] As such, in Haraway, received social distinctions, such as those of gender, turn out to be parasocial media-like distinctions. Representational reality is invariably contaminated, politically speaking, but this contamination is potentially exquisite, as Haraway and Hayles say. Your relation to it will depend on whether you see in it a failure of representation or a wager about other possible realities. If this situation is taken as the very worst, then you will surely bemoan how television animation wreaks havoc with the politics of representation, serving up a seemingly endless series of "paras" and "oids"—androids, ethnoids, gynoids, and other modes of paraexistence and paraconduct that occur alongside received social distinctions and appear somehow contrary to them without becoming contradictory enough to offer a firm stance.

By contrast, Haraway's wager is that if women are becoming somehow machinic, things have changed or are changing, and not only for the worse. Likewise, if self is becoming platformative, if platforms are becoming personlike, then something is changing. Not least among these changes is the emergence of gamic TV realities, which expand the space in front of the television into a networked environment: daily space becomes a media heterotopia. To play across heterogeneous media topologies, you have to become to some degree platformative, maybe splitting the difference between television set and mobile phone, to make something of the stuff of blink. Still, make no mistake: this is where everyone becomes vulnerable and exposed; and vulnerability and exposure, if rendered normative, can make for the worst kinds of dependency.

The lesson of the Pokémon Incident, in this respect, is not so much that television and animation can do neurological damage. Rather, the lesson is that when vulnerability to media takes on a normative value, a new field of rationality emerges around paradigms of dependency. This field of rationality becomes especially salient in contemporary discourses on media addiction, but the apparatus is a wide-reaching ensemble comprising media institutions, scientific studies, governmental measures, and aesthetic propositions that hinges on enacting a system of relations among them. In effect, insofar as vulnerability and dependency take on a normative value within the field of rationality produced through such an apparatus, this field shares terrain with or intersects the parasocial dimension of television as well as the effects of exposure integral to capitalism (increasingly evident in forms of precarious labor with affective connotations). What is to be done about these increasingly normativized forms of vulnerability? More specifically, what can television animation do?

Philip Pignarre and Isabelle Stengers formulate a response that resonates with contemporary new media in much the way that Haraway's cyborg manifesto resonated with 1980s new media: witchcraft. Above all, they argue, we need protection, but not in the form of the Hobbesian security apparatus in which we collectively overcome our vulnerability through military and economic might. Rather, we need protection from what they call "infernal alternatives," that is, "that set of situations that seem to leave no other choice than resignation or a slightly hollow sounding denunciation (such a denunciation is powerless because this situation offers no hold and the conclusion always comes back to the same thing: it is the whole 'system' that has to be destroyed)."[8] Debates about television and media have also tended toward infernal alternatives: the system must be reluctantly accepted, hollowly denounced, or completely dismantled. The result, as Pignarre and Stengers indicate, is a combination of "paranoia and depression," which comes of attributing "to capitalism the ensemble of operations of capture from which it profits, and to be seized by the powerlessness to resist it."[9]

The same is true of the situation of television media, which the tightening spiral of discourses on media addiction has reinvigorated. In fact, in this study, I introduced four infrastructure complexes to avoid establishing a massive and monolithic television complex, which would encourage recourse to infernal alternatives. While the term "complex" implies some degree of structural containment or constraint, working across four complexes reveals something of the pragmatic possibilities coursing through the affective solutions adhering to them.

Similarly, to counter such tendencies, Pignarre and Stengers advocate "the cultivation of sensitivity to what makes us vulnerable to the operations of capitalism. Notably, sensitivity to the 'gendered' dimensions of this vulnerability, for example the mobilization that implies scorn for the concern for consequences (care), suspected of sentimentalism." Ultimately, for Pignarre and Stengers, it is the pragmatism of witchcraft that deserves renewed consideration for its cultivation of sensitivity to what makes us vulnerable, without falling into "imprudent self-assurance of ideology critique, of demystification, of all those who make an enterprise out of the deconstruction of the appearances by which 'others' are had."[10]

Witchcraft, or something like it, is what arises on the inverse side of the screen–brain apparatus: a nonnormative take on vulnerability that is attentive to what makes us vulnerable to media and to what might prove therapeutic in affective terms. In such terms, the proliferation of nonhuman beings and parasocial relationships to them makes sense in a witchy way. It may be too soon to discount the abilities of magic girls and espers. Haraway's expansion of the cyborg manifesto into a species manifesto might well undergo a parallel expansion toward intensive alliances with nonspecies and into animism. In any event, the emergence of signaletic animism in the domain of expanded television media should be addressed in a less spectacular and more pragmatic fashion: the animism of anime is necessarily signaletic because it cultivates a sensitivity toward what makes us vulnerable, that is, the electromagnetic signal. Signaletic animism offers a way to approach that electromagnetic reality pragmatically, with an eye to what affords protection under conditions of vulnerability and with a sense of the magical powers of care for self and dependency on others, too often dismissed as sentimentalism.

ACKNOWLEDGMENTS

IF A NOVEL MAY BE LIKENED TO A DIALOGUE AMONG FRIENDS, SO TOO MAY AN ACADEMIC BOOK. THIS BOOK BEARS THE traces of so many exchanges with colleagues and students who are also friends that it feels like a long letter in reply to those whose thinking influenced mine, and whose encouragement made the ten-plus years devoted to this study feel worth the while. I constantly found myself citing them in this book. As replies go, however, this one also feels overdue: while I occasionally gave talks on topics related to this study, I have not previously published any of it. The inquiry unfolded as a book, as a movement of thought that did not lend itself to certain kinds of partition.

At the same time, because this movement of thought arose alongside union strikes, student demonstrations, and the other social movements and forms of protest that contributed to the call for general strike, it is not like a letter at all. It is like a society, or like a city situated within a society that still produces spaces and times for social activism—a city like Montreal. Some of the basic concerns of this book afford an indirect image of that urban activist situation: parasociality, improvisation, powers consistent with vulnerability, the question of what activist media might be and what obscures them. As such, my sense of gratitude extends not only to individuals but also to a situation, and when I consider the people to whom this book is beholden, what comes to mind are neighborhoods, clusters, and zones of activity and coalitions. Grateful as I am to teach within innovative departments and programs at McGill University such as East Asian studies, communications studies, and world cinemas, even more gratifying is the commitment of everyone within these institutional formations to make room for other arrangements across programs, departments, and universities.

I am fortunate to work (and to have worked) with truly brilliant and generous colleagues in Montreal: at McGill, Darin Barney, Brian Bergstrom, Jenny Burman, Michelle Cho, Michael Cowan, Ken Dean, Victor Fan, Yuri Furuhata, Sharon Hayashi, Adrienne Hurley, Becky Lentz, Xiao Liu, Tom Looser, Anne McKnight, Hajime Nakatani, Carrie Rentschler, Jonathan Sterne, Will Straw, and Alanna Thain. I have also worked with exceptional doctoral and postdoctoral students: Suzanne Beth, Erik Bordeleau, Marie-Pier Boucher, Marlowe Gardiner-Heslin, Annie Harrison, Inhye Kang, Gyewon Kim, Harumi Osaki, Martin Picard, Azra Rashid, Jen Spiegel, and Adam Szymanski. I am likewise indebted to my friends and colleagues at Concordia University and Université de Montréal: Bernard Bernier, Erin Manning, Brian Massumi, Livia Monnet, Josh Neves, Matthew Penney, Chris Salter, and Marc Steinberg. Yet such lists and institutional affiliations don't capture what is remarkable about how this situation affords intellectual community, improvisation, and activism. Brian, Erin, and Erik make the SenseLab and "Immediations" happen. Josh, Yuri, Marc, and Michelle make the Seminar on Political Theory and Media and "Porting Media" happen. Alanna and Michael work to activate the Moving Image Research Lab. Chris prolongs Hexagram. Carrie and Alanna reset and reboot the Institute for Gender, Sexuality, and Feminist Studies. Adrienne and kin trigger multitudes with the courage to find counteractualizations at a time when any form of activism is being institutionally conflated with terrorism, not least in universities. It is ultimately to such happenings that I feel most grateful, for they catalyzed the situations, passages, and crossings that provided inspiration for the movement from interaction to intra-action at the heart of this book.

I also thank those in New York and Cambridge who now seem a part of the Montreal situation, and whose thinking has profoundly affected mine: Harry Harootunian, Mellie Ivy, Sabu Koso, Tom Looser, Tomiko Yoda, and Alex Zahlten. The Montreal situation has forged equally important underground passages to Tokyo and Kyoto, where I have been blessed with conversations with and assistance from Jaqueline Berndt, Kotani Mari, Masumitsu Keiko, Nakagawa Shigemi, Narita Makoto, Ōtsuka Eiji, Tatsumi Takayuki, Tsuzura Junji, Ueno Toshiya, and Watanabe Tomoko. I thank Kadobayashi Takeshi and others with the Hyōshō bunkaron group who contributed to the animation event with Doi Nobuaki, Tsugata Nobuyuki, and Yamamura Kōji, as well as to Takayuki and the other organizers of the Science Fiction Writers of Japan who allowed for the dialogue with Aramaki Yoshio, Kasai Kiyoshi, and Kawamata Chiaki. I express my gratitude to Tonomura Tomi for organizing a seminar discussion on the Introduction to this book at the Eisenberg Institute for Historical Studies with Megan Ankerson and Lisa Nakamura; their comments inspired a radically different version. Michael Bourdaghs and Akira Lippit also provided extensive and productive comments. Conversations over the years with Brian Bergstrom, Brian

Massumi, Livia Monnet, Matthew Penney, and George Synder contributed profoundly to this work, even if they probably would not recognize their share.

Ultimately it is to my family that I am the most grateful: to Alex for his quick humor and love of mathematics and programming that extends into manga, games, and anime, and to Christine for sticking resolutely to the contrary direction, which makes for the perfect storm—and for the calm at the eye.

NOTES

Introduction

1. See Heinze's overview in "Radio and Television Consumption in Japan."

2. It would be impossible to provide references to the vast literature on any of these aspects of television, but to provide some key points of reference for this study, let me mention some of the English-language references that inform my approach even though I do not cite them extensively. In the context of the television set, I am thinking about the recent boom in platform studies (Ian Bogost and Nick Monfort, Matthew Fuller, Adrian MacKenzie, Marc Steinberg), which potentially renews and transforms the legacy of Marshall McLuhan. With respect to domestic and ambient viewing, John Fiske's *Television Culture* (1987), David Morley's *Family Television* (1986), Ien Ang's *Watching "Dallas"* (1991), Lynn Spiegel's *Make Room for TV* (1992), and Anna McCarthy's *Ambient Television* (2001) are relevant. I tend to cite Raymond Williams a good deal but rarely Stanley Cavell, yet Cavell's conceptualization of television in "The Fact of Television" is major influence on my account, precisely because he looks at television on the inverse side from Williams: monitoring instead of broadcasting, serialization instead of segmentation. Indeed, my account may be characterized in terms of finding an approach to television that comprises Williams and Cavell as two sides of the same coin.

3. See Segawa, *Chi-deji riken.*

4. In *La fin de la télévision,* for instance, Jean-Louis Missika dramatizes the idea that television is disappearing before our eyes, dividing it into three periods: paleotelevision, neotelevision, and posttelevision.

5. Notably Ōtsuka in *Teihon Monogatari shōhiron* and Azuma in *Gēmu teki riarizumu no tanjō.* In *Anime's Media Mix,* Steinberg shows that although the term "media mix" dates from the late 1980s, its constitutive moment is the 1960s, which also marks a new kind of multimedia storytelling.

6. Poniewozi, "Post-Television Era."

7. Zielinski, *Audiovisions.*

8. Yoshimi, "Television and Nationalism."

9. Feuer provides a nice description of this bias in her discussion of Herbert Zettl in "Concept of Live Television," 13.

10. Sobchack, *Address of the Eye*, 301.

11. Feuer, "Concept of Live Television," 14.

12. Manovich, *Language of New Media*, 302.

13. Philip Rosen offers one of the most nuanced treatments of the implications of indexicality and its multiple registers within film theory in *Change Mummified* (2001). Also, across a series of three books, David Norman Rodowick carefully tracks the philosophical implications of the erosion of indexicality as a ground for film theory with an eye to how it opens possibilities for truly philosophical inquiry in the wake of film theory: *The Virtual Life of Film* (2009), *Elegy for Theory* (2014), and *Philosophy's Artful Conversation* (2015).

14. See Buchan's introduction to *Pervasive Animation* for a succinct and incisive discussion of the stakes of the pervasive animation.

15. Recent works on animation in a more philosophical or ontological register are too numerous to cite, but it is worth noting a few key works, partly because they show how important animation was to the effort to open film studies to media studies. See, for instance, Sean Cubitt, *The Cinema Effect* (2004), Thomas Lamarre, *The Anime Machine* (2009), Eric Jenkins, *Special Affects* (2014), and essays in the 2014 collection edited by Karen Beckman, *Animating Film Theory*.

16. Although accounts of animation in the 1930s and early 1940s were centered on cinema (with pride of place given to Disney), they were highly philosophical in their line of inquiry, offering a rich dialogue with the more recent philosophical turn in animation studies. See, for instance, Eisenstein, *Eisenstein on Disney*; Hansen, "Of Mice and Ducks"; Imamura, "For the Sake of Japanese Cartoons."

17. On sound and music, see, for instance, Hansen's account of Adorno in "Of Mice and Ducks" as well as Imamura, "Theory of the Animated Sound Film." For an account of the use of color to resolve the problematic of compositing, see Lamarre, "First Time as Farce."

18. Chung provides a compelling account of how digital compositing of images is related to production in multiple sites in "Media Heterotopia."

19. See Sharp's account of 2-D and 3-D relations in anime in "Between Dimensions."

20. See Manovich's account of compositing in *Language of New Media*, 130–49, which is of interest because he sometimes seems to equate compositing with internal montage, and he sometimes considers compositing to be a different problematic.

21. Tsugata Nobuyuki adopts this framework in *Nihon animēshon no chikara*.

22. Japanese commentators Azuma Hiroki and Watanabe Daisuke have likewise turned to the notion of reset to describe the production of pathways across multiple media forms, resulting in diverse world lines, temporal loops, and multiple possible worlds. See Azuma, *Gēmu teki riarizumu no tanjō*, and Watanabe Daisuke, "*Kimi no na wa* no dai-hitto."

23. Morton, *Hyperobjects*, 1.

24. Deleuze, *Cinema 1*, 81; Marx and Engels, "Manifesto of the Communist Party," 476.

25. Shiga Nobuo, "Nyūmedia to eisei to konpyūta to no kanren," in *Shōwa terebi hōsōshi*, 1:316–21.

26. Williams, *Television*, 18.

27. In *The Production of Space* (1991), Henri Lefebvre makes a similar gesture: the production of space cannot be situated in the base or superstructure, and in fact shows the in-

adequacy of such a model (46). The focus of the production of distribution in this study parallels in many respects Lefebvre's focus on the production of space.

28. Marx, *Capital: Volume 1*, 473.

29. Marx, *Grundrisse*, 99

30. Deleuze and Guattari, *Anti-Oedipus*. Ian Buchanan provides a succinct account of the relation between the three syntheses and the three modes of production in *EPZ Deleuze and Guattari's "Anti-Oedipus"*; James Williams carefully shows how Deleuze's three synthesis were transformed into the three modes of production in *Anti-Oedipus* in *Gilles Deleuze's Philosophy of Time*.

31. I am deeply indebted here and in what follows to Jason Read's account in *Micropolitics of Capital*.

32. Two prime examples are Fuller's *Media Ecologies* and MacKenzie's *Wirelessness*.

33. Larkin, *Signal and Noise*, 19.

34. For two takes on this issue, see Steven Shaviro's account in *Universe of Things*, 50, in which he examines Harman's account in *Tool-Being*, 47.

35. Peters, *Speaking into the Air*, 201.

36. Peters, *Marvelous Clouds*; see especially chapter 2.

37. Buchanan draws out these connections in *EPZ Deleuze and Guattari's "Anti-Oedipus."*

38. Star and Ruhleder, "Steps Toward an Ecology of Infrastructure," 112.

39. Ibid., 113.

40. Ibid.

41. Latour, *Inquiry into Modes of Existence*, 93.

42. Latour, "Whose Cosmos," 451. See too his proposal for a Parliament of Things in *We Have Never Been Modern*.

43. Guattari, *Schizoanalytic Cartographies*, 48.

44. Furuhata, *Cinema of Actuality*.

45. Andrew, *André Bazin*, xiii

46. Rosen, *Change Mummified*.

47. Deleuze, *Cinema 1*.

48. Marotti, *Money, Trains, and Guillotines*.

49. See in particular Furuhata's account of Oshima Nagisa's *Ninja bugeichō* in *Cinema of Actuality*.

50. Furuhata, "Multimedia Environments," 56–79.

51. I am indebted to the media installation event by Kawai Masayuki, *Rhythm of Video Feedback*, performed at McGill University on February 29, 2016, and to Harashima Daisuke's discussion of it, which transformed the notion of glitch-error into glitch-rhythm in a manner similar to what I am presenting here.

52. See Fan's discussion in *Cinema Approaching Reality*.

53. See Rosen's careful delineation of the prolongation of indexical capture in *Change Mummified*.

54. Julie Turnock's discussion of the industrial formation of an ILM version of cinematic reality, in which special effects are used to make things look as if they are photographed, is a key point of reference in her *Plastic Reality*.

55. There are many other paths through television and animation. Among programs for the first twenty-five years of television, for instance, in *Terebi bangumi kotohajime*, historian Shiga Nobuo signals four influential animated series: the first *Tetsuwan Atomu* or *Astro Boy*

(1963–66), the first run of *Obake no Q-tarō* (1965–67), *Sazae-san* (1969–present), *Ijiwaru bāsan* (1970–71), and *Gegege no Kitarō* (1968–69), all highlighting a different set of concerns.

1. Population Seizure

1. Subsequent clinical reports and surveys found that about 5 percent of child viewers experienced neurological distress, a figure in keeping with general distribution of epileptiform photosensitivity. TV Tōkyō indicated that roughly 13 million viewers watched the episode, of which about 55 percent were school-age children. A conservative estimate would put the number of affected children at about 100,000. See Furushō et al., "Patient Background of the *Pokemon* Phenomenon," 553.

2. See Japan Commercial Broadcasters Association, "Picture Techniques Used in Broadcast Programs," trans. National Association of Broadcasters Japan, https://www.j-ba.or.jp/category /english/jba101020.

3. Harding, "TV Can Be Bad for Your Health," 265.

4. On March 29, 1997, there was an incident involving the episode "The Mysterious Father" *(Maboroshi no oyaji)* in which four children were taken to hospitals by ambulance after reportedly watching a scene in the episode with rapidly flashing red and white colors. Broadcasts were not suspended.

5. See Yadama Miyuki's explanatory video, "Terebi no mae no mina-san e" (To all of you in front of the television), *DrillSpin*, http://www.drillspin.com/person/view/ARDSAX161928.

6. "Jūbyō gurai me ga shimita tenmetsu hōhō, nichijōtekini terebi Pokemon jiken" (Techniques of transmitted light, used daily, arrest the eye for about ten seconds: the TV Pokémon Incident), *Asahi shinbun*, December 17, 1997.

7. Takahashi and Tsukahara, "*Pocket Monster* Incident," 632.

8. Foucault, "Confession of the Flesh," 194.

9. "'Jinken ni shinpai' Pokemon higai chōsa sezu Ayase-shi kyōin" (Teacher in Ayase city, "worried about human rights," not conducting polls on Pokémon victims), *Asahi shinbun*, December 18, 1997.

10. For an account of overlaps and differences between the account of the apparatus or *dispositif* in Foucault and in film theory, see contributions to *Cinema and Technology*, a 2011 special issue of *Semiotic Inquiry* edited by André Gaudreault and Martin Lefebvre, especially Frank Kessler, "Recadrages," and Will Straw, "Pulling Apart the Apparatus." Previously, in *Anime Machine*, I used Guattari's concept of the machine to reconsider the paradigm of the cinematographic apparatus in the context of animation to deal with social relations of production; here I address the social relations of distribution via the apparatus by drawing on Foucault, Guattari, and STS.

11. Takahashi Takeo et al., "Pokemon Seizures," 1.

12. Zielinski, *Audiovisions*, 19.

13. Bellour, "La querelle des dispositifs," 15.

14. In his 2008 account of the aesthetics and reception of Nigerian, Hausa, and Indian films in Nigeria, in *Signal and Noise*, Brian Larkin describes a *dispositif* that runs counter to that described by Bellour: brilliantly lighted outdoor venues and constant conversation, and movies produced with a quite different sensibility, one that is described in opposition to the impact of French art films in Africa. But then Bellour would surely consider such practices as belonging to a video-*dispositif*.

15. Tanizaki Jun'ichirō, "Tumor with a Human Face," 100.

16. Stringer, in "Original and Copy," evokes the Pokémon Incident in a footnote to his analysis of *Ringu*, 305.

17. Rotman, *Becoming Beside Ourselves*, 116.

18. Ibid., 107.

19. Anna McCarthy's study of television outside the home, *Ambient Television*, shows how the flexibility, adaptability, and complexity of TV technology allows it to enter into a variety of places, which recall the *dispositif* evoked in prior accounts.

20. For a summary of the documentary, see jsolodar, "Nintendo Knew about, Downplayed Seizure Risks: BBC Report," *Seizures from Video Games*, February 20, 2013, https://videogameseizures.wordpress.com/.

21. Said, *Orientalism*, 6.

22. While Foucault himself did not consider discourse analysis to be limited to texts (and his subsequent shift to *dispositif* makes the case more clearly), Kittler considers his discourse analysis to be an expression of an old European epoch enchanted with alphabetical writing and libraries; *Discourse Networks*, 369.

23. Foucault, "Truth and Power," 109.

24. Papapetros, "In/Animate Victims," 303. This essay draws from the introduction to his 2012 book, *On the Animation of the Inorganic*.

25. Papapetros, "In/Animate Victims," 300.

26. Ibid., 302.

27. Ibid., 303.

28. Tohkura Yoh'ichi, "Future of Communication Science and Technologies," 5.

29. Ibid.

30. Gombrich, *Aby Warburg*, 76.

31. Papapetros, "In/Animate Victims," 305.

32. Ibid.

33. Whitehead, *Process and Reality*, 68, cited in Wallack, *Epochal Nature of Process*, 83.

34. Tegmark, "Solid, Liquid, Gas, You," 30. See also Max Tegmark, "Consciousness as a State of Matter," preprint, ver. 3, March 18, 2015, https://arxiv.org/abs/1401.1219.

35. Anderson, *Imagined Communities*.

2. Neurosciences and Television

1. Kubey and Csikszentmihaly, "Television Addiction Is No Metaphor," 76.

2. A good example is Desmurget, *TV Lobotomie*, which dwells on statistical documentation showing how television negatively affects health and academic performance and promotes violence and fear. While his study largely follows the social behavior model, he nevertheless draws a good deal from cognitive studies and neuroscientific research and concludes that, because television is everywhere at all times, we need to control our intake.

3. Kubey and Csikszentmihaly, "Television Addiction Is No Metaphor," 80.

4. Schnabel, "Black Box," 767.

5. Ibid., 766.

6. Mori, *Gēmu nō no kyōfu*.

7. Helen Phillips, "Video Game 'Brain Damage' Claim Criticized," *New Scientist*, July 11, 2002, https://www.newscientist.com/.

8. Kubey and Csikszentmihaly, "Television Addiction Is No Metaphor," 80.

9. Acland, "Crack in the Electric Window," 170.

10. Ibid., 172.

11. For an overview of this initiative, see two essays by Koizumi, "Concept of 'Developing the Brain'" and "Brain-Science and Education."

12. Illes et al., "International Perspectives," 979. The cited source for this initiative is Koizumi, "Concept of 'Developing the Brain.'"

13. See, for instance, Hurley, *Revolutionary Suicide*; David H. Slater, "The Making of Japan's New Working Class," *Asia-Pacific Journal*, January 4, 2010, http://www.japanfocus.org/; Toivonen, "Don't Let Your Child Become a NEET!"; Bergstrom, *Young Boys Doing Terrible Things*; and D'Orangeville, *"Shonen," le monstre invisible*.

14. Illes et al., "International Perspectives," 979. The cited source is Takahashi and Tsukahara, *"Pocket Monster* Incident."

15. Connelly, *Neuropolitics*, 7.

16. Damasio, *Self Comes to Mind*, 19.

17. Lazzarato, *Making of Indebted Man*, 33.

18. Deleuze, "Brain Is the Screen," 366. Raymond Bellour provides a direct and succinct account of the stake of brain sciences in Deleuze's film theory in "Deleuze: The Thinking of the Brain." Pisters explicates and enlarges Deleuze's concept, offering an analysis of cinema based on the neuroimage, in *The Neuro-Image*. Elsaesser and Hagener provide an assessment of various approaches to the brain and the screen in the chapter "Cinema as Brain" in *Film Theory*.

19. Deleuze, *Cinema 2*, 211–12.

20. See, for instance, Massumi, "Too Blue," in *Parables for the Virtual*, 208–56.

21. Foucault, *Birth of Biopolitics*, 60.

22. Deleuze, *Francis Bacon*, 101.

23. See Munster, *Aesthesia of Networks*, 29; and Manning, *Relationscapes*, 124.

24. Massumi, *Parables for the Virtual*, 252.

25. Furushō et al., "Patient Background of the *Pokemon* Phenomenon," calculate schoolchildren as 55 percent of approximately 10 million viewers (553).

26. Ishida et al., "Photosensitive Seizures Provoked," 1340.

27. Takahashi and Tsukahara, *"Pocket Monster* Incident," place the figure at 200; Ishida et al., "Photosensitive Seizures Provoked," place the figure at 150.

28. See, for instance, Furushō et al., "Comparison Survey."

29. Ishida et al., "Photosensitive Seizures Provoked," 1343, calculate 55 percent of 10 million viewers, as does Furushō et al., "Patient Background of the *Pokemon* Phenomenon."

30. Both Takahashi and Tsukahara, *"Pocket Monster* Incident," and Harding, "TV Can Be Bad for Your Health," report isolating the effect of red–blue flash as soon as they examined the video the next day and quickly conducted tests to verify it.

31. Radford and Bartholomew, "Pokemon Contagion," 199. Radford later published a single-authored account making the same points, "Pokémon Panic of 1997."

32. Radford and Bartholomew, "Pokemon Contagion," 201.

33. Ibid., 200–201.

34. Bartholomew and Radford, *Martians Have Landed!*, 46, emphasis mine.

35. Zifkin and Kasteleijn-Nolst Trenité, "Pokemon Contagion," 1235.

36. Ibid.

37. Ibid., 1236.

38. "Pokemon no rokuga mite 42-sai dansei shisshin: netto ni 'utte' keiji" (Forty-two-year-old man blacks out watching a video of Pokémon; "now selling" notices appear online), *Asahi shinbun*, December 18, 1997.

39. Kasteleijn-Nolst Trenité et al., "Visual Stimuli in Daily Life."

40. See Covanis, "Photosensitivity"; Fisher et al., "Photic- and Pattern-Induced Seizures"; Kasteleijn-Nolst Trenité, "Photosensitivity"; and Verrotti et al., "Photosensitivity."

41. Harding and Takahashi, "Regulations," 46.

42. Takahashi Taeko et al., "Pokemon Seizures," 4.

43. Okamura et al., "Epilepsies after *Pocket Monster* Seizures."

44. Yamasaki et al., "Neural Basis," 1611.

45. Takada et al., "Epileptic Seizures Induced by Animated Cartoon," 1001.

46. Deleuze's conceptualization of singularity is also pertinent here, *The Logic of Sense*, 63. See too Steven Shaviro, "What Are Singularities," *Pinocchio Theory*, June 14, 2012, http://www.shaviro.com/. Burns and Kaiser provide a precise overview of its geopolitical relevance in "Introduction: Navigating Differential Futures," 8–9.

47. Erik Curiel and Peter Bokulich, "Singularities and Black Holes," *Stanford Encyclopedia of Philosophy*, ed. Edward N. Zalta, Fall 2012 edition, http://plato.stanford.edu/.

48. Vinge, "The Coming Technological Singularity"; Good, "Speculations Concerning the Ultraintelligent Machine."

49. Tegmark, "Will There Be a Singularity within Our Lifetime?," 30–33.

50. See also Chalmers, "Singularity."

51. Massumi, *Parables for the Virtual*, 252.

52. See, for instance, Latour and Woolgar, *Laboratory Life*.

53. Latour, *We Have Never Been Modern*, 5.

54. Massumi, *Parables for the Virtual*, 252.

55. Ibid.

56. DannoW, "The Mysterious Original Pokemon Red and Green Incident," *Pastebin*, February 21, 2010, http://pastebin.com/f71e6728f.

57. Massumi, *Parables for the Virtual*, 252–53.

58. Ibid., 253, emphasis his.

59. Sakai, "Modernity and Its Critique."

60. Kapur, "Out of Control," 123.

61. Radford and Bartholomew, "Pokemon Contagion," 202.

62. Zifkin and Kasteleijn-Nolst Trenité, "Pokemon Contagion," 1235.

3. This Stuff Called Blink

1. The pokémon seems to be Gengar and the episode appears to be number 24, which aired in Japan on September 2, 1997.

2. Bordwell, *Poetics of Cinema*, 332. Bordwell is citing McNeil, *Face*, 29, in the first sentence.

3. Bordwell, *Poetics of Cinema*, 330.

4. Ibid., 332, citing Kobayashi et al., "Jihatsusei shunmoku ni oyobosu ongaku eizō no kanshō kōka"; Tada Hideoki, "Eyeblink Rates"; and Tsuda and Suzuki, "Effects of Subjective Interest on Eyeblink Rates."

5. Bordwell, *Poetics of Cinema*, 335.

6. Ibid., 334; Bordwell, *Ozu and the Poetics of Cinema*, 173.

7. See Funatsuka et al., "Analysis of Photo-Pattern Sensitivity," for an overview of his team's clinical evaluations.

8. Barad, *Meeting the Universe Halfway*, 33.

9. Massumi, *Power at the End of the Economy*, 8.

10. The first major source is Harding and Jeavons, *Photosensitive Epilepsy*. Harding and Harding provide a succinct account in "Televised Material and Photosensitive Epilepsy."

11. Takahashi Yukitoshi et al., "Nonphotosensitive Video Game–Induced Partial Seizures."

12. "Jūbyō gurai me ga shimita tenmetsu hōhō, nichijōtekini terebi Pokemon jiken" (Techniques of transmitted light, used daily, arrest the eye for about ten seconds: The TV Pokémon Incident), *Asahi shinbun*, December 17, 1997.

13. Funatsuka et al., "Analysis of Photo-Pattern Sensitivity," 28.

14. Takahashi Tacko et al., "Pokemon Seizures," 9. Takahashi Takeo published a monograph in the same year, *Terebi eizō to hikari kanjusei hossa*, which provides an historical overview of research in Japan and abroad, the impact of the Pokémon Incident, the current state of guidelines in Japan, and various recommendations.

15. Takahashi et al., "Long-Wavelength Red Light Emission."

16. Takahashi and Tsukahara, "*Pocket Monster* Incident."

17. Shirakawa et al., "Study of the Effect of Color Photostimulation."

18. Takahashi Takeo et al., "Suppressive Efficacies by Adaptive Temporal Filtering System."

19. Parra et al., "Removal of Epileptogenic Sequences."

20. Parain and Lebas, "Point sur les écrans."

21. Harding and Takahashi, "Regulations," 46.

22. Acland makes this point succinctly in "Crack in the Electric Window."

23. See Ueno Toshiya, "Japanimation and Techno-Orientalism," 1997, http://www.to.or.at/ueno/japan.htm, which builds on Morley and Robins's chapter on techno-Orientalism in *Spaces of Identity*.

24. "The Playboy Interview: Marshall McLuhan," *NextNature.net*, December 12, 2009, http://www.nextnature.net/.

25. Brougère, "How Much Is a Pokémon Worth?," 189.

26. Gerber, "Images of Japan in the Digital Age," 108. See also Dobson's account of the treatment of Japan in *The Simpsons*, in particular his account of its staging of Pokémon Shock in the episode "Thirty Seconds over Tokyo." Dobson, "Mister Sparkle Meets the Yakuza."

27. Yano, "Panic Attacks," 133.

28. Ibid., 132.

29. Ministry of Posts and Telecommunications, "The Final Report of the 'Study Group on Broadcasting and Audio-Visual Sensory Perception,' June 1998," http://www.soumu.go.jp/main_sosiki/joho_tsusin/policyreports/english/group/broadcasting/final_report.html, chapter 1, section 2.

30. Lapoujade, *William James*, 18.

31. James, *Essays in Radical Empiricism*, 2–3.

32. Ibid., 86.

33. Lapoujade, *William James*, 18–20.

34. Ibid., 28n1.

35. See, for instance, Damasio's account of James in *Self Comes to Mind* and Austin's in *Zen and the Brain*.

36. Hornborg provides a succinct statement of this problem in "Submitting to Objects," 245.

37. Cytowic, *Synesthesia*, 61–63.

38. See in particular the images and explanation in Funatsuka et al., "Analysis of Photo-Pattern Sensitivity," 30.

39. My account of semblance and nonsensuous similarity is inspired by Brian Massumi's discussion, which builds on that of Walter Benjamin. See, for instance, Massumi, *Semblance and Event*, 105. Two essays by Benjamin are particularly important in this context: "On Semblance" and "On the Mimetic Faculty."

40. Cytowic, *Man Who Tasted Shapes*, 96.

41. Susan Greenfield, "Computers May Be Altering Our Brains," *Independent*, August 12, 2011, http://www.independent.co.uk/.

42. Stanislas Dehaene, "Your Brain on Books," *Scientific American*, November 17, 2009, https://www.scientificamerican.com/.

43. Read, *Politics of Transindividuality*, 104–5.

44. It is striking the degree to which contemporary discussions of social media addiction and the Internet repeat discourses on television, particularly when it comes to their emphasis on the relation between attention and distraction, which is addressed in detail in chapter 8. See, for instance, Carr, *Shallows*. For a quick overview of the basic issues, see Nir Eyal, "Who's Really Addicting You to Technology?," *LinkedIn*, February 9, 2016, https://www.linkedin.com/.

4. A Thousand Tiny Blackouts

1. Haddon, *Curious Incident*, 116–17.

2. Deleuze's account of three syntheses in *Difference and Repetition* is the inspiration for my account. See also Steven Shaviro's accounts on his blog, *Pinocchio Theory*, "The Connective and Disjunctive Syntheses" (July 7, 2008) and "The Third (Conjunctive) Synthesis" (July 14, 2008), http://www.shaviro.com/. In *Semblance and Event*, also building on William James, Massumi speaks of disjunctive relations (separative transition; pragmatic) and conjunctive relations (mutual inclusion; speculative). In effect, in working across these two sets of relations toward a pragmatic-speculative philosophy, Massumi is addressing the same problematic that I am addressing under the rubric of disjunctive synthesis, which happens between connective and conjunctive syntheses.

3. In his review of Žižek's book on Deleuze, Daniel Smith addresses the relation between Deleuze's three syntheses and Kant's, which is precisely the distinction I am making here. See Smith, "Inverse Side of Structure," 641–42.

4. Andrew, "Cognitivism," 2.

5. Joseph and Barbara Anderson, "The Myth of Persistence of Vision Revisited," 3. This essay is a return to an essay that they had written in 1978, "The Myth of Persistence of Vision."

6. See, for instance, Haber and Hershenson, *Psychology of Visual Perception*, and Nichols and Lederman, "Flicker and Motion in Film," 96, both of which are cited in Rod Munday, "The Moving Image," in *Lectures: Visual Perception 8*, http://visual-memory.co.uk/.

7. Munday, "Moving Image."

8. Seitz et al., "Visual Experience," 55.

9. Anderson and Anderson, "Myth of Persistence of Vision Revisited," 8–9.

10. Ibid., 9.

11. Ibid., 10

12. Nichols and Lederman, "Flicker and Motion in Film," 96.

13. Munday, "Moving Image."

14. In the second volume of his trilogy on film theory, *Elegy for Theory*, Rodowick provides a succinct summary of his account of photographic ontology in the first volume, *Virtual Life of Film*.

15. Evans, "Reality Programming," 207–8.

16. Ibid., 207; emphasis mine.

17. See Shaviro's account in *Universe of Things*.

18. Monnet works across psychoanalysis and Deleuze to provide an insightful account of the politics of active involunterism in "Anatomy of Permutational Desire."

19. Kubey and Csikszentmihaly, "Television Addiction Is No Metaphor," 76.

20. Mander, *Four Arguments*.

21. Kubey and Csikszentmihaly, "Television Addiction Is No Metaphor," 76.

22. Lang, "Limited Capacity Model," 48.

23. terry33, "How TV Affects Brainwaves," *TV Smarter*, February 21, 2009, http://tvsmarter.wordpress.com/.

24. Hirahara and Murase, "Human Information Science," 11.

25. Foucault, *Hermeneutics of the Subject*, 222–23.

5. Media Genealogy and Transmedia Ecology

1. See, for instance, Jean-Louis Missika, *La fin de la télévision* (2006); Amanda Ott, *Television Will Be Revolutionized* (2007); Marc Leverette, Brian L. Ott, and Cara Louise Buckley, eds., *It's Not TV* (2008); Graeme Turner and Jinna Tay, eds., *Television Studies after TV* (2009); and Denise Mann, *Wired TV* (2014).

2. Viret, *Idées reçues sur la télévision de demain*.

3. Okumura Kenta, *Soredemo terebi wa shinanai*, 211. See again Feuer's critique of liveness in "Concept of Live Television."

4. Selznick, *Global Television*, 3.

5. The general outline for such an account may be found in Lamarre, "Regional TV."

6. See, for instance, Gilder, *Life after Television*.

7. Mann, "When Television and New Media Work Worlds Collide."

8. See Steinberg, *Anime's Media Mix*.

9. Murphy, *How Television Invented New Media*, 26.

10. See Sterne's account in *MP3*, 14–17.

11. Peters brilliantly prolongs such an approach to media as environment (and vehicle) in the second chapter of *Marvelous Clouds*, in which he develops a contrast between humans and dolphins on the basis of how their environment operates as a medium to shape their technical condition of possibilities.

12. Williams, *Television*, 13.

13. Ibid., 18.

14. Miller, *Emergency Broadcasting*, 187–88.

15. In "Flow and Mobile Media," Oswald and Packer contest the tendency to associate broadcast with fixity, and the digital with fluidity (278) likewise centered on Raymond Williams's account of television and flow.

16. For an overview of the information revolution as the second great transformation, see Ichida and Boutang, "Against the Closure of the World."

17. Turkle, *Second Self* and *Life on the Screen*; Chun, *Control and Freedom*.

18. Galloway, *Protocol*.

6. A Little History of Japanese Television

1. See, for instance, Katō Hidetoshi's fine historical overview of Japanese television, "Japan," 170, as well as Takayanagi, *Terebi kotohajime*.

2. Ibid. A fuller history of Japan's technological progress appears in Satō Gentei's *Terebitō antena monogatari*.

3. Kasza, *The State and the Mass Media in Japan*, 6.

4. Nippon Hōsō Kyōkai Hōsō Bunka Kenkyūjo, *Terebi shichō no 50-nen*, 14.

5. Williams, *Television*, 21.

6. In his account of the moving panorama in *Illusions in Motion* (2013), Erkki Huhtamo makes the case for treating various technological devices as floating signifiers.

7. Williams, *Television*, 18.

8. Ibid., 17.

9. Ibid., 18.

10. Ibid., 18–19.

11. Nippon Hōsō Kyōkai Hōsō Bunka Kenkyūjo, *History of Broadcasting in Japan*, 231.

12. Darin Barney has significantly complicated this paradigm across several works, including *Prometheus Wired* (2000) and *Communication Technology* (2005); the latter is the source of my observation here.

13. Anderson, *Imagined Communities*.

14. "Matsutaro Shoriki: Japan's Citizen Kane," *Economist*, December 22, 2012, http://www.economist.com/.

15. Nippon Hōsō Kyōkai Hōsō Bunka Kenkyūjo, *Terebi shichō no 50-nen*, 16.

16. Chun, *Nation of a Hundred Million Idiots*, 62–63.

17. See Arima Tetsuo, *Nihon terebi to shīaiei*.

18. An unabashed renewal of the Grand Crescent appears in Asō Tarō's 2006 speech entitled "Arc of Freedom and Prosperity," which policy has been renewed and expanded by the second Abe Shinzō government. See Harano Jōji, "Behind the New Abe Diplomacy: An Interview with Cabinet Advisor Yachi Shōtarō," June 27, 2013, http://www.nippon.com/.

19. Ivy provides a detailed analysis of these rhetorical operations of national purity in "In/Comparable Horrors."

20. Yoshimi, "Television and Nationalism," 468.

21. Chun, *Nation of a Hundred Million Idiots*, 134–41.

22. Ibid., 139.

23. Ibid., 141.

24. Ibid., 154.

25. Yoshimi, "Television and Nationalism," uses this turn of phrase in the title of his essay.

26. Ibid., 477.

27. Ibid., 475.

28. Deleuze, "Postscript on Control Societies," 177.
29. Yoshimi, "Television and Nationalism," 475.
30. Ibid., 476.
31. Ibid., 478.
32. Ibid., 462.
33. Ibid., 474.
34. Chun, *Nation of a Hundred Million Idiots.*
35. Furu, "Research on 'Television and the Child' in Japan."
36. I draw here on Debaise's foreword to *La philosophie des possessions.*
37. Foucault, "Subject and Power," 332.
38. Yoshimi, "Television and Nationalism," 481.
39. Ibid., 484.
40. Ibid.
41. Ibid.
42. "New NHK Chief: 'Comfort Women' Only Wrong Per 'Today's Morality'; Programming Must Push Japan's Territorial Stances," *Japan Times,* January 25, 2014, http://www.japantimes .co.jp/.
43. Okumura Kenta, *Soredemo terebi wa shinanai.*
44. Agamben, *State of Exception.*
45. Although this emphasis runs throughout his work, Yoshimi's famous work in this respect may well be *Toshi no naka no doramaturugī: Tōkyō no sakariba no shakaishi* (1987). For an example in English, see Yoshimi, "Evolution of Mass Events in Prewar Japan."
46. Yoshimi, "From Street Corner to Living Room."

7. Television and New Media

1. In "The Fact of Television," Cavell considers the importance in television of monitoring as the material condition of television and of switching as the lack of distinction between live and playback, which I see intensified in the ability of the television to internally switch from receiver to monitor and hence to switch between broadcast, VCR, and games, for instance.

2. In linguistics, heterarchy refers to a diagram in which connections between nodes is nonhierarchical, and because elements are unranked, there is potential for the emergence of diverse ways of relating or ranking them. See Carole L. Crumley, "Heterarchy," *International Encyclopedia of Social Sciences,* 2008, http://www.encyclopedia.com/, and "Remember How to Organize."

3. Morris-Suzuki, *Beyond Computopia.*

4. Furuhata, "Multimedia Environments," 64.

5. Masuyama, *Terebi gēmu bunkaron,* 33. Masuyama dates *Magnet TV* to 1966, while the Whitney Art Museum dates it 1965. I am basing my discussion on the exemplar at the Whitney (http://collection.whitney.org/object/6139).

6. Katō, *Communication Policies in Japan,* 50.

7. Ibid.

8. Higuchi and Troutt, *Life Cycle Management,* xvii.

9. Ibid., 51.

10. In *Two Bits* (2008), in the context of new media, specifically free software movements, Chris Kelty pushes this question of the public sphere to its limit, arriving at a notion of re-

cursive publics, which is probably as close as we can get to a public sphere in the context of television and new media. Yet as Jacques Rancière *(Politics of Aesthetics)* points out, such formations would remain vacuous if not grounded in a distribution of the sensible, which is what is at stake here.

11. Anne Friedberg offers something of an overview in "The End of Cinema." In *Death 24× a Second*, Laura Mulvey addresses the pause effect enabled by DVD players, relating it to transformations in the experience of motion and stillness in moving images. Like these two accounts, I will stress how the VCR allows for acting on the image, stopping on movement.

12. This is the focus of Hilderbrand's study *Inherent Vice*.

13. In *Understanding the Global TV Format*, Albert Moran with Justin Malbon provide an account of the rise of television formats, which might be considered holding patterns that assemble what Raymond Williams calls flow and segmentation; a format is a flowing set of segments.

14. Rodowick, *Virtual Life of Film*, 26, emphasis his.

15. See "ODYSSEY tai PONG," in Uemura, Hosoi, and Nakamura, *Famicon to sono jidai*, 27–33.

16. See "Kasetto shiki bideo gēmu bijinesu," in Uemura, Hosoi, and Nakamura, *Famicon to sono jidai*, 45–46.

17. "Home PONG gēmu to omocha shijō," in Uemura, Hosoi, and Nakamura, *Famicon to sono jidai*, 69–70.

18. "Tasha kaihatsu gēmu sofuto no tōjō," in Uemura, Hosoi, and Nakamura, *Famicon to sono jidai*, 115–18.

19. Murphy, *How Television Invented New Media*, 27.

20. Triclot, *Philosophie des jeux vidéos*, 159.

21. Cited in Koehler, *Power-Up*, 39.

22. I draw here on Porter Abbott's account in *Cambridge Introduction to Narrative*.

23. "Donkī Kongu no yakuwari," in Uemura, Hosoi, and Nakamura, *Famicon to sono jidai*, 111–14.

24. Bogost and Monfort, *Racing the Beam*, 27–28.

25. Ibid., 28

26. Shiga Nobuo, *Ima, nyū media no jidai*.

27. Ibid., 11; also cited in Watanabe Midori, *Gendai terebi hōsōgaku*, 177.

28. Watanabe Midori, *Gendai terebi hōsōgaku*, 178.

29. Hidaka, *Nihon no hōsō no ayumi*, 261.

30. Shiga Nobuo, "Nyūmedia to eisei to konpyūta to no kanren," in *Shōwa terebi hōsōshi*, 1:316–21.

31. Ibid., 1:317.

32. Masuyama, *Terebi gēmu bunkaron*, 82.

33. Shiga, "Nyūmedia to eisei to konpyūta to no kanren," 1:319.

34. Anthony Ramirez, "The Games Played for Nintendo's Sales," *New York Times*, December 21, 1989, http://www.nytimes.com/.

35. Carla Lazzareschi, "Atari Sues Nintendo, Accuses Rival of Monopolizing Games," *Los Angeles Times*, February 1, 1989, http://articles.latimes.com/.

36. Ibid.

37. Ramirez, "Games Played for Nintendo's Sales."

38. Nakamura, "Media Concentration in Japan," 201. See too Hayashi, "The Dilemmas of Reforming Japan's Broadcasting System."

39. Nippon Television Holdings, "Basic Knowledge about Television in Japan," *Nippon TV Holdings*, May 2006, http://www.ntvhd.co.jp/english/ir/annual/annual/2006-05.pdf.

40. Hirano, "Sliding Back the Screens," 218.

8. Sociality or Something Like It

1. Studies of otaku cultures have so proliferated over the past two decades that it is impossible to cite them all, but the collection edited by Galbraith et al., *Debating Otaku in Contemporary Japan*, provides both a good overview of writing to date and interpretations of key issues.

2. Deleuze, "Postscript on Control Societies," 177.

3. See in particular the end of Lecture 5 in Foucault, *Psychiatric Power*.

4. Williams, "Structures of Feeling."

5. See Abbott, *Cambridge Introduction to Narrative*.

6. Ōtsuka, "World and Variation."

7. In *Otaku: Japan's Database Animals*, Azuma largely addresses the two-tiered structure of database consumption, but in *Gēmu teki riarizumu no tanjō*, he turns to questions of story.

8. See Azuma's monograph on Derrida, *Sonzaiteki, yūbinteki*, as well as Kadobayashi's assessment of Azuma's media theory in "Media Theory."

9. Derrida, "Living On."

10. See, for instance, Yoda's account in "Girlscape."

11. See Ōtsuka, *Media-mikkusu-ka suru Nihon*, and Steinberg's account in "Converging Contents and Platforms."

12. Azuma, "Animalization of Otaku Culture," 187.

13. See, for instance, Azuma, *Ippan ishi nīten zero*.

14. Michael Cowan presents a cogent, informative account of the rise of discourses on nervous stimulation in *Cult of the Will*.

15. I am drawing on Chun, *Nation of a Hundred Million Idiots*, 3; see also 160–65 for a more detailed account.

16. Foucault, *Birth of Biopolitics*, 247.

17. Crawford, *World beyond Your Head*, 9–10.

18. Crawford knowingly draws on a long tradition of concern about nervous stimulation, noting the work of Georg Simmel, for instance. It is worth nothing that a similar argument arises in the context of transportation: in *The Railway Journey* (1986), Wolfgang Schivelbusch evokes the same argument when he describes how the perceptual shock of traveling at speed on trains made travelers withdraw into reading books.

19. Crawford, *World beyond Your Head*, 22–23.

20. Ibid., 27

21. Ibid., 149

22. Ibid., 95–96, 177.

23. Ibid., 253.

24. The reference is to James J. Gibson's theories of the ecology of perception.

25. Crawford, *World beyond Your Head*, 253.

26. Massumi, *Power at the End of the Economy*, 11–12.

27. See Baudrillard, "Personalization or the Smallest Marginal Difference," chapter 6 of *Consumer Society*.

28. For an overview, see Macmillan, "Michel Foucault's Techniques of the Self."

29. Chun, *Nation of a Hundred Million Idiots,* 170 and n25.

30. Avenell, *Making Japanese Citizens,* 81–82.

31. Ibid., 82.

32. Katō, "Kyozō no sekai: terebi to jinrui," in *Media no shūhen,* 259.

33. Ibid., 261.

34. Ibid., 259.

35. See, for instance, Voci, *China on Video.*

36. Katō, "Kyozō no sekai," 266.

37. Ibid., 257.

38. Ibid.

39. Katō, *Communication Policies in Japan,* 50.

40. Foucault, *Foucault Reader,* 213.

41. Excellent introductions to Simondon's thought appear in Combes, *Gilbert Simondon,* and Read, *Politics of Transindividuality.*

42. Simondon, *Du mode d'existence des objets techniques,* 252: "The machine remains in the obscure zones of our civilization, at all social levels."

43. Read, *Politics of Transindividuality,* 106.

44. Bazin, *André Bazin's New Media,* 40.

45. Watanabe Takesato, *Terebi,* 10.

46. See Rodowick, *Virtual Life of Film,* and Rosen, *Change Mummified.*

47. Wells, *Understanding Animation,* 25.

48. See the essays in Dobson and Seaton, *Japanese Popular Culture and Contents Tourism.*

49. See chapter 4 of Part II of Hatakeyama Kenji and Kubo Masakazu, *Pokemon sutōrī,* which discusses the relation of the animated series to the overall series. Their book is the standard reference for the *Pokémon* series, and although this is my first citation of their book, I have drawn on it repeatedly.

50. See, for instance, Okada Toshio's discussion of generations of otaku in *Otakugaku nyūmon,* 55–62.

51. Ibid., 56–57.

52. Ibid., 58–59.

53. Ibid., 60–61.

54. Discussions of the tastes or practices of different generations run the risk of making them appear to be natural. But generations are produced, at once institutionally and discursively, primarily at the intersection of schools (dividing children by age with greater insistence in the postwar era) and marketing (tightening and multiplying consumer niches with demographic statistics).

55. Ani Maitra and Rey Chow provide an example in their account of government database initiatives to track populations in India in "What's 'In'?"

56. See Massumi, *Ontopower*; Povinelli, "Rhetorics of Recognition."

57. Morikawa Kaichirō, *Shuto no tanjō,* 2003.

58. Okada makes this association between *chōnin* culture (townspeople of the Edo period) and otaku culture near the end of his lectures on otaku, in *Otakugaku nyūmon,* 353–54. Azuma offers a scathing critique of this stance vis-à-vis Edo Japan in *Otaku: Japan's Database Animals.*

59. See Massumi, *Semblance and Event,* 166–67.

9. Platformativity and Ontopower

1. Yoshimi, for instance, uses this phrase as the title for the previously cited essay translated into English, "From Street Corner to Living Room."

2. Condry, *Soul of Anime*, 58.

3. In his introduction to a special issue on platforms and power, "Politics, Power, and 'Platformativity,'" in *Culture Machine*, Joss Hands uses the term "platformativity" to refer to political uses of platforms in an era in which Internet infrastructures are increasingly invisible, which allows for media platforms to make, openly and visibly, a diverse range of interventions (2).

4. See Cheah, "Mattering," and Kirby, *Judith Butler*.

5. See Cheah, "Crises of Money."

6. Kristeva's account of abjection thus strives to deconstruct the sovereign authority invested in bodies; *Powers of Horror*, 1982.

7. Nakazawa, *Poketto no naka no yasei*, chapter 4, "Pokemon no tegara," which might be translated as "Masterful feats with Pokémon," to render his central concern.

8. Nakazawa, *Poketto no naka no yasei*.

9. Ivy, "Art of Cute Little Things."

10. Allison, *Millennial Monsters*.

11. Hornborg provides a brilliant account of what is at stake for Marxist critiques of global capitalism in distinguishing fetishism and animism in "Submitting to Objects."

12. See Shaviro's account of Graham Harman, particularly in the Introduction and chapter 2 of *Universe of Things*, 2014.

13. Bao, *Fiery Cinema*, 26.

14. Condry, *Soul of Anime*, 56.

15. Hatakeyama Chōko and Matsuyama Masako, *Monogatari no hōsō keitairon*, 3.

16. Ibid., 86.

17. Azuma, *Otaku: Japan's Database Animals*, 42–48.

18. Lamarre, *Anime Machine*, 150–51, 195–96.

19. Steinberg, *Anime's Media Mix*, 130–32.

20. Lamarre, *Anime Machine*, 201; Condry, *Soul of Anime*, 206.

21. For a more extended account of how animation techniques in anime contribute to stopping on motion and "releasing" the character across media, see Lamarre, *Anime Machine*, chapter 15.

22. Tsugata Nobuyuki adopts this framework in *Nihon animēshon no chikara*.

23. Hagimoto Haruhiko riffs on this analogy brilliantly in chapter 5 of his 1969 book, *Omae wa tada no genzai ni suginai: terebi ni nani ga kanōka*, which Muraki Yoshihiko and Konno Tsutomu edited and expanded in 2008. This also implies a different take on the putative liveness of television.

24. Crawford, *World beyond Your Head*, 22–23.

25. Steinberg, *Anime's Media Mix*, 65–67; see also Steinberg, "Copying Atomu," 2013.

26. Steinberg expands on the problem of closed platforms in the contemporary context in "Converging Contents and Platforms."

27. Masuyama, *Terebi gēmu bunkaron*, 144–46.

28. Itō, Introduction to *Personal, Portable, Pedestrian*, 1.

29. See especially chapter 8 of Donna Haraway, *When Species Meet* (2008).

30. For an account of resource extraction related to cell phones, see Nicole Shukin, *Animal Capital* (2009), chapter 3. For an account of the implications of using cute and exotic animals in mobile phone ad campaigns, see Berland, "Animal and/as Medium."

31. Steinberg addresses the use of cute characters with mobile phones in East Asia, as does Hjorth, "Odours of Mobility."

10. The Family Broadcast Complex

1. Steven Shaviro, "The Connective and Disjunctive Syntheses," *Pinocchio Theory*, July 7, 2008, http://www.shaviro.com/.

2. Steven Shaviro, "The Third (Conjunctive) Synthesis," *Pinocchio Theory*, July 14, 2008, http://www.shaviro.com/.

3. I am expanding on Guattari's initial presentation of the infrastructure complex in *Schizoanalytic Cartographies* in accordance with his subsequent discussions of how the base–superstructure dichotomy returns, scrambled at the point of dissipation of energies, within so-called psychological complexes.

4. Otsuka Eiji, "World and Variation," 105. While Shin-chan's Chokobi also recall the Bikkuriman chocolates of the late 1980s, their model of media mix is like that of Kamen Rider snacks, not the Bikkuriman chocolates, which, as Otsuka points out, were not linked to a prior television series or manga.

5. This incident occurs in the second volume of the manga.

6. This incident occurs in the first *Crayon Shin-chan* movie.

7. Ōtsuka talks about such overlaps between manga and anime in *Mikkī no shoshiki*.

8. In *Aniparo to yaoi*, Nishimura Mari presents the history of *aniparo* or "anime parody" in the context of Japan's largest "amateur" comic market convention, Comiket. These parodies of anime were not parodic in the usual sense but rather sincere and ambitious episodes based on characters from popular anime series or television shows as well as other sources, typically rearticulated around love affairs between young male characters. The importance of television and especially television anime in inspiring such production reconfirms the central role of television and animation in "expanding" media mix to include fan production. Gradually, professionally published manga produced by publishing houses would adopt so-called amateur conventions, which were inflected by anime conventions.

9. Eco, "Does the Audience Have Bad Effects on Television?," 87.

10. Ibid., 94–95.

11. Ibid., 98.

12. Ibid., 99.

13. Ibid., 99.

14. Ibid., 101.

15. Ibid., 99.

11. The Home Theater Complex

1. Libido is not a drive from one point (a subject) to another (an object) but the introduction of a temporal lag (affect) between action and reaction (or crudely, stimulus and response), which temporally establishes a polarization into a subject effect and an object effect.

2. See Manning and Massumi's account of improvisation, on which I draw here, in *Thought in the Act*, 92–95.

3. See, for instance, the case involving a "cursed piano" in volume 7, where the investigation hinges on a tape recorder.

4. Stengers, "Introductory Notes," 183–96.

5. Tokugi, "OVA no jūgo nen," 307.

6. Ibid.

7. See Lamarre, "Scan Lines."

8. Tokugi, "OVA no jūgo nen," 311.

9. Ibid., 310, 314.

12. The Game Play Complex

1. For the sake of ease, I am removing the prefix ".hack//" from titles in the franchise—for instance, *Quarantine* instead of *.hack//Quarantine*.

2. See Lev Manovich, "Understanding Meta-Media," *C-Theory.net*, October 26, 2005, http://www.ctheory.net/, and Massumi's response to it in *Semblance and Event*, 81.

3. Massumi, *Semblance and Event*, 103.

4. RPGFan, "Creator's Talk Interview #4: Daisuke Uchiyama," trans. Chris Winkler and Eve C, *RPGFan*, n.d. http://www.rpgfan.com/.

5. IGNP S2, "E3 2003: .hack Interview," *IGN*, May 16, 2003. http://www.ign.com/.

6. Steinberg, *Anime's Media Mix*, 149–53.

7. Guattari, *Schizoanalytic Cartographies*, 17.

8. Ibid.

9. Dyer-Witheford and de Peuter, *Games of Empire*, xxvi.

10. Aarseth, *Cybertext*.

11. Galloway, *Gaming*, 3.

12. Gonzalo Frasco, "Simulation versus Representation," *Ludology.org*, 2001, http://www.ludology.org/.

13. Dyer-Witheford and de Peuter, *Games of Empire*, xvi.

14. Galloway, *Protocol*.

15. Azuma, *Otaku: Database Animals*.

16. Azuma, *Gēmu teki riarizumu*, 114.

17. See especially his account of *shasei*, where Azuma draws on Ōtsuka's account of "anime–manga-like realism" to draw a distinction between a sort of genuine copying or copying of reality *(genjitsu no shasei)* and a fictional kind of copying or copying of fiction *(kyokō no shasei)*; *Gēmu teki riarizumu*, 54–57.

18. Massumi, *Semblance and Event*, 52.

19. Ibid., 46. Gerow makes a similar point about participation in the context of Japanese television, in "Kind Participation."

13. The Portable Interface Complex

1. Wada-Marciano, "Global and Local Materialities of Anime," 250.

2. Lacan, "Seminar on 'The Purloined Letter,'" in *Écrits*, 6–48. This seminar not only affords the basic diagrams for the imaginary and symbolic but also provides the point of reference for Deleuze and Guattari for their Lacan-inspired machinic reading of the unconscious, although they will transform Lacan's cybernetic bias toward structure and autopoeisis into heterogenic capture.

3. The widely cited text is Joseph Campbell, *The Hero with a Thousand Faces* (1949).

Michael Nitsche provides a succinct overview of the monomyth in *Video Game Spaces,* 60–65. For a fine account of both Campbell's and Jung's engagement with fascism, see Ellwood, *Politics of Myth.* I am indebted to Ellwood's account in my delineation of the risks of the monomyth this chapter.

4. Foucault, "Of Other Spaces," 24.

5. Ibid.

6. Fans have tracked down the images used to create Yaso-Inaba, whose train station and principal intersections appear to be based on Ishiwa onsen, a small town with hot springs to the north of Mount Fuji.

7. Mladen Dolar provides the best overview of Žižek's account of the acoustic master in *A Voice and Nothing More.* Because I have opted to eliminate from this study a fuller discussion of Žižek's and Dolar's transformation of Michel Chion's account of acousmatic being, I will allow Merleau-Ponty's and Whitney's evocation of the mother's smile as a point of departure (instead of the paternal voice) to stand in for that discussion. Also, in the Conclusion, I introduce the signaletic being, which is intended to evoke an affective problematic deeper than either the mother's smile or the father's voice, which is precisely what I believe is at stake in *Persona 4*: the interval between immediacy and affect or affective temporality and prolongation.

8. Cheah, "Crises of Money," 193.

9. Ibid., 194.

10. Whitney, "Dependency Relations," 556.

11. Ibid., 565.

12. Ibid., 557.

13. Ibid., 560.

14. Ibid., 563, 560.

15. Lazzarato, "From Capital-Labour to Capital-Life," 95.

16. Whitney, "Dependency Relations," 570.

17. See Bakhtin, "Epic and Novel."

18. See Ōtsuka, "World and Variation."

19. Lamarre, *Anime Machine,* 120–21.

20. Merleau-Ponty, *Phenomenology of Perception,* 154.

21. Whitney, "Affects, Images,"190, emphasis hers. For the sake of readability, I have eliminated the page numbers that Whitney provides for the quotations within this passage, which derive from Merleau-Ponty, *Phenomenology of Perception,* 116, 117, 120, and 145–46.

22. Whitney, "Affects, Images," 193.

23. Ibid., 195; Merleau-Ponty, *Phenomenology of Perception,* 118–19.

24. Merleau-Ponty, *Phenomenology of Perception,* 154.

25. Lazzarato, "From Capital-Labour to Capital-Life," 191.

26. Whitney, "Affects, Images," 206.

27. I am indebted to Vicki Kirby's reading of Merleau-Ponty in *Quantum Anthropologies.*

Conclusion

1. Pickering, *Mangle of Practice.*

2. Lyotard, *Postmodern Explained,* 75–80.

3. Such is Thorne's objection in "To the Political Ontologists," 105–6.

4. Naveh and Bird-David, "Animism, Conservation and Immediacy," 37.

5. Morrison, "Animism," 39.
6. For a fuller account, see Lamarre, "Animation and Animism."
7. Haraway, "Cyborg Manifesto"; Hayles, "Unfinished Work," 159.
8. Pignarre and Stengers, *Capitalist Sorcery,* 24.
9. Ibid., 49.
10. Ibid., 45.

BIBLIOGRAPHY

Aarseth, Espen J. *Cybertext: Perspectives on Ergodic Literature.* Baltimore, Md.: Johns Hopkins University Press, 1999.

Abbott, H. Porter. *The Cambridge Introduction to Narrative.* Cambridge: Cambridge University Press, 2008.

Acland, Charles R. "The Crack in the Electric Window." *Cinema Journal* 51, no. 2 (2012): 169–73.

Agamben, Giorgio. *State of Exception.* Chicago: University of Chicago Press, 2005.

Allison, Anne. *Millennial Monsters: Japanese Toys and the Global Imagination.* Durham, N.C.: Duke University Press, 2006.

Anderson, Benedict. *Imagined Communities: Reflections on the Origin and Spread of Nationalism.* New York: Verso Books, 2006.

Anderson, Joseph, and Barbara Anderson. "The Myth of Persistence of Vision Revisited." *Journal of Film and Video* 45, no. 1 (1993): 3–12.

Anderson, Joseph, and Barbara Fisher. "The Myth of Persistence of Vision." *Journal of the University Film Association* 30, no. 4 (1978): 3–8.

Andrew, Dudley. *André Bazin.* Rev. ed. Oxford: Oxford University Press, 2013.

———. "Cognitivism: Quests and Questionings." *Iris* 9 (1989): 1–10.

Ang, Ien. *Watching "Dallas": Soap Opera and the Melodramatic Imagination.* New York: Methuen, 1991.

Arima Tetsuo. *Nihon terebi to shīaiei: hakkutsusareta Shōriki fairu* (Japanese television and the CIA: the "Shōriki file" unearthed). Tokyo: Shinchōsha, 2006.

Austin, James H. *Zen and the Brain: Toward an Understanding of Meditation and Consciousness.* Cambridge, Mass.: MIT Press, 1998.

Avenell, Simon. *Making Japanese Citizens: Civil Society and the Mythology of the Shimin in Postwar Japan.* Berkeley: University of California Press, 2010.

Azuma Hiroki. "The Animalization of Otaku Culture." Trans. Yuriko Furuhata and Marc Steinberg. In *Mechademia 2: Circuits of Desire* (2007): 175–87.

Azuma Hiroki. *Gēmu teki riarizumu no tanjō: dōbutsuka suru posutomodan 2* (The birth of gamic realism: animalized postmodern 2). Tokyo: Kōdansha, 2007.

———. *Ippan ishi nīten zero: Rusō, Furoito, Gūguru* (General Will 2.0: Rousseau, Freud, Google). Tokyo: Kōdansha, 2011.

———. *Otaku: Japan's Database Animals.* Minneapolis: University of Minnesota Press, 2009.

———. *Sonzaiteki, yūbinteki: Jakku Derida ni tsuite* (Ontological, postal: on Jacques Derrida). Tokyo: Shinchōsha, 1998.

Bakhtin, Mikhail. "Epic and Novel." Trans. Caryl Emerson and Michael Holquist. In *The Dialogic Imagination: Four Essays by M. M. Bakhtin,* ed. Michael Holquist, 259–422. 1941; repr. Austin: University of Texas Press, 2010.

Bao, Weihong. *Fiery Cinema: The Emergence of an Affective Medium in China, 1915–1945.* Minneapolis: University of Minnesota Press, 2015.

Barad, Karen. *Meeting the Universe Halfway: Quantum Physics and the Entanglement of Matter and Meaning.* Durham, N.C.: Duke University Press, 2007.

Barney, Darrin. *Communication Technology.* Vancouver: UBC Press, 2005.

———. *Prometheus Wired: The Hope for Democracy in the Age of Network Technology.* Chicago: University of Chicago Press, 2000.

Bartholomew, Robert, and Benjamin Radford. *The Martians Have Landed! A History of Media-Driven Panics and Hoaxes.* Jefferson, N.C.: McFarland, 2012.

Baudrillard, Jean. *The Consumer Society: Myths and Structures.* London: Sage, 1998.

Bazin, André. *André Bazin's New Media.* Ed. and trans. Dudley Andrew. Berkeley: University of California Press, 2014.

Beckman, Karen, ed. *Animating Film Theory.* Durham, N.C.: Duke University Press, 2014.

Bellour, Raymond. "Deleuze: The Thinking of the Brain." *Cinema* 1 (2010): 81–94.

———. "La querelle des dispositifs." *Art Press* 262 (1999): 48–52.

Benjamin, Walter. "On Semblance." *Selected Writings.* Vol. 1, *1913–1926.* Cambridge, Mass.: Harvard University Press, 1996.

———. "On the Mimetic Faculty." *Selected Writings.* Vol. 2, *1927–1934.* Cambridge, Mass.: Harvard University Press, 1999.

Bergstrom, Brian. *Young Boys Doing Terrible Things: Fictions of Youth, Crime, and Japan after Shōnen A.* Ph.D. diss., University of Chicago, 2018.

Berland, Jody. "Animal and/as Medium: Symbolic Work in Communicative Regimes." *Global South* 3, no. 1 (2009): 42–65.

Bogost, Ian, and Nick Monfort. *Racing the Beam: The Atari Video Computer System.* Cambridge, Mass.: MIT Press, 2009.

Bordwell, David. *Ozu and the Poetics of Cinema.* Princeton, N.J.: Princeton University Press, 1988.

———. *The Poetics of Cinema.* London: Routledge, 2008.

Brougère, Gilles. "How Much Is a Pokémon Worth? Pokémon in France." In *Pikachu's Global Adventure: The Rise and Fall of Pokémon,* ed. Joseph Jay Tobin, 187–208. Durham, N.C.: Duke University Press, 2004.

Buchan, Suzanne, ed. *Pervasive Animation.* New York: Routledge, 2013.

Buchanan, Ian. *EPZ Deleuze and Guattari's "Anti-Oedipus": A Reader's Guide.* London: Bloomsbury, 2008.

Burns, Lorna, and Birgit Kaiser. "Introduction: Navigating Differential Futures, (Un)making

Colonial Pasts." In *Postcolonial Literatures and Deleuze: Colonial Pasts, Differential Futures*, ed. Lorna Burns and Birgit Kaiser, 1–17. Amsterdam: Springer, 2012.

Campbell, Joseph. *The Hero with a Thousand Faces*. Princeton, N.J.: Princeton University Press, 1949.

Carr, Nicolas. *The Shallows: What the Internet Is Doing to Our Brains*. New York: Norton, 2010.

Cavell, Stanley. "The Fact of Television." *Daedulus* 111, no. 4 (1982): 75–96.

Chalmers, David J. "The Singularity: A Philosophical Analysis." *Journal of Consciousness Studies* 17 (2010): 7–65.

Cheah, Pheng. "Crises of Money." *Positions: East Asia Cultures Critique* 16, no. 1 (2008): 189–219.

———. "Mattering." *Diacritics* 26, no. 1 (1996): 108–39.

Chun, Jayson Makoto. *"A Nation of a Hundred Million Idiots"? A Social History of Japanese Television*. New York: Routledge, 2007.

Chun, Wendy. *Control and Freedom: Power and Paranoia in the Age of Fiber Optics*. Cambridge, Mass.: MIT Press, 2008.

Chung, Hye Jean. "Media Heterotopia and Transnational Filmmaking: Mapping Real and Virtual Worlds." *Cinema Journal* 51, no. 4 (2012): 87–109.

Combes, Muriel. *Gilbert Simondon and the Philosophy of the Transindividual*. Cambridge, Mass.: MIT Press, 2013.

Condry, Ian. *The Soul of Anime: Collaborative Creativity and Japan's Media Success Story*. Durham, N.C.: Duke University Press, 2012.

Connelly, William. *Neuropolitics: Thinking, Culture, Speed*. Minneapolis: University of Minnesota Press, 2002.

Covanis, Athanasios. "Photosensitivity in Idiopathic Generalized Epilepsies." *Epilepsia* 9 (2005): 67–72.

Cowan, Michael. *Cult of the Will: Nervousness and German Modernity*. University Park: Pennsylvania University Press, 2008.

Crawford, Michael. *The World beyond Your Head: Becoming Individual in an Age of Distraction*. New York: Farrar, Straus and Giroux, 2015.

Crumley, Carole L. 2005. "Remember How to Organize: Heterarchy across Disciplines." In *Nonlinear Models for Archaeology and Anthropology*, ed. Christopher S. Beekman and William S. Baden, 35–50. Aldershot, U.K.: Ashgate Press, 2005.

Cubbit, Sean. *The Cinema Effect*. Cambridge, Mass.: MIT Press, 2004.

Cytowic, Richard. *The Man Who Tasted Shapes: A Bizarre Medical Mystery Offers Revolutionary Insights in Reasoning, Emotion, and Consciousness*. New York: Putman, 1993.

———. *Synesthesia: A Union of the Senses*. Cambridge, Mass.: MIT Press, 2002.

Damasio, Antonio. *Self Comes to Mind: Constructing the Conscious Brain*. New York: Random House Vintage Books, 2010.

Debaise, Didier, ed. *La philosophie des possessions*. Paris: Presses du Réel, 2011.

Deleuze, Gilles. "The Brain Is the Screen: An Interview with Gilles Deleuze." Trans. Marie Therese Guirgis. In *The Brain Is the Screen: Deleuze and the Philosophy of Cinema*, ed. Gregory Flaxman, 365–73. Minneapolis: University of Minnesota Press, 2000.

———. *Cinema 1: The Movement-Image*. Trans. Hugh Tomlinson and Barbara Habberjam. Minneapolis: University of Minnesota Press, 1986.

———. *Cinema 2: The Time-Image*. Trans. Hugh Tomlinson and Robert Galeta. Minneapolis: University of Minnesota Press, 1989.

———. *Difference and Repetition*. New York: Columbia University Press, 1994.

———. *Francis Bacon: The Logic of Sensation*. Trans. Daniel W. Smith. Minneapolis: University of Minnesota Press, 2003.

———. *The Logic of Sense*. Trans. Mark Lester with Charles Stivale. New York: Columbia University Press, 1990.

———. "Postscript on Control Societies." In *Negotiations: 1972–1990*, 177–82, trans. Martin Joughin. New York: Columbia University Press, 1997.

Deleuze, Gilles, and Félix Guattari. *Anti-Oedipus: Capitalism and Schizophrenia*. Minneapolis: University of Minnesota Press, 1983.

Derrida, Jacques. "Living On." In *Deconstruction and Criticism*, ed. Harold Bloom et al., 62–142. New York: Continuum, 1979.

Desmurget, Michel. *TV Lobotomie: La vérité scientifique sur les effects de la télévision*. Paris: Max Milo Éditions, 2011.

Dobson, Hugo. "Mister Sparkle Meets the Yakuza: Depictions of Japan in *The Simpsons*." *Journal of Popular Culture* 39, no. 1 (2006): 44–68.

Dobson, Hugo, and Philip Seaton, eds. *Japanese Popular Culture and Contents Tourism*. Special issue, *Japan Forum* 27, no. 1 (2015).

Dolar, Mladen. *A Voice and Nothing More*. Cambridge, Mass.: MIT Press, 2006.

D'Orangeville, Akané. *"Shonen," le monstre invisible*. M.A. thesis, University of Montreal, 2010.

Dyer-Witheford, Nick, and Greig de Peuter. *Games of Empire: Global Capitalism and Video Games*. Minneapolis: University of Minnesota Press, 2009.

Eco, Umberto. "Does the Audience Have Bad Effects on Television?" In *Apocalypse Postponed*, trans. and ed. Robert Lumley, 87–102. London: British Film Institute, 1994.

Eisenstein, Sergei. *Eisenstein on Disney*. Kolkata, India: Seagull Books, 1986.

Ellwood, Robert. *The Politics of Myth: A Study of CG Jung, Mircea Eliade, and Joseph Campbell*. Albany, N.Y.: SUNY Press, 1999.

Elsaesser, Thomas, and Malte Hagener. *Film Theory: An Introduction through the Senses*. New York: Routledge, 2010.

Evans, William. "Reality Programming: Evolutionary Models of Film and Television Viewership." In *Moving Image Theory: Ecological Considerations*, ed. Joseph D. Anderson and Barbara Fisher Anderson, 200–214. Carbondale: Southern Illinois University Press, 2005.

Fan, Victor. *Cinema Approaching Reality: Locating Chinese Film Theory*. Minneapolis: University of Minnesota Press, 2015.

Feuer, Jane. "The Concept of Live Television: Ontology as Ideology." In *Regarding Television*, ed. E. Ann Kaplan, 12–22. Frederick, Md.: University Publications of America, 1983.

Fisher, Robert S., Graham Harding, Giuseppe Erba, Gregory L., Barkley, and Arnold J. Wilkins. "Photic- and Pattern-Induced Seizures: A Review for the Epilepsy Foundation of America Working Group." *Epilepsia* 46, no. 9 (2005): 1426–41.

Fiske, John. *Television Culture*. New York: Methuen, 1987.

Foucault, Michel. *The Birth of Biopolitics: Lectures at the Collège de France, 1978–79*. Trans. Graham Burchell. New York: Palgrave Macmillan, 2008.

———. "The Confession of the Flesh." In *Power/Knowledge: Selected Interviews and Other Writings, 1972–1977*, ed. and trans. Colin Gordon, 194–228. New York: Pantheon Books, 1980.

———. *The Foucault Reader*. Ed. Paul Rabinow. New York: Pantheon, 1982.

———. *The Hermeneutics of the Subject: Lectures at the Collège de France, 1981–82*. Trans. Graham Burchell. New York: Palgrave Macmillan, 2005.

———. "Of Other Spaces: Utopias and Heterotopias." Trans. Jay Miskowiec. *Diacritics* 16, no. 1 (1986): 22–27.

———. *Psychiatric Power: Lectures at the Collège de France, 1973–1974.* Trans. Graham Burchell. New York: Macmillan, 2008.

———. "The Subject and Power." In *Power: Essential Works of Michel Foucault, 1954–1984, Volume 3*, ed. James B. Faubion, 326–48. New York: New Press, 2000.

———. "Truth and Power." In *Power/Knowledge: Selected Interviews and Other Writings, 1972–1977*, ed. and trans. Colin Gordon, 109–33. New York: Pantheon Books, 1980.

Friedberg, Anne. "The End of Cinema: Multimedia and Technological Change." In *Reinventing Cinema Studies*, ed. Christine Gledhill and Linda Williams, 438–52. London: Arnold, 2000.

Fuller, Matthew. *Media Ecologies: Materialist Energies in Art and Technoculture.* Cambridge, Mass.: MIT Press, 2005.

Funatsuka Makoto, Fujita Michinari, Shirakawa Seigo, Oguni Hirokazu, and Ōsawa Makiko. "Analysis of Photo-Pattern Sensitivity in Patients with Pokemon-Related Symptoms." *Pediatric Neurology* 28, no. 1 (2003): 28–36.

Furu Takeo. "Research on 'Television and the Child' in Japan." *Studies in Broadcasting*, no. 3, 51–81. Tokyo: Nippon Hōsō Kyōkai.

Furuhata, Yuriko. *Cinema of Actuality: Japanese Avant-Garde Filmmaking in the Season of Image Politics.* Durham, N.C.: Duke University Press, 2013.

———. "Multimedia Environments and Security Operations: Expo '70 as a Laboratory of Governance." *Grey Room* 54 (2014): 56–79.

Furushō, Jun'ichi, Suzuki Masakazu, Tazaki Izumi, Satō Hiroyuki, Yamaguchi Katsuhiko, Īkura Yōji, Kumagai Kōmei, Kubagawa Tetsuji, and Hara Tsunekatsu. "Comparison Survey of Seizures and Other Symptoms of Pokemon Phenomenon." *Pediatric Neurology* 27, no. 5 (2002): 350–55.

Furushō, Jun'ichi, Yamaguchi Katsuhiko, Īkura Yōji, Kogure Tatsuya, Suzuki Masakazu, Konishi Sachiko, Shimizu Gorō, Nakayama Yasuko, Itō Keiko, Sakamoto Yasutoshi, Ishikawa Atsushi, Ezaki Sōsuke, Nawata Jun, and Kumagai Kōmei. "Patient Background of the *Pokemon* Phenomenon: Questionnaire Studies in Multiple Pediatric Clinics." *Acta Paediatrica Japonica* 40 (1998): 550–54.

Galbraith, Patrick W., Thiam Huat Kam, Björn-Ole Kamin, and Christopher Gerteis, eds. *Debating Otaku in Contemporary Japan: Historical Perspectives and New Horizons.* London: Bloomsbury, 2015.

Galloway, Alexander. *Gaming: Essays on Algorithmic Culture.* Minneapolis: University of Minnesota Press, 2006.

———. *Protocol: How Control Exists after Decentralization.* Cambridge, Mass.: MIT Press, 2004.

Gaudreault, André, and Martin Lefebvre, eds. *Cinema and Technology.* Special issue, *Semiotic Inquiry* 31, no. 1–3 (2011).

Gerow, Aaron. "Kind Participation: Postmodern Consumption and Capital with Japan's Telop TV." In *Television, Japan, and Globalization,* ed. Yoshimoto Mitsuhiro, Eva Tsai, and Jung-Bong Choi, 117–49. Ann Arbor: Center for Japanese Studies, University of Michigan Press, 2010.

Gilder, George. *Life after Television: The Coming Transformation of Media and the American Life.* New York: Norton, 1994.

Gombrich, Ernst. *Aby Warburg: An Intellectual Biography*. Chicago: Chicago University Press, 1986.

Good, I. J. "Speculations Concerning the Ultraintelligent Machine." In *Advances in Computers*, ed. F. Alt and M. Ruminoff, 6:31–88. London: Academic Press, 1965.

Guattari, Félix. *Schizoanalytic Cartographies*. Trans. Andrew Goffey. London: Bloomsbury, 2013.

Haber, Ralph Norman, and Maurice Hershenson. *The Psychology of Visual Perception*. 2nd ed. London: Holt, Rinehart and Winston, 1980.

Haddon, Mark. *The Curious Incident of the Dog in the Night-Time*. Toronto: Anchor Canada, 2004.

Hagimoto Haruhiko, Muraki Yoshihiko, and Konno Tsutomu. *Omae wa tada no genzai ni suginai: terebi ni nani ga kanōka* (You're nothing but in the present: what is made possible by television). 1969; repr., Tokyo: Asahi Shinbun Shuppan, 2008.

Hands, Joss. "Politics, Power, and 'Platformativity.'" *Culture Machine* 14 (2013). https://www.culturemachine.net/.

Hansen, Miriam. "Of Mice and Ducks: Benjamin and Adorno on Disney." *South Atlantic Quarterly* 92, no. 1 (1993): 27–61.

Haraway, Donna. "A Cyborg Manifesto: Science, Technology and Socialist-Feminism in the Late Twentieth Century." In *Simians, Cyborgs, and Women: The Reinvention of Nature*, 149–81. New York: Routledge, 1991.

———. *When Species Meet*. Minneapolis: University of Minnesota Press, 2008.

Harding, Graham F. A. "TV Can Be Bad for Your Health." *Nature Medicine* 4, no. 3 (1998): 265–67.

Harding, Graham F. A., and P. A. Harding. "Televised Material and Photosensitive Epilepsy." *Epilepsia* 40 (1999, suppl. 415-69): 65–69.

Harding, Graham F. A., and Peter M. Jeavons. *Photosensitive Epilepsy*. London: MacKeith Press, 1994.

Harding, Graham F. A., and Takahashi Takeo. "Regulations: What Next?" *Epilepsia* 45 (2004, suppl. 1): 46–48.

Harman, Graham. *Tool-Being: Heidegger and the Metaphysics of Objects*. Chicago, Ill.: Open Court Publishing, 2002.

Hatakeyama Chōko and Matsuyama Masako. *Monogatari no hōsō keitairon: shikakerareta animēshon bangumi* (On the morphology of broadcast narrative: how animation programs are laid out). Kyōto: Sekai Shisōsha, 2006.

Hatakeyama Kenji and Kubo Masakazu. *Pokemon sutōrī* (Pokémon story). Tokyo: Nikkei BP, 2000.

Hayashi Kaori. "The Dilemmas of Reforming Japan's Broadcasting System: Ambivalent Implications of Its Liberalization." In *Television and Public Policy: Change and Continuity in an Era of Global Liberalization*, ed. David Ward, 131–48. New York: Lawrence Erlbaum Associates, 2008.

Hayles, N. Katherine. "Unfinished Work: From Cyborg to Cognisphere." *Theory, Culture, Society* 23, no. 7–8 (2006): 159–66.

Heinze, Ulrich. "Radio and Television Consumption in Japan: A Trilateral Intercultural Comparison with the U.K. and Germany." *Electronic Journal of Contemporary Japanese Studies* 11, no. 2 (2011) http://www.japanesestudies.org.uk/.

Hidaka Ichirō. *Nihon no hōsō no ayumi* (The advance of Japanese broadcasting). Tokyo: Ningen no Kagakusha, 1991.

Higuchi Toru and Marvin Troutt. *Life Cycle Management in Supply Chains: Identifying Innovations through the Case of the VCR*. Hershey, N.Y.: IGI Publishing, 2008.

Hilderbrand, Lucas. *Inherent Vice: Bootleg Histories of Videotape and Copyright*. Durham, N.C.: Duke University Press, 2009.

Hirahara, Tatsuya, and Murase Hiroshi. "Human Information Science: Opening Up Communication Possibilities for the Future." *NTT Technical Review* 1, no. 2 (2003): 10–12.

Hirano, Chalinee. "Sliding Back the Screens: Civil Society and the Erosion of Bureaucratic Control of Television in Japan." In *Television, Regulation, and Civil Society in Japan*, ed. Philip Kitley, 205–25. London: Routledge, 2003.

Hjorth, Larissa. "Odours of Mobility: Mobile Phones and Japanese Cute Culture in the Asia-Pacific." *Journal of Intercultural Studies* 26, no. 1–2 (2005): 39–55.

Hornborg, Alf. "Submitting to Objects: Animism, Fetishism, and the Cultural Foundations of Capitalism." In *The Handbook of Contemporary Animism*, ed. Graham Harvey, 244–59. London: Routledge, 2014.

Huhtamo, Erkki. *Illusions in Motion: Media Archaeology of the Moving Panorama and Related Spectacles*. Cambridge, Mass.: MIT Press, 2013.

Hurley, Adrienne. *Revolutionary Suicide and Other Desperate Measures: Narratives of Youth and Violence in Japan and the United States*. Durham, N.C.: Duke University Press, 2012.

Ichida Yoshihiko and Yann Moulier Boutang. "Against the Closure of the World: What Is at Stake in the New 'Great Transformation.'" Trans. Christine Lamarre. In *Translation, Biopolitics, Colonial Difference*, ed. Naoki Sakai and Jon Solomon, 235–50. Hong Kong: University of Hong Kong Press, 2006.

Ikeda Nobuo, Nishi Kazuhiko, Hayashi Kōichirō, Yamada Hajime, and Hara Junjirō. *Netto ga terebi o nomikomu hi = Sinking of TV* (The day the Net swallowed television). Tokyo: Yōsensha, 2006.

Illes, Judy, Colin Blakemore, Mats G. Hansson, Takao K. Hensch, Alan Leshner, Gladys Maestre, Pierre Magistretti, Rémi Quirion, and Piergiorgio Strata. "International Perspectives on Engaging the Public in Neuroethics." *Neuroscience* 6 (2005): 977–82.

Imamura Taihei. "For the Sake of Japanese Cartoons." In *Mechademia 9: Origins* (2014): 107–24.

———. "A Theory of the Animated Sound Film." *Review of Japanese Culture and Society* 22 (2010): 44–51.

Ishida Shigenobu, Yamashita Yūshirō, Matsuishi Toyojirō, Ōshima Masachika, Ōshima Hiroharu, Katō Hirohisa, and Maeda Hisao. "Photosensitive Seizures Provoked While Viewing *Pocket Monster*, a Made-for-Television Animation Program in Japan." *Epilepsia* 39, no. 12 (1998): 1340–44.

Ito, Mizuko. "Introduction." In *Personal, Portable, Pedestrian: Mobile Phones in Japanese Life*, ed. Mizuko Ito, Daisuke Okabe, and Misa Matsuda, 1–16. Cambridge, Mass.: MIT Press, 2005.

Ivy, Marilyn. "The Art of Cute Little Things: Nara Yoshitomo's Parapolitics." *Mechademia 5: Fanthropologies* (2010): 3–29.

———. "In/Comparable Horrors: Total War and the Japanese Thing." *Boundary 2* 32, no. 2 (2005): 137–49.

James, William. *Essays in Radical Empiricism*. 1912; repr., Mineola, N.Y.: Dover, 2003.

Jenkins, Eric S. *Special Affects: Cinema, Animation and the Translation of Consumer Culture*. Edinburgh: Edinburgh University Press, 2014.

Kadobayashi Takeshi. "The Media Theory and Strategy of Azuma Hiroki." In *Media Theory in Japan,* ed. Marc Steinberg and Alex Zahlten, 80–100. Durham, N.C.: Duke University Press, 2017.

Kapur, Jyotsna. "Out of Control: Television and the Transformation of Childhood in Late Capitalism." In *Kid's Media Culture,* ed. Marsha Kinder, 122–36. Durham, N.C.: Duke University Press, 1999.

Kasteleijn-Nolst Trenité, Dorothée G. A. "Photosensitivity, Visually Sensitive Seizures and Epilepsies." *Epilepsy Research* 70S (2006): S269–79.

Kasteleijn-Nolst Trenité, Dorothée G. A., Gerrit Van Der Beld, Ingrid Heynderickx, and Paul Groen. "Visual Stimuli in Daily Life." *Epilepsia* 45 (2004): 2–6.

Kasza, Gregory J. *The State and the Mass Media in Japan, 1918–1945.* Berkeley: University of California Press, 1988.

Katō Hidetoshi. *Communication Policies in Japan.* Paris: Unesco, 1978.

———. "Japan." In *Television: An International History,* ed. Anthony Smith with Richard Paterson, 169–81. Oxford: Oxford University Press, 1998.

———. *Media no shūhen* (In the environs of media). Tokyo: Bungei Shunjū, 1976.

Kelty, Chris. *Two Bits: The Cultural Significance of Software.* Durham, N.C.: Duke University Press, 2008.

Kessler, Frank. "Recadrages: pour une pragmatique historique du dispositif cinématographique." In *Cinema and Technology,* ed. André Gaudreault and Martin Lefebvre. Special issue, *Semiotic Inquiry* 31, no. 1–3 (2011): 15–32.

Kirby, Vicki. *Judith Butler: Live Theory.* New York: Continuum, 2006.

———. *Quantum Anthropologies: Life at Large.* Durham, N.C.: Duke University Press, 2011.

Kittler, Friedrich. *Discourse Networks.* Stanford, Calif.: Stanford University Press, 1990.

Kobayashi Niina, Masaka Hiroki, Hoshino-Saitō Satoko, and Yamazaki Katsuo. "Jihatsusei shunmoku ni oyobosu ongaku eizō no kanshō kōka" (The effect of appreciating music videos on spontaneous eyeblink). *Japanese Journal for Physiological Psychology and Psychophysiology* 17, no. 3 (1999): 183–91.

Koehler, Chris. *Power-Up: How Japanese Video Games Gave the World an Extra Life.* Indianapolis, Ind.: BradyGames, 2005.

Koizumi Hideaki. "Brain-Science and Education in Japan." In *Neuroscience in Education: The Good, the Bad, and the Ugly,* ed. Sergio Della Sala and Mike Anderson, 1–20. Oxford: Oxford University Press, 2012.

———. "The Concept of 'Developing the Brain': A New Natural Science for Learning and Education." *Brain and Development* 26 (2004): 434–41.

Kristeva, Julia. *Powers of Horror: An Essay on Abjection.* Trans. Leon S. Roudiez. New York: Columbia University Press, 1982.

Kubey, Robert, and Mihaly Csikszentmihaly. "Television Addiction Is No Metaphor." *Scientific American,* February 2002, 74–80.

Lacan, Jacques. *Écrits.* Trans. Bruce Fink. New York: Norton, 1977.

Lamarre, Thomas. "Animation and Animism." In *Animals and Animality in the Literary Field,* ed. Bruce Boehrer, Molly Hand, and Brian Massumi. Durham, N.C.: Duke University Press, in press.

———. *The Anime Machine: A Media Theory of Animation.* Minneapolis: University of Minnesota Press, 2009.

———. "The First Time as Farce: Digital Animation and the Repetition of Cinema." In *Cin-*

ema Anime: Critical Engagements with Japanese Animation, ed. Steven T. Brown, 161–88. New York: Palgrave Macmillan, 2006.

———. "Regional TV: Affective Media Geographies." *Asiascape: Digital Asia* 2 (2015): 93–126.

———. "Scan Lines: How Cyborgs Feel." In *Simultaneous Worlds: Global Science Fiction Cinema*, ed. Jennifer Feeley and Sarah Ann Welles, 3–28. Minneapolis: University of Minnesota Press, 2015.

Lang, Annie. "The Limited Capacity Model of Mediated Message Processing." *Journal of Communication* 50, no. 1 (2000): 46–70.

Lapoujade, David. *William James, Empiricisme et pragmatisme*. Paris: Presses Universitaires de France, 1997.

Larkin, Brian. *Signal and Noise: Media, Infrastructure, and Urban Culture in Nigeria*. Durham, N.C.: Duke University Press, 2008.

Latour, Bruno. *An Inquiry into Modes of Existence*. Cambridge, Mass.: Harvard University Press, 2013.

———. *We Have Never Been Modern*. Trans. Catherine Porter. Cambridge, Mass.: Harvard University Press, 1993.

———. "Whose Cosmos, Which Cosmopolitics? Comments on the Peace Terms of Ulrich Beck." *Common Knowledge* 10, no. 3 (2004): 450–62.

Latour, Bruno, and Steve Woolgar. *Laboratory Life: The Construction of Scientific Facts*. 2nd ed. Princeton, N.J.: Princeton University Press, 1986.

Lazzarato, Maurizio. "From Capital-Labour to Capital-Life." *Ephemera* 4, no. 3 (2004): 187–208.

———. *The Making of the Indebted Man: An Essay on the Neoliberal Condition*. Trans. Joshua David Jordan. Los Angeles: Semiotext(e), 2012.

Lefebvre, Henri. *The Production of Space*. Trans. Donald Nicholson-Smith. Oxford: Blackwell, 1991.

Leverette, Marc, Brian L. Ott, and Cara Louise Buckley, eds. *It's Not TV: Watching HBO in the Post-Television Era*. New York: Routledge, 2008.

Lotz, Amanda. *The Television Will Be Revolutionized*. New York: New York University, 2007.

MacKenzie, Adrian. *Wirelessness: Radical Empiricism in Network Cultures*. Cambridge, Mass.: MIT Press, 2010.

Macmillan, Alexandre. "Michel Foucault's Techniques of the Self and the Christian Politics of Obediance." *Theory, Culture, and Society* 28, no. 4 (2011): 3–25.

Maitra, Ani, and Rey Chow. "What's 'In'? Disaggregating Asia through New Media Actants." In *Routledge Handbook of New Media in Asia*, ed. Larrisa Hjorth and Olivia Khoo, 17–27. London: Routledge, 2015.

Mander, Jerry. *Four Arguments for the Elimination of Television*. New York: William Morrow, 1978.

Mann, Denise. "When Television and New Media Work Worlds Collide." In *Wired TV: Laboring Over an Interactive Future*, ed. Denise Mann, 1–31. New Brunswick, N.J.: Rutgers University Press, 2014.

———, ed. *Wired TV: Laboring Over an Interactive Future*. New Brunswick, N.J.: Rutgers University Press, 2014.

Manning, Erin. *Relationscapes: Movement, Art, Philosophy*. Cambridge, Mass.: MIT Press, 2009.

Manning, Erin, and Brian Massumi. *Thought in the Act: Passages in the Ecology of Experience*. Minneapolis: University of Minnesota Press, 2014.

Manovich, Lev. *The Language of New Media*. Cambridge, Mass.: MIT Press, 2001.

Marotti, William. *Money, Trains, and Guillotines: Art and Revolution in 1960s Japan*. Durham, N.C.: Duke University Press, 2013.

Marx, Karl. *Capital: Volume 1*. Trans. Ben Fowkes. London: Penguin, 1976.

———. *Grundrisse*. Trans. Martin Nicolaus. London: Penguin, 1993.

Marx, Karl, and Friedrich Engels. "The Manifesto of the Communist Party." In *The Marx–Engels Reader*, 2nd ed., ed. Robert C. Tucker, 469–500. 1847–48; repr., New York: Norton, 1978.

Massumi, Brian. *Ontopower: War, Powers, and the State of Perception*. Durham, N.C.: Duke University Press, 2015.

———. *Parables for the Virtual: Movement, Affect, Sensation*. Durham, N.C.: Duke University Press, 2002.

———. *The Power at the End of the Economy*. Durham, N.C.: Duke University Press, 2015.

———. *Semblance and Event: Activist Philosophy and the Occurent Arts*. Cambridge, Mass.: MIT Press, 2011.

Masuyama Hiroshi. *Terebi gēmu bunkaron: intarakutibu media no yukue* (A cultural theory of television games: where interactive media is going). Tokyo: Kōdansha, 2001.

McCarthy, Anna. *Ambient Television: Visual Culture and Public Space*. Durham, N.C.: Duke University Press, 2001.

McNeil, Daniel. *The Face: A Natural History*. Boston: Little, Brown, 1998.

Merleau-Ponty, Maurice. *Phenomenology of Perception*. 1945; repr., New York: Routledge, 1965.

Miller, Edward D. *Emergency Broadcasting and 1930s Radio*. Philadelphia, Pa.: Temple University Press, 2003.

Missika, Jean-Louis. *La fin de la télévision*. Paris: Seuil, 2006.

Monnet, Livia. "Anatomy of Permutational Desire, Part II: Bellmer's Dolls and Oshii's Gynoids." *Mechademia 6: User Enhancement* (2011): 153–69.

Moran, Albert, and Justin Malbon. *Understanding the Global TV Format*. Bristol, U.K.: Intellect Books, 2006.

Mori Akio. *Gēmu nō no kyōfu* (The horror of the Game Brain). Tokyo: Nippon Hōsō Shuppan Kyōkai, 2002.

Morikawa Kaichirō. *Shuto no tanjō: moeru toshi Akihabara* (Birth of a personapolis: Akihabara, a city fanning the flames of fandom). Tokyo: Gentōsha, 2003.

Morley, David. *Family Television: Cultural Power and Domestic Leisure*. 1986; repr., London: Routledge, 2005.

Morley, David, and Kevin Robins. *Spaces of Identity: Global Media, Electronic Landscapes, and Cultural Boundaries*. London: Routledge, 1995.

Morrison, Kenneth M. "Animism and a Proposal for a Post-Cartesian Anthropology." In *The Handbook of Contemporary Animism*, ed. Graham Harvey, 38–52. London: Routledge, 2014.

Morris-Suzuki, Tessa. *Beyond Computopia: Information, Automation, and Democracy in Japan*. New York: Kegan Paul International, 1988.

Morton, Timothy. *Hyperobjects: Philosophy and Ecology after the End of the World*. Minneapolis: University of Minnesota Press, 2013.

Mulvey, Laura. *Death 24× a Second: Stillness and the Moving Image*. London: Reaktion, 2006.

Munster, Anna. *An Aesthesia of Networks: Conjunctive Experience in Art and Technology*. Cambridge, Mass.: MIT Press, 2013.

Murphy, Sheila C. *How Television Invented New Media*. New Brunswick, N.J.: Rutgers University Press, 2011.

Nakamura Kiyoshi. "Media Concentration in Japan: The Measurement Issues." *Waseda Global Forum* 7 (2010): 193–216.

Nakazawa Shin'ichi. *Poketto no naka no yasei: Ima koko ni ikiru kodomo* (The wilds in your pocket: children living in the here and now). Tokyo: Shinchōsha, 2004.

Naveh, Danny, and Nurit Bird-David. "Animism, Conservation and Immediacy." In *The Handbook of Contemporary Animism*, ed. Graham Harvey, 27–37. London: Routledge, 2014.

Nichols, Bill, and Susan J. Lederman. "Flicker and Motion in Film." In *The Cinematic Apparatus*, ed. Teresa de Lauretis and Stephen Heath, 96–105. New York: St Martin's Press, 1980.

Nippon Hōsō Kyōkai Hōsō Bunka Kenkyūjo. *Terebi shichō no 50-nen* (Fifty years of television audiences). Tokyo: NHK Shuppan, 2003.

———. *The History of Broadcasting in Japan*. Tokyo: Nippon Hōsō Kyōkai, 1967.

Nishimura Mari. *Aniparo to yaoi*. Tokyo: Ōta shuppan, 2002.

Nitsche, Michael. *Video Game Spaces: Image, Play, and Structure in 3D Worlds*. Cambridge, Mass.: MIT Press, 2008.

Okada Toshio. *Otakugaku nyūmon: tōdai "otaku bunkaron zemi" kōshiki tekisuto* (Introduction to otakuology: the official text of the Seminar on Otaku Culture at the University of Tokyo). Tokyo: Shinchōsha, 1996.

Okamura, Akihisa, Watanabe Kazuyoshi, Negoro Tamiko, Ishikawa Tatsuya, Ishiguro Yoshiko, Takenaka Junko, and Takada Hiroyuki. "Epilepsies after *Pocket Monster* Seizures." *Epilepsia* 46, no. 6 (2005): 980–82.

Okumura Kenta. *Soredemo terebi wa shinanai: Eizō seisaku no genba de ikiru* (Television nevertheless does not die: living on the actual site of image production). Tokyo: Gijutsuhyōronsha, 2013.

Oswald, Katherine, and Jeremy Packer. "Flow and Mobile Media: Broadcast Fixity to Digital Fluidity." In *Communication Matters: Materialist Approaches to Media, Mobility and Networks*, ed. Jeremy Packer and Stephen B. Crofts Wiley, 276–87. London: Routledge, 2013.

Ōtsuka Eiji. *Media-mikkusu-ka suru Nihon* (Media-mixed Japan). Tokyo: Īsuto puresu, 2014.

———. *Mikkī no shoshiki: sengo manga no senjika kigen* (The Mickey Mouse format: the wartime origins of postwar manga). Tokyo: Kadokawa shoten, 2013.

———. *Teihon Monogatari shōhiron*. Tokyo: Kadokawa, 2001.

———. "World and Variation: The Reproduction and Consumption of Narrative." In *Mechademia 5: Fanthropologies* (2010): 99–116.

Papapetros, Spyros. "In/Animate Victims: Cultural Reactions to Animation." *Communications and Critical/Cultural Studies* 9, no. 3 (2012): 300–306.

———. *On the Animation of the Inorganic: Art, Architecture, and the Extension of Life*. Chicago: University of Chicago Press, 2012.

Parain, Dominique, and Axel Lebas. "Le point sur les écrans de télévision et les séquences vidéo des dessins animés." *Épilepsies* 20, no. 3 (2008): 175–78.

Parra, J., S. N. Kalitzin, H. Stroink, E. Dekker, C. de Wit, and F. H. Lopes da Silva. "Removal of Epileptogenic Sequences from Video Material: The Role of Color." *Neurology* 64 (2005): 787–91.

Peters, John Durham. *The Marvelous Clouds: Toward a Philosophy of Elemental Media*. Chicago: University of Chicago Press, 2015.

————. *Speaking into the Air: A History of the Idea of Communication.* Chicago: University of Chicago Press, 2012.

Pickering, Andrew. *The Mangle of Practice: Time, Agency, and Science.* Chicago: University of Chicago Press, 2010.

Pignarre, Philippe, and Isabelle Stengers. *Capitalist Sorcery: Breaking the Spell.* Ed. and trans. Andrew Goffey. New York: Palgrave Macmillan, 2011.

Pisters, Patricia. *The Neuro-Image: A Deleuzian Film-Philosophy of Digital Screen Culture.* Stanford, Calif.: Stanford University Press, 2012.

Poniewozi, James. "The Post-Television Era Has Begun." *Time,* October 30, 2014.

Povinelli, Elizabeth A. "The Rhetorics of Recognition in Geontopower." *Philosophy and Rhetoric* 48, no. 4 (2015): 428–42.

Radford, Benjamin. "The Pokémon Panic of 1997." *Skeptical Inquirer* 25, no. 3 (2001). http://www.csicop.org/.

Radford, Benjamin, and Robert Bartholomew. "Pokemon Contagion: Photosensitive Epilepsy or Mass Psychogenic Illness?" *Southern Medical Journal* 94, no. 2 (2011): 197–204.

Rancière, Jacques. *The Politics of Aesthetics: The Distribution of the Sensible.* Trans. Gabriel Rockhill. New York: Continuum, 2004.

Read, Jason. *The Micropolitics of Capital: Marx and the Prehistory of the Present.* Albany, N.Y.: SUNY Press, 2003.

————. *The Politics of Transindividuality.* London: Brill, 2015.

Rodowick, David. *Elegy for Theory.* Cambridge, Mass.: Harvard University Press, 2014.

————. *Philosophy's Artful Conversation.* Cambridge, Mass.: Harvard University Press, 2015.

————. *The Virtual Life of Film.* Cambridge, Mass.: Harvard University Press, 2007.

Rosen, Philip. *Change Mummified: Cinema, Historicity, Theory.* Minneapolis: University of Minnesota Press, 2001.

Rotman, Brian. *Becoming Beside Ourselves: The Alphabet, Ghosts, and Distributed Human Being.* Durham, N.C.: Duke University Press, 2008.

Said, Edward. *Orientalism: Western Perceptions of the Orient.* New York: Vintage, 1978.

Sakai, Naoki. "Modernity and Its Critique: The Problem of Universalism and Particularism." In *Postmodernism and Japan,* ed. Masao Miyoshi and H. D. Harootunian, 93–122. Durham, N.C.: Duke University Press, 1989.

Satō Gentei, ed. *Terebitō antena monogatari: "i" no ji hatsueizō kara dejitaru hōsō made* (The story of the television tower antenna: from the first transmission of the kana "i" to digital broadcast). Tokyo: Ribun Shuppan, 2005.

Schivelbusch, Wolfgang. *The Railway Journey: The Industrialization of Time and Space in the 19th Century.* Berkeley: University of California Press, 1986.

Schnabel, Jim. "The Black Box." *Nature,* June 10, 2009, 765–68.

Segawa Kōsuke. *Chi-deji riken: denpazoku kanryō ugomeku terebi jijō* (Digital terrestrial television and special interests: why television is swarming with broadcast-group bureaucracies). Tokyo: Gendai Shokan, 2008.

Seitz, Aaron R., Jose E. Nanez, Steven R. Holloway, and Takeo Watanabe. "Visual Experience Can Substantially Alter Critical Flicker Fusion Thresholds." *Human Psychopharmocology Clinical Experiements* 20 (2005): 55–60.

Selznick, Barbara. *Global Television: Co-producing Culture.* Philadelphia: Temple University Press, 2008.

Sharp, Jasper. "Between Dimensions—3D Computer Generated Animation in Anime." In *Ga-Netchu: The Manga Anime Syndrome*, 120–33. Berlin: Deutsches Filminstitut DIF, 2008.

Shaviro, Steven. *The Universe of Things*. Minneapolis: University of Minnesota Press, 2015.

Shiga Nobuo. *Ima, nyū media no jidai: jōhō kakumei ga shakai o kaeru* (Now is the era of new media: the information revolution is changing society). Tokyo: Asahi Shinbunsha, 1984.

———. *Shōwa terebi hōsōshi* (A history of broadcast television in the Shōwa era). 2 vols. Tokyo: Hayakawa Shobō, 1990.

———. *Terebi bangumi kotohajime: sōseiki no terebi bangumi 25-nenshi* (Television programs in the beginning: a history of the first twenty-five years of television programming). Tokyo: Nippon Hōsō Shuppan Kyōkai, 2008.

Shirakawa Seigo, Funatsuka Makoto, Ōsawa Makiko, Fujita Michinari, and Oguni Hirokazu. "A Study of the Effect of Color Photostimulation from a Cathode-Ray Tube (CRT) Display on Photosensitive Patients: The Effect of Alternating Red–Cyan Flicker Stimulation." *Epilesia* 42, no. 7 (2001): 922–29.

Shukin, Nicole. *Animal Capital: Rendering Life in Biopolitical Times*. Minneapolis: University of Minnesota Press, 2009.

Simondon, Gilbert. *Du mode d'existence des objets techniques*. 1958; repr., Paris: Aubier, 1989.

Smith, Daniel. "The Inverse Side of Structure: Žižek on Deleuze on Lacan." *Criticism* 46, no. 4 (2004): 635–50.

Sobchack, Vivian. *The Address of the Eye: A Phenomenology of Film Experience*. Princeton, N.J.: Princeton University Press, 1992.

Spiegel, Lynn. *Make Room for TV: Television and the Family Ideal in Postwar America*. Chicago: University of Chicago Press, 1992.

Star, Susan Leigh, and Karen Ruhleder. "Steps Toward an Ecology of Infrastructure: Design and Access for Large Information Spaces." *Information Systems Research* 7, no. 1 (1996): 111–34.

Steinberg, Marc. *Anime's Media Mix: Franchising Toys and Characters in Japan*. Minneapolis: University of Minnesota Press, 2012.

———. "Converging Contents and Platforms: Niconico Video and Japan's Media Mix Ecology." In *Asian Video Cultures: In the Penumbra of the Global*, ed. Joshua Neves and Bhaskar Sarkar, 91–113. Durham, N.C.: Duke University Press, 2017.

———. "Copying Atomu." *Mechademia 8: Tezuka's Manga Life* (2013): 127–36.

Stengers, Isabelle. "Introductory Notes on an Ecology of Practices." *Cultural Studies Review* 11, no. 1 (2005): 183–96.

Sterne, Jonathan. *MP3: The Meaning of a Format*. Durham, N.C.: Duke University Press, 2012.

Straw, Will. "Pulling Apart the Apparatus." In *Cinema and Technology*, ed. André Gaudreault and Martin Lefebvre. Special issue, *Semiotic Inquiry* 31, no. 1–3 (2011): 59–74.

Stringer, Julien. "The Original and Copy: Nakata Hideo's *Ring* (1998)." In *Japanese Cinema: Texts and Contexts*, ed. Alstair Phillips and Julian Stringer, 296–307. New York: Routledge, 2007.

Tada Hideoki. "Eyeblink Rates as a Function of the Interest Value of Video Stimuli." *Tōhoku Psychologica Folia* 45 (1986): 107–13.

Takada Hiroyuki, Asō Kōsaburō, Watanabe Kazuyoshi, Okumura Akihisa, Negoro Tamiko, and Ishikawa Tatsuya. "Epileptic Seizures Induced by Animated Cartoon, *Pocket Monster*." *Epilepsia* 40, no. 7 (1999): 997–1002.

Takahashi Takeo. *Terebi eizō to hikari kanjusei hossa: sono nōha shindan to bōshisaku* (TV images and photosensitive seizures: EEG diagnosis and preventive measures). Tokyo: Shinkō igaku shuppansha, 1999.

Takahashi Takeo and Tsukahara Yasuo. "*Pocket Monster* Incident and Low Luminance Visual Stimuli: Special Reference to Deep Red Flicker Stimulation." *Acta Paediatrica Japonica* 40 (1998): 631–37.

Takahashi Takeo, Kamijō Ken'ichi, Takaki Yōko, and Yamazaki Toshimasa. "Suppressive Efficacies by Adaptive Temporal Filtering System on Photoparoxysmal Response Elicited by Flickering Pattern Stimulation." *Epilepsia* 43, no. 5 (2002): 530–34.

Takahashi Takeo, Tsukuhara Yasuo, Nomura Masahide, and Matsuoka Hiroo. "Pokemon Seizures." *Neurological Journal of Southeast Asia* 4 (1999): 1–11.

Takahashi Yukitoshi, Shigematsu Hideo, Kubota Hidemoto, Inoue Yūshi, Fujiwara Tateki, Yagi Kazuichi, and Seino Masakazu. "Nonphotosensitive Video Game–Induced Partial Seizures." *Epilepsia* 36, no. 8 (1995): 837–41.

Takahashi, Y., T. Ozawa, H. Nakamura, S. Yamada, H. Okamoto, S. Yajima, K. Gotō, and N. Kondō. "Long-Wavelength Red Light Emission from TV and Photosensitive Seizures." *Acta Neurologica Scandinavica* 103 (2001): 114–19.

Takayanagi Kenjirō. *Terebi kotohajime: I no ji ga utsutta hi* (Television in the beginning: the day the kana 'i' appeared on the screen). Tokyo: Yūhikaku, 1986.

Tanizaki Jun'ichirō. "The Tumor with a Human Face." In *Shadows on the Screen: Tanizaki Jun'ichirō on Cinema and Oriental Aesthetics,* trans. and ed. Thomas Lamarre, 86–101. Ann Arbor: Center for Japanese Studies, University of Michigan Press, 2005.

Tegmark, Max. "Solid, Liquid, Gas, You: A New Theory of Consciousness." *New Scientist,* no. 2964 (April 12–18, 2014): 29–31.

———. "Will There Be a Singularity within Our Lifetime?" In *What Should We Really Be Worried About? Real Scenarios that Keep Scientists Up at Night,* ed. John Brockman, 30–33. New York: Harper Perennial, 2013.

Thorne, Christian. "To the Political Ontologists." In *Dark Trajectories: Politics of the Outside,* ed. Joshua Johnson, 97–121. Miami, Fla.: [NAME] Publications, 2013.

Tohkura Yoh'ichi. "Future of Communication Science and Technologies in Information Society." Plenary Lecture at the 18th International Congress on Acoustics, Kyoto, Japan, April 4–9, 2004.

Toivonen, Tuukka. "Don't Let Your Child Become a NEET! The Strategic Foundations of a Japanese Youth Scare." *Japan Forum* 23, no. 3 (2011): 407–29.

Tokugi Yoshiharu. "OVA no jūgo nen" (Fifteen years of original video animation). In *Zusetsu terebi anime zensho* (The complete book of television animation, illustrated), ed. Misono Makoto. Tokyo: Hara shobō, 1999.

Triclot, Mathieu. *Philosophie des jeux vidéos.* Paris: Éditions La Découverte, 2011.

Tsuda Kenroku and Suzuki Naoto. "Effects of Subjective Interest on Eyeblink Rates and Occurrences of Body Movements." *Japanese Journal of Physiological Psychology and Psychophysiology* 8, no. 1 (1990): 31–37.

Tsugata Nobuyuki. *Nihon animēshon no chikara: hachijūgo nen no rekishi o tsuranuku futatsu no jiku* (The power of Japanese animation: two axes running through an eighty-five-year history). Tokyo: NTT shuppan, 2004.

Turkle, Sherry. *Life on the Screen.* New York: Simon and Schuster, 2011.

———. *The Second Self: Computers and the Human Spirit*. New York: Simon and Schuster, 1984.

Turner, Graeme, and Jinna Tay, eds. *Television Studies after TV: Understanding Television in the Post-Broadcast Era*. New York: Routledge, 2009.

Turnock, Julie. *Plastic Reality: Special Effects, Technology, and the Emergence of 1970s Blockbuster Aesthetics*. New York: Columbia University Press, 2014.

Uemura Masayuki, Hosoi Kōichi, and Nakamura Akinori. *Famicon to sono jidai: terebi gēmu no tanjō* (The Nintendo family computer and its era: the birth of television games). Tokyo: NTT shuppan, 2013.

Verrotti, Alberto, Francesca Beccaria, Federica Fiori, Alessandra Montagnini, and Giuseppe Capovilla. "Photosensitivity: Epidemiology, Genetics, Clinical Manifestations, Assessment, and Management." *Epileptic Disorders* 14, no. 4 (2012): 349–62.

Vinge, Vernor. "The Coming Technological Singularity." *Whole Earth Review* 81 (1993): 88–95.

Viret, Gérald-Brice. *Idées reçues sur la télévision de demain*. Paris: Éditions Le Cavalier Bleu, 2015.

Voci, Paola. *China on Video: Smaller-Screen Realities*. London: Routledge, 2010.

Wada-Marciano, Mitsuyo. "Global and Local Materialities of Anime." In *Television, Japan, and Globalization*, ed. Yoshimoto Mitsuhiro, Eva Tsai, and JungBong Choi, 241–58. Ann Arbor: Center for Japanese Studies, University of Michigan Press, 2010.

Wallack, F. Bradford. *The Epochal Nature of Process in Whitehead's Metaphysics*. Albany, N.Y.: SUNY Press, 1980.

Watanabe Daisuke, "*Kimi no na wa* no dai-hitto wa naze 'jiken' na no ka? Sekai-kei to bishōjo gēmu no bunmyaku kara yomitoku" (Why was the box office hit of *Your Name* an "event"? A close reading based on the contexts of the world type genre and beautiful girl games). *Real Sound*, September 8, 2016, http://realsound.jp/movie/2016/09/post-2675.html.

Watanabe Midori. *Gendai terebi hōsōgaku: genba kara no messēji* (A study of contemporary television broadcasting: a message from on site). Tokyo: Waseda Daigaku Shuppanbu, 1989.

Watanabe Takesato. *Terebi: "yarase" to "jōhō sōsa"* (Television: "faking" and "manipulating information"). Tokyo: Sanseidō, 1995.

Wells, Paul. *Understanding Animation*. New York: Routledge, 1998.

Whitehead, Alfred North. *Process and Reality, Corrected Edition*. Ed. David Ray Griffin and Donald W. Sherburne. New York: Free Press, 1978.

Whitney, Shiloh. "Affects, Images and Childlike Perception: Self–Other Difference in Merleau-Ponty's Sorbonne Lectures." *PhaenEx* 7, no. 2 (2012): 185–211.

———. "Dependency Relations: Corporeal Vulnerability and Norms of Personhood in Hobbes and Kittay." *Hypatia* 26, no. 3 (2011): 554–74.

Williams, James. *Gilles Deleuze's Philosophy of Time: A Critical Introduction and Guide*. Edinburgh: Edinburgh University Press, 2011.

Williams, Raymond. "Structures of Feeling." In *Marxism and Literature*, 128–35. Oxford: Oxford University Press, 1977.

———. *Television: Technology and Cultural Form*. New York: Schocken Books, 1975.

Yamasaki, Takao, Gotō Yoshinobu, Kinukawa Naoko, and Tobimatsu Shōzō. "Neural Basis of Photo/Chromatic Sensitivity in Adolescence." *Epilepsia* 49, no. 9 (2008): 1611–18.

Yano, Christine R. "Panic Attacks: Anti-Pokémon Voices in Global Markets." In *Pikachu's Global Adventure: The Rise and Fall of Pokémon*, ed. Joseph Tobin, 108–40. Durham, N.C.: Duke University Press, 2004.

Yoda, Tomiko. "Girlscape: The Marketing of Media Ambiance in Japan." In *Media Theory in Japan,* ed. Marc Steinberg and Alex Zahlten, 173–99. Durham, N.C.: Duke University Press, 2017.

Yoshimi Shun'ya. "The Evolution of Mass Events in Prewar Japan." *Senri Ethnological Studies* 40 (1995): 85–99.

———. "From Street Corner to Living Room: Domestication of TV Culture and National Time/Narrative." Trans. Jodie Beck. *Mechademia 9: Origins* (2014): 126–42.

———. "Television and Nationalism: Historical Change in the National Domestic TV Formation of Postwar Japan." *European Journal of Cultural Studies* 6, no. 4 (2003): 459–87.

———. "Terebi ga ie ni yatte kita: terebi no kūkan, terebi no jikan" (Television has come into the home: the space and time of television). *Shisō* 12, no. 956 (2003): 26–48.

———. *Toshi no doramaturugī: Tōkyō sakariba no shakaishi* (Dramaturgy of the city: a social history of Tokyo and its areas of activity). Tokyo: Kōbundō, 1987.

Zielinski, Siegfried. *Audiovisions: Cinema and television as entr'actes in history.* Amsterdam: Amsterdam University Press, 1999.

Zifkin, Benjamin, and Dorothée G. A. Kasteleijn-Nolst Trenité. "Pokemon Contagion: A Letter to the Editors." *Southern Medical Journal* 94, no. 12 (2001): 1235–36.

INDEX

THOMAS LAMARRE teaches East Asian studies and communications studies at McGill University. His publications on the history of media and thought include *The Anime Machine: A Media Theory of Animation* (Minnesota, 2009).